Slavoj Žižek was born in Ljubljana, Slovenia, in 1949, and is a professor at the European Graduate School, International Director of the Birkbeck Institute for the Humanities, Birkbeck College, University of London, and a senior researcher at the Institute of Sociology, University of Ljubljana. He has been a visiting professor at Columbia University, New York, and the University of Paris VIII, as well as at a number of other prestigious institutions on both sides of the Atlantic.

In his home country, he was a prominent political figure in the 1980s. He wrote a regular column for the newspaper *Mladina* and, in 1990, finished fifth in the election for Slovenia's four-person presidency. His international reputation as a writer and philosopher was secured in 1989 with the publication of *The Sublime Object of Ideology*, a book which applied the author's pioneering distillation of Lacan, Hegel and Marx to an analysis of agency and modern ideology. A string of much lauded works have followed, including *For They Know Not What They Do* (1991), *The Ticklish Subject* (1999), *Welcome to the Desert of the Real* (2002), *The Parallax View* (2006) and *In Defense of Lost Causes* (2008).

As well as providing original insights into psychoanalysis, philosophy and radical political theory, he has, through employing his extraordinary scholarship to the examination of popular entertainment, established himself as a witty and deeply moral cultural critic. He has been the subject of two feature-length documentaries, *Slavoj Žižek: The Reality of the Virtual* (2004) and *Žižek!* (2005). He also presented and wrote the three-part British TV documentary *A Pervert's Guide to Cinema* (2006).

His compelling, charismatic presence and puckish sense of the absurd have prompted the press to dub him 'the Elvis of cultural theory' and an 'intellectual rock star'. However, these jocular monikers belie a seriousness of purpose that has been nothing short of startling in an era marked by despondency and disengagement on the Left. More than an academic or theorist, Žižek has the gravitas and drive of a breed once thought extinct: the revolutionary. He has made phil[...] generation of politically committed re[...]

A series of classic philosophical texts from Verso

The four pillars of Slavoj Žižek's work are (Lacanian) psychoanalysis, (Hegelian) philosophy, a (Marxist) theory of ideology, and (Christian) theology. The structure of this scholarly edifice is mapped out in the titles of 'The Essential Žižek', four central interventions into each of these fields. The focus of *The Sublime Object of Ideology* is the importance of Lacan's work to philosophy and contemporary political struggle; *The Ticklish Subject* examines German Idealism and the unsurpassable horizon of our thinking; *The Plague of Fantasies* anatomizes the ideological mechanisms that shape our daily experience; and *The Fragile Absolute* explores the emancipatory core of Christianity.

Also available from Verso by the same author:

In Defense of Lost Causes
Welcome to the Desert of the Real
Iraq: The Borrowed Kettle
Revolution at the Gates, Žižek on Lenin: The 1917 Writings
Lacan: The Silent Partners

THE PLAGUE OF FANTASIES

SLAVOJ ŽIŽEK

VERSO
London • New York

First edition published by Verso 1997
This edition published by Verso 2008
© Slavoj Žižek 1997

5 6 7 8 9 10

Verso
UK: 6 Meard Street, London W1F 0EG
US: 20 Jay Street, Suite 1010, Brooklyn, NY 11201
www.versobooks.com
Verso is the imprint of New Left Books

ISBN-13: 978-1-84467-303-2

British library Cataloguing in Publication Data
A catalogue record for this book is available from the British Library
Library of Congress Cataloging-in-Publication Data
A catalog record for this book is available from the Library of Congress

Typeset by Hewer UK Ltd, Edinburgh
Printed in the US by Maple Vaill

Contents

Preface to the New Edition:
My Own Private Austria

When we think we really know a close friend or relative, it often happens that, all of a sudden, this person does something – utters an unexpectedly vulgar or cruel remark, makes an obscene gesture, casts a cold indifferent glance where compassion was expected – making us aware that we do not really know him; we become suddenly aware that there is a total stranger in front of us. At this point, the fellow man changes into a Neighbour. This is what happened in a devastating way with the notorious Austrian criminal Josef Fritzl: from being a kind and polite *fellow man*, he suddenly changed into a monstrous *Neighbour* – to the great surprise of the people who met him on a daily basis and simply could not believe that this was the same person.

Freud's idea of the 'primordial father' (*Urvater*), which he developed in *Totem and Taboo*, is usually met with ridicule – and justly so, if we take it as an anthropological hypothesis arguing that, at the very dawn of humanity, the 'ape-men' lived in groups dominated by an all-powerful father who kept all women for his own exclusive sexual (ab)use, and that, after the sons gathered and rebelled, killing the father, he returned to haunt them as a totemic figure of symbolic authority, giving rise to feelings of guilt and imposing the prohibition of incest. What if, however, we read the duality of the 'normal' father and the primordial father of unlimited access to incestuous enjoyment not as a fact of the earliest history of humanity, but as a libidinal fact, a fact of 'psychic reality', which accompanies, as an obscene shadow, 'normal' paternal authority, prospering in the dark underground of unconscious fantasies? This obscene underground is discernible through its effects – in myths, dreams, slips of the tongue, symptoms ... and, sometimes, it enforces its direct perverse realization (Freud noted that perverts realize what hysterics only fantasize about).

Does not the very architectural arrangement of the Fritzl household – the 'normal' ground and upper floors supported (literally and libidinally) by the windowless underground space of total domination and unlimited *jouissance* – embody the 'normal' family space redoubled by the secret domain of the obscene 'primordial father'? Fritzl created in his cellar his own utopia, a private paradise in which, as he told his lawyer, he spent hours on end watching TV and playing with the youngsters while his daughter Elisabeth prepared dinner. In this self-enclosed space, even the language the inhabitants shared was a kind of private language: it is reported that the two sons, Stefan and Felix, communicate in a bizarre dialect, with some of the sounds they utter being 'animal-like'. The Fritzl case thus validates Lacan's pun on perversion as *père-version* – it is crucial to note how the secret underground apartment complex concretizes a very precise ideologic-libidinal fantasy, an extreme version of father-domination-pleasure nexus. One of the mottos of May '68 was 'All power to the imagination' – and, in this sense, Fritzl is also a child of '68, ruthlessly realizing his fantasy.

This is why it is misleading, even outright wrong, to describe Fritzl as 'inhuman' – if anything, he was, to use Nietzsche's phrase, 'human, all too human'. No wonder Fritzl complained that his own life had been 'ruined' by the discovery of his secret family. What makes his reign so chilling is precisely the way his brutal exercise of power and his *usufruit* of the daughter were not just cold acts of exploitation, but were accompanied by an ideologico-familial justification (he was simply doing what a father should do, namely protecting his children from drugs and other dangers of the outside world), as well as by occasional displays of compassion and human consideration (he did take the sick daughter to hospital, etc.). These acts were not chinks of warm humanity in his armour of coldness and cruelty, but parts of the same protective attitude that made him imprison and violate his children.

Fritzl claimed that he noted Elisabeth wanted to escape her home – she was returning home late, looking for a job, had a boyfriend, was possibly taking drugs, and he wanted to protect her from all that. The contours of the obsessional strategy are clearly recognizable here: 'I'll protect her from the dangers of the outside world even if it means destroying her'. According to the media, Fritzl defended himself thus: 'If it weren't for me, Kerstin wouldn't be alive today. I'm no monster. I could have killed them all. Then there would have been no trace. No one would have found me out.' What is crucial here is the underlying premiss: as a father, he had the right to exercise total power over his children, including sexual abuse and killing; it was thanks to his goodness that he showed some consideration and allowed them to survive. And, as every psychoanalyst can confirm, we often find traces of such an attitude even in the most 'normal' and caring fathers: all of a sudden, the kind father explodes into a father-Thing, convinced that his children owe him everything, their very existence, that they are absolutely indebted to him, that his power over them is limitless, that he has the right to do whatever he wants in order to take care of them.

One should avoid here the trap of putting the blame on patriarchal authority as such, seeing in Fritzl's monstrosity the ultimate consequence of paternal Law, as well as the opposite trap of putting the blame on the disintegration of paternal Law. The attitude in question is neither simply a component of 'normal' paternal authority (the measure of its success is precisely the ability to set the child free, to let her go into the outside world), nor merely a sign of its failure (in the sense that the void of the 'normal' paternal authority is supplemented, filled in, by the ferocious figure of the all-powerful 'primordial father'); it is, rather, both simultaneously – a dimension which, under 'normal' circumstances, remains virtual, was actualized in the Fritzl case.

The attempts to point the finger at Austrian particularities make the same ideological error as those who dream of an 'alternative modernity' to the predominant liberal–capitalist one: by way of shifting the blame to contingent Austrian circumstances, they want to legitimize and proclaim the innocence of paternity as such, that is, they refuse to see the potential for such acts in the very notion of paternal authority. So instead of making miserable attempts to blame this terrible crime on Austria's Nazi history or the Austrians' excessive sense of orderliness and respectability, one should rather link the figure of Fritzl to a much more respectable Austrian myth, that of the von Trapp family immortalized in *The Sound of Music*: another family living in their secluded castle, with the father's benevolent military authority protecting them from the Nazi evil outside, and the generations strangely mixed up together (Sister Maria, like Elisabeth, being a generation between father and children . . .). One can imagine the frightened children gathered around the mother, Elisabeth, in fear of the storm that is the father's imminent arrival, and the mother calming them down with a song about 'some of their favourite things', such as much loved TV shows or the toys brought by father, on which they should focus their minds.

In the last years of the Communist regime in Romania, Nicolae Ceauşescu was asked by a foreign journalist how he justified the constraints on foreign travel imposed on Romanian citizens. Was this not a violation of their human rights? Ceauşescu answered that these constraints existed in order to protect an even higher and more important human right, the right to safety, which would have been threatened by too much free travel. Was he not reasoning here like Fritzl, who also protected his children's 'more fundamental' right to live in a safe home, where they would be protected from the dangers of the outside world? In other words, to use Peter Sloterdijk's terms, Fritzl protected his children's right to live in a safe self-enclosed sphere – while, of course, reserving for himself the right to transgress the barrier all the time, even visiting Thai sex-tourist resorts, the very embodiment of the kind of danger he wanted to protect his children from. Remember that Ceauşescu also saw himself as a caring paternal authority, a father protecting his nation from foreign decadence – as in all authoritarian regimes, the basic relationship between the ruler and his subjects was, whatever else it might be, one of unconditional love.

In caring for his own household, the city of Bucharest, Ceauşescu made a proposal which strangely recalls the architecture of Fritzl's house: in order to solve the problem of the polluted river which runs through the city, he wanted to dig beneath the existing river bed *another* wide channel into which all the dirt would be directed, so that there would have been two rivers, the deep one with all the pollution, and the surface one for the happy citizens to enjoy . . . Such a two-level distinction is constitutive of every ideology, as was made clear in John Carpenter's *They Live* (1988), one of the neglected masterpieces of the Hollywood Left. The film tells the story of John Nada (Spanish for 'Nothing'!), a homeless labourer who finds work on a Los Angeles construction site. One of the other workers, Frank Armitage, takes him to spend the night in a local shantytown. While being shown around that night, he notices some odd behaviour at a small church across the street. Investigating it the next day, he accidentally stumbles on several boxes, hidden in a secret compartment in a wall, full of sunglasses. When he later puts on a pair for the first time, he notices that a publicity billboard now simply displays the word 'OBEY', while another urges the viewer to 'MARRY AND REPRODUCE'. He also sees that paper money now bears the words 'THIS IS YOUR GOD'. He soon discovers that many people in the city are actually aliens and then, once they realize he can see them for what they are, the police arrive. Nada escapes and returns to the construction site to talk over his discoveries with Armitage, who is initially uninterested in his story. The two fight as Nada attempts to convince him, and then to force him, to put on the sunglasses. When he finally does so, Armitage joins together with Nada and they get in contact with the group from the church, who are organizing the resistance. At the group's meeting they learn that the aliens' primary method of control is a signal sent out over television that ensures that the general public cannot see them for what they are. In the final battle, after destroying the aliens' broadcasting antenna, Nada is mortally wounded; as his last dying act, he gives the aliens the finger. With the signal now turned off, people are startled to find the aliens in their midst.

There is a series of features one should take note of here, first among them the direct link made between the classic Hollywood sub-genre of the 'invasion of the body snatchers' – aliens amongst us who, invisible to our gaze, are running our lives – and class antagonism, ideological domination and exploitation. One cannot but be impressed by the down-to-earth depiction of the miserable shantytown lives of poor workers. Then, of course, there is the beautifully naive *mise-en-scène* of ideology: through the critico-ideological glasses, we directly see the Master-Signifier beneath the chain of knowledge – we learn to see dictatorship *in* democracy. This could remind us of the not-so-well-known fact that, in the 1960s, the leadership of the Communist Party of America, in order to account for its failure to mobilize the workers, seriously entertained the idea that the US population was being controlled by the secret use of drugs distributed through the air and the water supply. But we do not need aliens, secret drugs or gasses – the *form* of ideology does the work without them. It is because of this form that the depicted scene nonetheless stages our reality. Look at the front page of our daily newspapers: every title, even and especially when it pretends simply to inform, is an implicit injunction. When you are asked to choose between liberal democracy and fundamentalism, it is not only that one term is obviously preferred – what is more important, and the true injunction, is that you see this as the only true alternative, ignoring any third option.

Marxists accept this aspect of the struggle for dictatorship; they render the struggle visible and openly practise it. Why? Let us return to the film: once you put the glasses on and see directly the Master-Signifier, it no longer determines you. Which means that, before you see the ideological injunction through the glasses, you also saw it, but were unaware of the fact. To refer to the fourth missing term of Rumsfeldian epistemology, the injunctions were your 'unknown knowns'. This is why really seeing them hurts. When the hero tries to convince his friend to put the glasses on, the friend resists, and a long fight follows, worthy of *Fight Club* (another masterpiece of the Hollywood Left). The violence staged here is positive violence, a condition of liberation – the lesson is that our liberation from ideology is not a spontaneous act, an act of discovering our true Self. We learn in the film that, when one looks for too long at reality through critico-ideological glasses, one gets a bad headache: it is very painful to be deprived of the ideological surplus-enjoyment. To see the true nature of things, we need the glasses: it is not that we have to take off ideological glasses in order to see reality directly as it is – we are 'naturally' in ideology, our natural sight is ideological.

There is a further feature which makes this scene with ideologico-critical spectacles contemporary: in it, the ideological injunction is hidden, so that it can only be directly seen through the glasses. Such a relationship between the visible and the invisible is predominant in contemporary 'consumerist' societies, in which we, the subjects, are no longer interpellated on behalf of some big ideological identity, but directly as subjects of pleasures, so that the implied ideological identity is invisible. This is how the discourse of the university functions: its truth, the Master's injunction, is hidden beneath the bar. In the traditional discourse of the Master, where we are directly interpellated, the relationship is (almost symmetrically) inversed – the explicit text addresses us as followers of a great cause, while the implied message delivered between the lines concerns the obscene surplus-enjoyment with which we will be bribed if we subject ourselves to the cause: become a good Fascist . . . and you can steal from, beat and lynch the Jews; become a Catholic priest, serve God . . . and you can play with young boys as your treat; get properly married . . . and an occasional discreet affair is tolerated. We can thus imagine the kind of inverted ideological spectacles that would spell out this implicit obscene message: for example, a nationalist–populist party electoral poster which asks you to sacrifice yourself for your country, but which, when viewed through the glasses, shows you how you will profit from it, the spoils of your sacrifice – being allowed to humiliate foreigners, and so on, as part of your patriotic duty. Or imagine a poster in a small town in the American South, during the Ku Klux Klan era, calling on you to be a good Christian and defend Western civilization, but which when seen through the glasses declares that you are allowed to rape black women, lynch black men . . . There is yet another way to imagine the functioning of the ideological glasses:

when you are shown a scene of starving children in Africa, and asked to do something to help them, the true message visible through the glasses would be something like 'Don't think, don't politicize, forget about the true causes of their poverty, just act, contribute money, so that you will not have to think!'

Back to the long fight between Nada and Armitage, which starts with Nada saying to Armitage: 'I'm giving you a choice. Either put on these glasses or start eatin' that trash can.' (The scene takes place amongst overturned trash cans.) The fight, which goes on for an overwhelming ten minutes, with occasional pauses for an exchange of friendly smiles, is in itself totally irrational – why does Armitage not agree to put the glasses on, just to satisfy his friend? The only explanation is that he *knows* his friend wants him to see something dangerous, to access a prohibited knowledge which will totally spoil the relative peace of his daily life.

Are we then dealing here with the simple opposition between reality and its fantasy supplement? The topology is more complex: what precedes fantasy is not reality but a *hole* in reality, its *point of impossibility* filled in with fantasy. Lacan's name for this point is, of course, the *objet petit a*. The twisted topology of this object, which is the true focus of *The Plague of Fantasies*, is well worth examining more closely.

When confronted with statistics about the low percentage of voters who supported him, the Republican presidential candidate Mike Huckabee (a figure who seems to have stepped right out of an old populist Frank Capra film, if not from a Dickens novel) said on 8 February 2008 at the Conservative Political Action Conference: 'I know the pundits and I know what they say, the math doesn't work out. Well I didn't major in math, I majored in miracles. And I still believe in those, too.' This is worth quoting not just to make fun of the standard of political debate in the US; in a negative way, it points to a central component of Alain Badiou's thought, which, precisely, brings together mathematics and miracles. When we talk about miracles, we should, of course, bear in mind Lacan's qualification that the only 'irrationality' he admits exists is that of the irrational numbers in mathematics – in a homologous way, the only 'miracles' that a radical materialist admits exist are the mathematical ones. A 'miracle' is simply the sudden emergence of the New, which is irreducible to its preceding conditions, of something which retroactively 'posits' its conditions: every authentic act creates its own conditions of possibility.

What, on a closer look, is this irrational element? As Badiou pointed out, what defines a 'world' is primarily not its positive features, but the way its structure relates to its own inherent (point of) impossibility.[1] Classical mathematics dismissed the square root of -1 as an irrelevant externality, as nonsense to be ignored, while modern mathematics makes this impossible calculable, marking it with the letter I ('imaginary number'): mathematics historically splits and remakes itself by creating constants that occupy these impossible places: the square root of -1 is baptized an imaginary number, which is then used in a new space of calculations. (Things are similar with Cantor's conceptualization of different modalities of the infinite: the transfinite, etc.)

The same holds for capitalism: its dynamics of perpetual self-revolutionizing relies on the endless postponing of its point of impossibility (final crisis, collapse). What is for other, earlier, modes of production a dangerous exception is for capitalism normality: crisis is in capitalism *internalized*, taken into account, as the point of impossibility which pushes it to continuous activity. Capitalism is structurally always in crisis – this is why it is expanding all the time: it can only reproduce itself by way of 'borrowing from the future'; by way of escaping into the future. The final settling of accounts when all debts would be paid cannot ever arrive. Marx had a name for the social point of impossibility: 'class struggle'.

And, perhaps, one should extend this to the very definition of humanity: what ultimately distinguishes man from animal is not a positive feature (speech, tool-making, reflexive thinking, or whatever), but the rise of a new point of impossibility designated by Freud and Lacan as *das Ding*, the impossible-real ultimate reference point of desire. The often noted

1   See Alain Badiou, *Logiques des mondes*, Paris: Editions du Seuil, 2007.

experimental difference between humans and apes acquires here all its weight: when an ape is confronted with an object beyond its reach which it repeatedly fails to obtain, it will abandon it and move on to a more modest object (say, a less attractive sexual partner), whereas a human will persist in its effort, remaining transfixed by the impossible.

This is why the subject as such is hysterical: the hysterical subject is precisely a subject who poses *jouissance* as an absolute; he responds to the absolute of *jouissance* in the form of unsatisfied desire. Such a subject is capable of relating to a term that is off-limits; even more radically, it is a subject that can only exist insofar as it relates to a term that is 'out-of-play'. Hysteria is thus the elementary 'human' way of installing a point of impossibility in the guise of absolute *jouissance*. Is Lacan's *il n'y a pas de rapport sexuel* not also such a point of impossibility constitutive of being human?

When cognitivists, from Dennett onwards, try to explain consciousness, they enumerate a whole series of specifically human capacities which 'cannot really function without consciousness'. What if, however, instead of focusing on what is possible only with consciousness, we should change the terrain and ask: what is the specific point of impossibility of consciousness? What is it that we *cannot* do with consciousness? How is consciousness related to what, a priori, we *cannot* become conscious of? And what unsurpassable failure gave birth to consciousness? Is consciousness at its zero level not consciousness of a failure – of hitting a wall of radical impossibility? Here, the topic of mortality re-emerges: when Heidegger claims that only man (not an animal) is mortal, this, again, means that death is the ultimate possibility of the impossibility of a human being, its inherent point of impossibility, something one calculates with, and relates to, in contrast to an animal for which death is simply external.

This point is the *objet a*, that which is *subtracted* from reality (as it's impossible) and thus gives it consistency – if it gets included in reality, it causes a catastrophe. In what sense does the *objet a* (surplus-enjoyment) frame reality? Think for example of the 'production of a couple' motif that frames a Hollywood narrative about a big historical event like a war or natural catastrophe: this motif is, quite literally, the film's ideological surplus-enjoyment. Although we directly enjoy the spectacular shots of the disaster (battles, the gigantic wave which destroys cities, the Titanic sinking . . .), the surplus-enjoyment is provided by the sub-narrative of the couple which forms a 'frame' for the spectacular event – the asteroid which hits earth in *Deep Impact* materializes the daughter's rage at her father's new marriage; in *Reds*, the October Revolution serves to reunite the lovers; the ferocious dinosaurs in *Jurassic Park* embody the father-figure's aggressive rejection of paternal authority and care, and so on. It is this frame (through which we perceive the spectacular event), with its surplus-enjoyment, that 'bribes' us libidinally into accepting the ideology of the story.

The hero of *Perfume* (Patrick Süskind's novel and Tom Tykwer's film) is one instance of a subjectivity ruined by such catastrophic inclusion. Lacan supplemented Freud's list of partial objects (breast, faeces, penis) with two further objects: voice and gaze. Perhaps, we should add another object to this series: smell. Süskind's *Perfume* seems to point in this direction. Grenouille, the novel's unfortunate hero, is without any odour, so that others cannot smell him; but he himself possesses an extraordinary sense of smell, such that he is able to detect people far away. When his ideal woman accidentally dies he tries to recreate, not her in her bodily existence (*Perfume* is a true anti-*Frankenstein*), but her odour, by killing twenty-five pretty young women and scratching the surface of their skin to extract their odours, mixing them into the ideal perfume. This irresistible perfume is the ultimate *odor di femina*, the extracted 'essence' of femininity: whenever ordinary humans smell it, they suspend all rational restraint and engage in the bliss of a sexual orgy. When, towards the novel's end, Grenouille is arrested for murdering the twenty-five virgins and sentenced to public execution, it is enough for him to wave a napkin soaked in the ultimate perfume in front of the gathered crowd, who, instantly forgetting their cries for his death, start undressing and engaging in acts of depravity. The extracted femininity is what Lacan called the *objet petit a*, the object-cause of desire, that which is 'in you more than you' and thus makes me desire you; this is why Grenouille has to kill the virgins in order to extract from them their essence; or, as Lacan put it: 'I love you, but there is something in you more than yourself that I love, *objet petit a*, so I destroy you.'

Grenouille's fate is tragic, however: being odourless, he is a *pure subject*, without an object-cause of desire in himself, and as such is never desired by others. What he gains from this predicament is direct access to the object-cause of desire: while ordinary individuals desire another person because of the lure of the *objet a* in them, he has direct access to this object. Ordinary individuals can only desire insofar as they become victims of an illusion: they think they desire another person because of him or her, that is, they are not aware that their desire is caused by the essence/odour which has nothing to do with the person as such. Since Grenouille can bypass the person and directly target the object-cause of desire, he can avoid this illusion – this is why eroticism is for him a ridiculous game of lures. The price he pays for it, however, is that he cannot ever accept the inverse illusion that someone loves him: he is always aware that it is not him but his perfume that makes people adore him. The only way out of this predicament, the only way to posit himself as an object of the others' desire, is suicidal: in the final scene of the novel, he spills perfume on himself and is then literally torn apart and devoured by a bunch of thieves, beggars and whores.

And is this violent reduction of the thing to its *objet a* not also an example of what Badiou calls *subtraction*? One subtracts from the thing its decentred core, leaving behind its dead body. The opposite of this subtraction, and also a way to generate the *objet a*, is *protraction*. An example from cinema is a formal procedure of Tarkovsky's which, given his Soviet origins, cannot but ironically evoke the (in)famous dialectical 'law' of the transformation of quantity into quality, supplementing it with a kind of 'negation of the negation' (which was excluded by Stalin from the list of these 'laws' as being too Hegelian, not properly 'materialist'):

Tarkovsky proposed that if a take is lengthened, boredom naturally sets in for the audience. But if the take is extended even further, something else arises: curiosity. Tarkovsky is essentially proposing giving the audience time to inhabit the world that the take is showing us, not to *watch* it, but to *look* at it, to explore it.[2]

Perhaps the ultimate example of this procedure is the famous scene in Tarkovsky's *Mirror* in which the heroine, who works as a proofreader for a daily newspaper in the Soviet Union of the mid-1930s, runs through the rain from her home to the printing office fearing that she has missed an obscene misprint of Stalin's name. (Tarkovsky refers here to the legend according to which, at the time of the darkest purges, an issue of *Pravda* was almost printed in which Stalin was misspelled as 'Sralin' – the shitter, from the verb 'srat', to shit. At the scene's end, relieved that the fatal mistake had not taken place, the actress whispers the word into her friend's ear.) Sean Martin is right to emphasize the scene's unexpectedly immediate physical beauty:

> it is as if Tarkovsky were content just to watch Margarita Terekhova running through the rain, down steps, across yards, into corridors. Here, Tarkovsky reveals the presence of beauty in something that is apparently mundane and, paradoxically (given the period), also potentially fatal for Maria if the mistake she thinks she's made has gone to press.[3]

This effect of beauty is generated precisely by the excessive length of the scene: instead of just watching Maria running and, immersed in the narrative, worrying whether she will arrive on time to prevent the catastrophe, we are seduced into looking at the scene, taking note of its phenomenal features, the intensity of movements, and so on.

2   Sean Martin, *Andrei Tarkovsky*, Harpenden: Pocket Essentials, 2005, p. 49.
3   Ibid., p. 135.

The third figure of the *objet a*, after *subtraction* and *protraction*, is that of *obstruction*: the *objet a* as the agent of the Cunning of Reason, the obstacle which always perturbs the realization of our goals. Another example from cinema: the libidinal focus of the Coen brothers' *No Country for Old Men* (2007) is the figure of the pathological hired killer played by Javier Bardem – a ruthless killing machine, with an ethics of his own, sticking to his word, a figure of what Kant called diabolical Evil. When, at the film's end, he puts pressure on the hero's wife to choose heads or tails (which will decide whether she lives or dies), she replies that he should not hide behind the flip of a coin – it is his will that decides whether to kill her. He replies that she does not understand: he, his will, *is* like the coin. The key to this figure is the fact that it is not a real-life person, but a fantasy-entity – the embodiment of the pure object-obstacle, that unfathomable 'x' of blind fate – which always, in a weird mixture of chance and inexorable necessity, as the necessity of a chance (a stroke of bad luck), intervenes to undermine the fulfilment of subjects' plans and intentions, guaranteeing that, one way or another, things will always somehow go wrong.

One should locate the figure played by Bardem as the opposite of the resigned old sheriff (Tommy Lee Jones), who complains constantly about the craziness and violence of the present age – it is to him that the film's title refers. The sheriff is the Master rendered impotent, the failed paternal authority, while the Bardem figure embodies the cause of his collapse. The proper way to read *No Country for Old Men* is therefore first to imagine the same story *without* the Bardem character: just the triangle of the hero who runs away with the money after stumbling upon the site of the gang-sters' gunfight; the mafia hiring a freelancer (Woody Harrelson) to get the money back; and the sheriff observing their interplay from a sensible distance, playing one off against the other, and guaranteeing the happy (or at least just) outcome. The Bardem figure is the fourth element, the *objet a* that ruins the game.

Another way to put it would be to say that the *objet a* prevents the letter from arriving at its destination – but does it? Is there not a Cunning of Reason at work here, so that through the very fact of the letter having missed its true destination we are compelled to change our perspective and redefine the destination? The 2001 Darwin Award for the most stupid act of self-annihilation was conferred on an unfortunate woman from the Romanian countryside who woke up in the midst of her own funeral procession – after realizing what was going on and crawling out of her coffin, she ran away in blind terror only to be hit by a truck on a busy road and killed instantly. So she was put back into the coffin and the funeral procession carried on as before ... Is this not the ultimate example of what we call fate – of a letter arriving at its destination?

The fate of Nikolai Bukharin's 'testament', a letter he wrote to his wife Anna Larina in 1938, on the eve of his execution, is a tragic case of how a letter always arrives at its destination. The letter disappeared into the secret Soviet archives and was delivered to Anna Larina only in 1992:

Bukharin, on the eve of his fateful trial, exhorted her to 'Remember that the great cause of the USSR lives on, and *this* is the most important thing. Personal fates are transitory and wretched by comparison.' She read it in a world in which the USSR had just fallen.[4]

Bukharin's letter *did* arrive at its destination – did reach Anna Larina – at precisely the right moment; one can even say that it was delivered as soon as possible, that is, as soon as the historical situation made it possible that its delivery would produce a truth-effect. Bukharin perceived his tragic fate as being insignificant in comparison to the thriving of the great historical cause of the USSR – the continuity of this cause guaranteed that his death was not meaningless. Read after the USSR had disappeared, the letter confronts us with the meaninglessness of Bukharin's death: there is no big Other to redeem it, he literally died in vain.

The general lesson of this is that, in order to interpret a scene or an utterance, sometimes the key thing to do is to *locate its true addressee*. In one of the best Perry Mason novels, the lawyer witnesses a police interrogation of a couple in the course of which the husband tells the policeman in unexpectedly great detail what happened, what he saw, and what else

---

4   Nikolai Bukharin, *Philosophical Arabesques*, London: Pluto Press, 2005, p. 29.

he thinks also happened – why this excess of information? The explanation: the couple had committed the murder, and since the husband knew that he and his wife would soon be arrested and separated from each other, he used this opportunity to tell her the (false) story they should both cling to – the true addressee of his endless talk was thus not the police, but his wife.

Subtraction, protraction, obstruction: three versions of the same excessive/lacking object, an object that is never in its own place, always missing it and in excess of it. The relationship between anorexia and bulimia is one of the supreme examples of such an identity of lack and excess: anorexics as a rule turn into bulimics, and then in order to punish themselves return to anorexia. Bulimics eat to excess, while for anorexics *all* food is already an excess, a disgusting foreign body to be expelled. Which is why the two coincide: they both lack the 'common measure' of the normal habit of eating; they both bear witness to the imbalance introduced into the animal rhythm of digestion by the emergence of subjectivity – and the object-cause of this imbalance is precisely the *objet a*, surplus-enjoyment.

Introduction

Let us imagine ourselves in the standard situation of male-chauvinist jealousy: all of a sudden, I learn that my partner has had sex with another man – OK, no problem, I am rational, tolerant, I accept it . . . but then, irresistibly, images start to overwhelm me, concrete images of what they were doing (why did she have to lick him right *there*? Why did she have to spread her legs *so wide*?), and I am lost, sweating and quivering, my peace gone for ever. This *plague of fantasies* of which Petrarch speaks in *My Secret*, images which blur one's clear reasoning, is brought to its extreme in today's audiovisual media. Among the antagonisms that characterize our epoch (world-market globalization versus the assertion of ethnic particularisms, etc.), perhaps the key place belongs to the antagonism between the abstraction that increasingly determines our lives (in the guise of digitalization, speculative market relations, etc.) and the deluge of pseudo-concrete images. In the good old days of traditional *Ideologiekritik*, the paradigmatic critical procedure was to regress from 'abstract' (religious, legal . . .) notions to the concrete social reality in which these notions were rooted; today, it seems more and more that the critical procedure is forced to follow the opposite path, from pseudo-concrete imagery to abstract (digital, market . . .) processes which effectively structure our living experience.

This book approaches systematically, from a Lacanian viewpoint, the presuppositions of this 'plague of fantasies'. The first chapter ('The Seven Veils of Fantasy') elaborates the contours of the psychoanalytic notion of *fantasy*, with a special consideration of the way ideology has to rely on some phantasmic background. The second chapter ('Love Thy Neighbour? No, Thanks!') deals with the ambiguous relationship between fantasy and *jouissance*: the way in which fantasy animates and structures enjoyment, while simultaneously serving as a protective shield against its excess. The third chapter ('Fetishism and Its Vicissitudes') focuses on the impasses in the notion of *fetishism* as the paradigmatic case of phantasmic seduction, from its religious origins to its postmodern upheavals. The last chapter ('Cyberspace, Or, The Unbearable Closure of Being') directly tackles the topic of *cyberspace* as the latest version of the 'plague of fantasies', endeavouring to sketch the answer to the question of how ongoing digitalization will affect the status of subjectivity. The three appendices to these four main chapters analyse three examples of the *irrepresentability* of the Real as the inherent obverse of the 'plague of fantasies': the failure in representing the sexual act in cinema ('From the Sublime to the Ridiculous: The Sexual Act in Cinema'); the inscription of subjectivity in the breakdown of the melodic line in music ('Robert Schumann: The Romantic Anti-Humanist'); and the foreclosure of the content of the moral Law in modern (Kantian) ethics ('The Unconscious Law: Towards an Ethics Beyond the Good').

1 The Seven Veils of Fantasy

'The truth is out there'

When, a couple of years ago, the disclosure of Michael Jackson's alleged 'immoral' private behaviour (his sexual games with underage boys) dealt a blow to his innocent Peter Pan image, elevated beyond sexual and racial differences (or concerns), some penetrating commentators asked the obvious question: what's all the fuss about? Wasn't this so-called 'dark side of Michael Jackson' always here for all of us to see, in the video spots that accompanied his musical releases, which were saturated with ritualized violence and obscene sexualized gestures (blatantly so in the case of *Thriller* and *Bad*)? The Unconscious is outside, not hidden in any unfathomable depths – or, to quote the *X Files* motto: 'The truth is out there'.

Such a focusing on material externality proves very fruitful in the analysis of how fantasy relates to the inherent antagonisms of an ideological edifice. Do not the two opposed architectural designs of *Casa del Fascio* (the local headquarters of the Fascist party), Adolfo Coppede's neo-Imperial pastiche (1928) and Giuseppe Teragni's highly modernist transparent glasshouse (1934–36) reveal, in their simple juxtaposition, the inherent contradiction of the Fascist ideological project which simultaneously advocates a return to pre-modern organicist corporatism and the unheard-of mobilization of all social forces in the service of rapid modernization? An even better example is provided by the great projects of public buildings in the Soviet Union of the 1930s, which put on top of a flat multistorey office building a gigantic statue of the idealized New Man, or a couple: in the span of a couple of years, the tendency to flatten the office building (the actual workplace for living people) more and more became clearly discernible, so that it changed increasingly into a mere pedestal for the larger-than-life statue – does not this external, material feature of architectural design reveal the 'truth' of the Stalinist ideology in which actual, living people are reduced to instruments, sacrificed as the pedestal for the spectre of the future New Man, an ideological monster which crushes actual living men under his feet? The paradox is that had anyone in the Soviet Union of the 1930s said openly that the vision of the Socialist New Man was an ideological monster squashing actual people, they would have been arrested immediately. It was, however, allowed – encouraged, even – to make this point via architectural design . . . again, 'the truth is out there'. What we are thus arguing is not simply that ideology also permeates the alleged extra-ideological strata of everyday life, but that this materialization of ideology in external materiality reveals inherent antagonisms which the explicit formulation of ideology cannot afford to acknowledge: it is as if an ideological edifice, if it is to function 'normally', must obey a kind of 'imp of perversity', and articulate its inherent antagonism in the externality of its material existence.

This externality, which directly embodies ideology, is also occluded as 'utility'. That is to say: in everyday life, ideology is at work especially in the apparently innocent reference to pure utility – one should never forget that in the symbolic universe, 'utility' functions as a reflective notion; that is, it always involves the assertion of utility as meaning (for example, a man who lives in a large city and owns a Land Rover does not simply lead a no-nonsense, 'down-to-earth' life; rather, he owns such a car in order to *signal* that he leads his life under the sign of a no-nonsense, 'down-to-earth' attitude). The unsurpassed master of such analysis, of course, was Claude Lévi-Strauss, whose semiotic triangle of preparing food (raw, baked, boiled) demonstrated how food also serves as 'food for thought'. We probably all remember the scene from Buñuel's *Phantom of Liberty* in which relations between eating and excreting are inverted: people sit on their lavatories around the table, pleasantly talking, and when they want to eat, they silently ask the housekeeper, 'Where is that place ... you know?' and sneak away to a small room in the back. So, as a supplement to Lévi-Strauss, one is tempted to propose that shit can also serve as a *matière-à-penser*: do not the three basic types of lavatory form a kind of excremental correlative-counterpoint to the Lévi-Straussian triangle of cooking?

In a traditional German lavatory, the hole in which shit disappears after we flush water is way in front, so that the shit is first laid out for us to sniff at and inspect for traces of some illness; in the typical French lavatory, on the contrary, the hole is in the back – that is, the shit is supposed to disappear as soon as possible; finally, the Anglo-Saxon (English or American) lavatory presents a kind of synthesis, a mediation between these two opposed poles – the basin is full of water, so that the shit floats in it – visible, but not to be inspected. No wonder that Erica Jong, in the famous discussion of different European lavatories at the beginning of her half-forgotten *Fear of Flying*, mockingly claims: 'German toilets are really the key to the horrors of the Third Reich. People who can build toilets like this are capable of anything.' It is clear that none of these versions can be accounted for in purely utilitarian terms: a certain ideological perception of how the subject should relate to the unpleasant excrement which comes from within our body is clearly discernible – again, for the third time, 'the truth is out there'.

Hegel was among the first to interpret the geographical triad Germany-France-England as expressing three different existential attitudes: German reflective thoroughness, French revolutionary hastiness, English moderate utilitarian pragmatism; in terms of political stance, this triad can be read as German conservatism, French revolutionary radicalism and English moderate liberalism; in terms of the predominance of one of the spheres of social life, it is German metaphysics and poetry versus French politics and English economy. The reference to lavatories enables us not only to discern the same triad in the most intimate domain of performing the excremental function, but also to generate the underlying mechanism of this triad in the three different attitudes towards excremental excess:

ambiguous contemplative fascination; the hasty attempt to get rid of the unpleasant excess as fast as possible; the pragmatic approach to treat the excess as an ordinary object to be disposed of in an appropriate way. So it is easy for an academic to claim at a round table that we live in a post-ideological universe – the moment he visits the restroom after the heated discussion, he is again knee-deep in ideology. The ideological investment of such references to utility is attested by their *dialogical* character: the Anglo-Saxon lavatory acquires its meaning only through its differential relation to French and German lavatories. We have such a multitude of lavatory types because there is a traumatic excess which each of them tries to accommodate – according to Lacan, one of the features which distinguishes man from the animals is precisely that with humans the disposal of shit becomes a problem.

The same goes for the different ways in which one washes dishes: in Denmark, for example, a detailed set of features opposes the way dishes are washed to the way they do it in Sweden, and a close analysis soon reveals how this opposition is used to index the fundamental perception of Danish national identity, which is defined in opposition to that of Sweden.[1] And – to reach an even more intimate domain – do we not encounter the same semiotic triangle in the three main hairstyles of the female sex organ's pubic hair? Wildly grown, unkempt pubic hair indexes the hippie attitude of natural spontaneity; yuppies prefer the disciplinary procedure of a French garden (one shaves the hair on both sides close to the legs, so that all that remains is a narrow band in the middle with a clear-cut shave line); in the punk attitude, the vagina is wholly shaven and furnished with rings (usually attached to a perforated clitoris). Is this not yet another version of the Lévi-Straussian semiotic triangle of 'raw' wild hair, well-kept 'baked' hair and shaved 'boiled' hair? One can see how even the most intimate attitude towards one's body is used to make an ideological statement.[2] So how does this material existence of ideology

---

1   See Anders Linde-Laursen, 'Small Differences – Large Issues', *The South Atlantic Quarterly* 94: 4 (Fall 1995), pp. 1123–44.

2   The most obvious case – which, for that very reason, I left out – is, of course, that

relate to our conscious convictions? Apropos of Molière's *Tartuffe*, Henri Bergson has emphasized how Tartuffe is funny not on account of his hypocrisy, but because he gets caught in his own mask of hypocrisy:

> He immersed himself so well into the role of a hypocrite that he played it, as it were, sincerely. This way and only this way he becomes funny. Without this purely material sincerity, without the attitude and speech which, through the long practice of hypocrisy, became for him a natural way to act, Tartuffe would be simply repulsive.[3]

Bergson's expression of 'purely material sincerity' dovetails perfectly with the Althusserian notion of Ideological State Apparatuses – of the external ritual which materializes ideology: the subject who maintains his distance towards the ritual is unaware of the fact that the ritual already dominates him from within. As Pascal put it, if you do not believe, kneel down, act *as if* you believe, and belief will come by itself. This is also what Marxian 'commodity fetishism' is about: in his explicit self-awareness, a capitalist is a common-sense nominalist, but the 'purely material sincerity' of his deeds displays the 'theological whimsies' of the commodity universe.[4] This 'purely material sincerity' of the external ideological ritual, not the depth of the subject's inner convictions and desires, is the true *locus* of the fantasy which sustains an ideological edifice.

The standard notion of the way fantasy works within ideology is that of a fantasy scenario which obfuscates the true horror of a situation: instead of a full rendering of the antagonisms which traverse our society, we indulge in the notion of society as an organic Whole, kept together by forces of solidarity and co-operation . . . Here also, however, it is much more productive to look for this notion of fantasy where one would not expect to find it: in marginal and, again, apparently purely utilitarian situations. Let us simply recall the safety instructions prior to the takeoff

---

of the ideological connotation of different positions in the sexual act; that is, of the implicit ideological statements we are making by doing 'it' in a certain position.

3   Henri Bergson, *An Essay on Laughter,* London: Smith, 1937, p. 83.

4   For a more detailed elaboration of the paradoxes of fetishism, see Chapter 3 below.

of an aeroplane – are they not sustained by a phantasmic scenario of how a possible plane crash will look? After a gentle landing on water (miraculously, it is always supposed to happen on water!), each of the passengers puts on the life-jacket and, as on a beach toboggan, slides into the water and takes a swim, like a nice collective lagoon holiday experience under the guidance of an experienced swimming instructor. Is not this 'gentrifying' of a catastrophe (a nice soft landing, stewardesses in dance-like style graciously pointing towards the 'Exit' signs . . .) also ideology at its purest? However, the psychoanalytic notion of fantasy cannot be reduced to that of a fantasy-scenario which obfuscates the true horror of a situation; the first, rather obvious thing to add is that the relationship between fantasy and the horror of the Real it conceals is much more ambiguous than it may seem: fantasy conceals this horror, yet at the same time it creates what it purports to conceal, its 'repressed' point of reference (are not the images of the ultimate horrible Thing, from the gigantic deep-sea squid to the ravaging twister, phantasmic creations *par excellence*?).[5] Furthermore, one should specify the notion of fantasy with a whole series of features.[6]

5   The example of conservatism's reference to the horrifying origins of power (their prohibition against talking about these origins, which precisely creates the Horror of the 'primordial crime' by means of which power was instituted) perfectly expresses the radically ambiguous functioning of the Horrible with respect to the fantasy-screen: Horror is not simply and unambiguously the unbearable Real masked by the fantasy-screen – the way it focuses our attention, imposing itself as the disavowed and, for that reason, all the more operative central point of reference. The Horrible can also function as the screen itself, as the thing whose fascinating effect conceals something 'more horrible than horror itself', the primordial void or antagonism. For example, is not the anti-Semitic demonic image of the Jew, the Jewish plot, such an evocation of the ultimate Horror which, precisely, is the phantasmic screen enabling us to avoid confrontation with the social antagonism?

The logic of the horror which functions as a screen masking the void can also be illustrated by the uncanny power of the motif of a ship drifting along alone, without a captain or any living crew to steer it This is the ultimate horror not the proverbial ghost in the machine, but the machine in the ghost: there is *no* plotting agent behind it, the machine just runs by itself, as a blind contingent device. At the social level, this is also what the notion of a Jewish or Masonic conspiracy conceals: the horror of society as a contingent mechanism blindly following its path, caught in the vicious cycle of its antagonisms.

6 We can leave aside the feature which acquired commonplace status: the answer to the question 'Who, where, how is the (fantasizing) subject inscribed into the phantasmic narrative?' is far from obvious; even when the subject himself appears within his narrative, this is not automatically his point of identification – that is, he by no means necessarily

Fantasy's transcendental schematism

The first thing to note is that fantasy does not simply realize a desire in a hallucinatory way: rather, its function is similar to that of Kantian 'transcendental schematism': a fantasy constitutes our desire, provides its coordinates; that is, it literally 'teaches us how to desire'. The role of fantasy is thus in a way analogous to that of the ill-fated pineal gland in Descartes's philosophy, this mediator between *res cogitans* and *res extensa*: fantasy mediates between the formal symbolic structure and the positivity of the objects we encounter in reality – that is to say, it provides a 'schema' according to which certain positive objects in reality can function as objects of desire, filling in the empty places opened up by the formal symbolic structure. To put it in somewhat simplified terms: fantasy does not mean that when I desire a strawberry cake and cannot get it in reality, I fantasize about eating it; the problem is, rather: *how do I know that I desire a strawberry cake in the first place? This* is what fantasy tells me. This role of fantasy hinges on the fact that 'there is no sexual relationship', no universal formula or matrix guaranteeing a harmonious sexual relationship with one's partner: because of the lack of this universal formula, every subject has to invent a fantasy of his or her own, a 'private' formula for the sexual relationship – for a man, the relationship with a woman is possible only inasmuch as she fits his formula.

Recently, Slovene feminists reacted with a great outcry against a large cosmetics factory's publicity poster for sun lotion, depicting a series of

---

'identifies with himself'. (At a different level, the same goes for the subject's symbolic identity; the best way to render its paradox palpable is to paraphrase the standard disclaimer from the movie credits: 'Any resemblance to actual events or persons is purely accidental'· the gap between $ and S, between the void of the subject and the signifying feature which represents him, means that 'any resemblance of the subject *to himself* is purely accidental'. There is no connection whatsoever between the (phantasmic) real of the subject and his symbolic identity: the two are thoroughly *incommensurable*.) Fantasy thus creates a multitude of 'subject positions' among which the (observing, fantasizing) subject is free to float, to shift his identification from one to another. Here, talk about 'multiple, dispersed subject positions' is justified, with the proviso that these subject positions are to be strictly distinguished from the void that is the subject.

well-tanned women's behinds in tight bathing suits, accompanied by the slogan 'Each has her own factor'. Of course, this publicity is based on a rather vulgar double entendre: the slogan ostensibly refers to the sun lotion, which is offered to customers with different sun factors in order to suit customers' different skin types; however, its entire effect is based on its obvious male-chauvinist reading: 'Any woman can be had, if only the man knows her factor, her specific catalyst, what arouses her!' The Freudian point regarding fundamental fantasy would be that each subject, female or male, possesses such a 'factor' which regulates her or his desire: 'a woman, viewed from behind, on her hands and knees' was the Wolf Man's factor; a statue-like woman without pubic hair was Ruskin's factor; and so on. There is nothing uplifting about our awareness of this 'factor': such awareness can never be subjectivized; it is uncanny – even horrifying – since it somehow 'depossesses' the subject, reducing her or him to a puppet-like level 'beyond dignity and freedom'.

Intersubjectivity

The second feature concerns the radically intersubjective character of fantasy. The critical depreciation and abandonment of the term 'inter-subjectivity' in late Lacan (in clear contrast to his earlier insistence that the proper domain of psychoanalytic experience is neither subjective nor objective, but that of intersubjectivity) does not in any way involve an abandonment of the notion that the subject's relation to his/her Other and the latter's desire is crucial to the subject's very identity – paradoxically, one should claim that Lacan's abandonment of 'inter-subjectivity' is strictly correlative to the focusing of attention on the enigma of the impenetrable Other's desire ('*Che vuoi?*'). What the late Lacan does with intersubjectivity should be opposed to early Lacan's Hegelo-Kojèvian motifs of the struggle for recognition, of the dialectical connection between recognition of desire and desire for recognition, as well as to middle Lacan's 'structuralist' motif of the big Other as the anonymous symbolic structure.

Perhaps the easiest way to discern these shifts is by focusing on the changed status of the *object*. In early Lacan, the object is depreciated as to its inherent qualities; it counts only as a stake in the intersubjective struggles for recognition and love (the milk demanded by a child from the mother is reduced to a 'sign of love', that is, the demand for milk effectively aims at prompting the mother to display her love for the child; a jealous subject demands from his parents a certain toy; this toy becomes the object of his demand, because he is aware that it is also coveted by his brother, etc.). In late Lacan, on the contrary, the focus shifts to the object that the subject itself 'is', to the *agalma*, secret treasure, which guarantees a minimum of phantasmic consistency to the subject's being. That is to say: *objet petit a*, as the object of fantasy, is that 'something in me more than myself on account of which I perceive myself' as 'worthy of the Other's desire'.

One should always bear in mind that the desire 'realized' (staged) in fantasy is not the subject's own, but the *other's* desire: fantasy, phantasmic formation, is an answer to the enigma of '*Che vuoi?*' – 'You're saying this, but *what do you really mean by saying it?*' – which established the subject's primordial, constitutive position. The original question of desire is not directly 'What do I want?', but 'What do *others* want from me? What do they see in me? What am I to others?' A small child is embedded in a complex network of relations; he serves as a kind of catalyst and battlefield for the desires of those around him: his father, mother, brothers and sisters, and so on, fight their battles around him, the mother sending a message to the father through her care for the son. While he is well aware of this role, the child cannot fathom what object, precisely, he is to others, what the exact nature of the games they are playing with him is, and fantasy provides an answer to this enigma: at its most fundamental, fantasy tells me what I am to my others. It is again anti-Semitism, the anti-Semitic paranoia, which reveals this radically *intersubjective* character of fantasy in an exemplary way: fantasy (the social fantasy of the Jewish plot) is an attempt to provide an answer to 'What does society want from me?', to unearth the meaning of the murky events in which I am forced to participate. For that reason, the standard theory of 'projection', according to which the anti-Semite 'projects' on to the figure of the Jew the disavowed part of himself, is not sufficient: the figure of the 'conceptual Jew' cannot be reduced to the externalization of my (anti-Semite's) 'inner conflict'; on the contrary, it bears witness to (and tries to cope with) the fact that I am originally decentred, part of an opaque network whose meaning and logic elude my control.

This radical intersubjectivity of fantasy is discernible even in the most elementary cases, like that (reported by Freud) of his little daughter fantasizing about eating a strawberry cake – what we have here is by no means a simple case of the direct hallucinatory satisfaction of a desire (she wanted a cake, she didn't get it, so she fantasized about it . . .). That is to say: what one should introduce here is precisely the dimension of intersubjectivity: the crucial feature is that while she was voraciously eating a strawberry cake, the little girl noticed how her parents were deeply satisfied by this spectacle, by seeing her fully enjoying it – so what the fantasy of eating a strawberry cake is really about is her attempt to form an identity (of the one who fully enjoys eating a cake given by the parents) that would satisfy her parents, would make her the object of their desire . . .

One can clearly perceive the difference here from early Lacan, for whom the object is reduced to a token which is totally insignificant in itself, since it matters only as the point in which my own and the Other's desires intersect: for late Lacan, the object is precisely that which is 'in the subject more than the subject itself', that which I fantasize that the Other (fascinated by me) sees in me. So it is no longer the object which serves as the mediator between my desire and the Other's desire; rather, it is the Other's desire itself which serves as the mediator between the 'barred' subject $ and the lost object that the subject 'is' – that provides the minimum of phantasmic identity to the subject. And one can also see in what *la traversée du fantasme* consists: in an acceptance of the fact that *there is no secret treasure in me*, that the support of me (the subject) is purely phantasmic.

We can now see clearly, also, the opposition between Lacan and Habermas. Habermas insists on the difference between the subject-object relationship and intersubjectivity proper: in the latter, the other subject is precisely *not* one of the objects in my field of experience, but the partner in a dialogue, the interaction with whom, within a concrete life-world, forms the irreducible background of my experience of reality. What he represses thereby, however, is simply and precisely the *intersection* of these two relations – the level at which another subject is not yet the partner in intersubjective symbolic communication and/or interaction, but *remains an object*, a Thing, that which makes a 'neighbour' into a sleazy repulsive presence – *this* other *qua* the *object* which gives body to an unbearable excess of *jouissance* is the proper 'object of psychoanalysis'. Lacan's point is thus that symbolic intersubjectivity is *not* the ultimate horizon behind which one cannot reach: what precedes it is not a 'monadic' subjectivity, but a pre-symbolic 'impossible' relation to an Other which is the *real* Other, the Other as *Thing*, and not yet the Other located within the field of intersubjectivity.

The narrative occlusion of antagonism

The third point: fantasy is the primordial form of *narrative*, which serves to occult some original deadlock. The sociopolitical fantasy *par excellence*, of course, is the myth of 'primordial accumulation': the narrative of the two workers, one lazy and free-spending, the other diligent and enterprising, accumulating and investing, which provides the myth of the 'origins of capitalism', obfuscating the violence of its actual genealogy. Notwithstanding his emphasis on symbolization and/or historicization in the 1950s, Lacan is thus radically *anti-narrativist*: the ultimate aim of psychoanalytic treatment is *not* for the analysand to organize his confused life-experience into (another) coherent narrative, with all the traumas properly integrated, and so on. It is not only that some narratives are 'false', based upon the exclusion of traumatic events and patching up the gaps left by these exclusions – Lacan's thesis is much stronger: the answer to the question 'Why do we tell stories?' is that *narrative as such* emerges in order to resolve some fundamental antagonism by rearranging its terms into a temporal succession. It is thus the very form of narrative which bears witness to some repressed antagonism. The price one pays for the narrative resolution is the *petitio principii* of the temporal loop – the narrative silently presupposes as already given what it purports to reproduce (the narrative of 'primordial accumulation' effectively explains nothing, since it already presupposes a worker behaving like a full-blown capitalist).[7]

Let us elaborate on this gesture of the narrative resolution of antagonism apropos of the splitting of the domain of law into the neutral public Law and its obscene superego supplement. The problem with the definition of 'totalitarianism' as the eclipse of the neutral symbolic Law, so that the entire domain of law is 'stained' by the obscene superego,[8] is how we are to conceive the *prior* epoch – that is, where was the superego obscenity *before* the advent of 'totalitarianism'? Two opposed narratives suggest themselves here:

- The narrative according to which, with the advent of modernity, the law rooted in concrete traditional communities, and as such still permeated by *jouissance* of a specific 'way of life', gets split into the neutral symbolic Law and its superego supplement of obscene unwritten rules: it is only with the advent of modernity that the neutral judicial order of Law delivered of substantial *jouissance* emerges.
- The (Foucauldian) counter-narrative according to which, in the epoch of modernity, the rule of the traditional judicial Law is replaced by the web of disciplinary practices. Modernity involves the 'crisis of investiture', the inability of subjects to assume symbolic mandates: what prevents them from fulfilling the act of symbolic identification is the perception of a 'stain of enjoyment' in the big Other of the

7   The reference to narrative also enables us to differentiate between neurosis (hysteria) and perversion, since each involves a unique form of narrative: hysteria displays the linear narrative of origins (the neurotic's 'family myth'), while in perversion the narrative remains stuck in the same place and repeats itself indefinitely – that is to say, the perverse narrative is unable to 'progress' properly.

8   For such a notion of 'totalitarianism', see Chapter 6 of Slavoj Žižek, *For They Know Not What They Do*, London: Verso, 1991.

Law, the perception of the domain of law as permeated with obscene enjoyment. Consequently, the disciplinary exercise of power which supplants the pure symbolic Law is by definition stained with super-ego enjoyment (the fact that Schreber was possessed by the vision of the obscene God who wanted to use him as the feminine partner in the act of copulation is thus strictly correlative to the fact that he was the victim of a proto-Foucauldian disciplinary father).[9]

The problem is that these two narratives are, in their crucial aspects, mutu-ally exclusive: according to the first one, the neutral Law, delivered of the stain of enjoyment, emerged with modernity; while according to the second, modernity signals the 'crisis of investiture', the fact that Law is perceived as stained with superego enjoyment . . . The only solution to this deadlock, of course, is to conceive of these two narratives as the two complementary ideological gestures of resolving/obfuscating the under-lying deadlock which resides in the fact that the Law was smeared, stigmatized, by enjoyment *at the very moment of its emergence as the neutral-universal formal Law.* The very emergence of a pure neutral Law, free of its concrete 'organic' life-world support, gives birth to the obscene superego underside, since this very life-world support, once opposed to the pure Law, is all of a sudden perceived as obscene.[10]

It is easy to discern this same paradox in the standard New Age critique of Descartes: Descartes is accused of 'anthropocentrism' – however, does not Cartesian subjectivity (as correlative to the universe of modern science) involve the 'Copernican turn', does it not decentre man and reduce him to an insignificant creature on a small planet? In other words, what one should always bear in mind is how the Cartesian de-substantialization of the subject, its reduction to $, to the pure void of self-relating negativity,

9   As for the political stakes which overdetermine D.P. Schreber's psychosis, see Eric Santner, *My Own Private Germany,* Princeton, NJ: Princeton University Press, 1996.

10   An excellent example of this shift is provided by the novels of Walter Scott, espe-cially *Waverley,* a true epic of the inversion of tribal heroism into banditry; once Scottish society is subordinated to the bourgeois legal order, the very acts which hitherto epitomized the ethical generosity of clan society suddenly look like simple crimes.

is strictly correlative to the opposite reduction of man to a grain of dust in the infinity of the universe, to one among the endless objects in it: these are the two sides of the same process. In this precise sense, Descartes is radically anti-humanist; that is, he dissolves the Renaissance Humanist unity of man as the highest Creature, the summit of creation, into pure *cogito* and its bodily remainder: the elevation of the subject to the transcendental agent of the synthesis constitutive of reality is correlative to the abasement of its material bearer to one among the worldly objects. Although Descartes is also accused of patriarchal bias (the unmistakable male features of *cogito*), does not his formulation of *cogito* as pure thought which, as such, 'has no sex' mark the first break from pre-modern sexualized ontology? Descartes is also accused of conceiving the subject as the owner of natural objects, so that animals and the environment in general are reduced to mere objects available to be exploited, with no protection. However, is it not true that only when we confer upon them the status of property do natural objects become, for the first time, legally *protected* (as only a property can be)?

In all these (and other) cases, Descartes *set up the very standard by means of which one measures and rejects his positive doctrine on behalf of a post-Cartesian 'holistic' approach.* Narrativization is thus misrepresentational in both its versions: in the guise of the story of the progress from the primitive to the higher, more cultivated form (from primitive fetishistic superstition to the spiritual monotheistic religion or, in the case of Descartes, from primitive sexualized ontology to neutral modern thought), as well as in the guise of the story of historical evolution as regression or Fall (say, in the case of Descartes, from organic unity with nature to the exploitative attitude towards it; from the pre-modern spiritual complementarity of woman and man to the Cartesian identification of woman with the 'natural', etc.) – both versions obfuscate the absolute synchronicity of the antagonism in question.

Consequently, the paradox to be fully accepted is that when a certain historical moment is (mis)perceived as the moment of loss of some quality, upon closer inspection it becomes clear that the lost quality emerged only at this very moment of its alleged loss . . . This coincidence of emergence and loss, of course, designates the fundamental paradox of the Lacanian *objet petit a* which emerges as being-lost – narrativization occludes this paradox by describing the process in which the object is first given and then gets lost. (Although it may appear that the Hegelian dialectic, with its matrix of the mediatization of immediacy, is the most elaborate philosophical version of such a narrativization, Hegel was, rather, the first to provide the explicit formulation of this absolute synchronicity – as he put it, the immediate object lost in reflection 'only *comes to be* through being *left behind*'.[11]) The conclusion to be drawn from this absolute synchronicity, of course, is not that 'there is no history, since everything was already here from the very outset', but that the historical process does not follow the logic of narration: actual historical breaks are, if anything, *more* radical than mere narrative deployments, since what changes in them is the entire constellation of emergence and loss. In other words, a true historical break does not simply designate the 'regressive' loss (or 'progressive' gain) of something, but *the shift in the very grid which enables us to measure losses and gains.*[12]

The supreme example of this paradoxical coincidence of emergence and loss is provided by the notion of *history* itself – where, exactly, is its place; that is, which societies can be characterized as properly *historical*? On the one hand, pre-capitalist societies allegedly do not yet know history proper; they are 'circular', 'closed', caught in a repetitive movement predetermined

11 *Hegel's Science of Logic,* London: Allen & Unwin, 1969, p. 402.
12 Another way of formulating the same impasse is via the relationship between Althusser and Foucault: in contrast to Foucault, who conceives the relationship between judicial and disciplinary power as, *grosso modo,* that of historical succession (and thus underestimates the extent to which modern disciplinary power itself requires a 'judicial' supplement, and vice versa), Althusser endeavours (and ultimately foils) to think of the two aspects in a synchronous way, as the two constituents of the ideological process (the interpellation by the big Other stands for the 'judicial' aspect of power, while the Ideological State Apparatuses stand for the disciplinary 'micro-practices'), and thereby leaves out of consideration the historical shifts in the relationship between the two aspects. How are we to conceive of the two approaches, Foucauldian and Althusserian, together, so that we consider the historical passage as the shift in the very status of the split between the two aspects?

by tradition – so history must emerge *afterwards*, with the decay of 'closed' organic societies. On the other hand, the opposite cliché tells us that capitalism itself is no longer historical; it is rootless, with no tradition of its own, and therefore parasitical upon previous traditions, a universal order which (like modern science) can thrive anywhere, from Japan to Argentina, uprooting and slowly corroding all particular life-worlds based on specific traditions. So history is that which gets *lost* with the growth of capitalism, with its ultimate worldwide triumph, signalling the moment of the 'end of history' (Fukuyama's half-forgotten concept). The solution, again, is that *emergence and loss coincide*: the properly 'historical' is only a moment, even if this moment is properly unending and goes on for centuries – the moment of *passage* from pre-capitalist societies to a capitalist universal order.[13]

13   Following the Russian Formalists, David Bordwell has elaborated the distinction between story and plot: the story is the succession of events 'in itself', while the plot designates the way events are 'for itself', presented in the narrative. The clearest example of the gap between story and plot is, of course, the detective whodunit, where the plot progresses from traces of the crime to its final retelling as a consistent linear narrative. (Is not this distinction analogous to that between collection and set – to the fact that it is possible to construct a multitude of sets from the same collection?) The point of this distinction, of course, is that there is *stricto sensu* no story which simply precedes the plot: every story is already a 'plot', it involves a minimum of narrative organization, so that the distinction between story and plot is *internal to the plot*: 'story' (the 'true sequence of events') as opposed to plot always involves a minimum of naturalizing misrecognition of the devices of plot. For that reason, the example of the whodunit is misleading in so far as it suggests that the plot is a way of manipulating-repressing 'what really went on' (the story), as in the flashback procedures by means of which we gradually penetrate the true outline of the story. The point to make, rather, is that the story itself relies on a minimum of 'repression', and the plot (i.e. the way the story is manipulated in its presentation), in its very 'distortion' of the 'natural' succession of events, reveals the 'repressed' of the story (as in the Freudian distinction between the latent thought and manifest content of a dream, where the true secret, the unconscious desire, inscribes itself via the very distortion of the latent thought in the manifest content). When one retells a detective mystery in linear form, it loses its appeal, since what gets lost is precisely the element of mystery; this excess, produced by the shift from the linear narrative of a crime to the reconstruction of this crime via the deduction based on interpreting the traces, is not merely 'rhetorical', it reveals a 'truth' which disappears in the linear retelling.
    Incidentally, this holds not only in the case of mystery, where our interest is kept alive by the fact that we do not know what happened in the past, but perhaps even more in the opposite case of a tragic course of events which is rendered even more tragic when its ultimate catastrophic impact is presented to us in advance. In J.B. Priestley's *Time and the*

After the Fall

This brings us to the next feature, the problematic of the Fall. Contrary to the common-sense notion of fantasizing as an indulgence in the hallucinatory realization of desires prohibited by the Law, the phantasmic narrative does not stage the suspension-transgression of the Law, but *the very act of its installation*, of the intervention of the cut of symbolic castration – what the fantasy endeavours to stage is ultimately the 'impossible' scene of castration. For this reason, fantasy as such is, in its very notion, close to perversion: the perverse ritual stages the act of castration, of the primordial loss which allows the subject to enter the symbolic order. Or – to put it more precisely – in contrast to the 'normal' subject, for whom the Law functions as the agency of prohibition which regulates (access to the object of) his desire, for the pervert, *the object of his desire is Law itself* – the Law is the Ideal he is longing for, he wants to be fully acknowleged by the Law, integrated into its functioning … The irony of this should not escape us: the pervert, this 'transgressor' *par excellence* who purports to violate all the rules of 'normal' and decent behaviour, effectively longs for the very rule of Law.[14]

At the political level, let us recall the interminable search for the phantasmic point at which German history 'took the wrong turn' which

---

Conways, we see in Act I an evening gathering of young family members, brothers and sisters, dreaming about their future plans; in Act III, we see them twenty years later, all of them failures, leading miserable lives; Act III in then returns to the same evening as Act I, and presents its continuation, with the Conways dreaming about their bright future hopes … this minimal, elementary shift from story to plot (the reversal of temporal order) – the fact that after we have already witnessed their miserable failure, we see the Conways in Act III dreaming about their future – not only makes the situation much more depressing, but also conveys its truth: the fact that their hopes were in vain, that they were doomed to fail.

14   A further point about the pervert is that since, for him, the Law is not fully established (the Law is his *lost* object of desire), he supplements this lack with an intricate set of *regulations* (the masochistic ritual). The crucial point is, therefore, to bear in mind the opposition between Law and regulations (or 'rules'): the latter bear witness to the absence or suspension of Law.

ended up in Nazism: delayed national unification, due to the dismemberment of the German Empire after the Thirty Years War; the aestheticization of politics in the Romantic reaction to Kant (the theory of Jean-Luc Nancy and Philippe Lacoue-Labarthe); the 'crisis of investiture' and the Bismarckian state socialism in the second half of the nineteenth century; up to the report of the German tribes' resistance to the Romans which, allegedly, already displayed the features of *Volksgemeinschaft*...[15] Similar examples abound: when exactly, for example, did patriarchal repression coincide with the repression and exploitation of nature? The tenets of eco-feminism provide a multitude of 'regressive' determinations of this unique phantasmic moment of the Fall: the predominance of nineteenth-century Western capitalism; modern Cartesian science, with its objectivizing attitude towards nature; the noxious influence of the Greek rationalist Socratic Enlightenment; the emergence of great barbarian Empires; up to the passage from nomadic to agricultural civilization . . . And – Jacques-Alain Miller pointed out – is not Foucault himself also caught in the same phantasmic loop in his search for the moment when the Western order of sexuality emerged? He regresses further and further back from modernity, until he finally sets the limit where the Antique ethic of the 'care of the Self' disintegrates into the Christian ethic of confession: the fact that the tone of Foucault's last two books on pre-Christian ethics differs completely from his earlier probing into the complex of power, knowledge and sexuality – instead of his usual analyses of the material micro-practices of ideology, we get a rather standard version of the 'history of ideas' – bears witness to the fact that Foucault's Greece and Rome 'before the Fall' (into sexuality-guilt-confession) are purely phantasmic entities.

Against this background, it is possible to elaborate a precise theory of the Fall via a reference to Milton's *Paradise Lost*. Its first feature is that, for structural reasons, the Fall has never occurred in the present – Adam 'does not, strictly speaking, decide; he finds that he has decided. Adam discovers

15   I owe this example to Charity Snider, Columbia University.

his choice rather than makes it.'[16] Why is it like this? If the decision (the choice of the Fall) were to happen in the present, it would already presuppose what it gives birth to – the very freedom to choose: the paradox of the Fall is that it is an act which opens up the very space of decision. How is this possible? The second feature of the Fall is that it results from the choice to disobey in order to retain the erotic rapture of Eve, yet the paradox lies in the fact that 'because [Adam] disobeys he loses what he disobeyed in order to keep'.[17] Here we have, once again, the structure of castration: when Adam chooses to fall in order to retain *jouissance*, what he loses thereby is precisely *jouissance* – do we not encounter here the reversal of the structure of the 'states which are essentially by-products'? Adam loses X by directly choosing it, aiming to retain it . . . That is to say: what, precisely, is symbolic castration? It is the prohibition of incest in the precise sense of the loss of something which the subject never possessed in the first place. Let us imagine a situation in which the subject aims at X (say, a series of pleasurable experiences); the operation of castration does not consist in depriving him of any of these experiences, but adds to the series a purely potential, nonexistent X, with respect to which the actually accessible experiences appear all of a sudden as lacking, not wholly satisfying. One can see here how the phallus functions as the very signifier of castration: the very signifier of the lack, the signifier which forbids the subject access to X, gives rise to its phantom . . .

This paradox also enables us to define Paradise as the libidinal economy in which the paradox of the 'states which are essentially by-products' is not yet at work: in Paradise, the impossible coincidence of knowledge and *jouissance* persists. The assertion of some theologians (Aquinas among them) that there *was* sex in Paradise, that Adam and Eve *did* copulate, that their pleasure was even greater than ours (i.e. the pleasure of having sex after the Fall), the only and crucial difference being that, while copulating, they maintained proper measure and distance, and never lost self-control – this

16   I draw here on Henry Staten, *Eros in Mourning*, Baltimore, MD: Johns Hopkins University Press, 1995, p. 125.

17   Ibid., p. 124.

assertion unknowingly reveals the secret of Paradise: it was the kingdom of *perversity.* That is to say: does not the fundamental paradox of perversion reside in the fact that the pervert successfully avoids the deadlock of the 'states which are essentially by-products'? When the sadomasochistic pervert stages the scene in which he participates, he 'remains in control' at all times, maintains a distance, gives directions like a stage director, but his enjoyment is none the less much more intense than that of immediate passionate immersion.

So – what precise form did sexual activity assume in Eden? In the practice of homosexual fist-fucking, the man (usually associated with active penetration) must open himself up passively; he is penetrated in the region in which 'closure', resistance to penetration, is the natural reaction (one knows that the difficulty of fist-fucking is more psycho-logical than physical: the difficulty lies in relaxing the anal muscles enough to allow the partner's fist to penetrate – the position of the fisted one in fist-fucking is perhaps the most intense experience of passive opening available to human experience); on top of this opening oneself up to the other, whose organ literally enters my body and explores it from within, the other crucial feature is that this organ, precisely, is not the phallus (as in 'normal' anal intercourse) but the fist (hand), the organ *par excellence* not of spontaneous pleasure but of instrumental activity, of work and exploration. (No wonder fist-fucking, in its physical features, almost overlaps with the way a doctor examines the rectum for prostate cancer.) In this precise sense, fist-fucking is *Edenic*; it is the closest we can get to what sex was like before the Fall: what enters me is not the phallus, but a pre-phallic *partial object*, a hand (akin to hands running around as objects in the surrealistic nightmares in some of Buñuel's films) – we are back in a pre-lapsarian Edenic state in which, according to the speculations of some theologians, sex was performed as just another instrumental activity.

The impossible gaze

The fifth feature: on account of its temporal loop, the phantasmic narrative always involves an *impossible gaze*, the gaze by means of which the subject is already present at the act of his/her own conception. An exemplary case of this vicious cycle in the service of ideology is an anti-abortion fairy-tale written in the 1980s by a right-wing Slovene nationalist poet. The tale is set on an idyllic South Sea island where aborted children live together without their parents: although their life is nice and calm, they miss parental love and spend their time in sad reflection on how it is that their parents preferred a career or a luxurious holiday to themselves . . . The trick, of course, lies in the fact that the *aborted* children are presented as *having been born*, only born into an alternative universe (the lone Pacific island), retaining the memory of parents who 'betrayed' them – in this way they can direct at their parents a reproachful gaze which makes them guilty.[18]

Apropos of a phantasmic scene, the question to be asked is thus always: for which gaze is it staged? Which narrative is it destined to support? According to some recently published documents, the British General Michael Rose, head of the UNPROFOR forces in Bosnia, and his special team of SAS operatives, definitely had a 'hidden agenda' in Bosnia: under the pretence of maintaining a truce between the so-called 'warring factions', their secret task was also to place the blame on the Croats, and especially the Muslims (soon after the fall of Srebrenica, for example, Rose's operatives suddenly 'discovered', in northern Bosnia, some Serb bodies

18 What this reactionary fairy-tale relies on is the overlapping of the two lacks in the encounter of the enigma of the Other's desire. As Lacan puts it, the subject answers the enigma of the Other's desire (what does the Other want from me? What am I to the Other?) with his own lack, with proposing his own disappearance: when a small child is confronted by the enigma of his parents' desire, the fundamental fantasy to test this desire is the fantasy of his own disappearance (What if I die or disappear? How will my mother and father react?). In the Slovene fairy-tale, this phantasmic structure is realized: the children imagine themselves as nonexistent and, from this position, question their parents' desire ('Why did my mother prefer her career or a new car to me?').

allegedly slaughtered by the Muslims; their attempts to 'mediate' between Muslims and Croats actually inflamed the conflict between them, etc.); these diversions were intended to create the perception of the Bosnian conflict as a kind of 'tribal warfare', a civil war of everybody against everybody else in which 'all sides are equally to blame'. Instead of a clear condemnation of the Serb aggression, this perception was destined to prepare the terrain for an international effort of 'pacification' which would 'reconcile the warring factions'. From a sovereign state, the victim of aggression, Bosnia was suddenly transformed into a chaotic place in which 'powermad warlords' acted out their historical traumas at the expense of innocent women and children . . . Lurking in the background, of course, is the pro-Serbian 'insight' according to which peace in Bosnia is possible only if we do not 'demonize' one side in the conflict: responsibility is to be equally distributed, with the West assuming the role of the neutral judge elevated above local tribal conflicts.

The key point for our analysis is that General Rose's pro-Serb 'secret war' on the terrain itself was not trying to change the relations between military forces but, rather, to prepare the ground for a different narrative perception of the situation: 'real' military activity itself was here in the service of ideological narrativization.[19] And, incidentally, the key event which functioned as a kind of *point de capiton* in turning the held perspective on the Bosnian war hitherto upside down, and brought about its depoliticized (re)narrativization as a 'humanitarian catastrophe', was François Mitterrand's visit to Sarajevo in the summer of 1992. One is even tempted

19   Rose's bias was also clearly discernible in his curious, almost Lacanian, definition of the 'safety zones' which UNPROFOR was supposed to guarantee: in a TV interview, he stressed that one should define them in a 'flexible' way – if the Serbs occupy part of a safety zone, one simply redefines its boundaries, so that UNPROFOR now guarantees the restricted zone; in this way, no matter what the Serbs do, the security of these zones is always maintained . . . The arguments which made the fall of Srebrenica palpable also followed the same sophistic reasoning: first, the UN forces demanded that the besieged Bosnians in Srebrenica should disarm, since the UN can defend only civilian populations, not one army against another; then, after the Serbs attacked the almost defenceless civilian population of Srebrenica, UNPROFOR, of course, made it known that its limited forces could not protect a defenceless city from the well-armed Serb Army.

to postulate that General Rose was sent to Bosnia in order to realize Mitterrand's vision of the conflict on the ground. That is to say: until Mitterrand's visit, the predominant perception of the Bosnian conflict was still a *political* one: in dealing with Serb aggression, the key problem was the aggression of ex-Yugoslavia against an independent state; after Mitterrand left, the accent shifted towards a humanitarian aspect – down there, a savage tribal war is going on, and the only thing the civilized West can do is to exert its influence to assuage the inflamed passions and help the innocent victims with food and medicine.

Precisely through his display of compassion towards the suffering people of Sarajevo, Mitterrand's visit dealt the crucial blow to Bosnian interests – it functioned as the key factor of *political neutralization* in the international perception of the conflict. Or as vice-president of Bosnia and Herzegovina Ejup Ganic put it in an interview: 'First we were glad to receive Mitterrand, hoping that his visit signals a true concern of the West. All of a sudden, however, we grasped that we are lost.' However, the key point is that this gaze of the external innocent observer for whom the spectacle of 'tribal warfare in the Balkans' was staged, has the same 'impossible' status as the gaze of the aborted children born into a different reality in the Slovene anti-abortion fairy-tale: the gaze of the innocent observer is also in a way nonexistent, since this gaze is the impossible neutral gaze of someone who falsely *exempts* himself from his concrete historical existence – that is, from his actual involvement in the Bosnian conflict.

The same operation is easily discernible in the abundant media reports on the 'saintly' activities of Mother Teresa in Calcutta, which clearly rely on the phantasmic screen of the Third World. Calcutta is regularly presented as a Hell on Earth, the exemplary case of the decaying Third World megalopolis, full of social decay, poverty, violence and corruption, with its residents caught in terminal apathy (the facts are, of course, rather different: Calcutta is a city bursting with activity, culturally much more thriving than Bombay, with a successful local Communist government maintaining a whole network of social services). Into this picture of utter gloom, Mother Teresa brings a ray of hope to the dejected with the message that poverty is to be accepted as a way to redemption, since the poor, in enduring their sad fate with silent dignity and faith, repeat Christ's Way of the Cross ... The ideological benefit of this operation is double: in so far as she suggests to the poor and terminally ill that they should seek salvation in their very suffering, Mother Teresa deters them from probing into the causes of their predicament – from *politicizing* their situation; at the same time, she offers the rich from the West the chance of a kind of substitute-redemption by making financial contributions to her charitable activity. Again, all this works against the background of the phantasmic image of the Third World as Hell on Earth, as a place so utterly desolate that no political activity, only charity and compassion, can alleviate the suffering.[20]

The inherent transgression

In order to be operative, fantasy has to remain 'implicit', it has to maintain a distance towards the explicit symbolic texture sustained by it, and to function as its inherent transgression. This constitutive gap between the explicit symbolic texture and its phantasmic background is obvious in any work of art. Owing to the priority of place over the element which fills it up, even the most harmonious work of art is a priori fragmentary, lacking in regard to its place: the 'trick' of an artistic success resides in the artist's capacity to turn this lack into an advantage – skillfully to manipulate the central void and its resonance in the elements that encircle it. One can account in this way for the 'paradox of the Venus de Milo': today the statue's mutilation is no longer experienced as a deficiency, but, on the contrary, as a positive constituent of its aesthetic impact. A simple mental experiment confirms this conjecture: if we imagine the undamaged, complete statue (during the nineteenth century, art historians were actually busy 'complementing' it; in different 'reconstructions', the missing hand holds a spear, a torch, even a mirror ...), the effect is unmistakably

---

20   See Christopher Hitchens, *The Missionary Position,* London: Verso, 1995.

that of kitsch, the proper aesthetic impact is lost. What is significant in these 'reconstructions' is their very multiplicity: the object destined to fill the void is a priori secondary and, as such, exchangeable. A typically 'post-modern' counterpart to this nineteenth-century kitsch is provided by recent attempts to fill the void around which some canonical work is structured; again, the effect is inevitably that of obscene vulgarity. Take *Heathcliff*, a recent novel that deals with the central void of *Wuthering Heights*: what was Heathcliff doing between his disappearance from Wuthering Heights and his return as a rich man several years later? One of the earlier, more successful examples is the classic *film noir Killers*, based on Hemingway's short story of the same name: in its first ten minutes, the film faithfully follows the original story; what then ensues, however, is a prequel to it – an attempt to reconstruct the mysterious past traumatic experience that caused the 'Swede' to vegetate like the living dead, and calmly await his death.

Art is thus fragmentary, even when it is an organic Whole, since it always relies on the *distance towards fantasy*. In the 'unpublishable fragment' of her unfinished story 'Beatrice Palmato',[21] Edith Wharton provides a detailed X-rated description of a father–daughter incest, with mutual masturbation, cunnilingus and fellatio, as well as, of course, the act itself. It is easy to indulge in a quick psychoanalytic explanation, according to which this fragment offers the 'key' to Wharton's entire literary *œuvre* best condensed in the syntagm 'the "No" of the Mother' (the title of a sub-chapter in Erlich's book on Wharton). In Wharton's nuclear family it was her mother who acted as the agent of prohibition, while her father embodied a kind of prohibited knowledge, permeated with enjoyment. Further-more, it is easy here to play the game of child sexual abuse, and to point out that sufficient 'circumstantial evidence' suggests Wharton's childhood sexual abuse by her father as the traumatic event which marked the course of her life and literary career. It is also easy to emphasize the

21   The plot summary and the surviving fragment of 'Beatrice Palmato' are published in Gloria Erlich, *The Sexual Education of Edith Wharton,* Los Angeles: University of California Press, 1992.

ambiguity between fantasy and 'reality': it is practically impossible clearly to discern their respective parts (was paternal incest just her fantasy, or was this fantasizing triggered by 'real' sexual abuse?). In any case, this vicious cycle bears witness to the fact that Edith is not 'innocent': she participated in incest at the level of fantasy. Such an approach, however, fails to perceive that there is more truth in the artist's removal from fantasy than in its direct rendering: popular melodrama and kitsch are much closer to fantasy than 'true art'. In other words, in order to account for the distortion of 'original fantasy', it is not sufficient to refer to social prohibitions: what intervenes in the guise of these prohibitions is the fact that fantasy itself is a 'primordial lie', a screen masking the fundamental *impossibility* (in the case of Edith Wharton, of course, we are dealing with the phantasmic notion that doing it with one's father would really be 'it', the fully realized sexual relationship the woman is looking for in vain in her relationship with her husband or other partners). The artifice of 'true art' is thus to manipulate the censorship of the underlying fantasy in such a way as to reveal the radical falsity of this fantasy.

Let us further illustrate this gap between an explicit texture and its phantasmic support with an example from cinema. Contrary to its misleading appearance, Robert Altman's *MASH* is a perfectly conformist film – for all their mockery of authority, practical jokes and sexual escapades, the members of the MASH crew *perform their job exemplarily*, and thus present absolutely no threat to the smooth running of the military machine. In other words, the cliché which regards *MASH* as an anti-militarist film, depicting the horrors of the meaningless military slaughter which can be endured only through a healthy measure of cynicism, practical jokes, laughing at pompous official rituals, and so on, misses the point – this very distance is ideology. This dimension of *MASH* becomes even more tangible the moment one compares it to two other well-known films about military life, *An Officer and a Gentleman* and *Full Metal Jacket*. *MASH* and *An Officer* exhibit the two versions of the perfectly functioning military subject: identification with the military machine is supported either by ironic distrust, indulgence in practical jokes and sexual escapades (*MASH*), or by the awareness that behind the cruel drill sergeant there is a 'warm human person', a helping father-substitute who only feigns cruelty (in *An Officer and a Gentleman*), in strict analogy with the – profoundly anti-feminist – myth of a hooker who, deep in her heart, longs to be a good mother. *Full Metal Jacket*, on the other hand, successfully resists this ideological temptation to 'humanize' the drill sergeant or other members of the crew, and thus lays on the table the cards of the military ideological machine: the distance from it, far from signalling the limitation of the ideological machine, functions as its positive *condition of possibility*. What we get in the first part of the film is the military drill, the direct bodily discipline, saturated with the unique blend of a humiliating display of power, sexualization and obscene blasphemy (at Christmas, the soldiers are ordered to sing 'Happy birthday dear Jesus. . .') – in short, the superego machine of Power at its purest. This part of the film ends with a soldier who, on account of his overidentification with the military ideological machine, 'runs amok' and shoots first the drill sergeant, then himself; the radical, unmediated identification with the phantasmic superego machine necessarily leads to a murderous *passage à l'acte*. The second, main part of the film ends with a scene in which a soldier (Matthew Modine) who, throughout the film, has displayed a kind of ironic 'human distance' towards the military machine (on his helmet, the inscription 'Born to kill' is accompanied by the peace sign, etc. – in short, it looks as if he has stepped right out of *MASH*!), shoots a wounded Vietcong sniper girl. He is the one in whom the interpellation by the military big Other has fully succeeded; he is the fully constituted military subject.

The lesson is therefore clear: an ideological identification exerts a true hold on us precisely when we maintain an awareness that we are not fully identical to it, that there is a rich human person beneath it: 'not all is ideology, beneath the ideological mask, I am also a human person' is *the very form of ideology*, of its 'practical efficiency'. Close analysis of even the most 'totalitarian' ideological edifice inevitably reveals that not everything in it is 'ideology' (in the popular sense of the 'politically instrumentalized legitimization of power relations'): in every ideological edifice, there is a kind of 'trans-ideological' kernel, since, if an ideology is to become operative and effectively 'seize' individuals, it *has* to batten on and manipulate some kind of 'trans-ideological' vision which cannot be reduced to a simple instrument of legitimizing pretensions to power (notions and sentiments of solidarity, justice, belonging to a community, etc.). Is not a kind of 'authentic' vision discernible even in Nazism (the notion of the deep solidarity which keeps the 'community of people' together), not to mention Stalinism? The point is thus not that there is no ideology without a trans-ideological 'authentic' kernel but rather, that *it is only the reference to such a trans-ideological kernel which makes an ideology 'workable'.*

In one of his speeches to the Nazi crowd in Nuremberg, Hitler made a self-referential remark about how this very reunion is to be perceived: an external observer, unable to experience the 'inner greatness' of the Nazi movement, will see only the display of external military and political strength; while for us, members of the movement who live and breathe it, it is infinitely more: the assertion of the inner link connecting us . . . here again we encounter the reference to the extra-ideological kernel. Hitler's favourite Wagner opera was neither the overtly German *Meistersinger* nor *Lohengrin*, with its call to arms to defend Germany against the Eastern hordes, but *Tristan*, with its tendency to leave behind the Day (the daily life of symbolic obligations, honours and debts) and to immerse oneself in the Night, ecstatically to embrace one's own death. This 'aesthetic suspension of the political' (to paraphrase Kierkegaard) was at the very core of the phantasmic background of the Nazi attitude: at stake in it was 'something more than politics', an ecstatic aestheticized experience of Community.[22] So, paradoxically, the dangerous ingredient of Nazism is

22   For that reason, it is also erroneous to dismiss Nazi rituals as an 'inauthentic', faked imitation of pagan sacred rituals: Nazism actually *does* carry out the 'return of the repressed' of Christianity – of the pagan logic of the 'offering to obscure gods': 'This, re-enacting the most monstrous and supposedly superseded forms of the holocaust, is the drama of Nazism' (Jacques Lacan, *The Four Fundamental Concepts of Psycho-Analysis,* New York: Norton, 1978, p. 275), In other words, those who lament the loss of the authentic, 'primitive' relationship to the Sacred in our 'rationalist' and 'utilitarian' Western civilization have no right to become indignant about Nazi rituals . . .

not its 'utter politicization' of the whole of social life but, on the contrary, the suspension of the political through the reference to an extra-ideological kernel, much stronger than in a 'normal' democratic political order. Therein, perhaps, resides the problem with Judith Butler's question

> Does politicization always need to overcome *dis*identification? What are the possibilities of politicizing *dis*identification, this experience of *misrecognition*, this uneasy sense of standing under a sign to which one does and does not belong?[23]

Is not the attitude of the heroes of *MASH*, however, precisely that of an active *disidentification*? Of course, one can argue that *this* disidentification is something entirely different from the lesbian parodic imitation-subversion of feminine codes – none the less, the point remains that the difference is one between the two modes of disidentification, not between identification and its subversion. For that reason, an ideological edifice can be undermined by a too-literal identification, which is why its successful functioning requires a minimal distance from its explicit rules. Is not an exemplary case of such a subversion-through-identification provided by Jaroslav Hašek's *The Good Soldier Schweik*, the novel whose hero wreaks total havoc by simply executing the orders of his superiors in an overzealous and all-too-literal way? The inevitable conclusion to be drawn from this paradox is that the feature which effectively sustains identification, the famous Freudian-Lacanian *einziger Zug*, the unary feature, is not the obvious one, the big 'official' insignia, but a small feature, even the one of *marking a distance* from the official insignia. When a lesbian imitates-parodies-repeats-subverts the standard feminine code, does she not thereby, at a 'deeper' level, assert her 'true' queer identity, which requires such an ironic-subverting-parodizing attitude? A different example of the same logic is provided by the 'leader caught with his pants down': the solidarity of the group is strengthened by the subjects' common disavowal

23   Judith Butler, *Bodies That Matter,* New York: Routledge, 1994, p. 219.

of the misfortune that laid bare the Leader's failure or impotence – a shared lie is an incomparably more effective bond for a group than the truth. When, in an academic department, members of the inner circle surrounding a famous professor become aware of some flaw in him (he is addicted to drugs, a kleptomaniac, a sexual masochist pervert, he has stolen a key line of argumentation from a student, etc., etc.), this very knowledge of the flaw – coupled with the willingness to disavow this knowledge – is the true feature of identification which keeps the group together . . . (The catch, of course, is that the subject fascinated by the charismatic figure of a Leader is necessarily the victim of a kind of perspective-illusion: he [mis]perceives the 'because of' as 'in spite of': in his subjective experience, he adores the Leader *in spite of* the mark of his weakness, not because of it.)

The Duelists, Ridley Scott's extraordinary directorial début (based on a short story, 'The Duel', by Joseph Conrad), depicts the lifelong combat between two high-ranking soldiers, a true upper-class nobleman and an aspiring officer of middle-class origins – what keeps them forever apart is the difference in the way each of them relates to the upper-class code of honour: the aspiring middle-class officer doggedly follows this code and, for that very reason, generates a lasting impression of awkward ridicule; his counterpart, the nobleman, constantly violates the explicit rules of the official code, and thereby asserts his true upper-classness. The problem of the aspiring lower middle classes is that they misperceive the true cause of their failure: they think they are missing something, some hidden rule, and therefore feel compelled to follow all the rules even more closely. What they misperceive, however, is that the mysterious X which accounts for true upper-classness cannot be pinned down to a specific positive symbolic feature. Here we again encounter the *objet petit a*: when we are faced with two series of behaviour which cannot be distinguished by any clearly defined positive symbolic feature, yet the difference between the two is the unmistakable difference between true upper-classness and its clumsy imitation, that unfathomable X, the *je ne sais quoi* which accounts for this gap – in short, the object which makes the difference where one cannot establish any positive difference – this is precisely the *objet petit a* as the unfathomable object-cause of desire.

When the Clinton administration resolved the deadlock of gays in the US Army with the compromise 'Don't ask, don't tell!' (i.e. soldiers are not directly asked if they are gay, so they are also not compelled to lie and deny it, although they are not formally allowed in the Army – they are tolerated in so far as they keep their sexual orientation private, and do not actively endeavour to engage others in it), this opportunist measure was deservedly criticized for basically endorsing the homophobic attitude towards homosexuality: although the direct prohibition of homosexuality is not to be enforced, its very existence as a virtual threat compelling gays to remain in the closet affects their actual social status. In other words, what this solution amounted to was an explicit elevation of hypocrisy into a social principle, like the attitude towards prostitution in traditional Catholic countries – if we pretend that gays in the Army do not exist, it is as if they actually do not exist (for the big Other). Gays are to be tolerated, on condition that they accept the basic censorship concerning their identity.

While it is fully justified on its own level, the notion of censorship at work in this criticism, with its Foucauldian background of Power which, in the very act of censorship and other forms of exclusion, generates the excess it endeavours to contain and dominate, none the less seems to fall short at a crucial point. What it misses is the way in which censorship not only affects the status of the marginal or subversive force that the power discourse endeavours to dominate but, at an even more radical level, splits the power discourse itself from within. One should ask a naive, but nevertheless crucial question here: why does the Army community so strongly resist publicly accepting gays into its ranks? There is only one possible consistent answer: not because homosexuality poses a threat to the alleged 'phallic and patriarchal' libidinal economy of the Army community, but, on the contrary, because the libidinal economy of the Army community itself relies on a thwarted/disavowed homosexuality as the key component of the soldiers' male bonding.

From my own experience, I remember how the old infamous Yugoslav People's Army was homophobic to the extreme (when someone was discovered to have homosexual inclinations, he was instantly turned into a pariah, treated as a non-person, before being formally dismissed from the Army), yet at the same time, everyday army life was excessively permeated with the atmosphere of homosexual innuendo. Say, while soldiers were standing in line for their meal, a common vulgar joke was to stick a finger into the ass of the person ahead of you and then to withdraw it quickly, so that when the surprised person turned round, he did not know who among the soldiers sharing a stupid obscene smile behind his back did it. A predominant form of greeting a fellow soldier in my unit, instead of simply saying 'Hello!', was to say 'Smoke my prick!' ('*Pu i kurac!*' in Serbo-Croat); this formula was so standardized that it completely lost any obscene connotation and was pronounced in a totally neutral way, as a pure act of politeness.

References to homosexuality permeated even the (sometimes surprisingly complex) soldiers' practical jokes. Once, upon entering the large sleeping barracks, I witnessed a strange scene: three soldiers were holding another soldier's head firmly on a pillow, while a fourth soldier, using his half-erect penis as a stick, was beating the forehead of the soldier whose head was fixed on the pillow. The explanation of this strange ritualistic procedure involves a series of linguistic references and displacements worthy of Freud's famous case of the forgetting of the name Signorelli. In Serbo-Croat, the common term for testicles is not 'balls' but 'eggs' ('I'll squeeze your eggs!', not 'your balls'). Furthermore, the term for eggs 'over-easy' (unscrambled fried eggs) is 'eggs on the eye'. These two features provide the background for a standard Serbo-Croat vulgar riddle-joke: 'How do you make eggs on the eye? By putting the prick on the forehead!' All these elements combined account for the scene I witnessed in the barracks: after a particularly tasteless dinner, which was left uneaten by most of the soldiers, the unfortunate soldier, the victim of the practical joke, lying on his bed, loudly complained that he was still very hungry and wouldn't mind a simple meal, perhaps a pair of eggs on the eye; his fellow soldiers immediately seized the opportunity and provided him with 'eggs on the eye' by putting a prick on his forehead.

The key point not to be missed here is how this fragile coexistence of extreme and violent homophobia with a thwarted – that is, publicly unacknowledged, 'underground' – homosexual libidinal economy bears witness to the fact that the discourse of the military community can operate only by censoring its own libidinal foundation. At a slightly different level, the same goes for the practice of hazing (the ceremonial beating up and humiliating of the US Marines by their elder peers: sticking their medals directly on to their breast skin, etc.): when the public disclosure of these practices (somebody secretly shot them on video and made the tape public) caused such an outrage, what disturbed the public was not the practice of hazing itself (everybody was aware that things like this were going on) but the fact of rendering it public.

Outside the confines of military life, do we not encounter a strictly analogous self-censoring mechanism in contemporary conservative populism, with its sexist and racist bias? Recall the election campaigns of Jesse Helms, in which the racist and sexist message is not publicly acknowledged (on the public level, it is sometimes even violently disavowed), but is instead inarticulated 'between the lines', in a series of double-entendres and coded allusions. The point is that this kind of self-censorship (not openly admitting one's own fundamental message) is necessary if, in the present ideological conditions, Helms's discourse is to remain operative: if it were to articulate its racist bias directly, in a public way, this would make it unacceptable in the eyes of the predominant political discursive regime; if it were effectively to abandon the self-censored coded racist message, it would endanger the support of its targeted electoral body. Conservative populist political discourse is therefore an excellent example of a power discourse whose efficiency depends on the mechanism of self-censorship: it relies on a mechanism which is operative only in so far as it remains censored. Against the image, ever-present in cultural criticism, of a radical subversive discourse or practice 'censored' by Power, one is even tempted to claim that today, more than ever, the mechanism of censorship intervenes predominantly to enhance the efficiency of the power discourse itself.

The temptation to be avoided here is the old Leftist notion of 'better for us to deal with the enemy who openly admits his (racist, homophobic ...) bias than with the hypocritical attitude of publicly denouncing what one secretly and actually endorses'. This notion fatally underestimates the ideologico-political significance of keeping up *appearances*: an appearance is never 'merely an appearance', it profoundly affects the *actual* sociosymbolic position of those concerned. If racist attitudes were to be rendered acceptable for the mainstream ideologico-political discourse, this would radically shift the balance of the entire ideological hegemony. This is probably what Alain Badiou had in mind when[24] he mockingly designated his work a search for the 'good terror'. Today, in the face of the emergence of new racism and sexism, the strategy should be to *make such enunciations unutterable*, so that anyone relying on them automatically disqualifies himself (like, in our universe, those who refer approvingly to Fascism). One should emphatically *not* discuss 'how many people really died in Auschwitz', what are 'the good aspects of slavery', 'the necessity of cutting down on workers' collective rights', and so on; the position here should be quite unashamedly 'dogmatic' and 'terrorist': this is *not* a matter for 'open, rational, democratic discussion'.[25]

We are now in a position to specify the distinction between the Foucauldian interconnection between Power and resistance, and our notion of 'inherent transgression'. Let us begin via the matrix of the possible relations between Law and its transgression. The most elementary is

24   In a recent private conversation.

25   Towards the end of 1996, the Croat President Tudjman and his close advisers, in their overview of the situation in Croatia, referred to a 'Masonic-Jewish plot against Croatia', denouncing Western organizations and foundations (Amnesty International, Soros) as hand-in-glove with the enemies of Croatia, adding to this list even the BBC and Voice of America, warning against the penetration of paid subversives into every pore of Croat public and cultural life (incidentally, exactly the same list of enemies as twenty years ago, when the former Communist regime warned against the subversive ideological warfare of the West). The measure of ideologico-political 'regression' is the extent to which such propositions become acceptable in public discourse.

the simple relation of externality, of external opposition, in which transgression is directly opposed to legal Power, and poses a threat to it. The next step is to claim that transgression hinges on the obstacle it violates: without Law there is no transgression; transgression needs an obstacle in order to assert itself. Foucault, of course, in Volume I of *The History of Sexuality*, rejects both these versions, and asserts the absolute immanence of resistance to Power. However, the point of 'inherent transgression' is not only that resistance is immanent to Power, that power and counter-power generate each other; it is not only that Power itself generates the excess of resistance which it can no longer dominate; it is also not only that – in the case of sexuality – the disciplinary 'repression' of a libidinal investment eroticizes this gesture of repression itself, as in the case of the obsessional neurotic who derives libidinal satisfaction from the very compulsive rituals destined to keep the traumatic *jouissance* at bay.

This last point must be further radicalized: the power edifice itself is split from within: in order to reproduce itself and contain its Other, it has to rely on an inherent excess which grounds it – to put it in the Hegelian terms of speculative identity, Power is always-already its own transgression, if it is to function, it has to rely on a kind of obscene supplement. It is therefore not enough to assert, in a Foucauldian way, that power is inextricably linked to counter-power, generating it and being itself conditioned by it: in a self-reflective way, the split is always-already mirrored back into the power edifice itself, splitting it from within, so that the gesture of self-censorship is consubstantial with the exercise of power. Furthermore, it is not enough to say that the 'repression' of some libidinal content retroactively eroticizes the very gesture of 'repression' – this 'eroticization' of power is not a secondary effect of its exertion on its object but its very disavowed foundation, its 'constitutive crime', its founding gesture which has to remain invisible if power is to function normally. What we get in the kind of military drill depicted in the first part of *Full Metal Jacket*, for example, is not a secondary eroticization of the disciplinary procedure which creates military subjects, but the constitutive obscene supplement of this procedure which renders it operative. Judith Butler provides a perfect example of, again, Jesse Helms who, in his very formulation of the text of the anti-pornography law, displays the contours of a particular fantasy – an older man who engages in sadomasochistic sexual activity with another, younger man, preferably a child – which bears witness to his own perverted sexual desire.[26] Helms thus unwittingly brings to light the obscene libidinal foundation of his own crusade against pornography.

The empty gesture

How do these two levels, the public text and its phantasmic support, interact? Where do they intersect? Bertolt Brecht gave poignant expression to this point of intersection in his 'learning plays', notably in *Jasager*, where the young boy is asked to accord freely with what will in any case be his fate (to be thrown into the valley). As his teacher explains to him, it is customary to ask the victim if he agrees to his fate, but it is also customary for the victim to say yes … Every belonging to a society involves a paradoxical point at which the subject is ordered to embrace freely, as the result of his choice, what is anyway imposed on him (we *must* all love our country, our parents . . .). This paradox of willing (choosing freely) what is in any case necessary, of pretending (maintaining the appearance) that there is a free choice although in fact there isn't, is strictly co-dependent with the notion of an empty symbolic gesture, a gesture – an offer – which is meant to be rejected: what the empty gesture offers is the opportunity to choose the impossible, that which inevitably will *not* happen (in Brecht's case, the expedition turning round with the sick boy instead of getting rid of him by throwing him into the valley). And is not something similar part of our everyday mores? In John Irving's *A Prayer for Owen Meany*, after the little boy Owen accidentally kills John's (his best friend's, the narrator's) mother, he is, of course, terribly upset; so, to show how sorry he is, he discreetly delivers to John a gift of the complete collection of colour photos of baseball stars, his most precious

26   See Judith Butler, 'The Force of Fantasy', *Differences* 2:2 (1990).

possession; however, Dan, John's fastidious stepfather, tells him that the proper thing to do is to return the gift.

Let us imagine a more down-to-earth situation: when, after being engaged in a fierce competition for a promotion with my closest friend, I win, the proper thing to do is to offer to withdraw, so that he will get the promotion, and the proper thing for him to do is to reject my offer – this way, perhaps, our friendship can be saved ... What we have here is symbolic exchange at its purest: a gesture made to be rejected; the point, the 'magic' of symbolic exchange, is that although in the end we are back where we were at the beginning, the overall result of the operation is not zero but a distinct gain for both parties, the pact of solidarity. Of course, the problem is: what if the other to whom the offer to be rejected is made actually accepts it? What if, upon being beaten in the competition, I accept my friend's offer to get the promotion instead of him? A situation like this is properly catastrophic: it causes the disintegration of the semblance (of freedom) that pertains to social order – however, since, at this level, things in a way are what they seem to be, this disintegration of the semblance equals the disintegration of the social substance itself, the dissolution of the social link.

The need for the phantasmic support of the public symbolic order (materialized in the so-called unwritten rules) thus bears witness to the system's vulnerability: the system is compelled to allow for possibilities of choices which must never actually take place, since their occurrence would cause the system to disintegrate, and the function of the unwritten rules is precisely to prevent the actualization of these choices formally allowed by the system. In the Soviet Union of the 1930s and 1940s – to take the most extreme example – it was not only forbidden to criticize Stalin, *it was perhaps even more forbidden to announce this very prohibition*: to state publicly that it was forbidden to criticize Stalin. The system *needed* to maintain the *appearance* that one was allowed to criticize Stalin, the *appearance* that the absence of criticism (the fact that there was no opposition party or movement, that the Party got 99.99 per cent of the votes at elections ...), simply demonstrated that Stalin was effectively the best, and (almost) always right. In Hegel's terms, this appearance *qua* appearance was essential.

Or – to put it another way – the paradoxical role of unwritten rules is that, with regard to the explicit, public Law, they are simultaneously *transgressive* (they violate explicit social rules) *and more coercive* (they are additional rules which restrain the field of choice by prohibiting the possibilities allowed for – guaranteed, even – by the public Law). When universal human rights were proclaimed in the late eighteenth century, their universality, of course, concealed the fact that they privileged white men of property; however, this limitation was not openly admitted, it was coded in apparently tautological supplementary qualifications like 'all humans have rights, *in so far as they truly are rational and free*', which then implicitly excluded the mentally ill, 'savages', criminals, children, women . . . Fantasy designates precisely this unwritten framework which tells us how we are to understand the letter of the Law. And it is easy to observe how today, in our enlightened era of universal rights, racism and sexism reproduce themselves mainly at the level of the phantasmic unwritten rules which sustain and qualify universal ideological proclamations. The lesson of this is that – sometimes, at least – the truly subversive thing is not to disregard the explicit letter of Law on behalf of the underlying fantasies, but to *stick to this letter against the fantasy which sustains it.*[27] In other words, the act of taking the empty gesture (the offer to be rejected) literally – to treat the forced choice as a true choice – is, perhaps, one of the ways to put into

---

27   In (still Communist) Slovenia in the mid 1970s, there occurred a famous political incident known as 'the affair of the twenty-five delegates'. The unfortunate twenty-five 'delegates' (self-management newspeak for the members of the National Assembly) proposed as candidate for one of the two Slovene members of the collective Yugoslav Presidency an additional person, on top of the two 'official' candidates, so that the voters would have to choose two out of the three; they broke absolutely no rule, their procedure followed all formal rules, even the person they proposed was an absolutely faithful Party apparatchik – the unbearable trauma for the Power was the simple fact that another name emerged *outside the established unwritten rules of choosing the candidates.* So, immediately after this 'affair', there was a violent campaign in all public media against the unfortunate twenty-five 'delegates', accused of 'pseudo-democratic formalism', anti-Socialist activity, and so on – they were all forced to step down.

practice what Lacan calls 'traversing the fantasy': in accomplishing this act, the subject suspends the phantasmic frame of unwritten rules which tell him how to choose freely – no wonder the consequences of this act are so catastrophic.

It is therefore crucial to bear in mind the radical ambiguity of fantasy within an ideological space: fantasy works both ways, it simultaneously *closes the actual span of choices* (fantasy renders and sustains the structure of the forced choice, it tells us how we are to choose if we are to maintain the freedom of choice – that is, it bridges the gap between the formal symbolic frame of choices and social reality by preventing the choice which, although formally allowed, would, if in fact made, ruin the system) and *maintains the false opening*, the idea that the excluded choice might have happened, and does not actually take place only on account of contingent circumstances – as in Buñuel's *The Discreet Charm of the Bourgeoisie*, in which three upper-class couples try to dine together, but there is always an unforeseen incident (they misunderstand the date of the dinner; the police burst in, searching the place for drugs, etc., etc.). In this film, the role of the phantasmic frame is precisely to maintain the (mis)perception that the three couples *might* have succeeded in having the planned dinner together, and that what prevents this from happening is merely a series of unfortunate circumstances – what is thereby obfuscated is the fact that these unfortunate circumstances intervene necessarily, so that the dinner is, as it were, precluded by the very fundamental structure of the universe.

This void of the possible Otherness is what sustains hysterical desire (that is to say, desire *tout court*) – this non-acceptance of the ultimate closure, this vain hope that the Other Thing is waiting for us just around the corner. In my personal version of it, I am always afraid to miss the phone ringing, to be too late picking up the receiver; when a phone rings, I always expect it to be *the* call, and I am always disappointed when I hear the voice of the actual caller, whoever he or she is. There is no positive feature or content to identify this Call (a beloved person promising me sexual favours, a contract offering me a lot of money, or whatever) – it stands for pure, empty Otherness. And 'traversing the fantasy' involves precisely the acceptance of the traumatic fact of radical closure: there is no opening, contingency as such is necessary ... Bearing in mind that our capacity to desire involves the paradoxical structure of the forced choice (of the empty symbolic gesture of an offer to be rejected; of the gap between the explicit symbolic texture which guarantees the choice and the phantasmic obscene supplement which precludes it – that is, of the gap which separates the public symbolic space in which the subject dwells from the phantasmic kernel of his/her being), one can appreciate the radical character of 'traversing the fantasy': by means of this traversing, the gap is closed, the structure of the forced choice is suspended, the closure of being is fully accepted, the hysterical game of 'I offer you X (the opportunity to leave our community), on condition that you reject it', which structures our belonging to a community, is over. Once we move beyond desire – that is to say, beyond the fantasy which sustains desire – we enter the strange domain of *drive*: the domain of the closed circular palpitation which finds satisfaction in endlessly repeating the same failed gesture.

Drive's 'eternal return of the same'

The Freudian *drive* is thus another name for the *radical ontological closure*. Does not Nietzsche's famous 'Drunken Song' from the Fourth Part of *Zarathustra* ('*The world is deep, / And deeper than the day could read. / Deep is its woe –, / Joy – deeper still than grief can be: / Woe says: Hence! Go! / But joys all want eternity –, / – Want deep, profound eternity!*'[28]) express perfectly the excessive pleasure-in-pain at which late Lacan aims in his rehabilitation of drive? This Nietzschean 'eternity' is to be opposed to being-towards-death: it is the eternity of drive against the finitude of desire. The 'Yes!' of the 'eternal return of the same' thus aims at the same thing as Lacan's '*Encore!*' ('More!' – Nietzsche himself says in the preceding paragraph that 'the name of / this song / is "Once more" '), which is to be read (also) as

28   Friedrich Nietzsche, *Thus Spake Zarathustra*, Buffalo, NY: Prometheus Books, 1993, p. 338.

an evocation of the proverbial woman's 'More!' during the sexual act – it stands for *more of the same*, for the full acceptance of the pain itself as inherent to the excess of pleasure which is *jouissance*. The 'eternal return of the same' thus no longer involves the Will to Power (at least, not in the standard sense of the term): rather, it indexes the attitude of actively endorsing the passive confrontation with *objet petit a*, bypassing the intermediate role of the screen of fantasy. In this precise sense, the 'eternal return of the same' stands for the moment when the subject 'traverses the fantasy'.

According to the *doxa*, fantasy stands for the moment of closure: fantasy is the screen by means of which the subject avoids the radical opening of the enigma of the Other's desire – is 'traversing the fantasy' not therefore synonymous with confronting the opening, the abyss of the Other's impenetrable desire? What, however, if things are exactly inverted? What if it is fantasy itself which, in so far as it fills in the void of the Other's desire, sustains the (false) opening – the notion that there is some radical Otherness which makes our universe incomplete? And, consequently, what if 'traversing the fantasy' involves the acceptance of a radical ontological closure? The unbearable aspect of the 'eternal return of the same' – the Nietzschean name for the crucial dimension of *drive* – is the radical *closure* this notion implies: to endorse and fully assume the 'eternal return of the same' means that we renounce every opening, every belief in the messianic Otherness – here late Lacan parts with the 'deconstructionist' notion of spectrality, with the Derridean-Lévinasian problematic of the ontological crack or dislocation ('out-of-joint'), with the notion of the universe as not-yet-fully ontologically constituted. The point is thus to oppose the radical closure of the 'eternal' drive to the opening involved in the finitude/temporality of the desiring subject.

This closure of drive, of course, is not to be confused with the domain of pre-symbolic animal bodily instincts; crucial here is the basic and constitutive discord between drive and body: drive as eternal-'undead' disrupts the instinctual rhythm of the body. For that reason, drive as such is death drive: it stands for an unconditional impetus which disregards the proper needs of the living body and simply battens on it. It is as if some part of the body, an organ, is sublimated, torn out of its bodily context, elevated to the dignity of the Thing and thus caught in an infinitely repetitive cycle, endlessly circulating around the void of its structuring impossibility. It is as if we are not fit to fit our bodies: drive demands another, 'undead' body. 'The Unputrefied Heart', a poem by the Slovene Romantic poet France Prešeren, perfectly expresses the partial object of drive which is *libido*: years after a poet's death, his body is excavated for some legal reason; all parts of his corpse are long decayed, except the heart, which remains full of red blood and continues to palpitate in a mad rhythm – this undead organ which follows its path irrespective of the physical death stands for the blind insistence; it is drive itself, located beyond the cycle of generation and corruption. One is tempted to subtitle this poem 'Prešeren with Stephen King': is not such an undead partial organ one of the archetypal motifs of horror stories? Does it not index the point at which sublime poetry overlaps with repulsive horror?

The problem with Nietzsche, perhaps, is that in his praise of the body, he downplays – disregards, even – this absolute gap between the organic body and the mad eternal rhythm of drive to which its organs, 'partial objects', can be submitted. In this precise sense, drive can be said to be 'meta-physical': not in the sense of being beyond the domain of the physical, but in the sense of involving another materiality beyond (or, rather, beneath) the materiality located in (what we experience as) spatio-temporal reality. In other words, the primordial Other of our spatio-temporal bodily reality is not Spirit, but another 'sublime' materiality. Perhaps modern art provides the most pertinent case of this other materiality. When typical modernist artists speak about the Spiritual in painting (Kandinsky) or in music (Schoenberg), the 'spiritual' dimension they evoke points towards the 'spiritualization' (or, rather, 'spectralization') of Matter (colour and shape, sound) as such, *outside* its reference to Meaning. Let us recall the 'massiveness' of the protracted stains which 'are' yellow sky in late Van Gogh, or the water or grass in Munch: this uncanny 'massiveness' pertains neither to the direct materiality of the colour stains nor to the materiality of the depicted objects – it dwells in a kind of intermediate spectral domain of what Schelling called *geistige Körperlichkeit*. From the Lacanian perspective, it is easy to identify this 'spiritual corporeality' as materialized *jouissance*, '*jouissance* turned into flesh'.[29]

Fantasy, desire, drive

Desire emerges when drive gets caught in the cobweb of Law/prohibition, in the vicious cycle in which '*jouissance* must be refused, so that it can be reached on the inverted ladder of the Law of desire' (Lacan's definition of castration[30]) – and fantasy is the narrative of this primordial loss, since it stages the process of this renunciation, the emergence of the Law. In this precise sense, *fantasy is the very screen that separates desire from drive*: it tells the story which allows the subject to (mis)perceive the void around which drive circulates as the primordial loss constitutive of desire. In other words, fantasy provides a *rationale* for the inherent deadlock of desire: it constructs the scene in which the *jouissance* we are deprived of is concentrated in the Other who stole it from us. In the anti-Semitic ideological fantasy, social antagonism is explained away via the reference to the Jew as the secret agent who is stealing social *jouissance* from us (amassing profits, seducing our women . . .).[31] In 'traversing the fantasy', we find *jouissance* in the vicious cycle of circulating around the void of the (missing) object, renouncing the myth that *jouissance* has to be amassed somewhere else.

Hysteria provides the exemplary case of desire as a defence against *jouissance*: in contrast to the pervert who works incessantly to provide

---

29   Apropos of this material weight of Van Gogh's paintings, one can articulate the difference between traditional and modern painting: in traditional painting the stain is limited, located in the anamorphic element (the protracted-distorted skull in Holbein's *The Ambassadors,* etc.), whereas in Van Gogh the stain, in a way, spreads over and pervades the entire painting, so that every element within the frame is a depiction of some 'real object' and, simultaneously, a stain with its own material weight.

30   Jacques Lacan, *Écrits: A Selection,* New York: Norton, 1977, p. 324.

31   The paradigmatic case of the narrative which 'explains' how the *jouissance* we are deprived of is amassed in the Other is, of course, the neurotic myth of the primordial father [*Père-Jouissance*].

enjoyment to the Other, the neurotic-hysteric wants to be the object of the Other's *desire*, not the object of his *enjoyment* – she is well aware that the only way to remain desired is to *postpone* the satisfaction, the gratification of desire which would bring enjoyment. The hysteric's fear is that, in so far as she is the object of the Other's enjoyment, she is reduced to an instrument of the Other, exploited, manipulated by him; on the other hand, there is nothing a true pervert enjoys more than being an instrument of the Other, of his *jouissance*.[32] In a typical case of hysterical triangulation, while a wife can fully enjoy illicit sex only, her message to her lover is: if her husband learns of her affair and leaves her, she will also have to drop him ... What we encounter here is the basic neurotic strategy of snatching back from the other part of the *jouissance* he has taken from us: by cheating her husband, she steals back from him part of the *jouissance* he 'illegitimately' stole from her. That is to say: a neurotic has made the sacrifice of *jouissance* (which is why she is not a psychotic), which enables her to enter the symbolic order, but she is obsessed with the notion that the sacrificed *jouissance*, the *jouissance* 'taken' from her, is stored somewhere in the Other who is profiting from it 'illegitimately', enjoying in her place – so her strategy consists in getting at least part of it back by transgressing the Other's norms (from masturbating and cheating, up to speeding without getting a ticket).

In other words, the neurotic's basic notion is that the Other's authority

32   Is not the tendency to desire and enjoy the same object responsible for what Freud perceived as the 'universal tendency to debasement in the sphere of love'? Does not the paradigmatically modern endeavour to love, desire and enjoy the same object give rise to the superego pressure which makes the subject feel guilty if he does not love the object he enjoys? Perhaps, it would be productive to articulate the matrix of all possible combinations between the four fundamental modes of relating to a (libidinal) object: love, desire, *jouissance,* friendship. A *jouissance* entirely deprived of love and/or desire can none the less bear witness to an authentic act of friendship and solidarity (the melodramatic figure of a woman who goes to bed with her male colleague in distress, to comfort him). In *For the Moment,* a Canadian war melodrama, a promiscuous elderly woman with a heart of gold goes to bed with the hero, who is devastated by an impossible love affair; when the hero's love surprises the couple in bed, she is not jealous, since she immediately understands that her lover acted out of despair – sometimes, having sex with a third party can function as the proof of love.

is not 'legitimate': behind the facade of Authority, there is an obscene *jouissance* stolen from the neurotic (in the case of Dora, Freud's patient, her father is perceived by her as a dirty old man who, instead of loving her, 'castrated' her – turned her into an object of exchange and offered her to Mr K – in order to pursue his dirty affair with Mrs K). What the neurotic cannot stand is the idea that the Other is profiting from his sacrifice; he (typically the obsessional) is prepared to sacrifice everything *on condition that the Other does not profit from it,* that he does not amass the sacrificed *jouissance,* does not enjoy in his place. Through psychoanalytic treatment, the neurotic must be helped to stop blaming the Other (society, parents, church, spouse . . .) for his 'castration', and, consequently, to stop seeking retribution from the Other. (There, in the strategy of culpabilizing the Other, also resides the limitation of 'postmodern' identity politics, in which the deprived minority indulges in *ressentiment* by blaming, and seeking retribution from, the Other.) In the dialectic of Master and servant, the servant (mis)perceives the Master as amassing *jouissance,* and gets back (steals from the Master) little crumbs of *jouissance;* these small pleasures (the awareness that he can also manipulate the Master), silently tolerated by the Master, not only fail to present any threat to the Master but, in fact, constitute the 'libidinal bribery' which maintains the servant's servitude. In short, the satisfaction that he is able to dupe the Master is precisely what guarantees the servant's servitude to him.

Although both the neurotic and the pervert sacrifice enjoyment: although neither of the two is a psychotic directly immersed in *jouissance* – the economy of sacrifice is fundamentally different a neurotic is traumatized by the other's *jouissance* (an obsessional neurotic, for example, works like mad all the time *to prevent the Other from enjoying* – or, as they say in French, *pour que rien ne bouge pas dans l'autre*) – while a pervert posits himself as the object-instrument of the Other's *jouissance*; he sacrifices his *jouissance* to generate *jouissance* in the Other. In psychoanalytic treatment, the obsessional is active all the time, tells stories, presents symptoms, and so on, *so that things will remain the same,* so that nothing will really change, so that the analyst will remain immobile and will not effectively intervene

– what he is most afraid of is the moment of silence which will reveal the utter vacuousness of his incessant activity. In an intersubjective situation permeated with an undercurrent of tension, an obsessional who detects this undercurrent will talk continuously, to the distraction of those around him, in order to prevent the awkward silence in which the underlying conflict might emerge.[33]

The key point is thus clearly to delineate the specific intermediate status of perversion, between psychosis and neurosis, between the psychotic's foreclosure of the Law and the neurotic's integration into the Law. According to the standard view, the perverse attitude as the staging of the 'disavowal of castration' can be seen as a defence against the motif of 'death and sexuality', against the threat of mortality as well as the contingent imposition of sexual difference: what the pervert enacts is a universe in which, as in cartoons, a human being can survive any catastrophe; in which adult sexuality is reduced to a childish game; in which one is not forced to die or to choose one of the two sexes.[34] As such, the pervert's universe is the pure universe of the symbolic order, of the signifier's game running its course, unencumbered by the Real of human finitude. What this standard view (which persists within the confines of desire, Law and finitude as the ultimate horizons of human existence: the Law elevates to – or sublates into – a symbolic prohibition, the 'natural' barrier of mortality

33   One can also say that while the hysteric wants to keep the Other's desire (for her) alive, in order to avoid the fate of becoming the object of the Other's *jouissance,* the obsessional neurotic wants to obliterate his existence as an object of desire: whenever he discerns in his Other some signs of the latter's desire, he reacts with panic.

The difference between hysteria and obsessional neurosis also concerns their different historicity: hysteria was already known in Antiquity; it is, as it were, consubstannal with the very logic of symbolic identification, of recognizing oneself in the symbolic mandate that the social 'big Other' bestows on us; while obsessional neurosis is paradigmatically modern, and can arise only against the background of the phenomenon (mis)perceived as the 'decline of paternal authority', and whose consequence is the retreat from public life of direct manifestations of aggressivity (no more sacrifices, public punishments and tortures . . .). The repressed aggressive drives then return in the guise of obsessional compulsive symptoms – of the rituals destined to keep at bay the aggressivity which continues to lurk within the subjects.

34   See Louise Kaplan, *Feminine Perversions,* Harmondsworth: Penguin, 1993.

and sexual reproduction) leaves out of consideration is the unique short circuit between Law and *jouissance*: in contrast to the neurotic, who acknowledges the Law in order occasionally to take enjoyment in its transgressions (masturbation, theft . . .), and thus obtains satisfaction by snatching back from the Other part of the stolen *jouissance*, the pervert directly elevates the enjoying big Other into the agency of Law. As we have already seen, the pervert's aim is to *establish*, not to undermine, the Law: the proverbial male masochist elevates his partner, the Dominatrix, into the Lawgiver whose orders are to be obeyed. A pervert fully acknowledges the obscene-*jouissant* underside of the Law, since he gains satisfaction from the very obscenity of the gesture of installing the rule of Law – that is, of 'castration'. In the 'normal' state of things, the symbolic Law prevents access to the (incestuous) object, and thus creates the desire for it; in perversion, *it is the object itself* (say, the Dominatrix in masochism) *which makes the law*. Here the theoretical concept of masochism as perversion touches the common notion of a masochist who 'enjoys being tortured by the Law': a masochist *locates enjoyment in the very agency of the Law which prohibits the access to enjoyment.*

The truth of desire, the knowledge of fantasy

The opposition desire/drive coincides with the opposition truth/knowledge. As Jacques-Alain Miller emphasized, the psychoanalytic concept of 'construction' does not involve the (dubious) claim that the analyst is always right (if the patient accepts the analyst's proposed construction, that's OK; if the patient rejects it, this rejection is a sign of resistance which, consequently, again confirms that the construction has touched some traumatic kernel within the patient . . .). Rather, psychoanalytic treatment relies on the other side of the same coin, which is crucial in psychoanalysis – it is *the analysand who is always, by definition, in the wrong* (like the priest from Jutland who, at the end of Kierkegaard's *Either/Or*, repeatedly claims: 'You do not say "God is always in the right"; you say "Against God I am always in the wrong"'). In order to grasp this point, one should focus on the crucial distinction between construction and its counterpart, interpretation – this couple, construction/interpretation, is correlative to the couple knowledge/truth. That is to say: an interpretation is a gesture which is always embedded in the intersubjective dialectic of recognition between the analysand and the interpreter-analyst; it aims to bring about the effect of truth apropos of a particular formation of the unconscious (a dream, a symptom, a slip of the tongue . . .): the subject is expected to 'recognize' himself in the signification proposed by the inter-preter, precisely in order to subjectivize this signification, to assume it as 'his own' ('Yes, my God, that's me, I really wanted this . . .'). The very success of interpretation is measured by this 'effect of truth', by the extent to which it *affects the subjective position of the analysand* (stirs up memories of hitherto deeply repressed traumatic encounters, provokes violent resist-ance . . .). In clear contrast to interpretation, a construction (typically: that of a fundamental fantasy) has the status of a knowledge which can never be subjectivized – that is, it can never be assumed by the subject as the truth about himself, the truth in which he recognizes the innermost kernel of his being. A construction is a purely explanatory logical presup-position, like the second stage ('I am being beaten by my father') of the child's fantasy 'A child is being beaten' which, as Freud emphasizes, is so radically unconscious that it can never be remembered:

> This second phase is the most important and the most momentous of all. But we may say that in a certain sense it has never had a real exis-tence. It is never remembered, it has never succeeded in becoming conscious. It is a construction of analysis, but it is no less a necessity on that account.[35]

The fact that this phase 'never had a real existence', of course, indicates its status as the Lacanian *real*; the knowledge about it, a 'knowledge in the real', is a kind of 'acephalous', non-subjectivized knowledge: although it

---

35   Sigmund Freud, 'A Child is Being Beaten', *Standard Edition,* vol. 10, p. 185.

is a kind of 'Thou art that!' which articulates the very kernel of the subject's being (or, rather, for that very reason), its assumption *desubjectivizes* me – that is, I can assume my fundamental fantasy only in so far as I undergo what Lacan calls 'subjective destitution'. Or – to put it in yet another way – interpretation and construction stand to each other as do symptom and fantasy: symptoms are to be interpreted, fundamental fantasy is to be (re)constructed... However, this notion of 'acephalous' knowledge emerges rather late in Lacan's teaching – somewhere around the early 1970s, after the relationship between knowledge and truth has undergone a profound shift:

- 'Early' Lacan, from the 1940s to 1960s, moves within the co-ordinates of the standard philosophical opposition between the 'inauthentic' objectifying knowledge which disregards the subject's position of enunciation, and the 'authentic' truth in which one is existentially engaged, affected by it. In the psychoanalytic clinic, this opposition is perhaps best exemplified by the clear contrast between the obsessional neurotic and the hysteric: the obsessional neurotic *lies in the guise of truth* (while at the level of factual accuracy his statements are always true, he uses this factual accuracy to dissimulate the truth about his desire: say, when my enemy has a car accident because of a brake malfunction, I go to great lengths to explain to anyone who is willing to listen to me that I was never near his car and, consequently, am not responsible for the malfunction – true, but this 'truth' is propagated by me to conceal the fact that the accident realized my desire . . .), while the hysteric *tells the truth in the guise of a lie* (the truth of my desire articulates itself in the very distortions of the 'factual accuracy' of my speech: when, say, instead of 'I thereby open this session', I say 'I thereby close this session', my desire clearly comes out . . .). The aim of psychoanalytic treatment is thus to (re)focus attention from factual accuracy to hysterical lies, which unknowingly articulate the truth, and then to progress to a new knowledge which dwells in the place of truth; which, instead of dissimulating truth, gives rise to truth-effects – to what the Lacan of the 1950s called 'full speech', the speech in which subjective truth reverberates. As we have already emphasized, Lacan thus reinserts his theory into a long tradition, from Kierkegaard to Heidegger, of despising the mere 'factual truth'.

- From the late 1960s, however, Lacan increasingly focuses his theoretical attention on drive as a kind of 'acephalous' knowledge which brings about satisfaction. This knowledge involves neither an inherent relation to truth nor a subjective position of enunciation – not because it dissimulates the subjective position of enunciation, but because it is in itself non-subjectivized, ontologically prior to the very dimension of truth (although, of course, the very predicate 'ontological' thereby becomes problematic, since ontology is by definition a discourse on truth . . .). Truth and knowledge are thus related as desire and drive: interpretation aims at the truth of the subject's desire (the truth of desire is the desire for truth, as one is tempted to put it in a pseudo-Heideggerian way), while construction expresses the knowledge about drive. Is not the paradigmatic case of such an 'acephalous' knowledge that pertains to drive provided by *modern science*,[36] which exemplifies the 'blind insistence' of the (death) drive? Modern science follows its path (in microbiology, in manipulating genes, in particle physics . . .), cost what it may, satisfaction is provided by knowledge itself, not by any moral or communal goals that scientific knowledge supposedly serves. And are not all the 'ethical committees' which abound today and endeavour to establish rules for the proper conduct of gene manipulations, medical experiments, and so on, ultimately so many desperate attempts to reinscribe this inexorable drive-progress of science, which knows of no inherent limitation (in short: this *inherent* ethic of the scientific attitude), within the confines of human goals, to

36   See Jacques-Alain Miller, 'Retour de Granade: Savoir et satisfaction', *Revue de la cause Freudienne* 33, 1996.

provide them with a 'human face', a limitation or 'proper measure' that they are expected to obey? The commonplace wisdom today is that 'our extraordinary power to manipulate nature through scientific devices has run ahead of our faculty to lead a meaningful existence, to make a human use of this immense power' – at this point, the properly modern ethics of 'following the drive' clashes with the traditional ethics of leading a life regulated by proper measure and subordination of all its aspects to some notion of the Good. The problem is, of course, that the balance between the two can *never* be achieved: the notion of reinscribing scientific drive into the constraints of life-world is fantasy at its purest – perhaps the fundamental *Fascist* fantasy. Any limitation of this kind is utterly foreign to the inherent logic of science: science belongs to the Real and, as a mode of the Real of *jouissance*, it is indifferent to the modalities of its symbolization, to the way it will affect social life.

Of course, although the concrete organization of the scientific apparatus, up to its most abstract conceptual schemes, is socially 'mediated', this game of discerning a patriarchal (Eurocentric, male-chauvinist, mechanistic and nature-exploiting . . .) bias of modern science, in a way, *does not really concern science*, the *drive* which effectuates itself in the run of the scientific machine. Heidegger's position here seems utterly ambiguous; perhaps it is all too easy to dismiss him as the most sophisticated proponent of the thesis that science a priori misses the dimension of truth (didn't he claim that 'science doesn't think', that it is by definition unable to reflect its own philosophical foundation, the hermeneutic horizon of its functioning, and, furthermore, that this incapacity, far from playing the role of an impediment, is a positive condition of the possibility of its smooth functioning?). His more crucial point is, rather, that, as such, modern science at its most fundamental cannot be reduced to some limited ontic, 'socially conditioned' option (expressing the interests of a certain social group, etc.), but is, rather, the *real* of our historical moment, that which 'remains the same' in all possible ('progressive' and 'reactionary', 'technocratic' and 'ecological', 'patriarchal' and 'feminist') symbolic universes. Heidegger is thus well aware that all fashionable 'critiques of science', according to which science is a tool of Western capitalist domination, patriarchal oppression, and so forth, fall short of, and thus leave unquestioned, the 'hard kernel' of the scientific drive.[37] What Lacan forces us to add is that, perhaps, science is also 'real' in an even more radical sense: it is the first (and probably unique) case of a discourse which is *stricto sensu non-historical*, even in the most fundamental Heideggerian sense of the historicality of the epochs of Being – that is, whose functioning is inherently indifferent towards the historically determined horizons of the disclosure of Being. Precisely in so far as science 'doesn't think', *it knows*, ignoring the dimension of truth, and is, as such, drive at its purest . . . Lacan's supplement to Heidegger would thus be: why should this utter 'forgetting of Being', at

---

37   In order to get an idea of what Heidegger has in mind with *Gestell* as the essence of technique, it is instructive to cast a glance at the graveyards of outdated or used technical objects: piled-up mountains of used cars and computers, the famous aeroplane 'resting place' in the California desert . . . in these ever-growing piles of inert, dysfunctional 'stuff', which cannot but strike us with their useless, inert presence, one can, as it were, perceive the technological drive at rest. Let us recall how we experience the death of someone close to us: even if we directly witness his or her death, the trauma is redoubled, since often the most unbearable moment comes afterwards, when we visit the deceased's home and observe his private quarters: cupboards full of his clothes, shelves lined with his books, the bathroom with his toilet utensils . . . It is usually only at this moment – when we are compelled to acknowledge that the person to whom all this relates is no longer here, that all these personal belongings are now entirely *useless* – that we become fully aware of, fully take in, his final departure. Behind this, of course, is the fact that a person is in a way more 'here' in the material traces of his presence in his living environs than in the immediate presence of his bodily existence. And – at a totally different level, of course – is it not the same with the graveyards of used technology? It is only here, when its functioning is suspended, that we fully become aware of the ruthless technological drive which determines our lives.

Are we then condemned to the suffocating alternative of being dominated by technological drive, or of becoming aware of its meaninglessness through the confrontation with its useless debris? The third choice (which, perhaps, provides a superb example of what *spirit* is in the non-obscurantist meaning of the term) was invented by today's Japanese, in the guise of *chindogu,* the art of uselessly overfunctional objects, that is, of the objects-inventions which become meaningless and provoke laughter by their very excessive functionality, like glasses (binoculars) with electrically operated windscreen wipers to enable us to see clearly when it rains. Does not this Japanese trend confirm Kojève's insight into how the Japanese have added the touch of snobbery to capitalist functionalism?

work in modern science, be perceived only as the greatest 'danger'? Is there not within it an already perceptible 'liberating' dimension? Is not the suspension of ontological Truth in the unfettered functioning of science already a kind of 'passing through' the metaphysical closure?

Within psychoanalysis, this knowledge of drive, which can never be subjectivized, assumes the form of knowledge about the subject's 'fundamental fantasy', the specific formula which regulates his or her access to *jouissance*. That is to say: desire and *jouissance* are inherently antagonistic, even exclusive: desire's *raison d'être* (or 'utility function', to use Richard Dawkins's term) is not to realize its goal, to find full satisfaction, but to reproduce itself as desire. So how is it possible to couple desire and *jouissance*, to guarantee a minimum of *jouissance* within the space of desire? It is the famous Lacanian *objet petit a* that mediates between the incompatible domains of desire and *jouissance*. In what precise sense is *objet petit a* the object-cause of desire? The *objet petit a* is not what we desire, what we are after, but, rather, that which sets our desire in motion, in the sense of the formal frame which confers consistency on our desire: desire is, of course, metonymical; it shifts from one object to another, through all these displacements, however, desire none the less retains a minimum of formal consistency, a set of phantasmic features which, when they are encountered in a positive object, make us desire this object – *objet petit a* as the cause of desire is nothing other than this formal frame of consistency. In a slightly different way, the same mechanism regulates the subject's falling in love: the automatism of love is set in motion when some contingent, ultimately indifferent, (libidinal) object finds itself occupying a pre-given fantasy-place.

This notion of an impossible/real knowledge also allows us to tackle the question: is psychoanalysis, psychoanalytic knowledge, on the side of Law (the 'repressive' scientific gaze, objectifying, cataloguing, classifying, explaining sexuality away, and thus eliminating its excess) or on the side of its transgression – that is, does it provide a kind of initiatory knowledge about the secrets of *jouissance* hidden from the official public gaze? One should, rather, suggest the hypothesis that psychoanalytic knowledge is located at the intersection of Law and its transgression – an intersection which, of course, is an empty set. In the good old times of 'actually existing Socialism', every schoolchild was told again and again of how Lenin read voraciously, and of his advice to young people: 'Learn, learn, and learn!' – a classic joke from Socialism produces a nice subversive effect by using this motto in an unexpected context. Marx, Engels and Lenin were each asked which they preferred, a wife or a mistress. Marx, whose attitude in intimate matters is well known to have been rather conservative, answered, 'A wife'; Engels, who knew how to enjoy life, answered, of course, 'A mistress'; the surprise comes with Lenin, who answered 'Both, wife *and* mistress!' Is he dedicated to a hidden pursuit of excessive sexual pleasures? No, since he quickly explains: 'This way, you can tell your mistress that you're with your wife, and your wife that you are about to visit your mistress . . .' 'And what do you actually do?' 'Learn, learn and learn!' Psycho-analytic knowledge is definitely Leninist in this sense. Or – to put it in a slightly different way – the dialectic of Law and its transgression constitutes the domain of desire, while asexual (non-phallic) Leninist knowledge is constitutive of the domain of drive, which breaks out of the vicious cycle of desire supported by Law and involved in its transgression.

2 Love Thy Neighbour? No, Thanks!

Of fools and knaves

In his seminar on the ethics of psychoanalysis, Lacan elaborates the distinction between two types of contemporary intellectual, the *fool* and the *knave*:

> The 'fool' is an innocent, a simpleton, but truths issue from his mouth that are not simply tolerated but adopted, by virtue of the fact that this 'fool' is sometimes clothed in the insignia of the jester. And in my view it is a similar happy shadow, a similar fundamental 'foolery', that accounts for the importance of the left-wing intellectual.
>
> And I contrast this with the designation for that which the same tradition furnishes a strictly contemporary term, a term that is used in conjunction with the former, namely, 'knave' ... He's not a cynic with the element of heroism implied by that attitude. He is, to be precise, what Stendhal called an 'unmitigated scoundrel'. That is to say, no more than your Mr. Everyman, but your Mr. Everyman with greater strength of character.
>
> Everyone knows that a certain way of presenting himself, which constitutes part of the ideology of the right-wing intellectual, is precisely to play the role of what he is in fact, namely, a 'knave'. In other words, he doesn't retreat from the consequences of what is called realism; that is, when required, he admits he's a crook.[1]

1 Jacques Lacan, *The Ethics of Psychoanalysis,* London: Routledge, 1992, pp. 182–3.

In short, the right-wing intellectual is a knave, a conformist who refers to the mere existence of the given order as an argument for it, and mocks the Left on account of its 'utopian' plans, which necessarily lead to catastrophe; while the left-wing intellectual is a fool, a court jester who publicly displays the lie of the existing order, but in a way which suspends the performative efficiency of his speech. Today, after the fall of Socialism, the knave is a neoconservative advocate of the free market who cruelly rejects all forms of social solidarity as counterproductive sentimentalism, while the fool is a deconstructionist cultural critic who, by means of his ludic procedures destined to 'subvert' the existing order, actually serves as its supplement.[2]

What psychoanalysis can do to help us to break this vicious cycle of fool–knave is to lay bare its underlying libidinal economy – the libidinal profit, the 'surplus-enjoyment', which sustains each of the two positions. Two vulgar jokes about testicles from Eastern Europe illustrate the fool–knave opposition perfectly. In the first one, a customer is sitting at a bar, drinking whisky; a monkey comes dancing along the counter, stops at his glass, washes his balls in it, and dances away. Badly shocked, the customer orders another glass of whisky. The monkey strolls along again and does the same. Furious, the customer asks the bartender, 'Do you know why that monkey is washing his balls in my whisky?' The bartender replies, 'I have no idea – ask the gypsy, he knows everything!' The guest turns to the gypsy, who is wandering around the bar, amusing guests with his

2   Here we should recall a typical feminist deconstructionist analysis of a *film noir*: a detailed reading which triumphantly uncovers a sexist or patriarchal bias (the paranoiac fear of awakened feminine sexuality, etc.). Such an analysis not only presents no effective threat to the predominant sexist ideological hegemony; its very procedure of denouncing this hegemony enhances our (the spectator's) *jouissance* in the consumption of the object of analysis. One is tempted to invoke here Walter Benjamin's crucial distinction between the attitude that a cultural product assumes *towards* the dominant relations of production, and the position of this same product *within* these relations of production: a product whose explicit attitude is very critical towards the dominant relations of production often fits the frame of these relations perfectly. Or – to put it in terms of Lacan's opposition between the enunciated content and the position of enunciation – what, on the level of the enunciated content, is the critical rejection of an ideological hegemony can well involve the full endorsement of this same hegemony on the level of the position of enunciation.

violin and songs, and asks him, 'Do you know why that monkey is washing his balls in my whisky?' The gypsy answers calmly, 'Yes, sure!', and he starts to sing a melancholy song: 'Why does that monkey wash his balls in my whisky, oh why . . .' – the point, of course, is that gypsy musicians are supposed to know hundreds of songs and perform them at the customers' request, so the gypsy has understood the customer's question as a request for a song about a monkey washing his balls in whisky . . . The second joke takes place in medieval Russia, under the Tatar occupation, where a Tatar horseman encounters, on a lonely country road, a peasant with his young wife. The Tatar warrior not only wants to have sex with her, but – to add insult to injury, and to humiliate the peasant even further – he orders him to hold his (the Tatar's) balls gently in his hands, so that they will not get too dirty while he copulates with the wife on the dusty road. After the Tatar has finished with the sexual encounter and ridden away, the peasant starts to chuckle with pleasure; asked by his wife what is so funny about her being raped in front of her husband, he answers, 'Don't you get it, my love? I duped him – I didn't really hold his balls, they're covered in dust and dirt!'

So: if the conservative knave is not unlike the gypsy, since he also, in his answer to a concrete complaint ('Why are things so horrible for us . . . /gays, blacks, women/?'), sings his tragic song of eternal fate ('Why are things so bad for us people, O why?') – that is, he also, as it were, changes the tonality of the question from concrete complaint to abstract acceptance of the enigma of Fate – the satisfaction of the progressive fool, a 'social critic', is of the same kind as that of the poor Russian peasant, the typical hysterical satisfaction of snatching a little piece of *jouissance* away from the Master. If the victim in the first joke were a fool, he would allow the monkey to wash his balls in the whisky yet another time, but would add some dirt or sticky stuff to his glass beforehand, so that after the monkey's departure he would be able to claim triumphantly, 'I duped him! His balls are now even dirtier than before!'

It is easy to imagine a much more sublime version of the reversal performed by the gypsy musician – is not this same reversal at work in the subjective position of castrati singers, for example? They are made to 'cry to Heaven': after suffering a horrible mutilation, they are not supposed to bemoan their worldly misfortune and pain, and to look for the culprits responsible for it, but instead to address their complaint to Heaven itself. In a way, they must accomplish a kind of magic reversal and *exchange* all their worldly complaints for a complaint addressed to Divine Fate itself – this reversal allows them to enjoy their terrestrial life to the full . . . This is (the singing) *voice* at its most elementary: the embodiment of 'surplus-enjoyment' in the precise sense of the paradoxical 'pleasure in pain'. That is to say: when Lacan uses the term *plus-de-jouir*, one has to ask a naive but crucial question: in what does this surplus consist? Is it merely a qualitative increase of ordinary pleasure? The ambiguity of the French term is decisive here: it can mean 'surplus of enjoy-ment' as well as 'no more enjoyment' – the surplus of enjoyment over mere pleasure is generated by the presence of the very opposite of pleasure, that is, pain. Pain generates surplus-enjoyment via the magic reversal-into-itself by means of which the very material texture of our expression of pain (the crying voice) gives rise to enjoyment – and is not this what takes place towards the end of the joke about the monkey washing his balls in my whisky, when the gypsy transforms my furious complaint into a self-satisfying melody? What we find here is a neat exemplification of the Lacanian formula of the fetishistic object (minus phi under small a): like the castrato's voice, the *objet petit a* – the surplus-enjoyment – arises at the very place of castration. And does not the same go for love poetry and its ultimate topic: the lamentation of the poet who has lost his beloved (because she doesn't return his love, because she has died, because her parents do not approve of their union, and block his access to her . . .)? Poetry, the specific poetic *jouissance*, emerges when *the very symbolic articulation of this Loss gives rise to a pleasure of its own.*[3]

3   The same mechanism is already at work in the everyday attitude of the abandoned lover who desperately asks himself and his friends: 'O my God, why did she leave me? What did I do wrong? Did I say something? Did she meet another guy?' In order to reveal the modality of this questioning, it is sufficient to say to the mourning lover, directly and brutally: 'I know why she left you. Do you really want to know?' His answer will definitely be a desperate 'No!', since his question, precisely in so far as it remains unanswered, already provides a satisfaction of its own – that is, in a way, functions as its own answer.

Do we not find the same elementary ideological gesture inscribed into Jewish identity? Jews 'evacuate the law of *jouissance*', they are 'the people of the Book' who stick to the rules and allow for no ecstatic experience of the Sacred; yet, at the same time, they do find an excessive enjoyment precisely in their dealings with the Text of the Book: the 'Talmudic' enjoyment of how to read it properly, how to interpret it so that we can none the less have it our own way. Is not the tradition of lively debates and disputes which strike foreigners (Gentiles) as meaningless hairsplitting a neat example of how the very renunciation of the Thing-*jouissance* produces its own *jouissance* (in interpreting the text)? Maybe Kafka himself, as the Western 'Protestant' Jew, was shocked to discover this obscene aspect of the Jewish Law[4] – is not this *jouis-sense* in the Letter clearly discernible in the discussion between the priest and K. at the end of *The Trial*, after the parable on the door of the Law? What strikes one here is the 'senseless' detailed hairsplitting which, in precise contrast to the Western tradition of metaphorical-gnostic reading, undermines the obvious meaning not by endeavouring to discern beneath it layers of 'deeper' analogical meanings, but by insisting on a too-close, too-literal reading ('the man from the country was never ordered to come there in the first place', etc.).

Each of the two positions, that of fool and that of knave, is thus sustained by its own kind of *jouissance*: the enjoyment of snatching back from the Master part of the *jouissance* he stole from us (in the case of the fool); the enjoyment which directly pertains to the subject's pain (in the case of the knave). What psychoanalysis can do to help the critique of ideology is precisely to clarify the status of this paradoxical *jouissance* as the payment that the exploited, the servant, receives for serving the Master. This *jouissance*, of course, always emerges within a certain phantasmic field; the crucial precondition for breaking the chains of servitude is thus to 'traverse the fantasy' which structures our *jouissance* in a way which keeps us attached to the Master – makes us accept the framework of the social relationship of domination.

4   I owe this insight to Eric Santner, Princeton (private conversation).

Why jouissance *is not historical*

Jouissance concerns the very fundamentals of what one is tempted to call psychoanalytic ontology.[5] Psychoanalysis chances upon the fundamental ontological question: 'Why is there something instead of nothing?' apropos of the experience of the 'loss of reality [*Realitätsverlust*]', when some traumatic, excessively intense encounter affects the subject's ability to assume the full ontological weight of his world-experience. From the very outset of his teaching, Lacan emphasized the inherent and irreducible *traumatic* status of existence: 'By definition, there is something so improbable about all existence that one is in effect perpetually questioning oneself about its reality.'[6] Later, after the crucial turning point of his teaching, he links existence ('as such', one is tempted to add) to *jouissance* as that which is properly traumatic – that is, whose existence can never be fully assumed, and which is thus forever perceived as spectral, pre-ontological. In a key passage from 'Subversion of the Subject and Dialectic of Desire', for example, he answers the question 'What am I?'

> 'I' am in the place from which a voice is heard clamouring 'the universe is a defect in the purity of Non-Being'.
> And not without reason, for by protecting itself this place makes Being itself languish. This place is called *Jouissance*, and it is the absence of this that makes the universe vain.[7]

Jouissance is thus the ontological aberration, the disturbed balance (*clinamen*, to use the old philosophical term) which accounts for the passage from Nothing to Something; it designates the minimal *contraction* (in Schelling's sense of the term) which provides the density of the subject's reality.

---

5   See Nestor Braunsiein, *La Jouissance. Un concept lacanien,* Paris: Point Hors Ligne, 1992.

6   *The Seminar of Jacques Lacan, Book II. The Ego in Freud's Theory and in the Technique of Psychoanalysis,* Cambridge: Cambridge University Press, 1988, p. 226.

7   Jacques Lacan, *Écrits: A Selection,* New York: Norton, 1977, p. 317.

Someone can be happily married, with a good job and many friends, fully satisfied with his life, and yet absolutely hooked on some specific formation ('sinthom') of *jouissance*, ready to put everything at risk rather than renounce *that* (drugs, tobacco, drink, a particular sexual perversion . . .). Although his symbolic universe may be nicely set up, this absolutely meaningless intrusion, this *clinamen*, upsets everything, and there is nothing to be done, since it is only in this 'sinthom' that the subject encounters the density of being – when he is deprived of it, his universe is empty. At a less extreme level, the same holds for every authentic intersubjective encounter: when do I actually encounter the Other 'beyond the wall of language', in the real of his or her being? Not when I am able to describe her, not even when I learn her values, dreams, and so on, but only when I encounter the Other in her moment of *jouissance*: when I discern in her a tiny detail (a compulsive gesture, an excessive facial expression, a tic) which signals the intensity of the real of *jouissance*. This encounter with the real is always traumatic; there is something at least minimally obscene about it; I cannot simply integrate it into my universe, there is always a gulf separating me from it.

Jouissance is thus the 'place' of the subject – one is tempted to say: his 'impossible' Being-there, *Da-Sein*; and, for that very reason, the subject is always-already displaced, out-of-joint, with regard to it. Therein lies the primordial 'decentrement' of the Lacanian subject: much more radical and elementary than the decentrement of the subject with regard to the 'big Other', the symbolic order which is the external place of the subject's truth, is the decentrement with regard to the traumatic Thing-*jouissance* which the subject can never 'subjectivize', assume, integrate. *Jouissance* is that notorious *heimliche* which is simultaneously the most *unheimliche*, always-already here and, precisely as such, always already lost. What characterizes the fundamental subjective position of a *hysteric* (and one should bear in mind that for Lacan, the status of the subject as such is hysterical) is precisely the ceaseless questioning of his or her existence *qua* enjoyment – that is, the refusal fully to identify with the object that he or she 'is', the eternal wondering at this object: 'Am I really *that*?'

Another way to express the point is to say that *jouissance* designates the non-historical kernel of the process of historicization. Jacques-Alain Miller defines the analyst as the subject who, in contrast to us, 'common' individuals caught in the everyday symbolic circuit, no longer confounds what he hears [*j'ouis*] with what he enjoys [*jouir*]; Miller, of course, is alluding here to Lacan's famous wordplay from 'The Subversion of the Subject . . .' regarding the superego injunction *Jouis!* ('Enjoy!'), 'to which the subject can only reply *J'ouis* ('I hear'), the *jouissance* being no more than a half-heard innuendo'.[8] The subject can avoid this confusion only by 'traversing the fantasy', since it is precisely his fundamental fantasy which provides the frame anchoring his *jouissance* in that which he is able to hear/understand: when I achieve a distance towards the phantasmic frame, I no longer reduce *jouissance* to what I hear/understand, to the frame of meaning.

The most difficult and painful aspect of what Lacan calls 'separation' is thus to maintain the distance between the hard kernel of *jouissance* and the ways in which this kernel is caught in different ideological fields – *jouissance* is 'undecidable', 'free-floating'. The enthusiasm of fans for their favourite rock star and the religious trance of a devout Catholic in the presence of the Pope are libidinally *the same phenomenon*; they differ only in the different symbolic network which supports them. Sergei Eisenstein's provocatively entitled essay 'The Centrifuge or the Grail' aims precisely at emphasizing this 'unhistorical' neutrality of ecstasy (his name for *jouissance*): in principle, the ecstasy of a knight in the presence of the Grail, and the ecstasy of a lover in the presence of the beloved, are of the same nature as the ecstasy of the kolkhoz farmer in the presence of a new centrifuge for skimming milk. Eisenstein himself refers to St Ignatius of Loyola who, elaborating on the technique of religious ecstasy, acknowledges that the positive figure of God comes second, after the moment of 'objectless' ecstasy: first we have the experience of objectless ecstasy; subsequently this experience is attached to some historically determined representation – here we encounter an exemplary case of the Real as that which 'remains

8   Ibid., p. 319.

the same in all possible (symbolic) universes'. So, when someone, while describing his profound religious experience, emphatically answers his critics, 'You don't really understand it at all! There's more to it, something words cannot express!', he is the victim of a kind of perspective illusion: the precious *agalma* perceived by him as the unique ineffable kernel which cannot be shared by others (non-believers) is precisely *jouissance* as that which always remains the same. Every ideology attaches itself to some kernel of *jouissance* which, however, retains the status of an ambiguous excess. The unique 'religious experience' is thus to be split into its two components, as in the well-known scene from Terry Gilliam's *Brazil* in which the food on a plate is split into its symbolic frame (a colour photo of the course above the plate) and the formless slime of *jouissance* that we actually eat . . .

The philosophical consequence of this split, of this excess of *jouissance* which cannot be historicized, is that one should insist on the difference between historical and dialectical materialism. *Glengarry Glen Ross*, a film based on David Mamet's play, seems to confirm Hitchcock's well-known dictum: 'The better the villain, the better the movie'. On the one hand, the film provides a convincing description of the horrible and humiliating life of legwork endured by real-estate agents (ferocious competition, moral corruption, lies and humiliating adulation in the service of mere survival as a breadwinner . . .). However, is not the (libidinally) most satisfying part of the film the brief appearance of Alec Baldwin as a slick, politely cruel executive who humiliates the agents by bombarding them with aggressive wisecracks? It is the excessive enjoyment elicited by Baldwin's demeanour in this scene which accounts for the spectator's satisfaction in witnessing the humiliation of the poor agents. Such excessive enjoyment is the necessary support of social relationships of domination we see this in Oliver Stone's *Wall Street*, whose libidinal focus is undoubtedly the continuous wisecracking of the corrupted Gordon Gekko (Michael Douglas); or in the relationship between Burt Lancaster and Tony Curtis in *Sweet Smell of Success*, whose different yet complementary corruption is very indicative of the social crisis in America during the 1950s – but again, what truly fascinates the spectator is the way in which these two characters take excessive enjoyment in their utter corruption . . .

For the same reason, the standard feminist analyses of the *femme fatale* figure in the *noir* universe (all the well-known variations on how the *femme fatale* gives body to the fear of the emancipated femininity perceived as a threat to male identity, etc., etc.) seem somehow to miss the point, which is that the very features which critical analysis denounces as the product of the male paranoiac attitude (the Weiningerian image of woman as inherently evil; as the embodiment of a cosmic corruption, a fundamental flaw in the very ontological structure of the universe; as the seductress whose hatred and destruction of men express, in a perverted way, her awareness of how her identity depends on the male gaze, and who, therefore, secretly longs for her own annihilation as her only means of liberation) also account for the irresistible charm of this figure; as if all this theorizing is ultimately exercised in order to provide an alibi for our enjoyment of the *femme fatale*.

At a more fundamental level, the problem here concerns the tension between a historically specified act and its 'eternal' metaphysical dimension. *Film noir*, for example, combines the depiction of a specific historical moment (the decaying American megalopolis in the 1940s) with a properly 'metaphysical' vision of the corruption of the universe as such, with an attitude of disgust at Life itself in all its crawling and shrieking. Robert Penn Warren's *All the King's Men*, a unique *noir* novel, is inhabited by the same ambiguity: on the one hand a portrait of the inherent flaw in American populism, whose promise to redeem the poor terminates in political corruption and authoritarianism; on the other the profound belief in a fundamental Sin, consubstantial with human existence as such, combined with an attitude towards Life itself as a kind of evil nightmare. The point here, again, is that the historicist reduction of the ontological attitude to the distorted reflection of a concrete social constellation (as in the standard Marxist dismissal of 'ontological pessimism', and the feeling of universal decay, as the overblown misperception of the impasse which pertains to the subject's own historically specific class situation – the reading according to which the horrifying prospect of the cosmic catastrophe 'really means' the impossibility of imagining a way out of one's own specific historical deadlock...) is no less erroneous than the traditional metaphysical notion of concrete forms of decay as mere temporal exemplifications of universal ontological corruption, of 'the way of all flesh'.[9] In theology, Kierkegaard endeavours to resolve this false dilemma through his notion of a temporal Event (of the Incarnation) which, in its very singularity, provides the only gateway to Eternity.[10]

One is thus tempted to invert the standard notion according to which the atmosphere of ontological decay and catastrophe is to be read as the ideological 'exaggeration' (the overblown universalization) of a limited truth-content (of the impasse of the social situation of a certain class): here, more than anywhere else, Adorno's dictum 'In Freudian psychoanalysis, nothing is more true than its exaggerations' must be applied. When, for example, Pascal (a *noir* philosopher if there ever was one), in his melancholic pessimism, is said to express the social disintegration and loss of influence of the old nobility which accompanied the rise of the Absolutist monarchy, one should insist that the moment of truth is contained in this very 'exaggeration' of the ideological form with regard to its designated concrete social content. Perhaps one should evoke here the crucial Freudian distinction between latent dream-thoughts and the unconscious wish articulated in a dream: they are by no means the same, since the unconscious wish

9   Neil Jordan's *The Crying Game* is perhaps the ultimate example of this tension between historical and 'eternal', on account of the film's sudden and unexpected shift from a concrete historical terrain (the struggle between the IRA and the British Army in Northern Ireland) to the 'eternal' topic of the paradoxes of sexual identity and desire. And again, it is wrong to read this shift as an implicit demand for an even stronger historicization which relativizes even the apparently 'eternal' logic of sexual desire: the properly Kierkegaardian paradox, according to which Eternity is grounded in a concrete temporal, historical deed, must be fully assumed – in spite of its 'historicization', Eternity *remains* true Eternity, not just an illusion, not just the illusory eternalization of a concrete historical constellation.

10   Virginia Woolf captured this paradox nicely in her statement that, somewhere around 1910, a fundamental change in human nature occurred: her point is not simply that human nature is historical, culturally-socially conditioned, etc., etc., but, much more radically, that 'eternity' itself is bound to temporal shifts and divisions.

articulates itself through the very distortion of the latent dream-thought – through its translation from the everyday language of public communication into the dream-language (in Freud's dream about Irma's injection, for example, the latent dream-thought is simply Freud's aspiration to escape responsibility for the failure of Irma's treatment, a fully conscious concern which troubled him day and night, while the unconscious wish concerns a much more uncanny domain of primitive sexual fantasies and desires). Along the same lines, and precisely in so far as an ideological text has to be read as a ciphered formation of the unconscious, the reduction of its manifest content (Pascal's Jansenist theology) to its latent thought (the impasse of the social situation of the old nobility), while it is adequate, does not account for its impact, for the fascination it exerts on generations of readers – a third element must intervene, which, of course, is in the underlying economy of *jouissance.*

The philosopher who was the first to elaborate this non-historical kernel of historicity was F.W.J. Schelling: his relevance to today's debate on historicism resides in his notion of the primordial act of decision/ differentiation (*Ent-Scheidung*), of the gesture that opens up the gap between the inertia of the prehistoric Real and the domain of historicity, of multiple and shifting narrativizations. This act is thus a quasi-transcendental unhistorical condition of possibility and, simultaneously, a condition of the impossibility of historicization.[11] Every 'historicization', every symbolization, must 're-enact' this gap, this passage from the Real to history. Apropos of Oedipus, for example, it is easy to play the game of historicization, and to demonstrate how the Oedipal constellation is embedded in a specific patriarchal context, and so forth; it requires a far greater effort of thought to discern, in the very historical contingency of the Oedipus, one of the re-enactments of the gap which opens up the horizon of historicity. And does not the psychoanalytic clinical experience bear witness to the continuous struggle to secure an entry into the domain of historicity? Are not the patient's deadlocks so many monuments to the

---

11   See Chapter 1 of Slavoj Žižek, *The Indivisible Remainder,* London: Verso, 1996.

traumatic character of our entry into the domain of symbolic History, so many proofs that this entry can also fail (as in psychosis)? In short, what the historicists accept as primordially given, as the 'nature of things' ('in social life, everything results from the process of contingent construction'), is that which is at stake in a difficult uphill struggle; it has to be (re)gained by a continuous struggle; it never fully succeeds . . . Therein resides the key point: historicity is not the zero-level state of things secondarily obfuscated by ideological fixations and naturalizing misrecognitions; historicity itself, the space of contingent discursive constructions, must be sustained through an effort, assumed, regained again and again . . .

This non-historical kernel of *jouissance* is not something accessible only in 'metaphysical' or 'mystical' limit-experiences: it permeates our daily lives – one needs only the eyes to see it. On the rare occasions when, owing to various kinds of social obligations, I cannot avoid meeting my relatives who have nothing to do with Lacanian theory (or with theory in general), sooner or later the conversation always takes the same unpleasant turn: with barely concealed hostility and envy lurking beneath a polite surface, they ask me how much I earn by my writing and publishing abroad, and giving lectures around the world. Surprisingly, whichever answer I give sounds wrong to them: if I admit that I earn what, in their eyes, is a considerable sum of money, they consider it unjust that I earn so much for my empty philosophizing, while they, who are doing 'real work', have to sweat for a much lesser reward; if I tell them a small sum, they assert, with deep satisfaction, that even this is too much – who needs my kind of philosophizing in these times of social crisis? Why should we spend taxpayers' money on it? The underlying premiss of their reasoning is that, to put it bluntly, whatever I earn, I earn too much – why? It is not only that they consider my kind of work useless: what one can discern beneath this official, public reproach is the envy of enjoyment. That is to say: it soon becomes obvious what really bothers them: the notion that I actually *enjoy* my work. They possess a vague intuition of how I find *jouissance* in what I do; which is why, in their eyes, money is never a proper equivalent for my work. No wonder, then, that what I earn always oscillates between the two extremes of 'too little' and 'too much': such an oscillation is an unmistakable sign that we are dealing with *jouissance*. (In an analogous way, in the eyes of a racist, immigrant workers who steal our jobs are simultaneously lazy and overdiligent: they work excessively for low wages yet, simultaneously, they seem to work too little, to exploit our healthcare and welfare systems.)

The 'banality of Evil'?

An interesting phenomenon of post-Communist countries is the hatred of the Communist regime and its surviving representatives expressed precisely by the writers and journalists who not only were not involved in any serious dissident activity, but even 'collaborated' more than was necessary for (not only personal, but also professional) survival. In Slovenia, for example, an elderly poet regularity demands radical purges of the 'remainders of the past', and warns that although they have lost public power, Communists still secretly dominate economic and social life. Not so many years ago, however, this poet was quite a docile journalist who, among other things, highly praised the refined cultural taste of a Communist functionary now accused of organizing political show trials – which was definitely *not* necessary for professional survival. The explanation, of course, is that these people's animosity towards the Communist regime cannot be explained simply by the wrongs done to them – on the contrary, they hate the old regime because it humiliated them by extracting from them a 'surplus-obedience', a gesture of compliance which was accomplished out of a pure *jouissance* provided by their participation in the oppressive Communist ideological ritual. That is to say: how does one draw the line of separation between the obedience necessary for survival, and 'surplus-obedience'? There are, of course, no 'objective' criteria; it is also insufficient to say that we are dealing with 'surplus-obedience' when the subject did things which went beyond his own modest survival, and brought him excessive material and professional gains or power. The only acceptable notion is that even if the actual gesture of compliance was very modest, we are dealing with 'surplus-obedience' the moment the gesture of compliance provides the subject with a *jouissance* of its own.

At a more traumatic level, this reference to *jouissance* makes clear the inadequacy of Hannah Arendt's notion of the 'banality of Evil' from her famous report on the Eichmann trial – that is, how Eichmann, far from being driven by some demonic will to inflict suffering and destroy human lives, was simply a model civil servant doing his job, executing orders and not minding about their moral, etc., implications: what mattered to him was the pure 'boring' symbolic form of the Order, deprived of all imaginary – or, in Kantian terms, 'pathological' – vestiges (the horrors that its execution will entail, private motives of financial profit or sadistic satisfaction, etc., etc.). The fact remains however, that the execution of the Holocaust was treated *by the Nazi apparatus itself* as a kind of obscene dirty secret, not publicly acknowledged, resisting simple and direct translation into the anonymous bureaucratic machine. In order to account for the way executioners carried out the Holocaust measures, one should thus supplement the purely *symbolic* bureaucratic logic involved in the notion of the 'banality of Evil' with two other components: the *imaginary* screen of satisfactions, myths, and so on, which enable the subjects to maintain a distance towards (and thus to 'neutralize') the horrors they are involved in and the knowledge they have about them (telling themselves that Jews are only being transported to some new Eastern camps; claiming that just a small number of them were actually killed; listening to classical music in the evening and thus convincing themselves that 'after all, we are men of culture, unfortunately forced to do some unpleasant, but necessary things', etc.); and, above all, the *real* of the perverse (sadistic) *jouissance* in what they were doing (torturing, killing, dismembering bodies . . .). It is especially important to bear in mind how the very 'bureaucratization' of the crime was ambiguous in its libidinal impact: on the one hand, it enabled (some of) the participants to neutralize the horror and take it as 'just another job'; on the other, the basic lesson of the perverse ritual also applies here: this 'bureaucratization' was in itself a source of an additional *jouissance* (does it not provide an additional kick if one performs the killing as a complicated administrative-criminal operation? Is it not more satisfying to torture prisoners as part of some orderly procedure – say, the meaningless 'morning exercises' which served only to torment them – didn't it give another 'kick' to the guards' satisfaction when they were inflicting pain on their victims not by directly beating them up but in the guise of an activity officially destined to maintain their health?).

Therein also lies the interest of Goldhagen's much-discussed *Hitler's Willing Executioners*, a book whose rejection of all the standard versions of explaining how 'ordinary, decent' Germans were ready to participate in the Holocaust brings about an undeniable truth-effect.[12] One cannot claim that the vast majority did not know what was going on, that they were terrorized by the minority Nazi gang (a notion propagated by some Leftists in order to save the German 'people' from collective condemnation): they *did* know it; enough rumours and self-defeating denials were circulating. One cannot claim that they were grey, dispassionate bureaucrats blindly following orders in accordance with the German authoritarian tradition of unconditional obedience: numerous testimonies bear witness to the *excess of enjoyment* the executioners found in their enterprise (see the numerous examples of 'unnecessary' supplementary inflicting of pain or humiliation – urinating on an old Jewish lady's head, etc.). One cannot claim that the executioners were a bunch of crazy fanatics oblivious of even the most elementary moral norms: the very people who carried out the Holocaust were often able to behave honourably in their private or public lives, to engage in a diversified cultural life, to protest against social injustice, and so forth. One cannot claim that they were terrorized into submission, since any refusal to execute an order would be severely punished: before doing any 'dirty work', members of the police unit were regularly asked if they were able to do it, and those who refused were excused without any punishment. So although the book may be problematic in some of its historical research, its basic premiss is simply undeniable: the executioners *did have a choice*; they were on average fully responsible, mature, 'civilized' Germans.

12   See Daniel J. Goldhagen, *Hitler's Willing Executioners,* New York: Little, Brown & Co., 1996.

However, Goldhagen's explanation (the tradition of eliminationist anti-Semitism which was already fully established in the nineteenth century as the central ingredient of 'German ideology' and thus of German collective identity) is too close to the standard thesis on 'collective guilt' which allows for an 'easy way out' by reference to the collective destiny ('What could we do? The collective ideological heritage predetermined our actions!'). Furthermore, in his concrete descriptions (or, rather, in his interpretations of concrete testimonials) Goldhagen does not seem to take into account the way ideology and power function at the level of their 'microphysics'. One should fully agree with him that Arendt's notion of the 'banality of Evil' is insufficient, in so far as – to use Lacanian terms – it does not take into account the obscene, publicly unacknowledged surplus-enjoyment provided by executing orders, manifested in the 'unnecessary' excesses in this execution (as Goldhagen demonstrates, these excesses were not only not encouraged by superior officers – low-ranking soldiers were often even gently reprimanded for them, not from any compassion for Jews, but since such excesses were considered incompatible with the 'dignity' of a German soldier). Nevertheless, despite the public character of Nazi anti-Semitism, the relationship between the two levels, the text of the public ideology and its 'obscene' superego supplement, remained fully operative: Nazis themselves treated the Holocaust as a kind of collective 'dirty secret'. This fact not only posed no obstacle to the execution of the Holocaust – it precisely served as its libidinal support, since the very awareness that 'we are all together in it', that we participate in a common transgression, served as a 'cement' to the Nazi collective coherence.

Goldhagen's insistence that the executioners, as a rule, did not feel any 'shame' about what they were doing is thus misplaced: his point, of course, is that this absence of shame proves the extent to which their torturing and killing of Jews was integrated into their ideological awareness as totally acceptable. A close reading of the testimonials from his own book none the less demonstrates how the executioners *experienced their deeds as a kind of 'transgressive' activity*, as a kind of pseudo-Bakhtinian 'carnivalesque' activity in which the constraints of 'normal' everyday life were momentarily suspended – it was precisely this 'transgressive' character (transgressive with regard to the publicly acknowledged ethical norms of Nazi society itself) which accounted for the 'surplus-enjoyment' one got from excessively torturing the victims. The feeling of shame thus, again, in no way proves that the executioners were 'not wholly corrupted', that 'a minimum of decency persisted in them': on the contrary, this shame was the unmistakable sign of the excess of *enjoyment* they got from their acts.

So – if we return to the key element in Goldhagen's argumentation (prior to any engagement in raiding the ghetto and violently rounding up Jews, members of the German unit were explicitly asked if they felt able to accomplish this unpleasant task, and those who refused did not suffer any consequences): is it not reasonable to suppose that – to some extent, at least – we are dealing here with a situation of *forced choice*? For that reason, this choice was in a way even worse than open coercion: not only were the subjects forced to participate in repulsive obscene acts of violence, they even had to pretend they were doing it freely and willingly. (A minority which refused to participate was probably tolerated precisely to maintain the *semblance* of free choice.) But, again, our point is that this subtle coercion under the guise of free choice (you are free to choose and to reject participation, on condition that you make the right choice and decide freely to participate) in no way abolishes the subject's responsibility: one is responsible in so far as one *enjoys doing it*, and it is clear that the subtle (implicit) coercion generated the additional *jouissance* of being part of a larger, trans-individual body – of 'swimming in a collective Will'.

Heinrich Himmler made this point clear in his infamous statement that the Holocaust is one of the most glorious chapters of a German history which, unfortunately, will have to remain unwritten; the underlying notion of this statement is that one demonstrates one's true devotion to one's Fatherland not simply by doing noble things for it (by sacrificing one's life for it, etc.), but by being ready to accomplish horrible deeds for it when the necessity arises: that is, by giving preference to the demands of the Fatherland over petty concerns about personal integrity and honesty – the true hero is the one who is ready to dirty his hands for the noble Cause. Although one encounters the same logic in the Stalinist justification of the revolutionary terror, this in no way entails that Nazism mobilizes *jouissance* in the same way as Stalinism – that is, according to some universal 'totalitarian' mechanism.

The fundamental difference between the respective natures of Stalinist and Fascist 'totalitarianism' can be discerned through a tiny but significant detail: after the Fascist Leader finishes his public speech and the crowd applauds, the Leader acknowledges himself as the addressee of the applause (he stares at a distant point, bows to the public, or something similar), while the Stalinist leader (for example, the general secretary of the Party, after finishing his report to the congress) *stands up himself and starts to applaud.* This change signals a fundamentally different discursive position: the Stalinist leader is also compelled to applaud, since the true addressee of the people's applause is not himself, but the big Other of History whose humble servant-instrument he is . . . In so far as – according to Lacan – the position of the object-instrument of the big Other's *jouissance* is what characterizes the pervert's economy, one can also say that the difference is the one between the Fascist paranoiac and Stalinist pervert. With regard to 'being observed', for example, the paranoiac is convinced that he is observed during his sexual activity – he 'sees a gaze where, in reality, there is none' – while the pervert himself organizes the other's gaze to accompany his sexual activity (say, he asks a friend or an unknown person to watch him making love to his wife). And was it not the same with the notion of the plot against the regime? The paranoiac Nazis really believed in the Jewish conspiracy, while the perverted Stalinists actively organized/invented 'counterrevolutionary conspiracies' as pre-emptive strikes. The greatest surprise for the Stalinist investigator was to discover that the subject accused of being a German or American spy really was a spy: in Stalinism proper, confessions counted only in so far as they were false and extorted . . .

In what are we to ground this difference? With respect to the couple of Stalinism and Fascism, Heidegger silently grants priority to Fascism – at this point, we differ from him and follow Alain Badiou,[13] who claims

---

13   See Alain Badiou, *L'Éthique,* Paris: Hatier, 1993.

that despite the horrors perpetrated on its behalf (or rather, on behalf of the specific form of these horrors), Stalinist Communism was inherently related to a truth-event (of the October Revolution), while Fascism was a pseudo-event, a lie in the guise of authenticity. Badiou is referring here to the difference between *désastre* (the Stalinist 'ontologization' of the truth-event into a positive structure of Being) and *désêtre* (the Fascist imitation/staging of a pseudo-event called the 'Fascist Revolution'): *mieux vaut un désastre qu'un désêtre*, since *désastre* none the less remains inherently related to the truth-event whose disastrous consequence it is, while *désêtre* merely imitates the Event as an aesthetic spectacle deprived of the substance of Truth. For this very reason, the purges under Stalinism were so much more ferocious and, in a way, much more 'irrational' than Fascist violence: in Fascism, even in Nazi Germany, it was possible to survive, to maintain the appearance of a 'normal' everyday life, if one did not involve oneself in any oppositional political activity (and, of course, if one were not of Jewish origin . . .), while in the Stalinism of the late 1930s nobody was safe, *everyone* could be unexpectedly denounced, arrested and shot as a traitor. In other words, the 'irrationality' of Nazism was 'condensed' in anti-Semitism, in its belief in the Jewish plot; while Stalinist 'irrationality' pervaded the entire social body. For that reason, Nazi police investigators were still looking for proof and traces of actual activity against the regime, while Stalinist investigators were engaged in clear and unambiguous fabrications (invented plots and sabotages, etc.).

This violence inflicted by the Communist Power on its own members bears witness to the radical self-contradiction of the regime, to the inherent tension between its Communist project and the *désastre* of its realization: to the fact that at the origins of the regime there was an 'authentic' revolutionary project – incessant purges were necessary not only to erase the traces of the regime's own origins, but also as a kind of 'return of the repressed', a reminder of the radical negativity at the heart of the regime, a point perfectly expressed by Nikita Mikhalkov's *Burned by the Sun* (1994), the story of the last day of freedom of Colonel Kotov, a high-ranking member of the *nomenklatura*, a famous hero of the Revolution, happily married to a beautiful young wife. In the summer of 1936, Kotov is enjoying an idyllic Sunday at his datcha with his wife and daughter. Dmitri, a former lover of Kotov's wife, pays them an unexpected visit: what begins as a pleasant gathering – playing games, singing and rekindling old memories – turns into a nightmare . . . While Dmitri flirts with Kotov's wife and charms his daughter with stories and music, it soon becomes clear to Kotov that Dmitri is a NKVD agent who has come to arrest him as a traitor at the end of the day . . .[14]

Crucial here is the complete arbitrariness and nonsense of Dmitri's violent intrusion which disturbs the peace of the idyllic summer day: this idyll is to be read as emblematic of the new order in which the *nomenklatura* stabilized its rule, so that the intervention of the NKVD agent who disturbs the idyll, in its very traumatic arbitrariness – or, in Hegelese, 'abstract negativity' – bears witness to the fundamental falsity of this idyll, that is, to the fact that the new order is founded on the betrayal of the Revolution. The Stalinist purges of senior Party echelons relied on this fundamental betrayal: the accused were effectively guilty in so far as they, as members of the new *nomenklatura*, betrayed the Revolution. The Stalinist terror is thus not simply the betrayal of the Revolution – the attempt to erase the traces of the authentic revolutionary past; rather, it bears witness to a kind of 'imp of perversity' which compels the post-revolutionary new order to (re)inscribe its betrayal of the Revolution within itself, to 'reflect' or 'remark' it in the guise of arbitrary arrests and killings which threatened all members of the *nomenklatura* – as in psychoanalysis, the Stalinist confession of guilt conceals the true guilt. (As is well known, Stalin wisely recruited into the NKVD people of lower social origins who were thus able to act out their hatred of the *nomenklatura* by arresting and torturing senior apparatchiks.)

This inherent tension between the stability of the rule of the new *nomenklatura* and the perverted 'return of the repressed' in the guise of

14   The additional charm of the film lies in the implicit Oedipal frame grafted on to the political drama: the elder hero is the obscene father who steals his son's bride, and the son later returns as the avenger.

repeated purges of the ranks of the *nomenklatura* is at the very heart of the Stalinist phenomenon: purges are the very form in which the betrayed revolutionary heritage survives and haunts the regime. The dream of Gennadi Zyuganov, the Communist presidential candidate in 1996 (things would have turned out OK in the Soviet Union if only Stalin had lived at least five years longer and accomplished his final project of having done with cosmopolitanism and bringing about the reconciliation between the Russian State and the Orthodox Church – in other words, if only Stalin had realized his anti-Semitic purge . . .), aims precisely at the point of pacification at which the revolutionary regime would finally get rid of its inherent tension and stabilize itself – the paradox, of course, is that in order to reach this stability, Stalin's last purge, the planned 'mother of all purges' which was to take place in summer 1953 and was prevented by his death, would have had to succeed.

The poetry of ethnic cleansing

The same reference to *jouissance* enables us to cast a new light on the horrors of the Bosnian war, as they are reflected in Emir Kusturica's film *Underground*. As we know from philosophical phenomenology, the object of perception is constituted through the subject's attitude towards it. The most vivid illustration of this is a naked body: this body can provoke our sexual arousal; it can serve as the object of a disinterested aesthetic gaze; it can be the object of scientific (biological) inquiry; *in extremis*, among starving men, it can even be the object of culinary interest . . . Apropos of a work of art, one often encounters the same problem: when its political investment is too obvious, it becomes for all practical purposes impossible to suspend the political passion, and to assume a disinterested aesthetic attitude. And that is the trouble with *Underground*: one can approach it as an aesthetic object; in so far as politics involves passion no less than sex, one can approach it as an *enjeu* in our politico-ideological struggles; it can serve as the object of scientific interest (to the subject who is able to assume the gaze of a historian and study the film in order to learn something about the background of the Yugoslav crisis); *in extremis*, it can function as the object of a pure technical interest (how was it made?). As for the passionate reactions to which *Underground* gave rise, especially in France, it seems that its role as the *enjeu* in the political struggle about the meaning of the post-Yugoslav war totally eclipsed its inherent aesthetic qualities.

While, in the last analysis, I accept this perception, my point is a little more specific. The political meaning of *Underground* is not to be found primarily in its overt tendentiousness, in the way it takes sides in the post-Yugoslav conflict (heroic Serbs versus the treacherous, pro-Nazi Slovenes and Croats . . .) but, rather, in its very 'depoliticized' aestheticist attitude. That is to say: when, in his conversations with the journalists of *Cahiers du cinéma*, Kusturica insisted that *Underground* is not a political film at all but a kind of liminal trancelike subjective experience, a 'deferred suicide', he thereby unknowingly laid his true *political* cards on the table and indicated that *Underground* stages the 'apolitical' phantasmic background of the post-Yugoslav ethnic cleansing and war cruelties – how?

One often hears the warning that, in the case of the Bosnian war, one should avoid the cliché of the demonization of the Serbs. However, apart from the fact that this warning itself (based on the tendency to maintain an 'equidistance' towards all sides in the conflict – 'one cannot put all the blame on only one side; in this fraternal orgy of tribal killing, nobody is innocent') is one of the main clichés of the Bosnian war, it is interesting to discern, in this ambiguous demonization, the gap between 'official' and true desire. That is to say: in this very 'official', public condemnation of the Serbs and the contrasting compassion for the Bosnians, where the Serbs are perceived as invincible warriors and winners while the Bosnians are fixed in the role of suffering victims, the main endeavour of the West has been to keep this underlying phantasmic frame undisturbed. For this reason, the moment when the Serbs began to lose on the battlefield, the West instantly stepped up the pressure and finished the war: the Bosnians *had to remain victims* – the moment they were no longer losing, their image changed into that of fanatical Muslim fundamentalists . . . The truth of the so-called 'demonization of the Serbs' resided in the fascination with their victims, clearly perceptible in the Western attitude towards horrifying pictures of the mutilated corpses, of wounded and crying children, and so on: they were horrified by them, yet at the same time they 'couldn't take their eyes off them'.

Another predominant cliché is that the Balkan peoples are caught in the phantasmic whirlpool of historical myths. Kusturica himself endorses this view, stating, in an interview for *Cahiers du cinéma*: 'In this region, war is a natural phenomenon. It is like a natural catastrophe, like an earthquake which explodes from time to time. In my film, I tried to clarify the state of things in this chaotic part of the world. It seems that nobody is able to locate the roots of this terrible conflict.' What we find here, of course, is an exemplary case of 'Balkanism', functioning in a similar way to Edward Said's 'Orientalism': the Balkans as the timeless space on to which the West projects its phantasmic content. For that reason, one should avoid the trap of 'trying to understand'; what one should do is *precisely the opposite*; with regard to the post-Yugoslav war, one should accomplish a kind of inverted phenomenological reduction and put in parenthesis the multitude of *meanings*, the wealth of the spectres of the past which allow us to 'understand' the situation. One should resist the temptation to 'understand', and accomplish a gesture analogous to turning off the sound of a TV: all of a sudden, the movements of the people on screen, deprived of their vocal support, look like meaningless, ridiculous gesticulations. It is only such a suspension of 'comprehension' that renders possible the analysis of what is at stake – economically, politically, ideologically – in the post-Yugoslav crisis: of the *political* calculuses and strategic decisions which led to the war.

The weak point of the universal multiculturalist gaze does not reside in its incapacity to 'throw out the bathwater without losing the baby too': it is deeply wrong to assert that when one throws out the nationalist dirty water ('excessive' fanaticism), one should be careful not to lose the baby of the 'healthy' national identity – that is to say, one should trace the line of separation between the proper degree of 'healthy' nationalism which guarantees the necessary minimum of national identity, and 'excessive' (xenophobic, aggressive) nationalism. Such a common-sense distinction *reproduces the very nationalist reasoning which aims at getting rid of the 'impure' excess*. One is therefore tempted to propose an analogy with psychoanalytic treatment, whose aim is also not to get rid of the dirty water (of symptoms, of pathological tics) in order to keep the baby (the kernel of the healthy Ego) safe, but, rather, to throw out the baby (to suspend the patient's Ego) in order to confront the patient with his 'dirty water', with the symptoms and fantasies which structure his *jouissance*.[15] In the matter of national identity, one should also endeavour to throw out the baby (the spiritual purity of the national identity) in order to reveal the phantasmic support which structures the *jouissance* in the national Thing. And the merit of *Underground* is that it unknowingly reveals this dirty water.

Underground brings to the light of day the obscene 'underground' of the public, official discourse (represented in the film by the Titoist Communist regime). One should bear in mind that the 'underground' to which the film's title refers is not only the domain of 'deferred suicide', of the eternal orgy of drinking, singing and copulating, which takes place in the suspension of time and outside the public space; it also stands for the 'underground' workshop in which the enslaved workers – isolated from the rest of the world, and thus misled into thinking that World War II is still going on – work day and night and produce arms sold by Marko, the hero of the film, their 'owner' and the big Manipulator, the only one who mediates between the 'underground' and the public world. Kusturica is referring here to the old European fairy-tale motif of diligent dwarfs (usually controlled by an evil magician) who, during the night, while people are asleep, emerge from their hiding-place and accomplish their tasks (put the house in order, cook the meals . . .), so that when people wake up in the morning, they find their work magically done. Kusturica's

15 Such a reversal is crucial for the progress of psychoanalytic treatment: at the beginning, the patient wants to retain the consistency of his Self, and merely get rid of the embarrassing symptoms which disturb this consistency; in the course of analysis, however, it is the patient's Self which dissolves, while the patient is directly confronted with his symptom, deprived of the protective shield of his Self.

'underground' is the last embodiment of this motif, which comes down to us from Richard Wagner's *Rhinegold* (the Nibelungs who work in their underground caves, driven by their cruel master, the dwarf Alberich) to Fritz Lang's *Metropolis*, in which the enslaved industrial workers live and work deep beneath the earth's surface to produce wealth for the ruling capitalists.

This device of the 'underground' slaves dominated by a manipulative evil Master is set against the background of the opposition between the two figures of the Master: on the one hand, the 'visible' public symbolic authority; on the other, the 'invisible' spectral apparition. When the subject is endowed with symbolic authority, he acts as an appendage to his symbolic title – that is to say, it is the 'big Other', the symbolic institution, who acts through him: take, for example, a judge who may be a miserable and corrupt person, but the moment he puts on his robe and other insignia, his words are the words of Law itself . . . On the other hand, the 'invisible' Master (exemplified in the anti-Semitic figure of the 'Jew' who, invisible to the public eye, pulls the strings of social life) is a kind of uncanny double of public authority: he has to act in shadow, invisible to the public eye, irradiating a phantomlike, spectral omnipotence.[16]

The unfortunate Marko from Kusturica's *Underground* is to be located in this lineage of the evil magician who controls an invisible empire of enslaved workers: he is a kind of uncanny double of Tito as the public symbolic Master. The key question, however, is: how does Kusturica relate to this duality? The problem with *Underground* is that it falls into the cynical trap of presenting this obscene 'underground' from a benevolent distance. *Underground*, of course, is multilayered and extremely self-reflective. It plays with a mixture of clichés (the Serbian myth of a true man who, even when bombs are falling around him, calmly continues his meal); it is full of references to the history of cinema, up to Vigo's *Atalanta*, and to cinema as such (when the 'underground' war hero, who is presumed

16   See Slavoj Žižek, ' "I Hear You with My Eyes"; or, The Invisible Master', in *Gaze and Voice as Love Objects,* Durham, NC: Duke University Press, 1966.

dead, emerges from his hiding-place, he encounters cineastes shooting a film about his heroic death), as well as other forms of postmodern self-referentiality (recourse to the perspective of fairy-tales: 'There was once a land called . . .'; the passage from realism to pure fantasy: the idea of a network of underground tunnels beneath Europe, one of them leading directly from Berlin to Athens . . .). All this, of course, is meant in an ironic way; it is 'not to be taken literally' – however, *it is precisely through such self-distance that 'postmodern' cynical ideology functions.* Umberto Eco recently enumerated the series of features which define the kernel of the Fascist attitude: dogmatic tenacity, absence of humour, insensibility to rational argumentation . . . he could not have been more wrong. Today's neo-Fascism is more and more 'postmodern', civilized, playful, involving ironic self-distance . . . *yet no less Fascist for all that.*

So, in a way, Kusturica is right in his interview for *Cahiers du cinéma*: he *does* somehow 'clarify the state of things in this chaotic part of the world' by bringing its 'underground' phantasmic support to light. He thereby unknowingly provides the libidinal economy of the Serbian ethnic slaughter in Bosnia: the pseudo-Batailleian trance of excessive expenditure, the continuous mad rhythm of drinking-eating-singing-fornicating. And *that is the stuff of the 'dream' of the ethnic cleansers; therein lies the answer to the question 'How were they able to do it?'*. If the standard definition of war is that of 'a continuation of politics with the admixture of other means', then we can say that the fact that Radovan Karadžič the leader of the Bosnian Serbs, is a poet, is more than a gratuitous coincidence: ethnic cleansing in Bosnia was the continuation of (a kind of) *poetry* with the admixture of other means.

The desublimated neighbour

The fantasy which underlies the public ideological text as its non-acknowledged obscene support simultaneously serves as a screen against the direct intrusion of the Real. According to a popular racist and sexist myth, Italian men, during the sexual act, want the woman to whisper into their ears obscenities about what she has been doing with another man or men – only with the aid of this mythical support can they perform as the proverbial good lovers in reality. Here we encounter the Lacanian 'il n'y a pas de rapport sexuel' at its purest: the theoretically correct point of this myth is that even at the moment of the most intense bodily contact with each other, lovers are not alone, they need a minimum of phantasmic narrative as a symbolic support – that is, they can never simply 'let themselves go' and immerse themselves in 'that' . . . *Mutatis mutandis*, the same goes for religious or ethnic violence: the question to be asked is always 'What voices does a racist hear when he indulges in beating Jews, Arabs, Mexicans, Bosnians . . . ? What do these voices tell him?'

For animals, the most elementary form, the 'zero form', of sexuality is copulation; whereas for humans, the 'zero form' is *masturbation with fantasizing* (in this sense, for Lacan, phallic *jouissance* is masturbatory and idiotic); any contact with a 'real', flesh-and-blood other, any sexual pleasure that we find in touching *another* human being, is not something evident but inherently traumatic, and can be sustained only in so far as this other enters the subject's fantasy-frame. When, in the eighteenth century, masturbation became a moral problem with a distinctly modern twist,[17] what bothered the moralist sexologists was not primarily the non-productive loss of semen but, rather, the 'unnatural' way desire is aroused in masturbation – not by a real object but by a fantasized object created by the subject itself. When, for example, Kant condemns this vice as so unnatural that 'we consider it indecent even to call it by its proper name', his reasoning goes as follows: 'Lust is called unnatural if man is aroused to it, not by its real object, but by his imagination of this object, and so in a way contrary to the purpose of the desire, since he himself creates its object.'[18] The problem, of course, is that a minimum of 'synthesis of imagination' (to use Kant's own term) which (re-)creates its object is

17   I draw here on Thomas W. Laqueur, 'Masturbation, Credit and the Novel During the Long Eighteenth Century', *Qui Parle* 8: 2, 1995.
18   Immanuel Kant, *The Metaphysics of Morals,* Part II: The Doctrine of Virtue, II, 7, para. 424.

necessary for sexuality to function normally. This 'imagined part' becomes visible in an unpleasant experience known to most of us: in the middle of the most intense sexual act, it is possible for us all of a sudden to 'disconnect' – all of a sudden, a question can emerge: 'What am I doing here, sweating and repeating these stupid gestures?'; pleasure can shift into disgust or into a strange feeling of distance. The key point is that, in this violent upheaval, *nothing changed in reality*: what caused the shift was merely *the change in the other's position with regard to our phantasmic frame*. This is precisely what goes wrong in Kieslowski's *Short Film about Love*, a masterpiece on the (im)possibility of courtly love today: the hero, the young Tomek, practises voyeuristic masturbation (masturbating while observing the beloved woman through his 'rear window'); the moment he passes the phantasmic threshold of the window, and is seduced by the woman to the other side of the looking-glass as she offers herself to him, everything disintegrates and he is driven to suicide . . .

The same experience of 'desublimation' was already well known in the tradition of courtly love, in the guise of the figure of *die Frau-Welt* (the woman who stands for the world, terrestrial life): she looks beautiful from the proper distance, but the moment the poet or the knight serving her approaches her too closely (or when she beckons him to come nearer to her so that she can repay him for his faithful service), she turns her other, reverse side towards him, and what was previously the semblance of fascinating beauty is suddenly revealed as putrefied flesh, crawling with snakes and worms, the disgusting substance of life – as in the films of David Lynch, in which an object turns into the disgusting substance of life when the camera gets too close to it. The gap that separates beauty from ugliness is thus the very gap that separates reality from the Real: what constitutes reality is the minimum of idealization the subject needs in order to be able to sustain the horror of the Real.

We encounter the same decomposition in *Hamlet*, when Ophelia loses her status of the object of Hamlet's desire, and starts to embody for him the disgusting immortal movement of primordial life, of the cycle of generation and corruption in which Eros and Thanatos coincide, and every birth marks the beginning of decomposition – like the *Frau-Welt* when we get too close to her. In the course of this process, Hamlet's fantasy disintegrates, so that when Ophelia becomes, as it were, approachable in a direct way, without the screen of fantasy, he is no longer sure where she fits in, observing her with a strange detachment, as if she were a kind of alien. (In the graveyard scene in Act V, Hamlet recomposes his fantasy, and thereby reconstitutes himself as a desiring subject.)

Here we can see clearly how fantasy is on the side of reality, how it sustains the subject's 'sense of reality': when the phantasmic frame disintegrates, the subject undergoes a 'loss of reality' and starts to perceive reality as an 'irreal' nightmarish universe with no firm ontological foundation; this nightmarish universe is not 'pure fantasy' but, on the contrary, *that which remains of reality after reality is deprived of its support in fantasy*. So when Schumann's *Carnaval* – with its 'regression' to the dream-like universe in which intercourse between 'real people' is replaced by a kind of masked ball where one never knows what or who is hidden beneath the mask which laughs crazily at us: a machine, a slimy life-substance, or (undoubtedly the most horrifying case) simply the 'real' double of the mask itself – sets Hoffmann's *Unheimliche* to music, what we obtain is not the 'universe of pure fantasy' but, rather, the unique artistic rendering of the *decomposition* of the fantasy-frame. The characters musically depicted in *Carnaval* are like the ghastly apparitions strolling on the main Oslo street in Munch's famous painting, pale-faced and with a frail but strangely intense source of light within their eyes (signalling *gaze* as object replacing the looking eye): desubjectivized living dead, frail spectres deprived of their material substance.

No wonder, then, that, with regard to his beloved Clara, Schumann was literally a 'divided subject': desiring her proximity, yet simultaneously dreading her. No wonder that the reference to Beethoven's *An die ferne Geliebte* ('To the distant beloved') was crucial for him: Schumann's problem was that, in an obscure way, he desperately wanted his beloved Clara to remain at a proper distance in order to retain her sublime status, and thus avoid changing into a true *neighbour* who forces herself on us with her repellent crawl of life . . . In the letter to Clara, his future bride, of 10 May 1838 (at the very point when, after long years, they surmounted the obstacles to their union and were planning their imminent marriage), Schumann directly spills out the secret: 'Your presence here would, I believe, paralyse all my projects and my work, and this would really make me very unhappy.'[19] Even more uncanny is the dream he reports to Clara in his letter of 14 April 1838:

> I should tell you one of my dreams from the night before. I awoke and could not fall asleep again; I then identified myself more and more profoundly with you, with your dreams, with your soul, so that I suddenly shouted with all my power, from the deepest part of myself, 'Clara, I'm calling you!', and then I heard a cruel voice coming from somewhere near me: 'But Robert, I am near you!' I submerged into a kind of horror, as if ghosts met on a vast empty land. I did not call for you in this way again, it affected me too much.[20]

Do we not encounter here, in this hoarse and cruel voice, ambushing us in its very intrusive *overproximity*, the horrifying weight of the encounter of a neighbour in the Real of her presence? Love thy neighbour? No, thanks! And this split in Schumann, this radical oscillation between attraction and repulsion, between longing for the distant beloved and feeling estranged and repelled by her proximity, by no means exposes a 'pathological' imbalance within his psyche: such an oscillation is constitutive of human desire, so that the true enigma is, rather, how a 'normal' subject succeeds in covering it up and negotiating a fragile balance between the sublime image of the beloved and her real presence, so that the flesh-and-blood person can continue to occupy the sublime place and avoid the sad fate of turning into a repulsive excrement . . .

Jacques Rivette's film *La Belle noiseuse* focuses on the tense relationship

19   Quoted from Berthold Litzmann, *Clara Schumann, Fin Kunstlerleben*, vol. 1, Leipzig: Breitkopf & Hartel, 1902, p. 211.
20   Ibid., p. 206.

between the male painter (Michel Piccoli) and his model (Emmanuelle Béart): the model resists the artist, she actively provokes him, contests his approach, urges him on, and thus fully participates in the creation of the art object. In short, the model is literally 'the beautiful trouble-maker', the traumatic object which irritates and infuriates, rejecting its insertion into the series of ordinary objects – *ça bouge*, as they say in France. And what is art (the act of painting) if not an attempt to *dépose*, 'lay down', in the painting this traumatic dimension, to exorcize it by way of externalizing it in the object of art. In *La Belle noiseuse*, however, this pacification fails: at the end of the film, the artist immures the painting in a crack between two walls where it will stay for ever, unbeknownst to the future inhabitants of the house – why? The point is not that he failed to penetrate the secret of his model: he succeeded *too well* – that is to say, the finished product divulges *too much* about its model; it breaks through her veil of beauty and renders her visible as what she is in the Real of her being: the abhorrent cold Thing. No wonder, then, that when the model finally gets a view of the finished painting, she runs away in panic and disgust – what she sees out there is the kernel of her being, her *agalma*, turned into excrement. The true victim of the operation is thus not the painter, but the model herself: she was active; by her uncompromising attitude she provoked the artist into extracting from her and putting on canvas the kernel of her being, and she got what she asked for, which is always precisely *more* than she asked for – she got herself *plus* the excremental excess constitutive of the kernel of her being. For this precise reason, it was necessary that the painting be concealed for ever behind the wall, and not simply destroyed: any direct physical destruction would be to no avail; one can only bury it and thus keep it at bay, since what is 'laid down' in the painting is *stricto sensu* indestructible – it has the status of what Lacan, in *The Four Fundamental Concepts*, calls *lamella*, the mythical pre-subjective 'undead' life-substance, libido as an organ.

Orson Welles was extremely sensitive to the strange logic of this 'secret treasure', the hidden kernel of the subject's being which, once the subject discloses it to us, turns into a poisonous gift. To quote the epigraph to

Mr. Arkadin: 'A certain great and powerful king once asked a poet, "What can I give you of all that I have?" He wisely replied, "Anything, sir . . . except your secret."' Why? Because, as Lacan put it: *'I give myself to you . . . but this gift of my person . . . - Oh, mystery! is changed inexplicably into a gift of shit'* – the excessive opening up (disclosure of a secret, allegiance, obedience . . .) of one person to another easily reverts to an excremental repulsive intrusion. That is the meaning of the famous 'No trespassing!' sign shown at the beginning and end of *Citizen Kane*: it is highly hazardous to enter this domain of the utmost intimacy, as one gets more than one asked for – all of a sudden, when it is already too late to withdraw, one finds oneself in a slimy obscene domain . . . Most of us know from personal experience how unpleasant it is when a person in authority whom we deeply admire, and even want to know more about, grants our wish and takes us into his confidence, sharing with us his deepest personal trauma – the charisma evaporates all of a sudden, and we feel the impulse just to run away. Perhaps the feature which characterizes true friendship is precisely a tactful knowledge of when to stop, not going beyond a certain threshold and 'telling everything' to a friend. We do tell everything to a psychoanalyst – but precisely for that reason, he can never be our friend . . .

The neighbour's ugly voice

Heinrich Kleist's short story 'St Cecilia or the Power of the Voice' perfectly encapsulates the (singing) voice in its uncanny status of the embodiment of 'ugly' *jouissance*. It is set in a German town, torn between Protestants and Catholics, during the Thirty Years War. The Protestants plan to create slaughter in a large Catholic Church during a midnight Mass; four people are planted to start making trouble, and thus give the signal to the others to start the havoc. Things take a strange turn, however, when a beautiful nun, allegedly dead, miraculously awakens and leads the chorus in a beautiful song. This song mesmerizes the four thugs: they are unable to start making trouble and so, since there is no signal, the night passes peacefully. Even after the event, the four Protestant thugs remain numbed: they are locked in an asylum, where for years they just sit and pray all day long – only at midnight, every night, all of them promptly stand up and sing the sublime song they had heard on that fateful night ... Here, of course, horror arises, since what was originally the divine singing of nuns which exerted a miraculous redemptive-pacifying effect is now, in its repetition, a dreadfully repulsive obscene imitation.

In other words, what we have here is an exemplary case of the Hegelian tautology as the highest contradiction: 'Voice is ... voice' – that is to say, the ethereal-sublime voice of a church choir encounters itself in its otherness in the grotesque singing of the madmen. This grotesque singing inverts the standard version of the obscene turn, that of a gentle innocent girl's face which is distorted all of a sudden by rage and starts to swear, to spit out unspeakable blasphemies (the possessed girl in *The Exorcist*, etc.). This standard version reveals the underlying horror and corruption beneath the gentle surface: the semblance of innocence disintegrates; all of a sudden we perceive the intense obscenity behind it – what could be worse? Precisely what takes place in Kleist's story: the ultimate horror occurs not when the mask of innocence disintegrates, when a gentle girl's face starts to spit out profanities, but, rather, when the sublime text is (mis)appropriated by the wrong, corrupted speaker. In the standard version, we have the right object (a gentle innocent face) in the wrong place (engaged in blasphemous profanities); while in Kleist, we have the wrong object (brutal ugly thugs) in the right place (trying to imitate the sublime religious ritual).

At the level of ethnic identity, something similar happens when a subject who is not 'one of us' learns our language and endeavours to speak it, to behave as part of 'our' community: the automatic reaction of every proper racist is that the stranger, by doing this, steals from us the substance of our identity. In love relations, something similar happens when the proverbial husband buys a nice dress for his mistress and then, upon coming home, finds that his wife has discovered this dress among his things and, assuming that it is for her, has put it on, and enthusiastically shows herself off to him in it ... Does not something of the same order take place also in the famous scene from Hitchcock's *Vertigo* in which Midge, the hero's ordinary bespectacled friend, who is aware of his infatuation with the portrait of Carlotta, the long-dead fatal beauty, paints a picture which is the exact copy of the portrait of Carlotta, with the exception of the face – in place of Carlotta's face, she paints in her own ordinary bespectacled face. The view of it, of this wrong object (Midge's face) in the right place, of course, utterly depresses the hero – why?[21] In the standard version, sublime beauty is denounced as a lure, a false appearance beneath which the corrupted flesh reigns supreme – however, precisely as such, as a 'mere appearance', *appearance is saved*, while in the second case (from Kleist's story to Hitchcock's *Vertigo*) the sublime appearance, appropriated by the wrong subject, is, as it were, *undermined from within.*[22]

Strictly analogous is the relationship between the horrible content (wild promiscuity) behind the sublime mask of marriage and *same-sex marriage*, this traumatic point, the ultimate *bête noire*, of the Moral Majority. That is to say: why is same-sex marriage so traumatic for the Moral Majority attitude? Because it disturbs the premiss according to which homosexuals, seeking only quick promiscuous pleasures, are unable to engage in a profound personal relationship – the uncanny proximity of same-sex marriage to 'straight' marriage thus undermines the latter's uniqueness. The paradox is thus that the Moral Majority attitude secretly *wants* homosexuals to remain promiscuous pleasure-seekers: when they 'want more', marriage as the symbolic ritual asserting their deep personal commitment, the Moral Majority necessarily perceives this as an obscene travesty of the true marriage bond – like Kant, for whom the trial and execution of a

21   When Scottie is confronted with the portrait of Carlotta with Midge's ordinary bespectacled face painted in instead of Carlotta's face, is this not a clear case of confronting a gaze? Is not Midge's face not the point from which the painting, as it were, returns his gaze?

22   The scene from *Vertigo* thus in a sense condenses and announces the final deception of the hero: when, at the end of the film, he discovers that the girl he is trying to mould into the perfect copy of the lost Madeleine *is* Madeleine herself – that Madeleine herself was already a fake – it is not enough to say that he is deceived, since the copy no longer fits the lost ideal: it is the ideal itself which disintegrates, which is undermined from within.

monarch is an obscene travesty of justice and, as such, a *crimen inexpiabile* infinitely worse than a straight bloodthirsty rebellion . . .

A frog and a bottle of beer

So how are we to undermine the hold which the phantasmic *jouissance* exerts over us? Let us approach this issue via a specific problem: when a work of art comes under the spell of the proto-Fascist ideological universe, is this enough to denounce it as proto-Fascist? *Dune* (Herbert's novel, and especially Lynch's film) tells the story of how a corrupt imperial regime is replaced by a new authoritarian regime, obviously modelled on Muslim fundamentalism – is Lynch (and already Herbert himself) for that reason a misogynist proto-Fascist? This fascination is usually perceived as the 'eroticization' of power, so the question must be rephrased: how does a power edifice become eroticized – or, more precisely, sexualized? When ideological interpellation fails to seize the subject (when the symbolic ritual of a power edifice no longer runs smoothly, when the subject is no longer able to assume the symbolic mandate conferred upon him), it 'gets stuck' in a repetitive vicious cycle, and it is this 'dysfunctional' empty repetitive movement which sexualizes power, smearing it with a stain of obscene enjoyment. The point, of course, is that there never was a purely symbolic Power without an obscene supplement: the structure of a power edifice is always minimally inconsistent, so that it needs a minimum of sexualization, of the stain of obscenity, to reproduce itself. Another aspect of this failure is that a power relation becomes sexualized when an intrinsic ambiguity creeps in, so that it is no longer clear who is actually the master and who is the servant. What distinguishes the masochistic spectacle from a simple scene of torture is not merely the fact that in the masochistic spectacle, for the most part, violence is merely suggested; more crucial is the fact that the executioner himself acts as the servant's servant. When, in one of the most memorable *noir* scenes (from Nicholas Ray's *On Dangerous Ground*), in a lonely hotel room, Robert Ryan approaches a petty crook in order to beat him up, he desperately shouts: 'Why do you make me do it?', his face contorted in a unique expression of pleasure in pain, while the poor crook laughs back in Ryan's face and invites him: 'Come on! Beat me! Beat me!', as if Ryan himself were an instrument of his victim's enjoyment, this radical ambiguity confers on the scene the character of perverted sexuality.

This link between sexualization and failure is of the same nature as the link between matter and space curvature in Einstein: matter is not a positive substance whose density curves space, it is *nothing but* the curvature of space. By analogy, one should also 'desubstantialize' sexuality: sexuality is not a kind of traumatic substantial Thing, which the subject cannot attain directly; it is *nothing but* the formal structure of failure which, in principle, can 'contaminate' any activity. So, again, when we are engaged in an activity which fails to attain its goal directly, and gets caught in a repetitive vicious cycle, this activity is automatically sexualized – a rather vulgar everyday example: if, instead of simply shaking my friend's hand, I were to squeeze his palm repeatedly for no apparent reason, this repetitive gesture would undoubtedly be experienced by him or her as sexualized in an obscene way.

The obverse of this inherent sexualization of power due to the ambiguity (reversibility) of the relation between the one who exerts power and the one subjected to it – to the failure of the direct symbolic exercise of power – is the fact that sexuality as such (an intersubjective sexual relationship) always involves a relationship of power: there is no neutral symmetrical sexual relationship/exchange, undistorted by power. The ultimate proof is the dismal failure of the 'politically correct' endeavour to free sexuality of power: to define the rules of 'proper' sexual rapport in which partners should indulge in sex only on account of their mutual, purely sexual, attraction, excluding any 'pathological' factor (power, financial coercion, etc.): if we subtract from sexual rapport the element of 'asexual' (physical, financial . . .) coercion, which distorts the 'pure' sexual attraction, we may lose sexual attraction itself. In other words, the problem is that the very element which seems to bias and corrupt pure sexual rapport (one partner behaves violently towards the other; he forces his partner to accept him and indulge in sex with him because the partner is subordinated to him, financially dependent on him, etc.), may function as the very phantasmic support of sexual attraction – in a way, sex as such *is* pathological . . .

But, again: does not the open display of the repetitive sexualized rituals of power *sustain* the power edifice, even (and especially) under the false pretence of subverting it? Under what conditions is the staging of the hidden obscene supplement of a power edifice effectively 'subversive'? In the process of the disintegration of Socialism in Slovenia, the post-punk group Laibach staged an aggressive inconsistent mixture of Stalinism, Nazism and *Blut und Boden* ideology; many 'progressive' liberal critics accused them of being a neo-Nazi band – did they not effectively support what they pretended to undermine by mocking imitation, since they were obviously fascinated by the rituals they were staging? This perception thoroughly missed the point. A barely perceptible but none the less crucial line separated Laibach from 'true' totalitarianism: they staged (publicly displayed) the phantasmic support of power *in all its inconsistency*. The same goes for *Dune*: *Dune* is not 'totalitarian' in so far as it publicly displays the underlying obscene phantasmic support of 'totalitarianism' in all its inconsistency.

The ultimate example of this strange logic of subversion is provided by the 'Memoirs' of Daniel Paul Schreber, a turn-of-the-century German judge who described in detail his psychotic hallucinations about being sexually persecuted by the obscene God. We find in Schreber a true encyclopaedia of paranoiac motifs: persecution transposed from the doctor treating the psychotic on to God Himself; the theme of the catastrophic end of the world and its subsequent rebirth; the subject's privileged contact with God, who sends him messages encoded as sun rays . . . The multitude of readings covers an entire spectrum, from seeing in Schreber's 'Memoirs' a proto-Fascist text (the Hitlerian motif of universal catastrophe and the rebirth of a new, racially pure humanity) up to perceiving them as a proto-feminist text (the rejection of phallic identification, man's desire to occupy the feminine place in the sexual act) – this very oscillation between extremes is in itself a symptom worth interpreting. In his brilliant reading of Schreber's 'Memoirs', Eric Santner focuses on the fact that Schreber's paranoiac crises occurred at the time when he was close to assuming some position of judicial-political power.[23] The case of Schreber is thus to be located in what Santner calls the late-nineteenth-century 'crisis of investiture': the failure of assuming and performing a mandate of symbolic authority. So why did Schreber fall into psychotic delirium at the very moment when he was to assume the position of a judge – that is, the function of public symbolic authority? He was unable to come to terms with the stain of obscenity which formed an integral part of the functioning of symbolic authority: the 'crisis of investiture' breaks out when the enjoying underside of the paternal authority (in the guise of *Luder*, the obscene/ridiculous paternal double) traumatically affects the subject. This obscene dimension does not simply hinder the 'normal' functioning of Power; rather, it functions as a kind of Derridean supplement, as an obstacle which is simultaneously the 'condition of possibility' of the exercise of Power.

Power thus relies on an obscene supplement – that is to say, the obscene 'nightly' law (superego) necessarily accompanies, as its shadowy double, the 'public' Law.[24] As for the status of this obscene supplement, one should avoid both traps and neither glorify it as subversive nor dismiss it as a false transgression which stabilizes the power edifice (like the ritualized carnivals which temporarily suspend power relations), but insist on its *undecidable* character. Obscene unwritten rules sustain Power as long as they remain in the shadows; the moment they are publicly recognized, the edifice of Power is thrown into disarray. For that reason, Schreber is not 'totalitarian', although his paranoiac fantasy contains all the elements of a Fascist myth: what makes him truly subversive is the way he *publicly identifies* with the obscene phantasmic support of the Fascist edifice. To put it in psychoanalytic terms: Schreber identifies with the symptom of

23   See Eric Santner, *My Own Private Germany*, Princeton, NJ: Princeton University Press, 1996.

24   See Chapter 3 of Slavoj Žižek, *The Metastases of Enjoyment*, London: Verso, 1994.

Power, he displays it, stages it publicly, *in all its inconsistency* (for example, he displays its sexual phantasmic background which is the very opposite of pure Aryan masculinity: a feminized subject fucked by God . . .). And does not the same apply to the Weiningerian anti-feminist tradition which includes the figure of *femme fatale* in *film noir*? This figure displays the underlying obscene phantasmic support of 'normal' bourgeois femininity; there is nothing directly 'feminist' in it; all the desperate attempts of those who obviously like *noir* to discern in the figure of the *femme fatale* some redemptive qualities (a refusal to remain the passive object of male manipulation: the *femme fatale* wants to assert her control over men, etc.) somehow seem to miss the point, which is that *film noir* effectively undermines patriarchy simply by bringing to light the underlying phantasmic bric-à-brac in all its inconsistency.

A recent English publicity spot for a beer enables us to clarify this crucial distinction. The first part stages the well-known fairy-tale anecdote: a girl walks along a stream, sees a frog, takes it gently into her lap, kisses it, and, of course, the ugly frog miraculously turns into a beautiful young man. However, the story isn't over yet: the young man casts a covetous glance at the girl, draws her towards him, kisses her – and she turns into a bottle of beer, which the man holds triumphantly in his hand . . . For the woman, the point is that her love and affection (symbolized by the kiss) turn a frog into a beautiful man, a full phallic presence (in Lacan's mathemes, big Phi); for the man, it is to reduce the woman to a partial object, the cause of his desire (in Lacan's mathemes, the *objet petit a*). Because of this asymmetry, 'there is no sexual relationship': we have either a woman with a frog or a man with a bottle of beer – what we can never obtain is the 'natural' couple of the beautiful woman and man . . . Why not? Because the phantasmic support of this 'ideal couple' would have been the inconsistent figure of *a frog embracing a bottle of beer*.[25] This, then, opens up the possibility of

<hr/>

25 Of course, the obvious feminist point would be that what women witness in their everyday love experience is, rather, the opposite passage: one kisses a beautiful young man and, after one has come too close to him – that is to say, when it is already too late – one notices that he is in fact a frog . . .

undermining the hold a fantasy exerts over us through our very overiden-tification with it by *embracing simultaneously, within the same space, the multitude of inconsistent phantasmic elements*. That is to say: each of the two subjects is involved in his or her own subjective fantasizing – the girl fantasizes about the frog who is really a young man; the man about the girl who is really a bottle of beer. What Schreber (and Laibach and Lynch's *Dune*) oppose to this is not objective reality but the 'objectively subjective' underlying fantasy which the two subjects are never able to assume, something similar to a Magrittesque painting of a frog embracing a bottle of beer, with the title 'A man and a woman' or 'The ideal couple'.[26] And is this not the ethical duty of today's artist: to confront us with the frog embracing the bottle of beer when we are daydreaming about embracing our beloved?[27]

This inconsistency also allows us to draw a general conclusion about the notion of ideology. Ideology is not primarily the imaginary solution of real antagonisms ('class conflict'); rather, it consists in their symbolic solution: the elementary ideological gesture is the imposition of a signifier which starts to function as a kind of empty container for the multitude of mutually exclusive meanings – there is no ideology without such a 'pullback' from the signified content into the empty symbolic form. Recall the case of the aggressive 'hardwired' women in cyberpunk who revenge themselves against male violence to which they were exposed in their pre-cyber existence: it is easy to claim how they unite (at least) two contradictory ideological positions, the fetishized male fantasy of a non-castrated 'phallic' woman whose unleashed aggressivity poses a threat to the world, *and* a feminist rebellion against the brutal patriarchal system. The point not to be missed, however, is that their ideological appeal lies precisely *in* this 'inconsistent' combination, so that one and the same figure stands for the multiple, inconsistent 'contents': in ideology, one can have one's cake and

26   The association with the famous Surrealist 'dead donkey on a piano' is fully justi-fied here, since the Surrealists also practised a version of traversing the fantasy. (Incidentally, in recent Budweiser advertisements, a frog's tongue is stuck on to a bottle of beer.)

27   And, at a different level, did not Syberberg accomplish something similar in his *Parsifal,* by 'heinously' piling up inconsistent phantasmic fragments, from Marx through Romantic kitsch to Hitler?

eat it – that is, in this case, one can satisfy one's patriarchal fears and, at the same time, pay one's dues to one's feminist awareness. The 'pure' patriarchal ideology never existed: in order to be 'effective' as a social bond, it *always has to combine* a series of 'inconsistent' attitudes. The figure of the 'hardwired woman' is not simply an inconsistent bundle of two opposed ideological stances: it is in this very inconsistent bundle that *ideology* consists.

Exemplary here is Spielberg's *Star Wars* trilogy, which condenses (at least) three levels:[28] the Leftist motif of a Vietnam-like guerrilla against the US Empire (the victory of the Ewoks in the last part); the hippie New Age mythology (the wisdom of Yoda: 'The force be with you!'. . .); the moralism of the New Right (the return to simple basic virtues; from this aspect, the 'Evil Empire' is a metaphor for the Soviet Union). In order to account for the ideological background of *Star Wars*, one has to combine all three levels *under the dominant of the third level* – why? This third level involves a self-reflective moment: the infantilization of the spectator, that is, the return to the 'naive' spectator against the cynicism, reflectivity, and so on, of the 1960s and early 1970s – Spielberg himself often claims that his films are made for 'the kid in all of us'. The ideological theme of the grown-ups' redemption through their infantilization (the explicit topic of his *Peter Pan*) thus simultaneously produces a new subject position for the spectator.[29]

28   I draw here on Peter Biskind, 'Blockbusters', in Mark Crispin Miller, ed., *Seeing Through the Movies*, New York: Pantheon, 1990.

29   Even here, however, things are properly undecidable, since infantilization is a 'floating signifier' which can also function as part of a move *against* the patriarchal family and its violence, as in Spielberg's own *The Color Purple*: in this film, the infantilization of the heroine is intended to *subvert* the standard cliché about blacks as innocent children – infantilization is presented here not as the African-American's 'natural state' of childish innocence and irresponsibility but as a secondary reactive phenomenon, a desperate attempt to cope with the terrible trauma of suffering, of psychic and physical abuse. At a different level, Adorno was sensitive to the same phenomenon in his infamous rejection of jazz: he conceived jazz as the way African-Americans change their historical experience of pain into a circus performance intended to amuse their white masters, that is, precisely those who were the ultimate cause of their pain – what Adorno rejected was thus the element of black self-humiliation in jazz.

Ideological anamorphosis

The procedure which enables us to discern the structural inconsistency of an ideological edifice is that of the *anamorphic reading*. For example, is not the relationship between *le Nom-du-Père* and *le Non-du-Père* in Lacan a kind of theoretical anamorphosis?[30] The shift from *Nom* to *Non* – that is, the insight which makes us discern, in the positive figure of Father as the bearer of symbolic authority, merely the materialized/embodied negation – effectively involves a change in the subject's perspective: viewed from the right perspective, the Father's majestic presence becomes visible as a mere positivization of a negative gesture. One can also put it in Kantian terms: the anamorphic shift enables us to discern an apparently positive object as a 'negative magnitude', as a mere 'positivization of a void'. That is the elementary procedure of the critique of ideology: the 'sublime object of ideology' is the spectral object which has no positive ontological consistency, but merely fills in the gap of a certain constitutive impossibility.

The anti-Semitic figure of the Jew (to take *the* example of this sublime object) bears witness to the fact that the ideological desire which sustains anti Semitism is inconsistent, 'self-contradictory' (capitalist competition *and* pre-modern organic solidarity, etc.). In order to maintain this desire, a specific object must be invented which gives body to, externalizes, the cause of the non-satisfaction of this desire (the Jew who is responsible for social disintegration). The lack of positive ontological consistency in this figure of the Jew is proved by the fact that the true relationship of causality is inverted with regard to the way things appear within the anti-Semitic ideological space: it is not the Jew who prevents Society from existing (from realizing itself as a full organic solidarity, etc.); rather, it is social antagonism which is primordial, and the figure of the Jew comes second as a fetish which materializes this hindrance. In this sense, one can also say that the Jew (not actual Jews, but the 'conceptual Jew' in anti-Semitism)

---

30   See Hanna Gekle, *Tod im Spiegel: Zur Lacans Theorie des Imaginären,* Frankfurt: Suhrkamp, 1996.

is a Kantian 'negative magnitude': the positivization of the opposing force of 'evil' whose activity explains why the order of Good can never fully win. One of the most elementary definitions of ideology, therefore, is: a symbolic field which contains such a filler holding the place of some structural impossibility, while simultaneously disavowing this impossibility. In natural sciences, an example of such 'negative magnitude' is the infamous phlogiston (the ethereal stuff which allegedly serves as the medium for the transmission of light): this object merely positivizes the lack and inconsistency of our scientific explanation of the true nature of light. In all these cases, the basic operation is that of *giving negativity precedence over positivity*: prohibition is not a secondary obstacle which hinders my desire; desire itself is an attempt to fill the gap sustained by the prohibition. The (anti-Semitic figure of the) 'Jew' is not the positive cause of social imbalance and antagonisms: social antagonism comes first, and the 'Jew' merely gives body to this obstacle.

Kant is usually criticized for his formalism: for maintaining the rigid distinction between the network of formal conditions and the contingent positive content which provides the content for this formal network. There is, however, a critico-ideological use of this distinction: in the case of anti-Semitism, the main point is that the historical reality of Jews is exploited to fill in a pre-constructed ideological space which is in no way inherently connected with the historical reality of Jews. One falls into the ideological trap precisely by succumbing to the illusion that anti-Semitism really *is* about Jews.

Does not Lacan perform the same anamorphic shift of perspective in his famous reversal of Dostoyevsky ('If there is no God, nothing at all is permitted') - that is to say, in his reversal of (the common perception of) Law as the agency which represses desire into (the concept of) Law as that which effectively *sustains* desire? In this precise sense, the Hegelian dialectical reversal also always involves a kind of anamorphic shift of perspective: what we (mis)perceived as the obstacle (the Prohibition), the condition of impossibility, is actually a positive condition of possibility (of our desiring) - the wicked world about which the Beautiful Soul complains is the inherent condition of its own subjective position. (The same also goes for the relationship between Law and its transgression: far from undermining the rule of the Law, its 'transgression' in fact serves as its ultimate support. So it is not only that transgression relies on, presupposes, the Law it transgresses; rather, the reverse case is much more pertinent: Law itself relies on its inherent transgression, so that when we suspend this transgression, the Law itself disintegrates.)

In the history of modern philosophy, such an anamorphic shift condenses the operation of the line of 'over-orthodox' authors (from Pascal through Kleist and Kierkegaard to Brecht's learning plays) who subvert the ruling ideology by taking it more literally than it is ready to take itself – the uneasy, disturbing effect on the reader of *Pensées*, *The Prince of Homburg*, or *The Measure Taken* resides in the fact that they, as it were, disclose the hidden cards of the ideology they identify with (French Catholicism, German military patriotism, revolutionary Communism) and thus render it inoperative – that is, unacceptable to the existing order. These works violently confront us with the fact that ideology requires a distance towards itself in order to rule unimpeded: if ideology is to maintain its hold on us, we must experience ourselves as not fully in its grasp: 'I'm not merely a direct embodiment of . . . [Jansenism, Prussian patriotism, Communism]; beneath this ideological mask, there lurks a warm human person with his small sorrows and joys which have nothing to do with big ideological issues . . .'

What Pascal, Kleist and Brecht do is invert this (mis)perception: the apparently non-ideological experience of the 'warm human person' beneath the ideological mask is in itself false; it is here to obfuscate the fact that the ideological mask effectively runs the show. In Brecht's *The Measure Taken*, for example, individuals are violently reduced to their 'ideological mask', so that the very moment when the desperate hero, unable to endure any longer the sight of the suffering of the poor peasants, wants to shed his mask and show his true face in order to help them is denounced as false, as the moment of betrayal of the revolutionary Cause . . . Another aspect of this subversion was already emphasized by Pascal: one should reverse the Enlightenment notion according to which, to ordinary people unable to grasp the need for their religious belief, the truth of their religion has to be asserted in an authoritarian way, as a dogma which brooks no argument; while the enlightened elite is able to obey upon being convinced by good reasons (by analogy to the children, who must learn to obey without any explanation, in contrast to adults, who know why one should follow social obligations). The uncanny truth is, rather, that argumentation is for the crowd of 'ordinary people' who need the illusion that there are good and proper reasons for the order which they must obey, while the true secret known only to the elite is that the dogma of power is grounded only in itself: 'Custom is the whole of equity for the sole reason that it is accepted. That is the mystic basis of its authority.' 'It would therefore be a good thing for us to obey laws and customs because they are laws.'[31] Ideology is thus not only 'irrational obedience' beneath which critical analysis has to discern its true reasons and causes; it is also the 'rationalization', the enumeration of a network of reasons, masking the unbearable fact that the Law is grounded only in its own act of enunciation.

Another key philosopher and theologist to be inserted in this series is Nicolas Malebranche, the great Cartesian Catholic who, after his death, was excommunicated, and his books were destroyed, because of his very excessive orthodoxy – Lacan probably had figures like Malebranche in mind when he claimed that theologists are the only true atheists. In the best Pascalian tradition, Malebranche laid his cards on the table and 'revealed the secret' (the perverted truth) of Christianity: it was not that Christ came down to Earth in order to deliver people from sin, from the legacy of Adam's Fall; on the contrary, *Adam had to fall in order to enable Christ to come down to earth and dispense salvation.* Here Malebranche applies to God Himself the 'psychological' insight which tells us that the saintly figure who sacrifices himself for the benefit of others, to deliver them from their misery, secretly *wants* the others to suffer misery *so that he will be able to help them* – like the proverbial husband who works all day for his poor crippled wife, yet would probably

31   Blaise Pascal, *Pensées*, Harmondsworth: Penguin, 1966, pp. 46, 216.

abandon her if she were to regain her health and turn into a successful career woman. It is much more satisfying to sacrifice oneself for the poor victim than to enable the other to lose the status of victim and perhaps become even more successful than ourselves . . .

Malebranche develops this parallel to its ultimate conclusion, to the horror of the Jesuits who organized his excommunication: just as the saintly person uses the suffering of others to bring about his own narcissistic satisfaction in helping those in distress, so God also ultimately *loves only Himself*, and merely uses man to promulgate His own glory . . . From this reversal, Malebranche draws a consequence worthy of Lacan's above-mentioned reversal of Dostoyevsky ('*If God doesn't exist*, the father says, *then everything is permitted*. Quite evidently, a naive notion, for we analysts know full well that if God doesn't exist, then nothing at all is permitted any longer.'[32]): it is not true that if Christ had not come to earth to deliver humanity, everyone would have been lost – quite the contrary, *nobody* would be lost; that is, *every* human being had to fall so that Christ could come and deliver *some* of them . . . What further follows from this is the paradoxical nature of predestination and grace: divine grace is contingently disseminated, it has absolutely no correlation with our good deeds. The moment the link between grace and our deeds became directly perceptible, human freedom would be lost: God is not allowed to intervene directly in the universe; that is to say: grace has to remain masked, non-perceptible as such, as a direct divine intervention, since its direct transparency would change man into a slavish entity subordinated to God like an animal, and would deprive him of faith grounded in free choice.[33]

32   *The Seminar of Jacques Lacan, Book II: The Ego in Freud's Theory and in the Technique of Psychoanalysis*, p. 128.

33   An analogous operation of laying the (hidden) cards on the table is performed by Kierkegaard, who emphasized that the necessary consequence (the 'truth') of the Christian demand to *love one's enemy* is:

'the demand to *hate the beloved* out of love and in love . . . So high – humanly speaking to a kind of madness – can Christianity press the demand of love if love is to be the fulfilling of the law. Therefore it teaches that the Christian shall, if it is demanded, be capable of hating his father and mother and sister and beloved.' (Søren Kierkegaard, *Works of Love*, New York: Harper & Row, 1962, p. 114.)

However, although the dispensation of grace is not grounded in our good deeds but disseminated in an utterly contingent way, one should nevertheless endeavour to accomplish as many good deeds as possible – if and when divine grace touches us, our good deeds make us receptive to it, they enable us to recognize it and thus to profit from it . . . The achievement of Malebranche is thus to propose *a materialist theory of grace*: grace is distributed in a completely contingent way, not in accordance with human merits but following its own inherent proto-natural laws, like (to use Malebranche's own metaphor) the rain falling across a countryside, which can irrigate a field, and is thus spent in a productive way for human purposes, or fall on a barren hillside nearby and is thus spent in vain – one never knows, it is blind, like fate. This metaphor also makes it clear why one should none the less accomplish good deeds – like the peasant who should cultivate his field, so that when (and if) rain falls, it will bear fruit . . . In this precise sense, God is the Lacanian big Other: a machine which follows its inherent 'natural' laws and is (like Schreber's God) completely ignorant of human affairs. Malebranche is thus the theological counterpoint to the underlying ideology of J. Redfield's *The Celestine Prophecy*, the bible of the popular New Age mythology: not only do events in the world follow natural causal logic and express no inherent meaning, the dispensation of divine grace itself is a blind natural process with no inherent meaning . . .[34]

In other words, what Malebranche does here is something similar to Monty Python, who constantly practise such a reversal in order to reveal the underlying libidinal economy: they treat sex as a boring bureaucratic duty, and so on. At the very outset of the sex education scene from *The Meaning of Life*, the bored pupils who await the arrival of their teacher

---

Here Kierkegaard applies the logic of *hamamoration,* later articulated by Lacan, which relies on the split in the beloved between the beloved person itself and the true object-cause of my love for him, that which is 'in him more than himself' (for Kierkegaard: God) – sometimes, hatred is the only proof that I really love you.

34   See Nicolas Malebranche, *Treatise on Nature and Grace,* Oxford: Clarendon Press, 1992.

yawn and stare into space; when one of them close to the door shouts 'Teacher's coming!', they all of a sudden start to shout, make a noise with their chairs and tables, throw papers at each other ... all the usual commotion that the teacher is expected to be angry at and subdue. This reversal reveals the true economy of the situation: far from being a spontaneous outburst of energy constrained by school discipline, all the pupils' commotion is addressed to the teacher ... As in Malebranche, where Adam has to fall not on account of his autonomous *hubris* but in order to enable Christ's arrival, here also, the pupils make a noise and a commotion not on account of their autonomous spontaneity but in order to set in motion the teacher's disciplinary reprimand. (Here we have the Foucauldian interconnection of 'oppressive' power and resistance, of resistance in the service of power.)

One can now see in what sense all these 'over-orthodox' authors practise anamorphosis: when Pascal claims that reasons (to believe and obey) are for the crowd, while the elite knows that the law is based only in the act of its own enunciation – that we must obey it simply because 'law is law'; when Malebranche claims that Adam had to fall in order to make Christ's arrival possible (not vice versa); does not the effect of these propositions rely on an anamorphic shift of emphasis?

What lurks in the background, of course, is the fact that the God of Malebranche is Lacan's big Other at its purest: the order which regulates our universe, but remains purely virtual – is nowhere directly perceptible. The standard criticism of occasionalism (according to which not only is there no proof for occasionalism, but occasionalism even directly contradicts our sensible experience which tells us that physical bodies act directly upon our senses) thus presents no problem for Malebranche, since it is the key component of his argument *for* occasionalism – his point is that the knowledge of the true order of things (of divine causality) contradicts our sensible experience: if divine causality were to become directly observable, this would make us slaves of God and change God into a horrifying tyrant (this idea was later taken up by Kant, in his notion that it is only our epistemological limitation – our ignorance of noumenal causality –

which makes us free moral beings). One can never experience the symbolic 'big Other' *as such*: either – in our 'normal' everyday life – we are oblivious to the way in which it overdetermines our acts; or – in psychotic experience – we became aware of the big Other's massive presence, yet in a 'reified' way – not as a virtual Other, but as the materialized, obscene, superego Other (the God who bombards us with excessive *jouissance*, controls us in the Real). The only way to experience the big Other in the Real is thus to experience it as the superego agency, the horrible obscene Thing.

The object as a negative magnitude

The procedure of anamorphic reading thus reveals the role of 'negative magnitudes' in ideological formations. As the saying goes, desire is an infinite metonymy, it slides from one object to another. In so far as desire's 'natural' state is thus that of melancholy – the awareness that no positive object is 'it', its proper object, that no positive object can ever fill out its constitutive lack – the ultimate enigma of desire is: how can it be 'set in motion' after all? How can the subject – whose ontological status is that of a void, of a pure gap sustained by the endless sliding from one signifier to another – none the less get hooked on a particular object which thereby starts to function as the object-cause of his desire? How can infinite desire focus on a finite object? The reference to Kant is crucial here:

> the mediation of [this] infinity of the subject with the finiteness of desire may occur only through the intervention of what Kant ... introduced with so much freshness in the term *negative quantities*... Negative quantity, then, is the term that we shall find to designate one of the supports of what is called the castration complex, namely, the negative effect in which the phallus object enters into it.[35]

35   Jacques Lacan, *The Four Fundamental Concepts of Psycho-Analysis,* New York: Norton 1978, pp. 252–3.

The answer is thus that the object which functions as the 'cause of desire' must be in itself a metonymy of lack – that is to say, an object which is not simply lacking but, in its very positivity, gives body to a lack. The Lacanian *objet petit a* is such a 'negative magnitude', a 'something that stands for nothing', *a* above the 'minus phi' of castration. The Kantian opposition between *nihil privativum* and *nihil negativum* can thus be translated into the opposition between *objet petit a* and the Thing: *das Ding* is the absolute void, the lethal abyss which swallows the subject; while *objet petit a* designates that which remains of the Thing after it has undergone the process of symbolization. The basic premiss of the Lacanian ontology is that if our experience of reality is to maintain its consistency, the positive field of reality has to be 'sutured' with a supplement which the subject (mis)perceives as a positive entity, but is effectively a 'negative magnitude'. When, in psychotic experience, *objet petit a* is actually included in reality, this means that it no longer functions as a 'negative magnitude', but simply as another positive object: as for positive facts (objects of experience), there is nothing to distinguish a psychotic position from the position of a 'normal' subject; what a psychotic lacks is merely the dimension of 'negative' magnitude underpinning the presence of 'ordinary' objects.

The space for the ideological negative magnitude is opened up by the gap between collection and set. That is to say: at its most elementary level, ideology exploits the minimal distance between a simple *collection* of elements and the different *sets* one can form out of this collection. The moment we pass from a simple collection to a logically formed set, paradoxes and inconsistencies emerge: we can form, from a limited number of elements, two or more sets which share some of the elements (logical intersection), or we can construct a set with no elements (and, according to Lacan, the subject is precisely such an 'empty set' with regard to the set of signifiers which represent it); furthermore, we can then introduce an element which, in its very positivity, functions as a stand-in for this empty set. That is the secret of Poe's 'The Purloined Letter': the letter is invisible simply because we are searching in vain for it at the level of elements – the letter is a configuration (set) of the elements which we see all the time, only as parts of a different set . . .[36]

We are dealing with a *structure* in the strict sense of the term when one and the same collection is arranged in two sets: the 'structuralist' structure always consists of *two* structures; that is, it involves the difference between the 'obvious' surface structure and the 'true' concealed structure. Émile Benveniste[37] has demonstrated how the misleadingly 'obvious' opposition between the active and passive forms of the verb, with the neutral form as the intermediary, dissimulates the true opposition between the active and neutral forms, with regard to which the passive form is the third, mediating, supplementary term. And according to Lacan, it is the same with sexual orientations: the 'obvious' division into hetero- and homo-sexuality (which is further subdivided into gay and lesbian sexuality) dissimulates the true opposition between hetero-(lesbian) and homo-sexuality, which is further subdivided into gay and 'straight' sexuality. One can also say that this gap is constitutive of ideology: 'ideology' is the 'self-evident' surface structure whose function is to conceal the underlying 'unbalanced', 'uncanny' structure.

36   An exemplary case of how the subdivision of the collection accounts for the proper dynamics of the game is tennis, with its structure of game, set and match: although the point of the elementary unit of the game always remains the same (which of the two players will fail to return the ball), it is the internal articulation of this repetitive process into game, set and match (with, incidentally, its wholly 'irrational' counting of the points – 15, 30, 40 . . .) which makes the game interesting. Without this – that is, if one were to count the points in their simple accumulation – the game would lose its interest and became much duller . . . Do we not see the ultimate example of this gap between a mere collection and its organization into the set in our *calendar,* which combines two classifying principles: a day is always specified by two determinations: by its numerical place within the scope of a month (the 13th of September) and its place within the scope of a week (Friday)?

37   See Émile Benveniste, *Problèmes de linguistique générale,* Paris: Minuit, 1968.

3   Fetishism and Its Vicissitudes

Moving statues, frozen bodies

How does psychoanalysis relate to the shift from the traditional authority of wisdom passed on from generation to generation to the reign of expert knowledge – that is, to the predominance of the modern reflected attitude which lacks support in tradition? Psychoanalysis is neither a new version of the return to tradition against the excess of modern reflectivity ('we should open ourselves up to the spontaneity of our true Self, to its archaic, primordial forces' – it was Jung who achieved this anti-modernist inversion of psychoanalysis) nor just another version of the expert knowledge enabling us to understand, and thus rationally dominate, even our most profound unconscious processes. Psychoanalysis is, rather, a kind of modernist meta-theory of the impasse of modernity: why, in spite of his 'liberation' from the constraints of traditional authority, is the subject not 'free'? Why does the retreat of traditional 'repressive' Prohibitions not only fail to relieve us of guilt, but even reinforce it? Furthermore, today the opposition between tradition and expert knowledge is more and more reflectively 'mediated': the very 'return to traditional Wisdom' is increasingly handled by a multitude of *experts* (on transcendental meditation, on the discovery of our true Self . . .).

The exact opposite of this is so-called magic realism in literature, which also presupposes as its background the opposition between the traditional enchanted universe and modernity: magic realism presents the very process of modernization (the arrival of machines, the disintegration of old social structures) from the standpoint of the traditional 'enchanted' closed universe – from this viewpoint, of course, modernization itself looks like the ultimate magic . . .[1] And do we not find something similar in the New Age cyberspace cult which attempts to ground the return to old pagan wisdom in the highest technology? (Perhaps aesthetic post-modernism as such is a desperate attempt to infuse pre-modern enchantment into the process of modernization.) Thus we have a double movement of reflective mediation: (the return to) tradition itself becomes the object of modern expertise; modernization itself becomes the ultimate in (traditional) magic – is this not analogous to the opposition between movement and image, where the movement of life itself is conceived as the magic coming-alive of 'dead' images while, simultaneously, the 'dead' statue or photo is conceived as the 'frozen', immobilized movement of life?

This dialectic of mortification is crucial for our understanding of the underlying phantasmic background of ideological formations. It is deeply significant that photography, the medium of immobilization, was first perceived as involving the *mortification* of the living body. Similarly, the X-ray was perceived as that which renders the 'interior' of the body (the skeleton) directly visible. Remember how the media presented Roentgen's discovery of X-rays towards the end of the last century: the idea was that X-rays allow us to see a person who is still alive *as if he were already dead*, reduced to a mere skeleton (with, of course, the underlying theological notion of *vanitas*: through the Roentgen apparatus, we see 'what we truly are', in the eyes of eternity . . .). What we are dealing with here is the negative link between visibility and movement: in terms of its original phenomenological status, movement equals blindness; it blurs the contours of what we perceive: in order for us to perceive the object clearly,

---

1   See Franco Moretti, *Modern Epic,* London: Verso, 1996. And was not *Twin Peaks* a desperate attempt, interesting in its very ultimate failure, to produce a 'magic realism' within the very developed First World society? (This idea was suggested to me by Susan Willis.)

it must be frozen, immobilized – immobility makes a thing visible. This negative link accounts for the fact that the 'invisible man' from Whale's film of the same name becomes visible again at the very moment of his death: 'the person who has stopped being alive exists more fully than when actually alive, moving around before us'.[2] Plato's ontology and the Lacanian notion of the mirror-image which freezes motion like a jammed cinema reel overlap here: it is only immobility that provides a firm visible existence.[3]

Against this background, one can establish the contrast between the Gothic motif of a moving statue (or image) and its counterpoint, the inverse procedure of *tableaux vivants*. In his *Elective Affinities*, Goethe provides a nice description of the practice of *tableaux vivants* in eighteenth-century aristocratic circles: famous scenes from history or literature were staged for home amusement, with the living characters on stage remaining motionless – that is, resisting the temptation to move.[4] This practice of *tableaux vivants* is to be inserted into the long ideological tradition of conceiving a statue as a frozen, immobilized living body, a body whose movements are paralysed (usually by a kind of evil spell): the statue's immobility thus involves infinite pain – the *objet petit a* engendered by the stiffness of the living body, its freezing into the form of a statue, is usually a sign of pain miraculously filtered by the statue, from the trickle of blood on the garden statue in Gothic novels to the tears miraculously shed by every self-respecting statue of the Virgin Mary in Catholic countries. The last in this series is the figure of the street entertainer dressed up as a statue (usually as a knight in armour) who remains immobilized for long periods of time: he moves

2   Paul Virilio, *The Art of the Motor*, Minneapolis: University of Minnesota Press, 1995, p. 69.

3   In contrast to humans, some animals perceive only objects which are moving, and are thus unable to see us if we are absolutely frozen – what we have here is the opposition between pre-symbolic real life, which sees only movement, and the symbolized gaze, which can see only 'mortified', petrified objects.

4   In *Elective Affinities*, this immobility of *tableaux vivants* can be read as the metaphor for the very stiffness of the novel's heroes, who are unable to abandon themselves to passion.

(makes a bow) only when some passer-by throws money into his cup.[5] In contrast to this notion of the statue as a frozen, immobilized body, cinema was perceived at the beginning as the 'moving image', a dead image which miraculously comes alive – therein lies its spectral quality.[6] What lurks in the background is the dialectical paradox of the phenomenology of our perception: the immobility of a statue is implicitly conceived as the state of a living being frozen into immobility in an infinite pain; while the moving image is a dead, immobile object which magically comes alive – in both cases, the barrier which separates the living from the dead is transgressed. Cinema is a 'moving image', the continuum of dead images which give the impression of life by running at the proper speed; the dead image is a 'still', a 'freeze-frame' – that is, a stiffened movement.

5   An interesting accident concerning moving statues occurred in the last years of Socialism in Slovenia: at a crossroads near a small town north of the capital, Ljubljana, a small statue-head of Mary in a shrine allegedly started to move, and even shed tears. The local Communist administrators were delighted; they wanted to exploit the phenomenon economically – to attract religious tourists (perhaps as a sideshow to the flourishing business prompted by the regular appearances of Mary in Medjugorje, in nearby Croatia), construct hotels and leisure centres, and so on. Surprisingly, however, the local Catholic priest was violently opposed to the phenomenon; claiming that it was merely a case of mass hallucination, not a genuine miracle. For that reason, the official Party newspaper attacked him for his 'antisocial, noncooperative attitude' – why did he refuse to proclaim it as a miracle, and thereby help the community?

6   Thomas Elsaesser (on whom I draw here) made this point apropos of his well-argued rejection of the standard opposition between Lumière (the first 'realist,' precursor of *cinéma vérité*) and Méliès (the first 'fictionalist', founder of the narrative cinema). A careful observation reveals the tight and detailed narrative structure of Lumière's famous short 'documentaries' (most of them involving a clear structure of closure where the end echoes the beginning, etc.). Why was this narrative or fictional aspect of Lumière 'repressed'? Because it points towards a possible history of cinema which diverges from the one which was actualized and which we all know: Lumière outlined other possibilities of future development, possibilities which – from today's retroactive ideological reading, which is able to discern in the past only the 'germs' of the present – are simply invisible. One of the great tasks of the materialist history of cinema is therefore to follow Walter Benjamin and to read the 'actual' history of cinema against the background of its 'inherent negation', of the possible alternative histories which were 'repressed' and, from time to time, break in as 'returns of the repressed' (from Flaherty to Godard . . .), as in the well-known science-fiction motif of parallel universes where a traveller momentarily goes astray and wanders into another universe.

What we are dealing with here are the two opposed cases of the properly Hegelian paradox of a genus which is its own species – which comprises two species, itself and the species as such. It is incorrect to state that there are two kinds/species of pictures, moving and immobile: the picture 'as such' is immobile, frozen, and the 'moving picture' is its subspecies, the magic paradox of a 'dead' picture coming alive as a spectral apparition. On the other hand, the body as such is alive, moving, and the statue is the paradox of a living body painfully frozen into immobility . . .[7] A further Lacanian comment to be made is that the primordial point of fixation (or freeze) in what we see is *the gaze itself*: the gaze not only mortifies its object, it stands itself for the frozen point of immobility in the field of the visible. Does not Medusa's head exemplify a gaze which was transfixed when it came too close to the Thing and 'saw too much'? In a series of Hitchcock films, the effect of momentary immobilization is produced by the actor's direct gaze into the camera (Scottie in the nightmare sequence in *Vertigo*; the detective Arbogast while he is being slaughtered in *Psycho*; and the unfortunate Fane during his suicidal trapeze act in *Murder*).

Thus horror cuts both ways: what provokes horror is not only the discovery that what we took for a living human being is a dead mechanical doll (Hoffmann's Olympia) but also – perhaps even more – the traumatic discovery that what we took for a dead entity (a house, the wall of a cave . . .) is actually alive – all of a sudden, it starts to trickle, tremble, move, speak, act with (an evil) intent . . . So we have, on the one side, the 'machine in the ghost' (a ship which sails by itself, with no crew; an animal or a human

7   As is well known, at the beginning of cinema, the camera related to the stage precisely as if it were a theatrical stage: it stayed on this side of the barrier that separates the podium from the spectators, registering the action as if it were from the point of view of the theatrical spectator. It took some years for cinema as a specific art form to be born: this occurred at the moment in which the camera transgressed the barrier that separates it from the stage, invaded the actors' space, and started to move among them. One of the possible definitions of cinema is thus that it is a subgenre of the theatre – a theatrical performance in which the spectator, by means of his stand-in (camera), moves forward into the space he observes. In a kind of countermove, modern theatre sometimes endeavours to trespass the frontier between podium and public by surrounding the public with the actors, letting the actors mix with the public.

being which is revealed to be a complex mechanism of joints and wheels), and, on the other, the 'ghost in the machine' (some sign of *plus-de-jouir* in the machine giving rise to the effect of 'It's alive!'). The point is that both these excesses are desubjectivized: the 'blind' machine, as well as the 'acephalous' formless life-substance, are two sides of drive (unified in the alien-monster, a combination of machine and slimy life-substance). In literary fiction, one often encounters a person who appears to be just another person within the diegetic space, but is effectively a 'No-Man', the desubjectivized horror of the pure drive disguised as a normal individual. Numerous commentators, from Kierkegaard onwards, have pointed out that Mozart's Don Giovanni is actually 'characterless', a pure machine-like drive to conquer lacking any 'depth' of personality: the ultimate horror of this person resides in the fact that he is not a proper person at all.

This paradox of moving statues, of dead objects coming alive and/or of petrified living objects, is possible only within the space of the death drive which, according to Lacan, is the space between the two deaths, symbolic and real. For a human being to be 'dead while alive' is to be colonized by the 'dead' symbolic order; to be 'alive while dead' is to give body to the remainder of Life-Substance which has escaped the symbolic colonization ('lamella'). What we are dealing with here is thus the split between A and J, between the 'dead' symbolic order which mortifies the body and the non-symbolic Life-Substance of *jouissance*.

These two notions in Freud and Lacan are not what they are in our everyday or standard scientific discourse: in psychoanalysis, they both designate a properly monstrous dimension. Life is the horrible palpitation of the 'lamella', of the non-subjective ('acephalous') 'undead' drive which persists beyond ordinary death; death is the symbolic order itself, the structure which, as a parasite, colonizes the living entity. What defines the death drive in Lacan is this double gap: not the simple opposition between life and death, but the split of life itself into 'normal' life and horrifying 'undead' life, and the split of the dead into 'ordinary' dead and the 'undead' machine. The basic opposition between Life and Death is thus supplemented by the parasitical symbolic machine (language as a dead entity which 'behaves as if it possesses a life of its own') and its counterpoint, the 'living dead' (the monstrous Life-Substance which persists in the Real outside the Symbolic) – this split which runs within the domains of Life and Death constitutes the space of the death drive.[8] These paradoxes are grounded in the fact that, as Freud emphasizes repeatedly, *there is no notion or representation of death in the unconscious*: the Freudian *Todestrieb* has absolutely nothing to do with the Heideggerian *Sein-zum-Tode*. Drive is immortal, eternal, 'undead': the annihilation towards which the death drive tends is not death as the unsurpassable limit of man *qua* finite being. Unconsciously, we all believe we are immortal – there is no death-anxiety [*Todesangst*] in our unconscious, which is why the very phenomenon of 'consciousness' is grounded in our awareness of our mortality.

Kierkegaard's notion of 'sickness unto death' also relies on the difference between the two deaths. That is to say, the 'sickness unto death' proper, its despair, is to be opposed to the standard despair of the individual who is split between the certainty that death is the end, that there is no Beyond of eternal life, and his unquenchable desire to believe that death is not the last thing – that there is another life, with its promise of redemption and eternal bliss. The 'sickness unto death', rather, involves the opposite paradox of the subject who knows that death is not the end, that he has an immortal soul, but cannot face the exorbitant demands of this fact (the necessity to abandon vain aesthetic pleasures and work for his salvation), and therefore, desperately wants to believe that death *is* the end – that there is no divine unconditional demand exerting its pressure upon him:

> It is not that he cannot, through an unquenchable desire to overcome the limitation of death, bring his desire into line with the rational belief that he will not overcome it; it is rather that he cannot bring his

---

8   Within the domain of psychoanalysis, the compulsive neurotic provides an exemplary case of the reversal of the relationship between life and death: what he experiences as the threat of death, what he escapes from into his fixed compulsive rituals, is ultimately *life itself*, since the only endurable life for him is that of a 'living dead', the life of disavowed, mortified desire.

desire into line with what he fundamentally *knows* because of an unquenchable desire to *avoid the unpleasantness* implicit in the *ability* to overcome the limitation.[9]

The standard religious *je sais bien, mais quand même* is inverted here: it is not that 'I know very well that I am a mere mortal living being, but none the less I desperately want to believe that there is redemption in eternal life'; rather, it is that 'I know very well that I have an eternal soul responsible to God's unconditional commandments, but I desperately want to believe that there is nothing beyond death; I want to be relieved of the unbearable pressure of the divine injunction.' In other words, in contrast to the individual caught in the standard sceptical despair – the individual who knows he will die, but cannot accept it and hopes for eternal life – we have here, in the case of the 'sickness unto death', the individual who desperately wants to die, to disappear for ever, but knows that he cannot do it: that he is condemned to eternal life. The predicament of the individual 'sick unto death' is the same as that of the Wagnerian heroes, from the Flying Dutchman to Amfortas in *Parsifal*, who desperately strive for death, for the final annihilation and self-obliteration which would relieve them of the Hell of their 'undead' existence.

Troppo fisso!

Is not Lacan's *futur antérieur* his version of Marx's Thesis 11?[10] The repressed past is never known 'as such', it can become known only in the very process of its transformation, since the interpretation itself intervenes in its object and changes it: for Marx, the truth about the past (class struggle, the antagonism which permeates the entire past history) can become visible

---

9   Alastair Hannay, *Kierkegaard,* London: Routledge, 1991, p. 33.
10   'What is realized in my history is not the past definite of what was, since it is no more, or even the present perfect of what has been in what I am, but the future anterior of what I shall have been for what I am in the process of becoming' (Jacques Lacan, *Écrits: A Selection,* New York: Norton, 1977, p. 86).

only to a subject caught up in the process of its revolutionary transformation. What is at play here is the distinction between the subject of the enunciated and the subject of the enunciation: when, during psychoanalytic treatment, the analysand subjectively fully accepts the fact that his identification is that of a worthless scum or excrement, this very recognition is the unmistakable sign that he has effectively already overcome this identification. (Schelling made the same point apropos of the fundamental existential decision which concerns what I am in the kernel of my being: the moment this decision is explicitly taken, brought to consciousness, it is in reality already undone.) The key point not to be missed here is that this moment of *futur antérieur* is not *the* moment when a past situation is 'defrosted', caught in a transformational dynamic, but, on the contrary, the moment of 'deep freeze' elaborated by Walter Benjamin: as Benjamin emphasized in his *Theses*, the present appears to a revolutionary as a frozen moment of repetition in which the evolutionary flow is immobilized, and past and present directly overlap in a crystalline way. Furthermore, is not this moment of *Troppo fisso!* the very moment of 'non-dialectical excess', of 'exaggeration', when 'one particular moment stands for all'?

When, in *Purgatorio*, Dante focuses his gaze on the beloved Beatrice, oblivious of everything else, divine voices quickly reproach him for staring too fixedly ('troppo fisso!') – this *frozen gaze* which blurs the proper view of the totality of Being designates the original sin of looking.

> Tranced by the holy smile that drew me there
> into the old nets, I forgot all else –
> my eyes wore blinkers and I could not care.
> when suddenly my gaze was wrenched away
> and forced to turn left to those goddesses·
> 'He stares too fixedly!', I heard them say. (32: 4–9)

This fixation on the beloved object (or, more to the point, on some scene of the Other's *jouissance*) which congeals it, wrenches it from its context, and thus destabilizes, throws off the rails, the balanced flow of things, stands for the violent cut of anamorphosis which, at the visual level, sustains the gap between reality and the real. In so far as this 'Troppo fisso!' is negativity at its most elementary, it allows us a privileged access to the 'mechanism' of Hegelian dialectics.

Adorno's famous thesis that nothing is more true in Freud's theory than its exaggerations is to be taken literally, not reduced to the common-sense 'wisdom' according to which exaggeration in one direction corrects the existing opposite exaggeration, and thus re-establishes the proper balance. One has thus to abandon the textbook notion of the Hegelian dialectical process in which the first exaggeration is supplanted by the opposite one until, finally, the proper balance between the two is established, and each is reduced to its proper limited place, as in politics: one needs neither organic links that are too strong (which give us an inflexible corporate state unable to accommodate individual freedom, that is, the infinite right of subjectivity) nor a too-strong unilateral emphasis on abstract individual freedom (which leads to liberal anarchy and the disintegration of concrete social links, and as such gives rise to a mechanical state which is again experienced as an external power limiting the subjects' freedom), but the proper 'synthesis' of the two . . .

Hegel's point is not a new version of the yin/yang balance, but its exact opposite: 'truth' resides in the excess of exaggeration as such. That is to say: here one has to apply the fundamental Hegelian logical principle according to which the two species of the genus are the genus itself and its one species, so that we do not have the two exaggerations (finally reunited in a synthesis), but the balance as such and the disruptive 'exaggeration' which disturbs its poise. And of course, Hegel's point is the exact opposite of the standard wisdom: the harmonious balanced totality is not the 'truth' within which particular exaggerations, deprived of their excess, must find their proper place; on the contrary, *the excess of 'exaggeration' is the truth which undermines the falsity of the balanced totality.* In other words, in the choice between the Whole and its Part, one has to choose the Part and elevate it to the Principle of the Whole – this 'crazy' reversal introduces the dynamics of the process. One can also put it in terms of the opposition between 'being' and 'event', of the subject *qua* event, articulated by Alain Badiou:[11] the subject emerges in the event of 'exaggeration', when a part exceeds its limited place and explodes the constraints of balanced totality.

In the good old days of Socialism, one of the official Yugoslav philosophers developed a monster called the 'dialectical theory of meaning', in which he endeavoured to provide a 'dialectical synthesis' of all contemporary theories of meaning. After exposing all 'unilateral' theories of meaning (pragmatist, referential, syntactic, phenomenological . . .) to a detailed critique, he proposed a 'dialectical' definition of meaning as a 'complex' relationship in which a subject relates to an objective content via a set of syntactic rules which give rise to an intentional object within a practical pragmatic context . . . an entirely worthless theoretical monster. Why?

If we take a close look at each of these 'unilateral' theories of meaning, we soon discover that its moment of truth is to be found in its very 'exaggeration': what is of interest, and thus 'enlightening', in the syntactic theory of meaning is not the fact that syntactic structure also contributes to it, but the much more exclusive notion that what we perceive as 'meaning' can be *reduced* to an effect of syntactic interrelations; what is of interest in pragmatism is not a rather common-sense notion that the meaning of a term is always embedded in the use of this term within a concrete lifeworld context, but the much more radical thesis that the meaning of a term 'as such' is *nothing but* the multitude of its uses; what makes Oswald Ducrot's notion of argumentative *topoi* so interesting is not merely the premiss that each statement or predicate also has an argumentative dimension, that we use it in order to argue for some attitude towards the designated content – Ducrot claims that not only is the descriptive content of a predicate always accompanied by some argumentative attitude, but that this very 'descriptive content' is in itself nothing but a reified bundle of argumentative *topoi*;[12] and so forth. Again, the key Hegelian point not to be missed here is that the enlightening 'truth-effect' of each of these

11   See Alain Badiou, *L'Être et l'événement,* Paris: Seuil, 1988.
12   See Oswald Ducrot, *Le Dire et le dit,* Paris: Minuit, 1984.

theories resides not in the reduced kernel of truth beneath the false exaggeration ('not all meaning can be reduced to argumentative attitude, but a limited argumentative stance supplements its referential content in every statement we make . . .') but in the very 'unilateral' reductionist exaggeration.

Is not the whole point of Hegel, however, that one should pass from one position to the next through the self-resolution of its constrained character? Yes, but Hegel's point is that this passage occurs only and precisely when we fully assume the 'unilateral' reductionist gesture: Hegelian totality is not an organic Whole within which each element sticks to its limited place, but a 'crazy' totality in which a position reverts to its Other in the very movement of its excessive exaggeration – the dialectical 'link' of partial elements emerges only through their 'exaggeration'. Back to Ducrot: the Hegelian point to be made is not that each predicate has a descriptive as well as an argumentative aspect, but that the descriptive aspect itself emerges when an argumentative attitude is brought to its extreme, 'reified', and thus self-negates.

In the standard notion of the opposition between subject and object, the subject is conceived as the dynamic pole, as the active agent able to transcend every fixed situation, to 'create' its universe, to adapt itself to every new condition, and so on, in contrast to the fixed, inert domain of objects. Lacan supplements this standard notion with its obverse: the very dimension which defines subjectivity is a certain 'exaggerated', excessive, unbalanced *fixation* or 'freeze' which disturbs the ever-changing balanced flow of life, and can assume three forms, in accordance with the triad of Imaginary, Symbolic and Real:

• At the level of the Imaginary, Lacan – as is well known – locates the emergence of the ego in the gesture of the precipitous identification with the external, alienated mirror-image which provides the idealized unity of the Self as opposed to the child's actual helplessness and lack of coordination. The feature to be emphasized here is that we are dealing with a kind of 'freeze of time': the flow of life is suspended, the Real of the dynamic living process is replaced by a 'dead', immobilized image – Lacan himself uses the metaphor of cinema projection, and compares the ego to the fixed image which the spectator perceives when the reel gets jammed. So, already at this most elementary level, one has to invert the commonplace according to which an animal is caught in its environs, in the self-enclosed organic whole of *Innenwelt* and *Aussenwelt*, while man can transcend this closure, dialectically subvert the confines of his environs, build new, artificial environs, and so on – yes, but what makes this transcendence possible is precisely an *excessive fixation* on the mirror-image.

- The answer to this deadlock may seem to reside in the opposition between imaginary fixity and the dialectic fluidity and mediating power of the symbolic process: an animal remains stuck at the imaginary level, it is caught in the mirror-relationship to its environs, while man is able to transcend this closure by being engaged in the process of symbolization. It is the realm of 'symbolic fictions' which enables us to adapt ourselves to ever new situations, radically to change our self-perception, and so on. Is not the ultimate feature of the symbolic order found in its utter contingency? We can never derive the 'story we tell about ourselves' from our 'real situation', there is always a minimal gap between the real and the mode(s) of its symbolization ... Here however, again, the very plasticity of the process of symbolization is strictly correlative to – even grounded in – the excessive fixation on an *empty signifier*: to put it in a somewhat simplified way, I can change my symbolic identity precisely and only in so far as my symbolic universe includes 'empty signifiers' which can be filled in by a new particular content. For example, the democratic process consists of the elaboration of ever new freedoms and equalities (of women, of workers, of minorities ...); but throughout this process, the reference to the signifier 'democracy' is a constant, and the ideological struggle is precisely the struggle to impose an ever new meaning on this term (say, to claim that democracy which is not inclusive of democracy for women, which does not also preclude workers' enslavement, which does not also include respect for religious, ethnic, sexual, etc., minorities, is not true democracy . . .). The very plasticity of the signified content (the struggle for what democracy 'really means') relies on the fixity of the empty signifier 'democracy'. What characterizes human existence is thus the 'irrational' fixation on some symbolic Cause, materialized in a Master-Signifier to whom we stick regardless of the consequences, disregarding our most elementary interest, survival itself: it is the very 'stubborn attachment' to some Master-Signifier (ultimately a 'signifier without signified') which enables man to maintain free flexibility towards every signified content (the fact that I fear God absolutely enables me to overcome my fear of any worldly threat, etc.).

- According to this second commonplace, the self-transcending plasticity and freedom of man is grounded in the distance between 'things' and 'words', in the fact that the way we relate to reality is always mediated by a contingent symbolic process. Here again, however, a certain excessive fixity intervenes: according to psychoanalytic theory, a human subject can acquire and maintain a distance towards (symbolically mediated) reality only through the process of 'primordial repression': what we experience as 'reality' constitutes itself through the foreclosure of some traumatic X which remains the impossible-real kernel around which symbolization turns. What distinguishes man from animals is thus again the excessive fixation on the trauma (of the lost object, of the scene of some shattering *jouissance*, etc.); what sets the dynamism that pertains to the human condition in motion is the very fact that some traumatic X eludes every symbolization. 'Trauma' is that kernel of the Same which returns again and again, disrupting any symbolic identity.

So, at each of the three levels, the very dynamic, adaptive, self-transcending capacity which defines subjectivity is grounded in an excessive fixation.

The violence of interpretation

This paradox of truth-in-exaggeration also enables us to throw new light on the notion of interpretation. Paul de Man concludes his Preface to *The Rhetoric of Romanticism* with a very concise and far-reaching thesis: 'Reading as disfiguration, to the very extent that it resists historicism, turns out to be historically more reliable than the products of historical archeology.'[13] Interpretation is thus conceived as a violent act of disfiguring the interpreted text; paradoxically, this disfiguration supposedly comes much closer to the 'truth' of the interpreted text than its historicist contextualization. How?

Let us focus on Lacan's great readings of classical literary and philosophical texts (*Antigone*, Plato's *Symposium*, Kant's *Critique of Practical Reason*). These readings clearly represent a case of violent appropriation, irrespective of philological rules, sometimes anachronistic, often 'factually incorrect', displacing the work from its proper hermeneutic context; yet this very violent gesture brings about a breathtaking 'effect of truth', a shattering new insight – once one reads Lacan, an entirely new dimension of Plato's and Kant's work is revealed. The key point here is how this 'effect of truth' is strictly co-dependent with the violent gesture of 'anachronistic' appropriation: the only way to uncover the truth of Plato or Kant is to read them as 'our contemporaries'.

An illustrative case of such a productive 'violence of interpretation' is Walter Benjamin's reading of Goethe's *Elective Affinities* – not to mention the great modern stagings of Mozart and Wagner, in which a violent 'misreading' of the original content (notably that of Peter Sellars apropos of Mozart's *Così fan tutte*: the couple truly and traumatically in love are Alfonso and Despina, so the key *tragic* aria of the opera is Despina's 'Una donna a quindici anni') gives rise to a new perspective

13   Paul de Man, *The Rhetoric of Romanticism,* New York: Columbia University Press, 1984, p. 123.

on the opera itself.[14] Or – to put it in terms of the Hegelian critique of Kant – at this precise point, the opposition between 'for us' (the mere subjectivity of the external interpretative gesture) and the 'in-itself' (of the work's true content) is suspended, since the very violent gesture of subjective intervention, brutal rape even, brings us closer to the work In-itself than any objective historicist approach . . . One is thus tempted to say that the motto of the Lacanian reading of, say, Hegel is: 'Philosophers have hitherto only interpreted Hegel; however, the point is also to change him.'[15]

Why, then, is 'historical archaeology' insufficient? The first answer that comes to mind is: de Man, of course, is against it, since he is an extreme 'discursivist'. For him, historical 'reality' itself is dominated by 'rhetorical' tropes, so that the main ideological mechanism lies in the 'reification' of discursive operations as properties of (discursively constructed) 'reality'. We need only recall, from *The Resistance to Theory*, his famous definition of ideology as 'the confusion of linguistic with natural reality, of reference with phenomenalism'. Does this stance, however, effectively lead to the 'discursive idealism' of neglecting 'real battles', reducing the pathos of the real of history to the staging and playing out of rhetorical tropes? I want to argue that the opposite is the case: the true choice is not between 'naive historicist realism' (where every discursive formation is embedded in the context of material practices, and thereby depends on them) and 'textualist idealism' (*il n'y a pas de hors texts*, every 'direct' experience of reality involves the subject's blindness to the textual mechanisms which generate it. . .). Rather, it is through the very 'pullback' from direct experience of 'reality' to the textual mechanisms that we are brought closer to the traumatic

14   One can argue the point that Heidegger's famous readings of the history of metaphysics obey the same logic of the violence of interpretation: although philologists have long 'proven' the factual falsity of his claim that the early Greeks used the term for truth, *alethia,* in the sense of an 'unveiling', the effects of his (mis)reading are none the less extremely productive.

15   *Mutatis mutandis,* the 'Thesis eleven' of late Lacan concerning psychoanalytic practice would be: 'Psychoanalysts, inclusive of early Lacan, have hitherto only interpreted symptoms; however, the point is also to traverse fantasy.'

kernel of some Real 'repressed' in a constitutive way by so-called 'reality' itself. It is crucial here not to miss the emphasis of de Man's standard criticism of the naturalizing organicist attitude: what such an attitude misrecognizes is not merely the textual mechanisms that constitute it but the traumatic *social antagonism* ('class struggle') obfuscated by the experience of society as an aestheticized organic Whole. As Fredric Jameson emphasized, the desperate Formalist attempt to distinguish formal structure from any positive content is the unfailing index of the violent repression of some traumatic content – the last trace of this content is the frozen form itself.

In the false alternative between 'naive historicist realism' and 'discursive idealism', both sides accuse each other of 'fetishism': for historicist realists, discursive idealism fetishizes the 'prison-house of language', while for discursivists, every notion of pre-discursive reality is to be denounced as a 'fetish'. What makes this polemic of theoretical interest is the fact that these mutually exclusive uses of the term 'fetishism' point towards a certain split which cuts through the very heart of the notion of fetishism.

Marx opens his discussion of commodity fetishism in *Capital* with the statement: 'a commodity is, in the first place, an object outside us, a thing that by its properties satisfies human wants of some sort or another': this standard notion of fetishism relies on a clear common-sense distinction between what the object is 'in itself', in its external material reality, and the externally imposed fetishist aura, the 'spiritual' dimension, which adheres to it (for example, in 'primitive' fetishist religion, a tree which is 'in itself' merely a tree acquires an additional spectral dimension as the seat of the Spirit of the Forest – or, in commodity fetishism, an object which satisfies some human want also becomes the bearer of Value, the material embodiment of social relations). In German Idealism, however, (and in the radical versions of Hegelian Marxism, like Georg Lukács's *History and Class Consciousness*), *'objectivity' as such*, as the firm, stable, immediate, determinate Being opposed to the fluidity of subjective mediation, *is conceived (and denounced) as a 'fetish'*, as something 'reified', as the domain whose appearance of stable Being conceals its subjective mediation. From this perspective, the very notion of the object's external material being, directly identical to itself ('the way things really are'), is the ultimate fetish beneath which the critical-transcendental analysis should recognize its subjective mediation/production. The fetish is thus at one and the same time the false appearance of In-itself, and the imposition on this In-itself of some spiritual dimension foreign to it.

It may seem that this split simply indicates the opposition between materialism (which maintains the In-itself of reality, independent of subjective mediation) and idealism (which conceives of every material reality as something posited/mediated by the subject); on closer inspection, however, these two opposed poles reveal a profound hidden solidarity, a shared conceptual matrix or framework. For the Marxist historical materialist, the very ideal agency which allegedly 'posits' or mediates every material reality (the 'transcendental subject') is already a fetish of its own, an entity which 'abbreviates', and thus conceals, the complex process of sociohistorical praxis. For a deconstructionist 'semiotic materialist', the notion of 'external reality' is – no less than the notion of the 'transcendental subject' – a 'reified' point of reference which conceals the textual process which generates it. And this game can go on almost indefinitely: in a Marxist response to deconstructionism, the very notion of 'arche-writing' or Text is again dismissed as a fetish which conceals the process of historical material practice . . .

The theoretical problem behind these impasses is: how are we to conceive of some 'immediacy' which would not act as a 'reified' fetishistic screen, obfuscating the process which generates it? Lacan agrees with the German Idealist argument whereby any reference to 'external reality' falls short: our access to this 'reality' is always-already 'mediated' by the symbolic process. At this point, however, it is crucial to bear in mind the distinction between reality and the Real: the Real as 'impossible' is precisely the excess of 'immediacy' which cannot be 'reified' in a fetish, the unfathomable X which, although nowhere present, curves/distorts any space of symbolic representation and condemns it to ultimate failure. If we are to discern the contours of this Real, we cannot avoid the meanderings of the notion of fetishism.

From religion to the universe of commodities

How do Marx and Freud displace the notion of fetishism with regard to its previous anthropological use?[16] The first to systematize this term and locate it clearly was Charles de Brosses who, back in 1760, defined fetishism as the first, primitive, stage of religion involving the veneration of natural objects (stones, animals . . .). The notional background for fetishism thus lies in evolutionist universalism: 'fetishism' has a place within the notion of a universal human history progressing from the lower stage (the veneration of natural objects) to the abstract spiritualized stage (the purely spiritual God); it allows us to grasp the unity of human species, to recognize the Other, while none the less asserting our superiority. The fetishist Other is always 'lower' – that is to say, the notion of fetishism is strictly correlative to the gaze of the observer who approaches the 'primitive' community from the outside.

As such, the notion of fetishism seems to unite, inextricably, the critique of ideology and ideology itself: in the very gesture of rejecting ideology (criticizing the illusions and blindness of the 'primitive' Other, his veneration of false idols), the critique repeats the ideological gesture. It would be easy to level at Marx and Freud the criticism that their use of the term 'fetishism' also involves the same external gaze, and is thus no less ideological: does not Marx's critique of commodity fetishism rely on the utopian point of transparent social relations? Is this not the point from which he can observe his own society, as if from the outside, and thus

16   I draw here on Alfonzo Iacono, *Le Fétichisme, Histoire d'un concept*, Paris: PUF, 1992.
As for the analogy between Marx's and Freud's use of the notion of fetishism: in both cases, fetishism stands for a displacement (relations between men are displaced on to relations between things; the subject's sexual interest is displaced from the 'normal' sexual object to its substitute); this displacement is in both cases a 'regressive' shift of focus towards a 'lower' and partial element which conceals (and at the same time designates) the true point of reference. The analogy further consists in the fact that for Marx and Freud, the fetish is not simply a 'lower stage' of development (of society, of genital Oedipal sexuality), but a symptom of the inherent contradiction within the 'higher' stage itself: commodity fetishism, for example, reveals the crack in spiritual Christianity and in the 'mature' free individual of 'developed' society itself.

articulate its ideological blindness? Furthermore, does not Freud's notion of fetishism involve a reference to the 'normal' sexual relation? On the contrary: upon closer inspection, one can easily show how things are more complicated. Marx uses the notion of fetishism in an analogical way – he refers to the similarity between the notion of fetish in 'primitive' religions and the fetishism at the very core of our 'developed' society. His reasoning goes as follows: we, in our 'developed' Western society, tend to oppose our pure spiritual religion to the 'primitive's' veneration of natural objects; is it not the case, however, that the very foundation of our society involves the veneration of a material object (money, gold), which, in the process of exchange, is endowed with supranatural properties? The reference to external ('primitive') society thus serves to alienate us (in the Brechtian sense of *Verfremdung*) from our own society, so that we can discern the 'primitivism' in its very kernel. In contrast to the attitude of the traditional anthropologist, the attitude of Marx is thus not simply that of an external observer, but an intricate mixture of externality and internality: the reference to – the analogy with – the external Other enables us to achieve a critical distance from our own society . . .[17]

There is, however, a hidden teleology in Marx's notion of fetishism. That is to say: as is well known, Marx articulates the notion of commodity fetishism in comparison to four other social relations of production, two in existence and two fictional: the primitive familial organization of production; the feudal organization of production within the social frame of servitude and domination; Robinson Crusoe's solitary production on an island; and future Communist production. If we disregard for a moment the enigmatic role of the example of Crusoe (which, by its analogy with Communist production, points towards the fact that in Communism the dimension of the Social will also be abolished, that society will function as a unified common intellect), there is, beneath the appearance of a synchronous comparison, a clear teleological line of evolution from

17   This Marxian insight was already made by some South American natives themselves who, in a well-known anecdote, noticed that gold was the fetish of the Spaniards.

prehistoric familial production, through slave and feudal relations of direct interpersonal servitude and domination, and then through capitalist commodity fetishism to the future Communist transparency of the Social. Marx points out that in pre-capitalist modes of production, social relations of production are in a sense more transparent than they are in capitalism, since they are not displaced on to relations between things, but are experienced as direct relations between people (relations of domination between masters and servants); whereas in capitalism relations between people are experienced as free and equal – that is, domination *per se* is displaced on to 'relations between things'.

However, in order to distinguish properly between pre-capitalist societies of domination and post-capitalist society (Communism), we must introduce a further distinction, the notion of a certain 'fetishism' which is independent of the opposition between 'people' and 'objects': it designates the state in which the effect of a 'structure', of a network, is (mis)perceived as the direct property of an individual entity: in the case of commodity fetishism, the fact that a certain commodity functions as a 'general equivalent' is (mis)perceived as its direct pseudo-natural property, as with interpersonal relations in which (the example is Marx's own) subjects who hail a certain person as a King are not aware that this person is a King only in so far as they treat him as one, not vice versa. In order to characterize this inversion, Marx refers to the Hegelian notion of 'reflective determination': in commodity fetishism proper, as well as in fetishized intersubjective relations, the property which is actually a mere 'reflective determination' of an object or person is misperceived as its direct 'natural' property. From this analogy between commodity fetishism and fetishized interpersonal relations, one has to draw a paradoxical conclusion: what is displaced in commodity fetishism is *fetishism itself* namely, the previous *direct* 'fetishization' of intersubjective relations. Commodity fetishism is thus a strange intermediate stage between fetishized social relations and transparent social relations: a stage in which social relations are no longer fetishized, yet fetishism is transposed on to '(social) relations between things'.

One should therefore be careful not to miss the precise logic of the 'fetishist misrecognition'. It is easy to fall prey to the nominalist reduction of an institution to its individuals and their acts, in which and through which this institution exists: when one says 'America bombed Iraq', what this actually means is that President Bush's order set in motion the chain of command which led to the takeoff of the bombers . . . However, is not such a reduction also misleading? What 'actually took place' were, of course, merely individual acts; however, in order for individual acts, which are in their materiality negligible (a signature on a piece of paper, a phone call . . .), to have such enormous consequences (the killing of thousands of people, the destruction of hundreds of houses and bridges . . .), a symbolic order has to be operative, an order which is purely 'virtual' (it does not 'actually exist' anywhere), yet determines the fate of things. So the misrecognition at work here is not only the one criticized by nominalists (reifying hypostasis of the symbolic order) but also the one exemplified by the very nominalist reduction (as if, in an act like the American bombing of Iraq, we were dealing with direct 'relations between people' – that is to say: as if, in order to explain what 'actually took place', one is not compelled to take into account the efficiency of the symbolic institution . . .).

Fetishist 'reification' is thus double: not only are 'relations between people' reified in 'relations between things' (so that critical analysis must penetrate the reified surface and discern beneath it the 'relations between people' which actually animate it) – an even more tricky 'fetishist reification' is at work when we (mis)perceive the situation as simply involving 'relations between people', and fail to take into account the invisible symbolic structure which regulates these relations. An everyday bourgeois subject not only (mis)perceives money as a material object with the 'magic' property of functioning as the equivalent of all commodities; in his everyday consciousness, such a subject is usually well aware that money is merely a sign guaranteeing its owner the right to have at his disposal a part of the social product, and so on. What an everyday bourgeois subject effectively fails to perceive at a much more fundamental level, is the fact that money is precisely *not* merely a token of interpersonal relations but emerges as the materialization of the symbolic institution in so far as this institution is irreducible to direct interaction between 'concrete individuals'.

The fact that the most persistent fetishist misperception consists in the very reduction of the social structure to transparent 'relations between concrete individuals' is absolutely crucial for the Marxian critique of so-called 'utopian socialism' (in his *Theories on Surplus-Value*, the projected Volume IV of *Capital*, containing the systematic criticism of his 'bourgeois' predecessors). What Marx rejects here is the Utopian Socialist notion of a society in which money would no longer be fetishized, but would directly act as a fully transparent intermediary in the 'relations between people' – as a kind of neutral voucher attesting to the owner's right to a certain part of the social product. Here we have, as it were, Marx at his best, demonstrating how the distortion of a universal medium or instrument, apparently due to contingent-empirical circumstances, is inscribed into its very concept: for a priori reasons, it is not possible to have money as only a neutral voucher without the effects of fetishist inversion; it is not possible to have a perfect state-capitalist society in which the State acts as the collective capitalist, paying every one of its employees the 'full value' of his labour, his contribution to social productivity . . . Such a notion, the belief in such a possibility, is the most precise definition of 'utopia'.

The spectralization of the fetish

There is a strong temptation today to renounce the notion of fetishism, claiming that its basic mechanism (the obfuscation of the process of production in its result) is no longer operative in our era of a new kind of 'false transparency'. The paradigmatic case of this is the recent series of 'The making of . . .' films which accompany big-budget productions: *Terminator 2*, *Indiana Jones*, and so on: far from destroying the 'fetishist' illusion, the insight into the production mechanism in fact even strengthens it, in so far as it renders palpable the gap between the bodily causes and their surface-effect . . . In short, the paradox of 'the making of . . .' is the same as that of a magician who discloses the trick without dissolving the mystery of the magical effect. The same goes, more and more, for political campaign advertisements and publicity in general: where the stress was initially on the product (or candidate) itself, it then moved to the effect-image, and now shifts more and more to the making of the image (the strategy of making an advertisement is itself advertised, etc.). The paradox is that – in a kind of reversal of the cliché according to which Western ideology dissimulates the production process at the expense of the final product – the production process, far from being the secret locus of the prohibited, of what cannot be shown, of what is concealed by the fetish, serves as the fetish which fascinates with its presence.

At a somewhat different level, another sign of the same tendency is the fact that today failures themselves have lost their Freudian subversive potential, and are becoming more and more the topic of mainstream entertainment: one of the most popular shows on American TV is 'The best bloopers of . . .', bringing together fragments of TV series, movies, news, and so on, which were cut because something stupid occurred (the actor muddled his lines, slipped . . .). From time to time, one even gets the impression that the slips themselves are carefully planned so that they can be used in just such a show. The best indicator of this devaluation of the slip is the use of the term 'Freudian slip' ('Oh, I just made a Freudian slip!'), which totally suspends its subversive sting.

The central paradox (and perhaps the most succinct definition) of post-modernity is that the very process of production, the laying-bare of its mechanism, functions as the fetish which conceals the crucial dimension of the form, that is, of the social *mode* of production.[18] In a step further in

18   What about Derrida's key criticism of Marx, according to which, in his very probing description of the logic of spectrality in the commodity universe and in social life in general, Marx none the less counts on the revolutionary moment in which the dimension of spectrality as such will be suspended, since social life will achieve complete transparency? The Lacanian answer is that spectrality is not the ultimate horizon of our experience: there is a dimension beyond (or, rather, beneath) it, the dimension of drive attained when one 'traverses the fundamental fantasy' (see Slavoj Žižek, 'The Abyss of Freedom', in F.W.J. Schelling, *The Ages of the World*, Ann Arbor: University of Michigan Press, 1997). Furthermore, at this point one should turn the question on Derrida, who himself gets entangled in a necessary ambiguity apropos of the problem of how *la clôture métaphysique* relates to the

this discussion of Marx, one is thus tempted to propose a schema of three successive figures of fetishism, which form a kind of Hegelian 'negation of negation': first, traditional interpersonal fetishism (Master's charisma); then standard commodity fetishism ('relations between things instead of relations between people', that is, the displacement of the fetish on to an object); finally, in our postmodern age, what we witness as the gradual dissipation of the very materiality of the fetish. With the prospect of electronic money, money loses its material presence and turns into a purely virtual entity (accessible by means of a bank card or even an immaterial computer code); this dematerialization, however, only strengthens its hold: money (the intricate network of financial transactions) thus turns into an invisible, and for that very reason all-powerful, spectral frame which dominates our lives. One can now see in what precise sense production itself can serve as a fetish: the postmodern transparency of the process of production is false in so far as it obfuscates the immaterial virtual order which effectively runs the show . . . This shift towards electronic money also affects the opposition between capital and money. Capital functions as the sublime irrepresentable Thing, present only in its effects, in contrast to a commodity, a particular material object which miraculously 'comes to life', starts to move as if endowed with an invisible spirit. In one case, we have the excess of materiality (social relations appearing as the property of a pseudo-concrete material object); in the other, the excess of invisible spectrality (social relations dominated by the invisible spectre of Capital). Today, with the advent of electronic money, the two dimensions seem to collapse: money itself increasingly acquires the features of an invisible spectral Thing discernible only through its effects.

Again, the paradox is that with this spectralization of the fetish, with the progressive disintegration of its positive materiality, its presence

---

domain of Western thought. Derrida endlessly varies the motif of how, with regard to this *clôture*, we are neither wholly within nor wholly without, and so on – however, what about Japan or India or China? Are they an inaccessible Outside, and is deconstruction thus constrained to the West, or is *différance* a kind of 'universal' structure not only of language, but of life as such, also discernible in animal life?

becomes even more oppressive and all-pervasive, as if there is no way the subject can escape its hold . . . why? Crucial for the fetish-object is that it emerges at the intersection of the two lacks: the subject's own lack as well as the lack of his big Other. Therein lies Lacan's fundamental paradox: within the symbolic order (the order of differential relations based on a radical lack), the positivity of an object occurs not when the lack is filled but, on the contrary, when *two lacks overlap*. The fetish functions simultaneously as the representative of the Other's inaccessible depth *and* as its exact opposite, as the stand-in for that which the Other itself lacks ('mother's phallus'). At its most fundamental, the fetish is a screen concealing the liminal experience of the Other's impotence – the experience best epitomized by the vertiginous awareness that 'the secrets of the Egyptians were also secrets for the Egyptians themselves', or (as in Kafka's novels) that the all-pervasive spectacle of the Law is a mere semblance staged in order to fascinate the subject's gaze.[19]

Within the domain of psychoanalytic treatment, this ambiguity of the object which involves the reference to the two lacks becomes visible in the guise of the opposition between the fetish and the phobic object: in both cases we are fascinated, our attention is transfixed, by an object which functions as the stand-in for castration; the difference is that in the case of the fetish, the disavowal of castration succeeds; while in the case of the phobic object, this disavowal fails, and the object directly announces the dimension of castration.[20] Gaze, for example, can function as the fetish-object *par excellence* (nothing fascinates me more than the Other's gaze, which is fascinated in so far as it perceives that which is 'in me more than

19   It is easy to discern this redoubled lack already in the functioning of the religious fetish. According to the standard notion, 'primitive' religions confuse the material symbol of the spiritual dimension with the spiritual Thing itself: for a primitive fetishist, the fetishized object (a sacred stone, tree, forest) is 'sacred' in itself, in its very material presence, not only as a symbol of another spiritual dimension . . . Does not the true 'fetishist illusion' however, reside *in the very idea that there is a (spiritual) Beyond occluded by the presence of the fetish*? Is it not the ultimate sleight of hand of the fetish to give rise to the illusion that *there is something beyond it,* the invisible domain of Spirits?

20   See Paul-Laurent Assoun, *Le Regard et la voix*, Paris: Anthropos, 1995, vol. 2, p. 15.

myself', the secret treasure at the kernel of my being), but it can also easily shift into the harbinger of the horror of castration (the gaze of Medusa's head). The phobic object is thus a kind of reflection-into-self of the fetish: in it, the fetish as the substitute for the lacking (maternal) phallus turns into the harbinger of this very lack . . . The point not to be missed is that we are dealing with *one and the same* object: the difference is purely topological.[21] Phobia articulates the fear of castration, while in fetishist perversion (symbolic) castration is that which the subject is after, his object of desire. That is to say: even with the fetishist disavowal of castration, things are more ambiguous than they may seem. Contrary to the *doxa*, the fetish (or the perverse ritual which stages the fetishist scene) is not primarily an attempt to disavow castration and stick to the (belief in the) maternal phallus; beneath the semblance of this disavowal, it is easy to discern traces of the desperate attempt, on the part of the perverse subject, to *stage* the symbolic castration – to achieve separation from the mother, and thus obtain some space in which one can breathe freely. For that reason, when the fetishist staging of castration disintegrates, the Other is no longer experienced by the subject as castrated; its domination over the subject is complete . . .

The theoretical lesson of this is that one should invert the commonplace according to which fetishism involves the fixation on some particular content, so that the dissolution of the fetish enables the subject to accomplish the step towards the domain of symbolic universality, within which he is free to move from one object to another, sustaining towards each of them a mediated dialectical relationship. In contrast to this cliché, one should fully accept the paradoxical fact that the dimension of universality is always sustained by the fixation on some particular point.

21   This allows us also to throw new light on the relationship between the two fetish-objects in Richard Wagner: the ring in the *Ring* cycle and the Grail cup in *Parsifal;* the Grail is stable, immovable, it *remains in its place* and shows itself only from time to time, whereas the ring is out of place and *emulates around;* for this reason, the Grail brings incommensurable joy, whereas the ring brings disaster and doom to whomsoever possesses it . . . What one has to do, of course, is to assert the 'speculative identity' between the two: they are one and the same object conceived in a different modality.

Fetish between structure and humanism

According to the classic Althusserian criticism of the Marxist problematic of commodity fetishism, this notion relies on the humanist ideological opposition of 'human persons' versus 'things'. Is it not one of Marx's standard determinations of fetishism that, in it, we are dealing with 'relations between things (commodities)' instead of direct 'relations between people' – that in the fetishist universe, people (mis)perceive their social relations in the guise of relations between things? Althusserians are fully justified in emphasizing how, beneath this 'ideological' problematic, there is another, entirely different – *structural* – concept of fetishism already at work in Marx: at this level, 'fetishism' designates the short circuit between the formal/differential structure (which is by definition 'absent', i.e. it is never given 'as such' in our experiential reality) and a positive element of this structure. When we are victims of the 'fetishist' illusion, we (mis)perceive as the immediate/'natural' property of the fetish-object that which is conferred upon this object by virtue of its place within the structure. The fact that money enables us to buy things on the market is not a direct property of the object-money, but results from the structural place of money within the complex network of socioeconomic relations; we do not relate to a certain person as to a 'king' because this person is 'in himself' (on account of his charismatic character or something similar) a king, but because he occupies the place of a king within the set of socio-symbolic relations.

Our point, however, is that these two levels of the notion of fetishism are necessarily connected: they form the two constitutive sides of the very concept of fetishism; that is why one cannot simply devalue the first as ideological, in contrast to the second, which is properly theoretical (or 'scientific'). To make this point clear, one should reformulate the first feature in a much more radical way. Beneath the apparently humanist-ideological opposition between 'human beings' and 'things' lurks another, much more productive notion, that of the mystery of substitution and/or displacement: how is it ontologically possible that the innermost 'relations between people' can be displaced on to (or substituted by) 'relations between things'? That is to say: is it not a basic feature of the Marxian notion of commodity fetishism that 'things believe instead of us, in place of us'? The point worth repeating again and again is that in Marx's notion of fetishism the place of the fetishist inversion is not in what people think they are doing, but in their social activity itself: a typical bourgeois subject is, in terms of his conscious attitude, a utilitarian nominalist – it is in his social activity, in exchange on the market, that he acts *as if* commodities were not simple objects but objects endowed with special powers, full of 'theological whimsies'. In other words, people are well aware of how things really stand; they know very well that the commodity-money is nothing but a reified form of the appearance of social relations, that beneath the 'relations between things' there are 'relations between people' – the paradox is that in their social activity they act *as if* they do not know this, and follow the fetishist illusion. The fetishist belief, the fetishist inversion, is displaced on to things; it is embodied in what Marx calls 'social relations between things'. And the crucial mistake to be avoided here is the properly 'humanist' notion that this belief, embodied in things, displaced on to things, is nothing but a reified form of direct human belief: the task of the phenomenological reconstitution of the genesis of 'reification' is then to demonstrate how original human belief was transposed on to things . . .

The paradox to be maintained is that displacement is original and constitutive: there is no immediate, self-present living subjectivity to whom the belief embodied in 'social things' can be attributed, and who is then dispossessed of it. There are some beliefs, the most fundamental ones, which are from the very outset 'decentred' beliefs of the Other; the phenomenon of the 'subject supposed to believe' is thus universal and structurally necessary. From the very outset, the speaking subject displaces his belief on to the big Other *qua* the order of pure semblance, so that the subject never 'really believed in it'; from the very beginning, the subject refers to some decentred other to whom he imputes this belief. All concrete versions of this 'subject supposed to believe' (from small children for whose sake parents pretend to believe in Santa Claus, to the 'ordinary working people' for whose sake Communist intellectuals pretend to believe in Socialism) are stand-ins for the big Other.[22] So – the way one should answer the conservative platitude according to which every honest man has a profound need to believe in something is to say that every honest man has a profound need to find another subject who will believe in his place.

The subject supposed to believe

In order properly to determine the scope of this notion of the subject supposed to believe as the fundamental, constitutive feature of the symbolic order,[23] one should oppose it to another, better-known, notion, that of the *subject supposed to know*: when Lacan speaks of the subject supposed to know, one usually fails to notice how this notion is not the norm but the exception, which gains its value in contrast to the subject supposed to believe as the standard feature of the symbolic order. So – what is the 'subject supposed to know'?

22   The actuality of the *subject supposed to believe* in Stalinist 'totalitarianism' is perhaps best exemplified by the well-known incident concerning the Great Soviet Encyclopaedia which occurred in 1954, immediately after the fall of Beria. When Soviet subscribers received the volume of the Encyclopaedia which contained the entries under the letter B, there was, of course, a double-page article on Beria, praising him as the great hero of the Soviet Union; after his fall and denunciation as a traitor and spy, all subscribers received from the publishing house a letter asking them to cut out and return the pages on Beria; in exchange they were promptly sent a double-page entry (with photos) on the Bering Strait, so that when they inserted it into the volume, its wholeness was re-established; there was no blank to bear witness to the sudden rewriting of history . . . The mystery here is: *for whom* was this (semblance of) wholeness maintained, if every subscriber *knew* about the manipulation (since he had to perform it *himself*)? The only answer is, of course: *for the nonexistent subject supposed to believe* . . .

23   See Michel de Certeau, 'What We Do When We Believe', in *On Signs,* ed. Marshall Blonsky, Baltimore, MD: Johns Hopkins University Press, 1985, p. 200. See also Chapter 5 of Slavoj Žižek, *The Sublime Object of Ideology,* London: Verso, 2008.

In the TV series *Columbo*, the crime (the act of murder) is shown in detail in advance, so that the enigma to be resolved is not that of 'whodunit?', but of how the detective will establish the link between the deceptive surface (the 'manifest content' of the crime scene) and the truth about the crime (its 'latent thought') – how he will prove his or her guilt to the culprit. The success of *Columbo* thus attests to the fact that the true source of interest in the detective's work is the process of deciphering itself, not its result (the triumphant final revelation 'And the murderer is . . .' is completely lacking here, since we know who it is from the very outset). Even more crucial than this feature is the fact that not only do we, the spectators, know in advance who did it (since we actually see it) but, inexplicably, the detective Columbo himself immediately knows it: the moment he visits the scene of the crime and encounters the culprit, he is absolutely certain, he simply knows, that the culprit did it. His subsequent effort thus concerns not the enigma 'who did it?', but how he should prove this to the culprit.

This reversal of the 'normal' order has clear theological connotations: as in true religion, where I first believe in God and then, on the grounds of my belief, become susceptible to the proofs of the truth of my faith, here also, Columbo *first* knows, with a mysterious but none the less absolutely infallible certainty, who did it; and *then*, on the basis of this inexplicable knowledge, proceeds to gather proof . . . And, in a slightly different way, this is what the analyst *qua* 'subject supposed to know' is about: when the analysand enters into a transferential relationship with the analyst, he has the same absolute certainty that the analyst *knows* his secret (which can only mean that the patient *is* a priori 'guilty', that there *is* a secret meaning to be drawn from his acts). The analyst is thus not an empiricist, probing the patient with different hypotheses, searching for proofs, and so on; he embodies the absolute certainty (which Lacan compares with the certainty of Descartes's *Cogito ergo sum*) of the analysand's 'guilt', of his unconscious desire.

These two notions – that of the subject supposed to believe and that of the subject supposed to know – are not symmetrical, since belief and knowledge themselves are not symmetrical: at its most radical, the status of the (Lacanian) big Other *qua* symbolic institution is that of belief (trust), not that of knowledge, since belief is symbolic and knowledge is real (the big Other involves, and relies on, a fundamental 'trust').[24] Belief is always minimally 'reflective', a 'belief in the belief of the other' ('I still believe in Communism' is the equivalent of saying 'I believe there are still people who believe in Communism'), while knowledge is precisely *not* knowledge about the fact that there is another who knows.[25] For this reason, I can *believe* through the other, but I cannot *know* through the other. That is to say: owing to the inherent reflectivity of belief, when another believes in my stead, I myself believe through him; knowledge is not reflective in the same way – that is, when the other is supposed to know, I do not know through him.

According to a well-known anthropological anecdote, the 'primitives' to whom one attributed certain 'superstitious beliefs', when directly asked about them, answered that 'some people believe . . .', immediately displacing their belief, transferring it on to another. Again, are we not doing the same with our children: we go through the ritual of Santa Claus, since our children (are supposed to) believe in it and we do not want to disappoint them. Is this not also the usual excuse of the mythical crooked or cynical politician who turns honest? – 'I can't disappoint those [the mythical 'ordinary people'] who believe in it [or in me]'. Furthermore, is not this need to find another who 'really believes' also

24   For that precise reason, Lacan speaks of 'knowledge in the real', not of *belief* in the real. Another way to put it is to say that belief and knowledge relate to each other as do desire and drive: desire is also always reflective, a 'desire to desire', while drive is *not* 'drive to drive'.

25   The logic of 'subject supposed to know' is thus not 'authoritarian' (relying on another subject who knows on my behalf) but, on the contrary, productive of new knowledge: the hysterical subject who incessantly probes the Master's knowledge is the very model of the emergence of new knowledge. It is the logic of 'subject supposed to believe' which is effectively 'conservative' in its reliance upon the structure of belief which must not be put in question by the subject ('whatever you think you know, retain your belief, act as if you believe . . .').

what propels us in our need to stigmatize the Other as a (religious or ethnic) 'fundamentalist'? In an uncanny way, belief always seems to function in the guise of such a 'belief at a distance': in order for the belief to function, there *has to be* some ultimate guarantor of it, yet this guarantor is always deferred, displaced, never present *in persona*. How, then, is belief possible? How is this vicious cycle of deferred belief cut short? The point, of course, is that the subject who directly believes does not need to exist for the belief to be operative: it is enough precisely to *presuppose* its existence, that is, to *believe* in it – either in the guise of the mythological founding figure who is not part of our experiential reality, or in the guise of the impersonal 'one' ('one believes . . .'). The crucial mistake to be avoided here is, again, the properly 'humanist' notion that this belief embodied in things, displaced on to things, is nothing but a reified form of a direct human belief, in which case the task of the phenomenological reconstitution of the genesis of 'reification' would be to demonstrate how the original human belief was transposed on to things . . . The paradox to be maintained, in contrast to such attempts at phenomenological genesis, is that *displacement is original and constitutive*: there is no immediate, self-present living subjectivity to whom the belief embodied in 'social things' can be attributed, and who is then dispossessed of it.

Je sais bien, mais quand même . . . [I believe]: therein lies the dilemma – either we play the Jungian obscurantist game of 'don't let's focus on our superficial rational knowledge, let's embrace the profound archetypal beliefs which form the foundation of our being', or we embark on the difficult road of giving an account of these beliefs in knowledge. It was already Kierkegaard who expressed the ultimate paradox of belief: he emphasized that the apostle preaches the need to believe and asks that we accept his belief upon his word; he never offers 'hard proofs' destined to convince non-believers. For this reason, the church's reluctance to face material which may prove or disprove its claims is more ambiguous than it may appear. In the case of the Turin Shroud – which allegedly contains the contours of the crucified Jesus, and thus his almost photographic portrait

– it is too simple to read the Church's reluctance as expressing the fear that the shroud will turn out to be a fake from a later period – perhaps it would be even more horrifying if the shroud were proved to be authentic, since this positivist 'verification' of the belief would undermine its status and deprive it of its charisma. Belief can thrive only in the shadowy domain between outright falsity and positive truth. The Jansenists' notion of a miracle bears witness to the fact that they were fully aware of this paradox: for them, a miracle is an event which has the quality of a miracle only in the eyes of the believer – to the common-sense eyes of an infidel, it looks like a purely natural coincidence. It is thus far too simple to read this reluctance of the Church as an attempt to avoid the objective testing of the truth of a miracle: the point is, rather, that the miracle is inherently linked to the fact of belief – there is no neutral miracle to convince cynical infidels. The fact that the miracle appears as such only to believers is a sign of God's power, not of His impotence . . .[26]

The primordial substitution

This relationship of substitution is not limited to beliefs: the same goes for every one of the subject's innermost feelings and attitudes, including crying and laughing. We need only recall the old enigma of transposed/

26   A further interesting fact concerning the relationship between belief and knowledge is that attempts to 'demonstrate the existence of God' (i.e. to confer upon our assurance that 'God exists' the status of knowledge) as a rule emerge *when nobody seems to doubt His existence* (in short, when 'everybody believes'), not in times of the rise of atheism and the crisis of religion (who today is still seriously engaged in 'proving the existence of God'?). One is thus tempted to claim that, paradoxically, the very endeavour to demonstrate the existence of God introduces doubt – in a way, creates the very problem it purports to solve. According to the standard Hegelian notion, attempts to prove God's existence through reasoning bear witness to the fact that the Cause (our immediate faith in Him) is already lost – that our relationship to Him is no longer a 'substantial' faith but already a reflectively 'mediated' knowledge. In clear contrast to this notion, reflective knowledge seems rather to have the status of an 'excess' we indulge in when we are sure of our Faith (like a person in an emotional relationship who can allow himself to mock his partner gently, precisely when he is so sure of the depth of their relationship that he knows such superficial jokes cannot hurt it).

displaced emotions at work, from the so-called 'weepers' (women hired to cry at funerals) in 'primitive' societies, to the 'canned laughter' on a TV screen, and to adopting a screen persona in cyberspace. When I construct a 'false' image of myself which stands for me in a virtual community in which I participate (in sexual games, for example, a shy man often assumes the screen persona of an attractive promiscuous woman), the emotions I feel and 'feign' as part of my screen persona are not simply false: although (what I experience as) my 'true self' does not feel them, they are none the less in a sense 'true' – as when I watch a TV mini-series with canned laughter where, even if I do not laugh, but simply stare at the screen, tired after a hard day's work, I nevertheless feel relieved after the show . . .[27] This is what the Lacanian notion of 'decentrement', of the decentred subject, aims at: my most intimate feelings can be radically externalized; I can literally 'laugh and cry through another'.

And is not the primordial version of this substitution by means of which 'somebody else does it for me' the very substitution of a *signifier* for the subject? In such a substitution lies the basic, constitutive feature of the *symbolic order*: a *signifier* is precisely an object-thing which substitutes for me, acts in my place. The so-called primitive religions in which another human being can take upon himself my suffering, my punishment (but also my laughter, my enjoyment . . .) – that is, in which one can suffer and pay the price for a sin *through the Other* (up to prayer wheels which do the praying for you) are not as stupid and 'primitive' as they may seem – they harbour a momentous liberating potential. By surrendering my innermost content, including my dreams and anxieties, to the Other, a space opens up in which I am free to breathe: when the Other laughs for me, I am free to take a rest; when the Other is sacrificed instead of me, I am free to go on living with the awareness that I did atone for my guilt; and so on.

27   Before one gets used to 'canned laughter', there is none the less usually a brief period of uneasiness: the first reaction to it is one of shock, since it is difficult to accept that the machine out there can 'laugh for me'; there is something inherently obscene in this phenomenon. With time, however, one grows accustomed to it, and the phenomenon is experienced as 'natural'.

The efficiency of this operation of substitution is exemplified in the Hegelian reflective reversal: when the Other is sacrificed for me, *I sacrifice myself through the Other*; when the Other acts for me, *I myself act through the Other*; when the Other enjoys for me, *I myself enjoy through the Other*. Take the good old joke about the difference between Soviet-style bureaucratic Socialism and Yugoslav self-management Socialism: in Russia, members of the *nomenklatura*, the representatives of the ordinary people, drive themselves in expensive limousines, while in Yugoslavia, *ordinary people themselves ride in limousines through their representatives*. This liberating potential of mechanical rituals is also clearly discernible in our modern experience: every intellectual knows the redeeming value of being temporarily subjected to military drill, to the requirements of a 'primitive' physical job, or to some similar externally regulated labour – the very awareness that the Other regulates the process in which I participate, sets my mind free to roam, since I know I am *not involved*. The Foucauldian motif of the interconnection between discipline and subjective freedom thus appears in a different light: by submitting myself to some disciplinary machine, I, as it were, transfer to the Other the responsibility of main-taining the smooth running of things, and thus gain precious space in which to exercise my freedom.

The one who originally 'does it for me' is the signifier itself in its external materiality, from the 'canned prayer' in the Tibetan prayer wheel to the 'canned laughter' on our TV: the basic feature of the symbolic order *qua* 'big Other' is that it is never simply a tool or means of communication, since it 'decentres' the subject from within, in the sense of accomplishing his act for him. This gap between the subject and the signifier which 'does it for him' is clearly discernible in common everyday experience: when a person slips, *another* person standing next to him and merely observing the accident can accompany it with 'Oops!' or something similar. The mystery of this everyday occurrence is that when the other does it for me, instead of me, *its symbolic efficiency is exactly the same as it would have been had I done it directly*. Therein lies the paradox of the notion of the 'performative' or speech act: in the very gesture of accomplishing an act by uttering words, I am deprived of authorship; the 'big Other' (the symbolic institution) speaks through me. It is no wonder, then, that there is something puppet-like about people whose professional function is essentially performative (judges, kings . . .): they are reduced to a living embodiment of the symbolic institution: their sole duty is to 'dot the i's' mechanically, to confer the institutional cachet on some content elaborated by others. Later Lacan is fully justified in reserving the term 'act' for something much more suicidal and real than a speech act.

This mystery of the symbolic order is exemplified by the enigmatic status of what we call 'politeness': when, upon meeting an acquaintance, I say 'Glad to see you! How are you today?', it is clear to both of us that, in a way, I 'do not mean it seriously' (if my partner suspects that I am really interested, he may even be unpleasantly surprised, as though I were probing at something which is too intimate and of no concern to me – or, to paraphrase the old Freudian joke: 'Why are you saying you're glad to see me, when you're *really* glad to see me!?'). It would be wrong, however, to designate my act as simply 'hypocritical', since in another way, I *do* mean it: the polite exchange does establish a kind of pact between the two of us; in the same sense as I do 'sincerely' laugh through the canned laughter (the proof being the fact that I actually do 'feel relieved' afterwards).

If we radicalize the relationship of substitution (i.e. the first aspect of the notion of fetishism) in this way, then the connection between the two aspects, the opposition 'persons versus things', their relation of substitution ('things instead of people', or one person instead of another, or a signifier instead of the signified), and the opposition 'structure versus one of its elements', becomes clear: *the differential/formal structure occluded by the element-fetish, can emerge only if the gesture of substitution has already occurred.* In other words, the structure is always, by definition, a *signifying* structure, a structure of signifiers which are substituted for the signified content, not a structure of the signified. For the differential/formal structure to emerge, the real has to redouble itself in the symbolic register, a *reduplicatio* has to occur, on account of which things no longer count as what they directly 'are', but only with regard to their symbolic place. This primordial substitution of the big Other, the Symbolic Order, for the Real of the immediate Life-Substance (in Lacanian terms: of A – *le grand Autre* – for J – *jouissance*), gives rise to $, to the 'barred subject' who is then 'represented' by the signifiers – that is, on whose behalf signifiers 'act', who acts through signifiers . . .

Interpassivity

Against this background, one is tempted to supplement the fashionable notion of 'interactivity' with its shadowy and much more uncanny supplement/double, the notion of 'interpassivity'.[28] That is to say: it is commonplace to emphasize how, with the new electronic media, the passive consumption of a text or a work of art is over: I no longer merely stare at the screen, I increasingly interact with it, entering into a dialogic relationship with it (from choosing the programs, through participating in debates in a Virtual Community, to directly determining the outcome of the plot in so-called 'interactive narratives'). Those who praise the democratic potential of the new media generally focus on precisely these features: on how cyberspace opens up the possibility for the large major-ity of people to break out of the role of passive observer following the spectacle staged by others, and to participate actively not only in the spectacle itself, but more and more in establishing the very rules of the spectacle.

Is not the other side of this interactivity, however, interpassivity? Is not the necessary obverse of my interacting with the object instead of just passively following the show the situation in which the object itself takes from me, deprives me of, my own passive reaction of satisfaction (or mourning or laughter), so that it is the object itself which 'enjoys the show' instead of me, relieving me of the superego duty to enjoy myself? Do we not witness 'interpassivity' in a great number of today's

28   I draw here on Robert Pfaller's intervention at the symposium *Die Dinge lachen an unsere Stelle,* Linz (Austria), 8–10 October 1996.

publicity spots or posters which, as it were, passively enjoy the product instead of us? (Coke cans containing the inscription 'Ooh! Ooh! What taste!' emulate the ideal customer's reaction in advance.) Another strange phenomenon brings us closer to the heart of the matter: almost every VCR *aficionado* who compulsively records hundreds of movies (myself among them) is well aware that the immediate effect of owning a VCR is that one actually watches *fewer* films than in the good old days of a simple TV set without a VCR; one never has time for TV, so instead of losing a precious evening, one simply tapes the film and stores it for a future viewing (for which, of course, there is almost never time . . .). So although I do not actually watch films, the very awareness that the films I love are stored in my video library gives me a profound satisfaction and, occasionally, enables me simply to relax and indulge in the exquisite art of *far niente* – as if the VCR is in a way *watching them for me, in my place* . . . the VCR stands here for the 'big Other', for the medium of symbolic registration.[29]

Is not the Western liberal academic's obsession with the suffering in Bosnia the outstanding recent example of interpassive suffering? One can authentically suffer through reports on rapes and mass killings in Bosnia, while calmly pursuing one's academic career . . . Another standard example of interpassivity is provided by the role of the 'madman' within a pathologically distorted intersubjective link (say, a family whose repressed traumas explode in the mental breakdown of one of its members): when a group produces a madman, do they not shift on to him the obligation passively to endure the suffering which belongs to all of them? Furthermore, is not the ultimate example of interpassivity the 'absolute example' (Hegel) itself: that of Christ, who took upon himself the (deserved) suffering of humanity? Christ redeemed us all

29   It seems that today even pornography functions more and more in an interpassive way. X-rated movies are no longer primarily the means destined to excite the user in his (or her) solitary masturbatory activity: just staring at the screen where 'the action is' is sufficient – that is to say, it is enough for me to observe how others enjoy in my place.

not by acting for us, but by assuming the burden of the ultimate passive experience. (The difference between activity and passivity, of course, is often blurred; weeping as an act of public mourning is not simply passive, it is passivity transformed into an active ritualized symbolic practice.)

In the political domain, one of the recent outstanding examples of 'interpassivity' is the multiculturalist Leftist intellectual's 'apprehension' about how even the Muslims, the great victims of the Yugoslav war, are now renouncing the multi-ethnic pluralist vision of Bosnia and conceding to the fact that if the Serbs and Croats want their clearly defined ethnic units, they too want an ethnic space of their own. This Leftist's 'regret' is multiculturalist racism at its worst: as if the Bosnians were not literally *pushed* into creating their own ethnic enclave by the way that the 'liberal' West has threatened them in the last five years. What interests us here, however, is how the 'multi-ethnic Bosnia' is only the latest in the series of mythical figures of the Other through which Western Leftist intellectuals have acted out their ideological fantasies: this intellectual is 'multi-ethnic' through Bosnians, breaks out of the Cartesian paradigm by admiring Native American wisdom, and so on – just as in past decades, when they were revolutionaries by admiring Cuba, or 'democratic socialists' by endorsing the myth of Yugoslav 'self-management' Socialism as 'something special', a genuine democratic breakthrough . . . In all these cases, they have continued to lead their undisturbed upper-middle-class academic existence, while doing their progressive duty *through the Other*.

This paradox of interpassivity, of believing or enjoying through the other, also opens up a new approach to aggressivity: aggressivity is provoked in a subject when the other subject, through which the first subject believed or enjoyed, does something which disturbs the functioning of this transference. Look, for example, at the attitude of some Western Leftist academics towards the disintegration of Yugoslavia: since the fact that the people of ex-Yugoslavia rejected ('betrayed') Socialism disturbed the belief of these academics – that is, prevented them from persisting in their belief in 'authentic' self-management Socialism through the Other which realizes it – everyone who did not share their Yugo-nostalgic attitude was dismissed as a proto-Fascist nationalist.[30]

The subject supposed to enjoy

Did we not, however, confuse different phenomena under the heading 'interpassivity'? Is there not a crucial distinction between the Other taking over from me the 'dull' mechanical aspect of routine duties, and the Other taking over from me, and thus depriving me of, enjoyment? Is not 'to be relieved of one's enjoyment' a meaningless paradox, at best a euphemisn for simply being *deprived* of it? Is enjoyment not something which, precisely, *cannot* be done through the Other?

At the level of elementary psychological observation, one can answer this by recalling the deep satisfaction a subject (a parent, for example) can derive from the awareness that his or her beloved daughter or son is really enjoying something; a loving parent can literally enjoy through the Other's enjoyment. However, there is a much more uncanny phenomenon at work here: the only way really to account for the satisfaction and liberating potential of being able to enjoy through the Other – of being relieved of one's enjoyment and displacing it on to the Other – is to accept that enjoyment itself is not an immediate spontaneous state, but is sustained by a superego imperative: as Lacan emphasized again and again, the ultimate content of the superego injunction is 'Enjoy!'.

30   Here the case of Peter Handke is illustrative: for many long years he lived his authentic life interpassively, delivered of the corruption of Western consumerist capitalism, through the Slovenes (his mother was Slovene): for him, Slovenia was a country in which words related directly to objects (in the shops, milk was called simply 'milk', avoiding the pitfall of commercialized brand names, etc.) – in short, a pure phantasmic formation. Now, Slovene independence and willingness to join the European Union have unleashed in him a violent aggressivity: in his recent writings he dismisses Slovenes as Slaves of Austrian and German capital, selling their legacy to the West . . . all this because his interpassive game was disturbed – because the Slovenes no longer behave in a way which would enable him to be authentic through them. No wonder, then, that he has turned to Serbia as the last vestige of authenticity in Europe, comparing Bosnian Serbs laying siege to Sarajevo with Native Americans laying siege to a camp of white colonizers . . .

In order to grasp this paradox properly, one should first elucidate the opposition between the (public symbolic) Law and the superego. The public Law 'between the lines' silently tolerates – incites, even – what its explicit text prohibits (say, adultery), while the superego injunction which ordains *jouissance*, through the very directness of its order, hinders the subject's access to it much more efficiently than any prohibition. Let us recall the figure of the father who advises his son on sexual exploits: if the father warns him against it, formally prohibits him from dating girls, and so on, he of course, between the lines, only propels the son to do it – to find satisfaction in violating the paternal prohibition; if, on the contrary, the father, in an obscene way, directly pushes him to 'behave like a man' and seduce girls, the actual effect of this will probably be the opposite (the son's withdrawal, shame of the obscene father, even impotence . . .). Perhaps the briefest way to render the superego paradox is the injunction 'Like it or not, enjoy yourself!'

An attempt to resolve this same deadlock is the typical hysterical strategy of changing (suspending) the symbolic link while pretending that nothing has changed in reality: a husband, say, who divorces his wife and then continues to visit her house and the kids regularly as if nothing had happened, feeling not only as at home as before, but even more relaxed; since the symbolic obligation to the family is broken, he can now really take it easy and enjoy it. Against this background, it is easy to discern the liberating potential of being relieved of enjoyment: in this way, one is relieved of the monstrous *duty* to enjoy. On closer analysis, one would thus have to distinguish between two types of 'the Other doing (or, rather, enduring) it for me':[31]

- In the case of commodity fetishism, our belief is laid upon the Other: I think I do not believe, but I believe through the Other. The gesture of criticism here consists in the assertion of identity: no, it is *you* who believe through the Other (in the theological whimsies of commodities, in Santa Claus . . .).

- In the case of a video recorder viewing and enjoying a film for me (or of the canned laughter, or of the weepers who cry and mourn for you, or of the Tibetan prayer wheel) it is the other way round: you think you enjoyed the show, but the Other did it for you. The gesture of criticism here is that, no, it was *not you* who laughed, it was the Other (the TV set) who did it.

Is not the key to this distinction that we are dealing here with the opposition between belief and *jouissance*, between the Symbolic and the Real? In the case of (symbolic) belief, you disavow the identity (you do not recognize yourself in the belief which is yours); in the case of (real) *jouissance*, you misrecognize the decentrement in what you (mis)perceive as 'your own' *jouissance*. Perhaps the fundamental attitude which defines the subject is neither that of passivity nor that of autonomous activity: but precisely that of interpassivity. This interpassivity is to be opposed to the Hegelian *List der Vernunft* ('cunning of Reason'): in the case of the 'cunning of Reason', *I am active through the other* – that is, I can remain passive while the Other does it for me (like the Hegelian Idea which remains outside the conflict, letting human passions do the work for it); in the case of interpassivity, *I am passive through the other* – that is, I accede to the other the passive aspect (of enjoying), while I can remain actively engaged (I can continue to work in the evening, while the VCR passively enjoys for me; I can make financial arrangements for the deceased's fortune while the weepers mourn for me). This allows us to propose the notion of *false activity*, you think you are active, while your true position, as embodied in the fetish, is passive ... Do we not encounter something akin to this false activity in the paradox of Predestination (the very fact that things are decided in advance – that our attitude to Fate is that of a passive victim – urges us to engage ourselves in incessant frenetic activity) and in the typical strategy of the obsessional neurotic, which also involves a 'false activity': he is frantically active in order to prevent the real thing from happening (in a group situation in which some tension threatens to explode, the obsessional talks all the time, tells jokes, etc., in order to prevent the awkward moment of silence which would make the participants aware of the underlying tension)?[32]

The object which gives body to the surplus-enjoyment fascinates the subject, it reduces him to a passive gaze impotently gaping at the object; this relationship, of course, is experienced by the subject as something shameful, unworthy. Being directly transfixed by the object, passively submitting to its power of fascination, is ultimately unbearable: the open display of the passive attitude of 'enjoying it' somehow deprives the subject of his dignity. Interpassivity is therefore to be conceived as the primordial form of the subject's *defence* against *jouissance*: I defer *jouissance* to the Other who passively endures it (laughs, suffers, enjoys . . .) on my behalf. In this precise sense, the effect of the subject supposed to enjoy – the gesture of transposing one's *jouissance* to the Other – is perhaps even more primordial than that of the 'subject supposed to know', or the 'subject supposed to believe'. Therein lies the libidinal strategy of a pervert who assumes the position of the pure instrument of the Other's *jouissance*: for the (male) pervert, the sexual act (coitus) involves a clear division of labour in which he reduces himself to a pure tool of woman's enjoyment; he is doing the hard work, accomplishing the active gestures, while she, in transports of ecstasy, endures it passively and stares into space . . . In the course of the

---

32   It would be interesting to approach, from this paradox of interpassivity, Schelling's notion of the highest freedom as the state in which activity and passivity, being-active and being-acted-upon, harmoniously overlap: man reaches his acme when he turns his very subjectivity into the Predicate of an ever higher Power (in the mathematical sense of the term), that is, when he, as it were, yields to the Other, 'depersonalizes' his most intense activity and performs it as if some other, higher Power were acting through him, using him as its medium – like the mystical experience of Love, or like an artist who, in the highest frenzy of creativity, experiences himself as a medium through which some more substantial, impersonal Power expresses itself. (See Chapter 1 of Slavoj Žižek, *The Indivisible Remainder*, London: Verso, 1996.) This notion of the highest freedom designates the impossible point of perfect overlapping between passivity and activity in which the gap of inter- (activity or passivity) is abolished: when I am active, I no longer need another to be passive for me, in my place, since my very activity is already in itself the highest form of passivity; and vice versa: when, in an authentic mystical experience, I let myself go completely, adopt the passive attitude of *Gelassenheit*, this passivity is in itself the highest form of activity, since in it, the big Other itself (God) acts through me . . .

psychoanalytic treatment, the subject has to learn to accept directly his relationship to the object which gives body to his *jouissance*, bypassing the proxy who enjoys in his place, instead of him. The disavowed fundamental passivity of my being is structured in the fundamental fantasy which, although it is a priori inaccessible to me, regulates the way I relate to *jouissance*. For that precise reason, it is impossible for the subject to assume his fundamental fantasy without undergoing the radical experience of 'subjective destitution': in assuming my fundamental fantasy, I take upon myself the passive kernel of my being – the kernel the distance towards which sustains my subjective activity.

The substitution of the object for the subject is thus in a way even more primordial than the substitution of the signifier for the subject: if the signifier is the form of 'being active through another', the object is the form of 'being passive through another' – that is to say, the object is primordially that which suffers, endures it, for me, in my place: in short, that which *enjoys* for me. So what is unbearable in my encounter with the object is that in it, I see *myself* in the guise of a suffering object: what reduces me to a fascinated passive observer is the scene of *myself* passively enduring it. Far from being an excessive phenomenon which occurs only in extreme 'pathological' situations, interpassivity, in its opposition to interactivity (not in the standard sense of interacting with the medium, but in the sense of another doing it for me, in my place), is thus the feature which defines the most elementary level, the necessary minimum, of subjectivity: in order to be an active subject, I have to get rid of – and transpose on to the other – the inert passivity which contains the density of my substantial being. In this precise sense, the opposition signifier/object overlaps with the opposition interactivity/interpassivity: the signifier is interactive, it is active on my behalf, in my place, while the object is interpassive, it suffers for me. Transposing my very passive experience on to another is a much more uncanny phenomenon than that of being active through another: in interpassivity I am decentred in a much more radical way than I am in interactivity, since interpassivity deprives me of the very kernel of my substantial identity.

Consequently, the basic matrix of interpassivity follows from the very notion of subject as the pure activity of (self-)positing, as the fluidity of pure Becoming, devoid of any positive, firm Being: if I am to function as pure activity, I have to externalize my (passive) Being – in short: I have to be passive *through another*. This inert object which 'is' my Being, in which my inert Being is externalized, is the Lacanian *objet petit a*. In so far as the elementary, constitutive structure of subjectivity is hysterical – in so far, that is, as hysteria is defined by the question 'What for an object am I (in the eyes of the Other, for the Other's desire)?', it confronts us with interpassivity at its purest: what the hysterical subject is unable to accept, what gives rise to an unbearable anxiety in him, is the presentiment that the Other(s) perceive him in the passivity of his Being, as an object to be exchanged, enjoyed or otherwise 'manipulated'. Therein lies the 'ontological axiom' of Lacanian subjectivity: the more I am active, the more I must be passive in another's place – that is to say, the more there must be another object which is passive in my place, on my behalf. (This axiom is realized in its utmost simplicity in the proverbial senior manager who, from time to time, feels compelled to visit prostitutes to be exposed to masochistic rituals and 'treated as a mere object'.) What psychoanalysis is looking for in an active subject is precisely the fundamental fantasy which sustains his disavowed passivity.

The theoretical problem which arises here is the one formulated long ago by Adorno (and to which he proposed his solution of 'angstlose Passivität (passivity without anxiety)': is it possible for the subject to be passive towards the domain of objects, to acknowledge the 'primacy of the object', without falling prey to fetishism? In Lacanian terms, the same problem should be reformulated as: does *objet petit a* always and necessarily function as a fetishist object, as the object whose fascinating presence covers up the lack of castration (the small *a* over minus phi of castration, in Lacan's mathemes)?

Sexual difference

Crucial here is the reflective reversal of 'the Other does it for me, instead of me, in my place', into 'I myself am doing it through the Other': this reversal expresses the minimal condition of subjectivity – that is to say, the attitude which constitutes subjectivity is not 'I am the active autonomous agent who is doing it', but 'when another is doing it for me, I myself am doing it through him' (a woman who is doing it through her man, etc.). This reversal is repeatedly at work in the Hegelian dialectical process, in the guise of the reversal of determining reflection into reflective determination. As we know, determining reflection is the dialectical unity of positing and external reflection. At the level of the subject's activity, 'positing reflection' occurs when I am directly active; in 'external reflection', the Other is active and I merely observe it passively. When the Other does it for me, instead of me, when he acts as my proxy, my relationship to him becomes that of determining reflection – external and positing reflection already overlap in it (the very act of observing the Other doing it for me, the moment of external reflection, makes me aware that he is doing it for me – that, in this sense, I myself 'posited' his activity, that his activity is 'mediated' by my subjective position); it is only when I posit direct identity between the Other's activity and my own – when I conceive of myself as the truly active party, as the one who is doing it through the Other – that we pass from determining reflection to reflective determination (since, at this level, the Other's activity is not only determined by my reflection, but directly posited as my reflective determination). Or – to refer again to the Yugoslav joke – we are dealing here with the shift from 'representatives of the people who drive limousines in place of the ordinary people' to 'ordinary people themselves who drive limousines through their representatives' . . . In the domain of *jouissance*, this shift is a shift from the Other enjoying it instead of me, in my place, to myself enjoying it through the Other.

This paradox also allows us to throw some new light on sexual difference. When, at the outset of his argumentation for distributive justice,

John Rawls states that his hypothesis excludes the presence of envy in rational subjects, he thereby excludes desire itself in its constitutive mediation with the Other's desire. However, the logic of 'envy' is not the same for both sexes. How, then, does 'desire is the desire of the Other' differ in the case of men and women? The masculine version is, to put it simply, that of competition/envy: 'I want it because you want it, in so far as you want it' – that is to say, what confers the value of desirability on an object is that it is already desired by another. The aim here is the ultimate destruction of the Other, which, of course, then renders the object worthless – therein lies the paradox of the male dialectic of desire. The feminine version, on the contrary, is that of 'I desire through the Other', in both senses of 'let the Other do it (possess and enjoy the object, etc.) for me' (let my husband, my son . . . succeed for me), as well as 'I desire only what he desires, I want only to fulfil his desire' (Antigone, who wants only to fulfil the desire of the Other in accomplishing the proper burial of her brother).[33]

The thesis that a man tends to act directly and to take on board his act, while a woman prefers to act by proxy, letting another do (or manipulating another into doing) it for her, may sound like the worst cliché, which gives rise to the notorious image of woman as a congenital schemer hiding behind man's back.[34] What, however, if this cliché nevertheless points towards the feminine status of the subject? What if the 'original' subjective gesture, the gesture constitutive of subjectivity, is not that of autonomously 'doing something' but, rather, that of the primordial substitution, of withdrawing and letting another do it for me, in my place? Women, much more than men, are able to enjoy by proxy, to find

33   See Darian Leader, *Why Do Women Write More Letters Than They Post?*, London: Faber & Faber, 1966.

34   When it is applied to our everyday ideological perceptions of the relationship between women and men, the term 'cliché' is theoretically wrong. That is to say; when one denounces these perceptions as 'clichés', this is as a rule said in such a way that it allows us to dispense with a close analysis of *what, precisely, these 'clichés' are*. Within the social space, *everything* is ultimately a 'cliché' (i.e. a contingent symbolic formation not grounded in the immediate 'nature of things'). 'Clichés' should therefore be taken extremely seriously, and the problem with the term 'cliché' is that it is misleading in so far as one can always hear in front of it an imperceptible 'mere' ('cliché' *equals* 'mere cliché').

deep satisfaction in the awareness that their beloved partner enjoys (or succeeds, or has attained his or her goal in any other way).[35] In this precise sense, the Hegelian 'cunning of Reason' bears witness to the resolutely feminine nature of what Hegel calls 'Reason': 'Look for the hidden Reason (which realizes itself in the apparent confusion of egotistic direct motifs and acts)!' is Hegel's version of the notorious *Cherchez la femme!* This, then, is how reference to interpassivity allows us to complicate the standard opposition of man versus woman as active versus passive: sexual difference is inscribed into the very core of the relationship of substitution – woman can remain passive *while being active through her other*; man can be active *while suffering through his other*.[36]

The 'objectively subjective'

The ontological paradox – scandal, even – of these phenomena (whose psychoanalytic name, of course, is *fantasy*) lies in the fact that they subvert the standard opposition of 'subjective' and 'objective': of course, fantasy is by definition not 'objective' (in the naive sense of 'existing independently of the subject's perceptions'); however, it is not 'subjective' either (in the sense of being reducible to the subject's consciously experienced intuitions). Fantasy, rather, belongs to the 'bizarre category of the objectively subjective – the way things actually, objectively seem to you even if they don't seem that way to you'.[37] When, for example, the subject actually experiences a series of phantasmic formations which interrelate as so many permutations of each other, this series is never complete: it is always as if

35   In the case of men, the presupposed Other's enjoyment is, rather, the source of obsessive anxiety, the ultimate goal of compulsive rituals is precisely to keep the other mortified, that is, to prevent him from enjoying . . .

36   When, in his scheme of four discourses, Lacan puts $ (subject) under S1, (the master-signifier), is not one possible way to read this substitution to put Woman under Man – to conceive of man as woman's metaphorical substitute, as her proxy? (The opposite substitution, $ under *objet petit a,* would, of course, be woman as man's substitute.)

37   Daniel C. Dennett, *Consciousness Explained,* New York: Little, Brown & Co., 1991, p. 132. (Dennett, of course, evokes this concept in a purely negative way, as a nonsensical *contradictio in adjecto*.)

the actually experienced series presents so many variations on some under-lying 'fundamental' fantasy which is *never* actually experienced by the subject. (In Freud's 'A Child is Being Beaten', the two consciously experi-enced fantasies presuppose and thus relate to a third one, 'My father is beating me', which was never actually experienced and can only be retro-actively reconstructed as the presupposed reference of – or, in this case, the intermediate term between – the other two fantasies.) One can even go further and claim that, in this sense, the Freudian unconscious itself is 'objectively subjective': when, for example, we claim that someone who is consciously well disposed towards Jews none the less harbours profound anti-Semitic prejudices of which he is not consciously aware, do we not claim that (in so far as these prejudices express not the way Jews really are, but the way they appear to him) *he is not aware how Jews really seem to him*?

This brings us back to the mystery of 'fetishism': when, by means of a fetish, the subject 'believes through the other' (i.e. when the fetish-thing believes for him, in the place of him), we also encounter this 'bizarre cate-gory of the objectively subjective': what the fetish objectivizes is 'my true belief', the way things 'truly seem to me', although I never actually expe-rience them in this way; apropos of commodity fetishism, Marx himself uses the term 'objectively-necessary appearance'. So when a critical Marxist encounters a bourgeois subject immersed in commodity fetishism, the Marxist's comment to him is not 'Commodity may seem to you a magical object endowed with special powers, but it really is just a reified expression of relations between people'; the actual Marxist's comment is, rather, 'You may think that the commodity appears to you as a simple embodiment of social relations (that, for example, money is just a kind of voucher enti-tling you to a part of the social product), but *this is not how things really seem to you* – in your social reality, by means of your participation in social exchange, you bear witness to the uncanny fact that a commodity really appears to you as a magical object endowed with special powers.'

At a more general level, is this not a characteristic of the symbolic order as such? 'When I encounter a bearer of symbolic authority (a father, a judge . . .), my subjective experience of him can be that he is a corrupted weakling, yet I none the less treat him with due respect because *this is how he 'objectively appears to me'*. Another example: in Communist regimes, the semblance according to which people supported the Party and enthusiastically constructed Socialism was not a simple subjective semblance (nobody really believed in it) but, rather, a kind of 'objective semblance', a semblance materialized in the actual social functioning of the regime, in the way the ruling ideology was materialized in ideological rituals and apparatuses. Or, to put it in Hegelian terms: the notion of the 'objectively subjective', of the semblance conceived in the 'objective' sense, designates the moment when the difference between objective reality and subjective semblance is reflected within the domain of the subjective semblance itself. What we obtain in this reflection-into-semblance of the opposition between reality and semblance is precisely the paradoxical notion of objective semblance, of 'how things really seem to me'. Therein lies the dialectical synthesis between the realm of the Objective and the realm of the Subjective: not simply in the notion of subjective appearance as the mediated expression of objective reality, but in the notion of a semblance which objectivizes itself and starts to function as a 'real semblance' (the semblance sustained by the big Other, the symbolic institution) against the mere subjective semblance of actual individuals.

This is also one way of specifying the meaning of Lacan's assertion of the subject's constitutive 'decentrement': its point is not that my subjective experience is regulated by objective unconscious mechanisms which are 'decentred' with regard to my self-experience and, as such, beyond my control (a point asserted by every materialist) but, rather, something much more unsettling: I am deprived of even my most intimate 'subjective' experience, the way things 'really seem to me', that of the fundamental fantasy which constitutes and guarantees the kernel of my being, since I can never consciously experience and assume it . . . According to the standard view, the dimension which is constitutive of subjectivity is that of the phenomenal (self-)experience – I am a subject the moment I can say to myself: 'No matter what unknown mechanism governs my acts, perceptions and thoughts, nobody can take from me what I see and feel now.' Lacan turns this standard view around: the 'subject of the signifier' emerges only when a key aspect of the subject's *phenomenal* (self-)experience (his 'fundamental fantasy') becomes *inaccessible* to him; that is to say: is 'primordially repressed'. At its most radical, the Unconscious is the *inaccessible phenomenon*, not the objective mechanism which regulates my phenomenal experience.

The *prima facie* philosophical observation apropos of this paradox, of course, would be that modern philosophy long ago elaborated such a notion of 'objectively subjective'. That is the whole point of the Kantian notion of the 'transcendental' which precisely designates objectivity, in so far as it is 'subjectively' mediated/constituted: Kant emphasizes again and again that his transcendental idealism has nothing to do with the simple subjective phenomenalism – his point is not that there is no objective reality, that only subjective appearances are accessible to us. There definitely *is* a line which separates objective reality from mere subjective impressions, and Kant's problem is, precisely, how we pass from the mere multitude of subjective impressions to objective reality: his answer, of course, is: through transcendental constitution – through the subject's synthetic activity. The difference between objective reality and mere subjective impressions is thus internal to subjectivity, it is the difference between merely subjective and objectively subjective . . . This, however, is not what the Lacanian notion of fantasy aims at. To grasp this difference, one should introduce here the seemingly hairsplitting, but none the less crucial distinction between 'subjectively objective' and 'objectively subjective': the Kantian transcendentally constituted reality is *subjectively objective* (it stands for objectivity which is subjectively constituted/mediated), while fantasy is *objectively subjective* (it designates an innermost subjective content, a product of fantasizing, which, paradoxically, is 'desubjectivized', rendered inaccessible to the subject's immediate experience).

It would, however, be a serious misunderstanding to read this radical decentrement involved in the notion of fetishism (I am deprived of my innermost beliefs, fantasies, etc.) as 'the end of Cartesian subjectivity'. What this deprivation (i.e. the fact that a phenomenological reconstitution which would generate 'reified' belief out of the presupposed 'first-person' belief necessarily fails, the fact that substitution is original, the fact that even in the case of the most intimate beliefs, fantasies, etc., the big Other can 'do it for me') effectively undermines is the standard notion of the so-called 'Cartesian Theatre', the notion of a central Screen of Consciousness which forms the focus of subjectivity, where (at a phenomenal level) 'things really happen'.[38] In clear contrast, the Lacanian subject *qua* $, the void of self-referential negativity, is strictly correlative to the primordial decentrement: the very fact that I can be deprived of even my innermost psychic ('mental') content, that the big Other (or fetish) can laugh for me, believe for me, and so on, is what makes me $, the 'barred' subject, the pure void with no positive substantial content. The Lacanian subject is thus empty in the radical sense of being deprived of even the minimal phenomenological support: there is no wealth of experiences to fill in its void. And Lacan's premiss is that the Cartesian reduction of the subject to pure *cogito* already implies such a reduction of every substantial content, including my innermost 'mental' attitudes – the notion of 'Cartesian Theatre' as the original *locus* of subjectivity is already a 'reification' of the subject *qua* $, the pure void of negativity.

Two interconnected conclusions are thus to be drawn from this chapter. In contrast to the commonplace according to which the new media turn us into passive consumers who just stare blindly at the screen, one should claim that the so-called threat of the new media lies in the fact that *they deprive us of our passivity, of our authentic passive experience, and thus prepare us for the mindless frenetic activity*. In contrast to the notion that we are dealing with a subject the moment an entity displays signs of a phantasmic 'inner life' which cannot be reduced to external behaviour, one should claim that what characterizes subjectivity is rather *the gap which separates the two*: fantasy, at its most elementary, is inaccessible to the subject, and it is this inaccessibility which makes the subject 'empty'. We thus obtain a

38   For this notion of 'Cartesian Theatre', see Dennett, *Consciousness Explained.*

relationship which totally subverts the standard notion of the subject who directly experiences himself, his 'inner states': an 'impossible' relationship between the *empty, non-phenomenal subject* and the *phenomena which forever remain 'desubjectivized', inaccessible to the subject* – the very relationship registered by Lacan's formula of fantasy, $0 a.

4 Cyberspace, or, The Unbearable Closure Of Being

What is a symptom?

When one is dealing with a universal structuring principle, one always automatically assumes that – in principle, precisely – it is possible to apply this principle to all its potential elements, so that the principle's empirical non-realization is merely a matter of contingent circumstances. A symptom, however, is an element which – although the non-realization of the universal principle in it appears to hinge on contingent circumstances – *has* to remain an exception, that is, the point of suspension of the universal principle: if the universal principle were to apply also to this point, the universal system itself would disintegrate.

In the paragraphs on civil society in his *Philosophy of Right*, Hegel demonstrates how the growing class of 'rabble [*Pöbel*]' in modern civil society is not an accidental result of social mismanagement, inadequate government measures, or simple economic bad luck: the inherent structural dynamic of civil society necessarily gives rise to a class which is excluded from its benefits (work, personal dignity, etc.) – a class deprived of elementary human rights, and therefore also exempt from duties towards society, an element within civil society which negates its universal principle, a kind of 'non-Reason inherent in Reason itself' – in short, *its symptom*. Do we not witness the same phenomenon in today's growth of an underclass which is excluded, sometimes even for generations, from the benefits of liberal-democratic affluent society? Today's 'exceptions' (the homeless, the ghettoized, the permanently unemployed) are the symptom of the late-capitalist universal system, the permanent reminder of how the immanent logic of late capitalism works: the proper capitalist utopia is that through appropriate measures (affirmative action and other forms of state inter-vention for progressive liberals; the return to self-care and family values for conservatives), this 'exception' could be – in the long term and in principle, at least – abolished. And is not an analogous utopianism at work in the notion of a 'rainbow coalition': in the idea that, at some utopian moment to come, all progressive struggles (for gay and lesbian rights; for the rights of ethnic and religious minorities; the ecological struggle; the feminist struggle; and so on) will be united in a common 'chain of equivalences'?

The necessary failure here is structural: it is not simply that, because of the empirical complexity of the situation, all particular progressive fights will never be united, that 'wrong' chains of equivalences will always occur (say, the enchainment of the fight for African-American ethnic identity with patriarchal and homophobic attitudes), but, rather, that occurrences of 'wrong' enchainments are grounded in the very structuring principle of today's progressive politics of establishing 'chains of equivalences': the very domain of the multitude of particular struggles, with their contin-uously shifting displacements and condensations, is sustained by the 'repression' of the key role of economic struggle. The Leftist politics of the 'chains of equivalences' among the plurality of struggles is strictly correl-ative to the abandonment of the analysis of capitalism as a global economic system – that is, to the tacit acceptance of capitalist economic relations and liberal-democratic politics as the unquestioned framework of our social life.

In this precise sense, symptom turns a dispersed *collection* into a *system* (in the precise sense this term acquired in German Idealism): we are within a system the moment we breach the gap which separates the a priori form from its contingent content – the moment we envisage the *necessity* of what appears to be a contingent intrusion which 'spoils the game'. A system indicates the fact that 'there is One' (Lacan's *y a de l'un*), an inherent element which subverts the universal frame from within; to return to our example: the 'systemic' nature of late-capitalist political struggle means that the chain of equivalences of today's identity struggles is *necessarily* never completed, that the 'populist temptation' *always* leads to the 'wrong' chain of equivalences.

In a different field, a 'system' also underlies the series of Buñuel films which vary the motif of what Buñuel himself calls the 'inscrutable impossibility of the fulfilment of a simple desire'. In *The Criminal Life of Archibaldo de la Cruz*, the hero wants to accomplish a simple murder, but all his attempts fail; in *The Exterminating Angel*, after a dinner party, a group of rich people cannot cross the threshold and leave the house; in *The Discreet Charm of the Bourgeoisie*, we have the opposite case of three upper-class couples planning to dine together, but unexpected complications always prevent the fulfilment of this simple wish; in *Navarin*, where the narrative follows a pattern of endless on-the-road humiliations and entrapments, the idealist priest Navarin, to whom life is a sort of journey in the footsteps of Christ, witnesses how his hopes of liberation are dashed on the very road to freedom that he has chosen. His final insight, of course, is that what he has hitherto dismissed as mere distractions on his road to freedom – the contingent, unexpected humiliations and entrapments – provide the very framework of his actual experience of freedom. In other words, the structural role of these humiliations and entrapments which seem to pop up out of nowhere is the same as that of the unexpected complications which again and again prevent the group in *The Discreet Charm* from dining together . . . The ultimate example which, perhaps, provides the key to this entire series is, of course, *That Obscure Object of Desire*, in which a woman, through a succession of absurd tricks, postpones again and again the final moment of sexual reunion with her aged lover (when, for example, the man finally gets her into bed, he discovers beneath her nightgown an old-fashioned corset with numerous buckles which are impossible to undo) The charm of the film lies in this very nonsensical short circuit between the fundamental, metaphysical Limit and some trivial empirical impediment. Here we find the logic of courtly love and of sublimation at its purest: some common, everyday object or act becomes inaccessible or impossible to accomplish once it finds itself in the position of the Thing – although the thing should be easily within our grasp, the entire universe has somehow been adjusted to produce, again and again, an unfathomable contingency blocking access to it.[1]

The solution to this tension between the subject's goal (to sleep with the beloved; to have dinner together; to achieve freedom . . .) and the imbecilic contingent intrusions which prevent its realization again and again lies in the Hegelian insight into their ultimate speculative identity: it is the barrier of these intrusions which maintains the Goal in its elevated sublimity, so that – to revert to a Derridean formulation – the condition of impossibility of realizing the Goal is simultaneously its condition of possibility – or, to put it in Hegelese, in fighting the imbecilic contingency of the ways of the world, the Idea fights itself, the very resource of its strength. This *necessity of the utter, imbecilic contingency*, this enigmatic notion of an unexpected intrusion which none the less pops up with absolute inevitability (and has to pop up, since its non-arrival would entail the dissolution of the whole domain of the search for the Goal), is the highest speculative mystery, the true 'dialectical synthesis of contingency and necessity' to be opposed to platitudes about the deeper necessity which realizes itself through surface contingencies. One is tempted to contend that when Hegel makes his 'panlogistic' claim according to which 'Reason rules the world' (or 'what is actual is reasonable'), its actual content is this kind of necessary intrusion of a contingency: when one is sure that 'Reason rules the world', this means that one can be sure that a contingency will always emerge which will prevent the direct realization of our Goal.[2]

1   For a detailed account of this structure of sublimation, sec Chapter 4 of Slavoj Žižek, *The Metastases of Enjoyment,* London: Verso, 1994.

2   Furthermore, it would be productive to classify the multitude of 'irrational' impediments in Buñuel's films; they can be grouped in four categories which form a kind of Greimasian semiotic square: sexual impediment which prevents the consummation of the act of love, and thus proves that 'there is no sexual relationship' (*That Obscure Object of Desire*); religious impediment which prevents our access to spiritual freedom (*Navarin*); the

The other side of this necessity which realizes itself in the guise of a series of contingent intrusions which again and again prevent the universal notion or project from realizing itself (like the accidents which again and again prevent the three couples in *The Discreet Charm* . . . from dining together, like the unfortunate accidents which again and again prevent the abolition of African-American ghettos in the liberal-democratic project), is the necessity, the absolute certainty, that within the field of a universal Lie the 'repressed' truth will emerge in the guise of a particular contingent event. That is the basic lesson of psychoanalysis: in our everyday lives, we vegetate, deeply immersed in the universal Lie; then, all of a

---

impossibility of participating in a banal everyday social ritual, i.e. a dinner party (*The Discreet Charm of the Bourgeoisie*); the obverse impossibility of ending the social ritual and leaving the house after a dinner party (*The Exterminating Angel*); the criminal transgressive act, i.e. murder (*The Criminal Life of Archibaldo de la Cruz* – a true anti-Oedipus, since in contrast to Oedipus, who unknowingly murders his father, poor Archibaldo consciously wants to kill a series of women who are then actually killed, but by a miraculous accident which has nothing to do with him); finally, the sociopolitical impediment which prevents the realization of freedom and makes freedom forever 'phantomatic', i.e. that mysterious X on account of which revolutions always seem to go wrong (*The Phantom of Liberty*, precisely)

The first thing to do is to classify these examples into the couples of opposites: participation in a banal social ritual versus the act of leaving the place of this ritual; the sexual act (i.e. the act of creating life) versus killing (taking life); earthly anarchic freedom versus religious spiritual freedom. It is as if the same opposition is repeated three times, in three different powers/potencies – at the level of banal social rituals, of 'sinful' private acts, and of the endeavour to reach absolute Freedom. At each of the three levels, we can neither 'get out' nor 'stay in': it is impossible to participate in the banal social ritual, but it is also impossible to get out of it; it is impossible to make love, and also to kill; it is impossible to find fulfilment and spiritual freedom in Christian transcendence, but it is no less impossible to find it in social anarchy . . . The Lacanian name for such an inability to 'get out' *and* 'stay in' is, of course, the Real; this same paradox of the Real is at work in 'free associations' within the psychoanalytic cure (we never really have them, one never can fully suspend the pressure of inhibitions and 'let oneself go'; at the same time, *whatever one says* on the analytic couch is a free association, even if it was carefully planned or if it is a long line of strict logical reasoning) and in *jouissance: Jouissance* eludes us, it is beyond our reach, its full confrontation is lethal; at the same time, however, one can never get rid of it, its remainder sticks to us whatever we do. Along the same lines, the Kantian ethical injunction also has the status of the Real: it is impossible fully to realize one's ethical duty, yet it is also impossible to avoid the pressure of the call of duty.

sudden, some contingent encounter – a casual remark during a conversation, an incident we witness – brings to light the repressed trauma which shatters our self-delusion. Correlative to the illusion which tells us that the failure to realize our project is due to a mere unfortunate set of circumstances is the illusion which tells us that if we had not made that stupid contingent gesture (overheard that remark, taken that turn in the street and encountered that person . . .), everything would have remained OK; our universe would still be intact, instead of lying in ruins.

We can see how each of these two forms negates one of the two aspects of the ideological space curvature: the first one negates its false opening (demonstrating that the promise of opening will remain unfulfilled for necessary reasons); the second negates its false closure (demonstrating that the excluded externality will necessarily invade the inside). What we have here, of course, is the logical square of necessity, possibility, impossibility and contingency: the recurring impossibility (to dine together) negates the ideological form of possibility, the contingency (the contingent emergence of truth) negates the ideological form of universal necessity. And is not the notion of cyberspace a key symptom of our socioideological constellation? Does it not involve the promise of false opening (the spiritualist prospect of casting off our 'ordinary' bodies, turning into a virtual entity which travels from one virtual space to another) as well as the foreclosure of the social power relations within which virtual communities operate?

The virtual as real

One should adopt towards cyberspace a 'conservative' attitude, like that of Chaplin *vis-à-vis* sound in cinema: Chaplin was far more than usually aware of the traumatic impact of the voice as a foreign intruder on our perception of cinema. In the same way, today's process of transition allows us to perceive what we are losing and what we are gaining – this perception will become impossible the moment we fully embrace, and feel fully at home in, the new technologies. In short, we have the privilege of occupying the place of 'vanishing mediators'. Such a Chaplinesque attitude compels us to resist the seductive charm of the two contemporary myths about cyberspace, which are both based on the commonplace according to which we are today in the middle of the shift from the epoch of modernism (monological subjectivity, mechanistic Reason, etc.) to the postmodern epoch of dissemination (the play of appearances no longer grounded in reference to some ultimate Truth, the multiple forms of constructed Selves):

- In cyberspace, we witness a return to *pensée sauvage*, to 'concrete', 'sensual' thought: an 'essay' in cyberspace confronts fragments of music and other sounds, text, images, video clips, and so on, and it is this confrontation of 'concrete' elements which produces 'abstract' meaning . . . here, are we not again back with Eisenstein's dream of 'intellectual montage' – of filming *Capital*, of producing the Marxist theory out of the clash of concrete images? Is not hypertext a new practice of montage?[3]

- Today we are witnessing the move *from the modernist culture of calculation to the postmodernist culture of simulation.*[4] The clearest indication of this move is the shift in the use of the term 'transparency': modernist technology is 'transparent' in the sense of retaining the illusion of an insight into 'how the machine works'; that is to say, the screen of the interface was supposed to allow the user direct access to the machine behind the screen; the user was supposed to 'grasp' its workings – in ideal conditions, even to reconstruct it rationally. The postmodernist 'transparency' designates almost the exact opposite of this attitude of analytical global planning: the interface screen is supposed to conceal the workings of the machine, and to simulate our everyday experience as faithfully as possible (the Macintosh style of interface, in which written orders are replaced

3   On Eisenstein, see V.V. Ivanov, 'Eisenstein's Montage of Hieroglyphic Signs', in *On Signs,* ed. Marshall Blonsky, Baltimore, MD: The Johns Hopkins University Press, 1985, pp. 221–35.

4   See Sherry Turkle, *Life on the Screen: Identity in the Age of the Internet,* New York: Simon & Schuster, 1995.

by simple mouse-clicking on iconic signs . . .); however, the price of this illusion of a continuity with our everyday environs is that the user becomes 'accustomed to opaque technology' – the digital machinery 'behind the screen' retreats into total impenetrability, even invisibility. In other words, the user renounces the endeavour to grasp the functioning of the computer, resigning himself to the fact that in his interaction with cyberspace he is thrown into a non-transparent situation analogous to that of his everyday *Lebenswelt*, a situation in which he has to 'find his bearings', to act in the mode of tinkering [*bricolage*] by trial and error, not simply to follow some pre-established general rules – or, to repeat Sherry Turkle's pun, in the postmodernist attitude we 'take things at their interface value'.

If the modernist universe is the universe, hidden behind the screen, of bytes, wires and chips, of electric current, the postmodernist universe is the universe of naive trust in the screen which makes the very quest for 'what lies behind it' irrelevant. 'To take things at their interface value' involves a *phenomenological* attitude, an attitude of 'trusting the phenomena': the modernist programmer takes refuge in cyberspace as a transparent, clearly structured universe which allows him to elude (momentarily, at least) the opacity of his everyday environs, in which he is part of an a priori unfathomable background, full of institutions whose functioning follows unknown rules which exert domination over his life; for the postmodernist programmer, in contrast, the fundamental features of cyberspace coincide with those described by Heidegger as the constitutive features of our everyday life-world (the finite individual is thrown into a situation whose co-ordinates are not regulated by clear universal rules, so that the individual has gradually to find his way in it).

In both these myths, the error is the same: yes, we are dealing with a return to pre-modern 'concrete thought' or to the non-transparent life-world, but this new life-world already presupposes a background of the scientific digital universe: bytes – or, rather, the digital series – is the Real behind the screen; that is to say, we are never submerged in the play of appearances without an 'indivisible remainder'. Postmodernism focuses on the mystery of what Turkle calls the 'emergence' and Deleuze elaborated as the 'sense-event': the emergence of the pure appearance which cannot be reduced to the simple effect of its bodily causes;[5] none the less, this emergence is the effect of the digitalized Real.[6]

Apropos of the notion of interface, the temptation here, of course, is to bring it to the point of its self-reference: what if one conceives of *'consciousness' itself, the frame through which we perceive the universe, as a kind of 'interface'*? The moment we yield to this temptation, however, we accomplish a kind of foreclosure of the Real. When the user playing with the multiplicity of Internet Relay Chat (IRC) channels says to himself: 'What if real life (RL) itself is just one more IRC channel?'; or, with respect to multiple windows in a hypertext, 'What if RL is just one more window?', the illusion to which he succumbs is strictly correlative to the opposite one – to the common-sense attitude of maintaining our belief in the full reality outside the virtual universe. That is to say: one should avoid both traps, the simple direct reference to external reality outside cyberspace as well as the opposite attitude of 'there is no external reality, RL is just another window'.[7]

In the domain of sexuality, this foreclosure of the Real gives rise to the New Age vision of the new computerized sexuality, in which bodies mix in ethereal virtual space, freed of their material weight: a vision which is *stricto sensu* an ideological fantasy, since it unites the impossible – sexuality

5   See Gilles Deleuze, *The Logic of Sense,* New York: Columbia University Press, 1990.

6   Another trap to be avoided here is to sexualize too quickly the shift from the modernist culture of calculation to the postmodernist culture of simulation by calling it a shift from 'masculine' to 'feminine': from the male modernist attitude of control, domination, etc., to the postmodern feminine attitude of tinkering, dialogue with the machine . . . This way, we miss the crucial point: a cyborg monster has no sex, it is asexual in the sense of the Lacanian *lamella,* that is, it stands for what was lost in the human animal's entry into the order of sexuality.

7   This double trap is analogous to the double trap apropos of the notion of ideology: the simple reliance on pre-ideological external reality as the measure of ideological distortion is strictly correlative to the attitude of 'there is no external reality, all we are dealing with is the multitude of simulacra, of discursive constructs'. See Slavoj Žižek, 'Introduction', in *Mapping Ideology,* London: Verso, 1995.

(linked to the Real of the body) with the 'mind' decoupled from the body, as if – in today's universe, where our bodily existence is (perceived as) more and more threatened by environmental dangers, AIDS, and so on, up to the extreme vulnerability of the narcissistic subject to actual psychic contact with another person – we could reinvent a space in which we could fully indulge in bodily pleasures by getting rid of our actual bodies. In short, this vision is that of a state without lack and obstacles, a state of free floating in the virtual space in which desire nonetheless survives somehow . . .

The threatened frontier

Instead of indulging in these ideologies, it is far more productive to begin with how computerization affects the hermeneutic horizon of our everyday experience. This experience is based on the three lines of separation: between 'true life' and its mechanical simulation; between objective reality and our false (illusory) perception of it; between my fleeting affects, feelings, attitudes, and so on, and the remaining hard core of my Self. All these three boundaries are threatened today:

- Technobiology undermines the difference between 'natural' life-reality and 'artificially' generated reality: already in today's genetic technology (with the prospect of free choice of sex, hair colour, IQ . . .), living nature is posited as something technically manipulable; that is, in principle, nature as such coincides with a technical product. The circle is thus closed, our everyday hermeneutical experience is undermined: technology no longer merely *imitates* nature, rather, it reveals the underlying mechanism which *generates* it, so that, in a sense, 'natural reality' itself becomes something 'simulated', and the only 'Real' is the underlying structure of DNA.
- In so far as the VR apparatus is potentially able to generate experience of the 'true' reality, VR undermines the difference between 'true' reality and semblance. This 'loss of reality' occurs not only in

computer-generated VR but, at a more elementary level, already with the growing 'hyperrealism' of the images with which the media bombard us – more and more, we perceive only colour and outline, no longer depth and volume: 'Without visual limit there can be no, or almost no, mental imagery; without a certain blindness, no tenable appearance.'[8] Or – as Lacan put it – without a *blind spot* in the field of vision, without this elusive point from which the object returns the gaze, we no longer 'see something'; the field of vision is reduced to a flat surface, and 'reality' itself is perceived as a visual hallucination.

- The MUD (Multiple User Domains) technology in cyberspace undermines the notion of Self, or the self-identity of the perceiving subject: the standard motif of 'postmodern' writers on cyberspace, from Stone[9] to Turkle, is that cyberspace phenomena like MUD render the deconstructionist 'decentred subject' palpable in our everyday experience. The lesson is that one should endorse this 'dissemination' of the unique Self into a multiplicity of competing agents, into a 'collective mind', a plurality of self-images without a global co-ordinating centre, and disconnect it from pathological trauma: playing in Virtual Spaces enables me to discover new aspects of 'me', a wealth of shifting identities, of masks without a 'real' person behind them, and thus to experience the ideological mechanism of the production of Self, the immanent violence and arbitrariness of this production/construction.

These three levels follow one another logically: first, within 'objective reality' itself the difference between 'living' and 'artificial' entities is undermined; then the distinction between 'objective reality' and its appearance gets blurred; finally, the identity of the self which perceives something

8   Paul Virilio, *The Art of the Motor*, Minneapolis: University of Minnesota Press, 1995, p. 4.
9   See Allucquere Rosanne Stone, *The War of Desire and Technology*, Cambridge, MA: MIT Press, 1995.

(be it appearance or 'objective reality') explodes. This progressive 'subjec-tivization' is strictly correlative to its opposite, to the progressive 'exter-nalization' of the hard kernel of subjectivity. This paradoxical coincidence of the two opposed processes has its roots in the fact that today, with VR and technobiology, we are dealing with the loss of the surface which separates inside from outside. This loss jeopardizes our most elementary perception of 'our own body' as it is related to its environs; it cripples our standard phenomenological attitude towards the body of another person, in which we suspend our knowledge of what actually exists beneath the skin (glands, flesh . . .) and conceive the surface (of a face, for example) as directly expressing the 'soul'. On the one hand, inside is always outside: with the progressive implantation and replacement of our internal organs, techno-computerized prostheses (bypasses, pacemakers . . .) function as an internal part of our 'living' organism; the colonization of the outer space thus reverts to the inside, into 'endolocolonization',[10] the techno-logical colonization of our body itself. On the other hand, outside is always inside: when we are directly immersed in VR, we lose contact with reality – electro-waves bypass the interaction of external bodies and directly attack our senses: 'it is the eyeball that now englobes man's entire body'.[11]

Another aspect of this paradox concerns the way the progressive immo-bilization of the body overlaps with bodily hyperactivity: on the one hand I rely less and less on my proper body; my bodily activity is more and more reduced to giving signals to machines which do the work for me (clicking on a computer mouse, etc.); on the other hand, my body is strengthened, 'hyperactivated', through body-building and jogging, pharmaceutical means, and direct implants, so that, paradoxically, the hyperactive super-man coincides with the cripple who can move around only by means of prostheses regulated by a computer chip (like the Robocop). The prospect is thus that the human being will gradually lose its grounding in the concrete life-world – that is to say, the basic set of coordinates which

10   Virilio, *The Art of the Motor*, p. 113.
11   Ibid., p. 148.

determine its (self-) experience (the surface separating inside from outside, a direct relationship to one's own body, etc.). Potentially, total subjectivization (the reduction of reality to an electro-mechanically generated cyberspace 'window') coincides with total objectivization (the subordination of our 'inner' bodily rhythm to a set of stimulations regulated by external apparatuses). No wonder Stephen Hawking is emerging as one of the icons of our time: the mind of a genius (or so we are told), but in a body which is almost totally 'mediatized', supported by prostheses, speaking with an artificial, computer-generated voice. Hawking's active contact with his surroundings is limited to a weak pressure he is still able to exert with the fingers of his right hand. In short, his popular appeal cannot be separated from his debilitating illness – from the fact that his body, reduced to an immobile mass of flesh, kept functioning by mechanical prostheses and contacting the world through clicking a computer mouse, tells us something about the general state of subjectivity today.

At a more fundamental level, however, this 'derailment' – this lack of support, of a fixed instinctual standard, in the co-ordination between the natural rhythm of our body and its surroundings – characterizes man *as such*: man *as such* is 'derailed'; he eats more than is 'natural'; he is obsessed with sexuality more than is 'natural': he follows his drives with an excess far beyond 'natural' (instinctual) satisfaction, and this excess of drive has to be 'gentrified' through 'second nature' (man-made institutions and patterns). The old Marxist formula about 'second nature' is thus to be taken more literally than usual: the point is not only that we are never dealing with pure natural needs, that our needs are always-already mediated by the cultural process; moreover, *the labour of culture has to reinstate the lost support in natural needs,* to re-create a 'second nature' as the recompense for the loss of support in the 'first nature' – the human animal has to reaccustom itself to the most elementary bodily rhythm of sleep, feeding, movement.

What we encounter here is the loop of (symbolic) castration, in which one endeavours to reinstate the lost 'natural' co-ordination on the ladder of desire: on the one hand, one reduces bodily gestures to the necessary minimum (of clicks on the computer mouse . . .); on the other, one attempts to recover lost bodily fitness by means of jogging, body-building, and so on; on the one hand, one reduces the bodily odours to a minimum (by taking regular showers, etc.); on the other, one attempts to recover these same odours through toilet water and perfumes; and so on. This paradox is condensed in the phallus as the *signifier* of desire – as the point of inversion at which the very moment of 'spontaneous' natural power turns into an artificial prosthetic element. That is to say: against the standard notion of the phallus as the siege of male 'natural' penetrative-aggressive potency-power (to which one then opposes the 'artificial' playful prosthetic phallus), the point of Lacan's concept of the phallus as a *signifier* is that the phallus 'as such' *is* a kind of 'prosthetic', 'artificial' supplement: it designates the point at which the big Other, a decentred agency, supplements the subject's failure. When Judith Butler, in her criticism of Lacan, emphasizes the parallel between mirror-image (ideal-ego) and phallic signifier,[12] one should shift the focus to the feature they effectively share: both mirror-image and phallus *qua* signifier are 'prosthetic' supplements for the subject's foregoing dispersal/failure, for the lack of co-ordination and unity, in both cases, the status of this prosthesis is 'illusory', with the difference that in the first case we are dealing with imaginary illusion (identification with a decentred immobile image), while in the second, the illusion is symbolic; it stands for phallus as pure semblance. The opposition between the 'true', 'natural' phallus and the 'artificial' prosthetic supplement ('dildo') is thus false and misleading: phallus *qua* signifier is already 'in itself' a prosthetic supplement. (This status of phallus also accounts for Lacan's identification of woman with phallus: what phallus and woman share is the fact that their being is reduced to a pure semblance. In so far as feminity is a masquerade, it stands for phallus as the ultimate semblance.)

Back to the threatened limit/surface which separates inside from outside: the very threat to this limit determines today's form of the

---

12   See Chapter 2 of Judith Butter, *Bodies That Matter*, New York: Routledge, 1993.

hysterical question – that is to say: today, hysteria stands predominantly under the sign of vulnerability, of a threat to our bodily and/or psychic identity. We have only to recall the all-pervasiveness of the logic of victimization, from sexual harassment to the dangers of food and tobacco, so that the subject itself is increasingly reduced to 'that which can be hurt'. Today's form of the obsessional question 'Am I alive or dead?' is 'Am I a machine (does my brain really function as a computer) or a living human being (with a spark of spirit or something else that is not reducible to the computer circuit)?'; it is not difficult to discern in this alternative the split between A (*Autre*) and J (*jouissance*), between the 'big Other', the *dead* symbolic order, and the Thing, the *living* substance of enjoyment. According to Sherry Turkle, our reaction to this question goes through three phases: (1) the emphatic assertion of an irreducible difference: man is not a machine, there is something unique about him . . .; (2) fear and panic when we become aware of all the potential of a machine: it can think, reason, answer our questions . . ., (3) disavowal, that is, recognition through denial: the guarantee that there is some feature of man inaccessible to the computer (sublime enthusiasm, anxiety . . .) allows us to treat the computer as a 'living and thinking partner', since 'we know this is only a game, the computer is not really like that'.

Consider how John Searle's polemics against AI (his Chinese Room thought experiment) was 'gentrified' and integrated into the user's everyday attitude: Searle has proved that a computer cannot really think and understand language – *so, since there is the ontological-philosophical guarantee that the machine does not pose a threat to human uniqueness, I can calmly accept the machine and play with it* . . . Is not this split attitude, in which 'disavowal and appropriation are each tied to the other', a new variation on the old philosophical game of 'transcendental illusion' practised already by Kant apropos of the notion of teleology – since I know the computer cannot think, I can act, in my everyday life, *as if* it really *does?*[13]

13   Turkle, *Life on the Screen*, p. 126.

Identifications, imaginary and symbolic

This same ambiguity determines the way we relate to our screen personae:

- On the one hand, we maintain an attitude of external distance, of playing with false images: 'I know I'm not like that (brave, seductive . . .), but it's nice, from time to time, to forget one's true self and put on a more satisfying mask – this way you can relax, you are delivered of the burden of being what you are, of living with yourself and being fully responsible for it . . .'[14]
- On the other hand, the screen persona I create for myself can be 'more myself than my 'real-life' persona (my 'official' self-image), in so far as it reveals aspects of myself I would never dare to admit in RL. Say: when I play anonymously in MUD, I can present myself as a promiscuous woman and engage in activities which, were I to indulge in them in RL, would bring about the disintegration of my sense of personal identity . . .

These two aspects are, of course, inextricably intertwined: the very fact that I perceive my virtual self-image as mere play allows me to suspend the usual hindrances which prevent me from realizing my 'dark side' in RL, and to externalize all my libidinal potential freely. When a man who, in his RL social contacts, is quiet and bashful, adopts an angry, aggressive persona in VR, one can say that he thereby expresses the repressed side of himself, a publicly non-acknowledged aspect of his 'true personality' – that his 'electronic id is here given wing';[15] however, one can also claim that he is a weak subject fantasizing about more aggressive behaviour in order to avoid confronting his RL weakness and cowardice. Acting out a

14   Years ago, in a TV interview, one of the participants in a contest for the best 'Madonna lookalike' gave an appropriate answer to the journalist's patronizing question about how she felt being deprived of her true self in her total imitation of another person: 'For 364 days a year, I am forced to live with my true Self – it is a liberating experience to be able to get rid of it for at least one day!'

15   Turkle, *Life on the Screen,* p. 205.

fantasy scene in VR allows us to bypass the deadlock of the dialectic of desire and its inherent rejection: when a man bombards a woman with flirtatious promises about what sexual favours he would like to bestow on her, her best answer is 'Shut up, or you'll really have to do it!' In VR, I can do it, act it out, without really doing it, and thus avoid the anxiety connected with the RL activity – I can do it, and since I know I'm not really doing it, the inhibition or shame is suspended.

This is one way to read Lacan's dictum 'Truth has the structure of a fiction': I can articulate the hidden truth about my drives precisely in so far as I am aware that I am simply playing a game on the screen. In cyberspace sex, there is no 'face-to-face', just the *external* impersonal space in which everything, including my most intimate *internal* fantasies, can be articulated with no inhibitions . . . What one encounters here, in this pure 'flux of desire', is, of course, the unpleasant surprise of what the Frankfurt School called 'repressive desublimation': the universe, freed of everyday inhibitions, turns out to be a universe of unbridled sadomasochistic violence and will to domination . . .[16] The usual complaint against cybersex is that instead of the truly arousing and intensive encounter with another body, we get a distanced, technologically mediated procedure. However, is it not precisely this gap, this distance towards immediate *Erlebnis*, which can also *add* sexual arousal to a sexual encounter? People use pornography (or other technical sex devices) not only when they lack 'flesh-and-blood' partners but also in order to 'spice up' their 'real' sex life. The status of sexual supplement is thus again radically ambiguous and 'undecidable': it can spoil the game, yet it can also intensify enjoyment.

16   In other words, *computerization undermines performativity*. By claiming this, I am not resurrecting the myth of the good old pre-computerized times when words really counted. As Derrida – but also Lacan – emphasized again and again, the performative can always, for structural reasons, go wrong; it can arise only against the background of radical undecidability – the very fact that I have to rely on the other's word means that the other remains forever an enigma to me. What tends to get lost in virtual communities is this very abyss of the other, this very background of undecidability: in the 'wired universe', the very opaqueness of the other tends to evaporate. In this sense, the suspension of performativity in virtual communities is the very opposite of the suspension of performativity in the psychoanalytic cure, where I can tell my analyst anything, all my obscene fantasies about him, knowing that he will not be offended, that he will not 'take it personally'.

In order to conceptualize the two poles of this undecidability, Turkle resorts to the opposition between 'acting out' and 'working through' the difficulties of RL:[17] I can follow the escapist logic and simply act out my RL difficulties in VR, or I can use VR to become aware of the inconsistency and multiplicity of the components of my subjective identifications, and work them through. In this second case, the interface screen functions like a psychoanalyst: the suspension of the symbolic rules which regulate my RL activity enables me to stage-externalize my repressed content which I am otherwise unable to confront. (Here again, do we not encounter the logic of *acceptance through disavowal*: I accept my fantasies in so far as 'I know it's only a VR game'?) The same ambiguity is reproduced in the impact of cyberspace on community life. On the one hand there is the dream of the new populism, in which decentralized networks will allow individuals to band together and build a participatory grass-roots political system, a transparent world in which the mystery of the impenetrable bureaucratic state agencies is dispelled. On the other, the use of computers and VR as a tool to rebuild community results in the building of a community *inside* the machine, reducing individuals to isolated monads, each of them alone, facing a computer, ultimately unsure if the person she or he communicates with on the screen is a 'real' person, a false persona, an agent which combines a number of 'real' people, or a computer program ... Again, the ambiguity is irreducible.

However, this ambiguity, although irreducible, is not symmetrical. What one should introduce here is the elementary Lacanian distinction between imaginary projection-identification and symbolic identification. The most concise definition of symbolic identification is that it consists in assuming a mask which is more real and binding than the true face beneath it (in accordance with Lacan's notion that human feigning is the feigning of feigning itself: in imaginary deception, I simply present a false image of myself, while in symbolic deception, I present a true image and

17   Turkle, *Life on the Screen*, p. 200.

count on it being taken for a lie...[18]). A husband, for example, can maintain his marriage as just another social role and engage in adultery as 'the real thing'; however, the moment he is confronted with the choice of actually leaving his wife or not, he suddenly discovers that the social mask of marriage means more to him than intense private passion . . . The VR persona thus offers a case of imaginary deception in so far as it externalizes-displays a false image of myself (a timid man playing a hero in MUD . . .) and a symbolic deception in so far as it expresses the truth about myself in the guise of a game (by playfully adopting an aggressive persona, I disclose my true aggressivity).

In other words, VR confronts us, in the most radical way imaginable, with the old enigma of transposed/displaced emotions.[19] At a somewhat different level, we encounter the same paradox apropos of TinySex: what TinySex compels us to accept is the blurred line of separation between 'things' and 'mere words'. Their separation is not simply suspended, it is still here, but displaced – a third realm emerges which is neither 'real things' nor 'merely words', but demands its own specific (ethical) rules of conduct. Let us consider virtual sex: when I play sex games with a partner on the screen, exchanging 'mere' written messages, it is not only that the games can really arouse me or my partner and provide us with a 'real' orgasmic experience (with the further paradox that when – and if – I later encounter my partner in RL, I can be deeply disappointed, turned off: my on-screen experience can be in a sense 'more real' than the encounter in reality); it is not only that, beyond mere sexual arousal, my partner and I can 'really' fall in love without meeting in RL. What if, on the net, I rape my partner? On the one hand, there is a gap which separates it from RL – what I did remains in a sense closer to impoliteness, to rude, offensive

18   Or – to take a rather vulgar everyday example – being slightly overweight, I have at my disposal two strategies to conceal this fact. I can put on a shirt with vertical lines which makes me appear slender, or I can, on the contrary, put on a shirt with horizontal lines, counting on the fact that people I meet will (mis)perceive my overweight as the illusion created by my inappropriate dress: 'Look, this stupid shirt makes him look fat, whereas he is not really so fat!'

19   See Chapter 3 above.

talk. On the other hand, it can cause deep offence, even emotional catastrophe, which is not reducible to 'mere words' ... And – back to Lacan – what is this middle-mediating level, this third domain interposing itself between 'real life' and 'mere imagination', this domain in which we are not directly dealing with reality, but not with 'mere words' either (since our words do have real effects), if not *the symbolic order itself*?

Where is the 'decentred subject'?

When deconstructionist cyberspace ideologists (as opposed to the predominant New Age cyberspace ideologists) try to present cyberspace as providing a 'real-life', 'empirical' realization or confirmation of deconstructionist theories, they usually focus on how cyberspace 'decentres' the subject. Both Stone and Turkle approach this via the relationship between Multiple User Domains and post-traumatic Multiple Personality Disorder (MPD). There are four variations on the relationship between the Self and 'its' Body which violate the standard moral-legal norm of 'one person in one body':

- *many persons in a single body* (the 'pathology' of MPD): this version is 'pathological' in so far as there is no clear hierarchy between the plurality of persons – no One Person guaranteeing the unity of the subject;
- *many persons outside a single body* (MUD in cyberspace): these persons refer to the body which exists outside cyberspace, in 'reality', with the (ideological) presupposition that this body accommodates a 'true person' behind the multiple masks (screen personae) in VR;
- *many bodies in a single person*: this version is again 'pathological' in so far as many bodies immediately coalesce with a single collective person, and thereby violate the axiom 'one body – one person'. Take the fantasy of aliens, 'multiple bodies, but one collective mind'; or the case of hypnosis, in which the person of one body possesses another body – not to mention the popular image of 'totalitarian'

communities that function like an ant colony – the Centre (Party) totally controls their individual minds . . .

- *many bodies outside a single person* (institution, 'legal' – or, as they put it in France, 'moral' – person). This is how we 'normally' relate to an institution: we say 'the State, Nation, company, school . . . wants this', although 'we know very well' that the institution is not an actual living entity with a will of its own, but a symbolic fiction.

The temptation to be avoided here is to 'deconstruct' too hastily the limit which, in both cases, separates the 'normal' from the 'pathological'. The difference between the subject who suffers from MPD and the subject who plays in MUD does *not* lie in the fact that in the second case there still persists a kernel of Self firmly anchored in the 'true reality' outside the virtual play. The subject who suffers from MPD is rather too firmly anchored in 'true reality': what he lacks is, in a sense, lack itself: the void which accounts for the constitutive dimension of subjectivity. That is to say: the 'multiple Selves' externalized on the screen are 'what I want to be', the way I would like to see myself, the representations of my ideal ego; as such, they are like the layers of an onion: there is nothing in the middle, and the subject is this 'nothing' itself. It is therefore crucial to introduce here the distinction between 'Self' ('person') and subject: the Lacanian 'decentred subject' is *not* simply a multiplicity of good old 'Selves', partial centres; the 'divided' subject does *not* mean there are simply *more* Egos/Selves in the same individual, as in MUD. The 'decentrement' is the decentrement of the $ (the void of the subject) with regard to its content ('Self', the bundle of imaginary and/or symbolic identifications); the 'splitting' is the splitting between $ and the phantasmic 'persona' as the 'stuff of the I'. *The subject is split even if it possesses only one 'unified' Self,* since this split is the very split between $ and Self . . . In more topological terms: the subject's division is not the division between one Self and another, between two contents, but *the division between something and nothing,* between the feature of identification and the void.

'Decentrement' thus first designates the ambiguity, the oscillation between symbolic and imaginary identification – the undecidability as to where my true point is, in my 'real' self or in my external mask, with the possible implication that my symbolic mask can be 'more true' than what it conceals, the 'true face' behind it. At a more radical level, it points towards the fact that the very sliding from one identification to another, or among 'multiple selves', presupposes the gap between identification as such and the void of $ (the 'barred subject') which *identifies itself* – serves as the empty medium of identification. In other words, the very process of shifting among multiple identifications presupposes a kind of empty band which makes the leap from one identity to another possible, and this empty band is the subject itself.

To make the subject's 'decentrement' clearer, we should recall the 'agent' in cyberspace: a program which acts as my stand-in, performing a series of specific functions. An 'agent' works in both directions: on the one hand it can serve as my extension and act *for* me, scanning the immense conglomerate of information and picking out what interests me, accomplishing simple (or not so simple) tasks for me (sending messages, etc.); on the other, it can act *on* me and control me (for example, it can automatically check my blood pressure and warn me if it rises too much). Such a program which acts as my stand-in within the cyberspace provides an almost perfect illustration of the Lacanian concept of *ego* as opposed to the subject: a cyberspace agent is not 'another subject' but simply the subject's *ego*, ego as the subject's supplement – it is, of course, a kind of 'alter ego', but Lacan's point is that ego itself is always-already 'alter' with regard to the subject whose ego it is. For that reason, the subject entertains towards it the relationship of acceptance-through-disavowal described by Turkle: 'one knows very well it is merely a program, not a real living person', but for that very reason (i.e. because one knows that 'it's only a game') one can allow oneself to treat it as a caretaking partner . . . Here again we encounter the radical ambiguity of cyberspace supplements: they can improve our lives, delivering us of unnecessary burdens, but the price we pay is our radical 'decentrement' – that is to say, agents also 'mediatize' us. Since my cyberspace agent is an external program which acts on my behalf, decides what information I will see and read, and so on, it is easy to imagine the paranoiac possibility of *another* computer program controlling and directing my agent unbeknownst to me – if this happens, I am, as it were, dominated from within; my own ego is no longer mine.

One of the commonplaces about Romanticism is that it asserts madness as the positive foundation of 'normality': it is not madness which is a secondary and accidental distortion of normality; rather, it is normality itself which is nothing but gentrified/regulated madness (to quote Schelling) – in this way, Romanticism clearly announces the Freudian thesis that the 'pathological' provides the key to the 'normal'. Long before Romanticism, however, Malebranche adopted the same approach. In eighteenth-century Enlightenment thought, the blind man acted as the model enabling us to grasp the logic of vision: we can claim that we understand vision only when we can translate the act of seeing into a procedure accessible also to a person who, precisely, does *not* see.[20]

Along the same lines, Malebranche claims that the 'pathological' case of feeling a hand one does not have provides the key to explaining how a 'normal' person feels the hand he actually possesses – as in psychoanalysis, where the 'pathological' provides the key to the 'normal'. No wonder, then, that Malebranche, in effect, pre-empted Lacan's famous quip about madness ('A madman is not only a beggar who thinks he is a king, but also a king who thinks he is a king' – that is, who directly grounds his symbolic mandate in his immediate natural properties): in strict analogy, Malebranche claims that a madman is not only a person who feels his right hand without actually having one – that is, a person who can feel pain in his missing limbs – but also a person who feels a hand he *really* has, since when I claim to feel my hand directly, I confound two ontologically different hands: the material, bodily hand and the representation of a hand in my mind, which is the only thing I am actually aware of. A madman is not only a man who thinks he is a rooster, but also a man who thinks he is directly a man – that is to say, this material body he feels directly as his own. Here Malebranche evokes the problematic of the two bodies, the ordinary material one and the sublime one: the fact that I can fully feel the limb I do not have demonstrates that the hand I feel is not the corporeal hand but the idea of this hand planted in my mind by God. (In his piano music, Robert Schumann exploits the same gap with a melody which is expected to occur – whose structural place is constructed – but is then not actually played: for that reason, its presence is even more strongly felt – see Appendix II below.) And is not the *phallus* that strange bodily organ in which bodily and mental causality separate and at the same time strangely intermingle (its erection does not obey my conscious will, yet I can obtain involuntary erection by mere thoughts)? Perhaps this simultaneous separation/overlapping defines 'symbolic castration'. One can thus say that the phallus is the ultimate occasionalist object: the point at which the very gap that separates the series of mental causes from the series of bodily causes is inscribed into our body . . .

The phantasmic hypertext

Our first result is thus that cyberspace merely radicalizes the gap constitutive of the symbolic order: (symbolic) reality always-already was 'virtual'; that is to *say. every access to (social) reality has to be supported by an implicit phantasmic hypertext.* How does this hypertext work?

Ulu Grosbard's *Falling in Love* is usually dismissed as a failed remake of David Lean's *Brief Encounter*: what perhaps saves the film, however, is its overt self-reflective attitude: before we get to the final happy ending (the couple are reunited for good), all other known and possible endings are rehearsed. For a brief moment, it seems that the desperate heroine will attempt suicide; for a further brief moment, it seems that, a year after breaking up, the two lovers will accidentally meet again, just sadly say hello to each other, and then depart; and so on. Because of all this, the spectator is assured, at least twice, that what he sees is already the final scene of the film – unexpectedly, however, the film goes on . . . This implicit reference to (at least) two other possible outcomes is not a mere intertextual play, but relies on a deeper libidinal necessity: it is only against the background of the two phantasmic scenarios (suicide; the melancholic encounter after the break-up) that the couple can finally be reunited in 'real life'. At the level of fantasy, these two scenarios must occur if the final reunion in 'real life' is to be rendered acceptable. To put it in somewhat pathetic terms: the couple can be reunited in 'real life' only if, on the phantasmic level, they have gone through a double suicidal gesture, and accepted the loss. This allows us to supplement the standard notion according to which there is no reality without its phantasmic support: social reality (in this case: the reality of the couple's reunion) can occur only if it is supported by (at least) *two* fantasies, two phantasmic scenarios.

Let us test this hypothesis with some other examples. *Le Père humilié*, the last part of Paul Claudel's Coufontaine trilogy, analysed by Lacan as the exemplary case of the modern tragedy,[21] focuses on the relationship between the beautiful blind Pensée and the two brothers who love her, Orion and Orso. Orion's love for Pensée is absolute, true passion, but for that very reason, after a night of love, he leaves her for the battlefield, where he meets his violent death (what we encounter here, of course, is the standard I-Can't-Love-You-Unless-I-Give-You-Up motif). On the other hand, Orso's love for Pensée is the standard affectionate frame of mind, which lacks this unconditional dimension: more than anything else, he would like to live with her – that is to say, he actually prefers her to anyone or anything else, which is why he gets her (marries her and adopts Orion's son as his own), but has to renounce having sex with her . . . a nice version of 'there is no sexual relationship': either a lasting *mariage blanc*, or the consummated passion which has to end in tragedy. One is thus tempted to claim that Orion and Orso are two aspects of one and the same person, like the old gentleman's mistress in Buñuel's *Obscure Object of Desire*, who is played by two different actresses. In other words, do not these two versions embody the two scenarios which, on the phantasmic level, *have*

21   See Jacques Lacan, *Le Séminaire, livre VIII: Le transfert,* Paris: Éditions du Seuil, 1991.

to occur, if 'normal' marriage, which seemingly unites both aspects (I live with a woman that I love, and have a child with her), *is to take place?* Is not such a double renunciation the condition of what we call 'happiness'?

At a different level of political process, the same logic of a double phantasmic background is discernible in *Meet John Doe*, Frank Capra's key film and the turning point in his career: it marks the passage from the social populism of *Mr Deeds* and *Mr Smith* to the Christian attitude of *It's a Wonderful Life*. *Meet John Doe* is the story of an unemployed man (Gary Cooper), hired to impersonate a nonexistent fictional character fabricated by a manipulative journalist (Barbara Stanwyck) to arouse public compassion; the whole scam is orchestrated by Norton, the newspaper's owner and a big mogul, in order to advance his proto-Fascist dictatorial goals. The first uncanny feature of the film is that it presents the crowd not as the idealized community of compassionate common people but as an unstable, unreliable mob which oscillates between the two excesses of sentimental solidarity and violence (well before Freud, such a notion of the crowd had already been theorized by Spinoza). The further point is that Gary Cooper's character is presented not as an originally good and innocent man, thrown into a violent conflict by some dark manipulative forces or Fate itself (as in the two *Mr* films), but as an opportunistic loser who first agrees to participate in a scam, and is only gradually redeemed by taking the Cause he is compelled to personify seriously, so that he is finally ready to sacrifice his life in order to prove the seriousness of his commitment. The suicide motif in Capra is present more often than it may appear (it is also central to *It's a Wonderful Life*); but it is only in *Meet John Doe* that it assumes the key role as the only means left to Doe of proving that his Cause is not a fake.

This deadlock is clearly manifested by the obvious failure of the film's ending (the failed ending is the usual place at which the inconsistency of the work's ideological project becomes visible – what makes *Così fan tutte* central to Mozart's operatic project is the very failure of its finale). The ending of the film was decided on after a long period of hesitation in which a whole series of different endings were considered; the existing pseudo-Christological ending involves the ideological gesture of resolving the deadlock of the other endings under consideration.

In the first version the film ended with the convention scene, in which John Doe endeavours to denounce the scam, and with Norton's full victory over John Doe: when Doe attempts to explain to the crowd what actually took place, the electricity is cut off and his voice is not heard . . . In the second version, the truly Christological one, Doe fulfils his promise and actually kills himself – he jumps from the skyscraper, while Norton and others watch; the Colonel, Doe's friend, takes his body in his arms. (Significantly, this pietà composition inverts the one we see in the final version, where it is Doe himself who takes Anna's body into his arms.) In the third, Norton is broken down and promises that the true John Doe story will be printed in his papers . . .[22] The version we actually have – when Doe actually wants to commit suicide, the crowd of his followers who are watching talk him out of it, and together they vow to form a new, authentic John Doe movement, out of reach of Norton's manipulations – has thus to be read as the resolution of the deadlock to which the previously considered versions bear witness.

Each ending is unsatisfying in its own way: the first two (the defeat of Doe's Cause; Doe's death) are too bleak; the third one is too ridiculous in the simplicity of Norton's conversion to goodness. The first two versions are the only consistent ones, since they resolve the tension between the authenticity of Doe's Cause and the falsity of his story (the fact that he is a fake) in the only two possible ways: either Doe survives, and the Cause is lost and discredited; or the Cause is saved, but Doe has to pay for it with his life. Both these solutions, however, were unacceptable to the Hollywood ideological framework. Capra wanted it both ways (Doe alive, as well as his Cause saved), so his problem was how to spare Doe's life without making his vow to kill himself an empty gesture not to be taken seriously. The solution was that the common people, the

22   See Joseph McBride, *Frank Capra: The Catastrophe of Success,* New York: Simon & Schuster, 1992.

members of his movement, were the only ones who could effectively convince him not to take his life.

The ending we actually see is thus to be read against the background of the other endings considered, as in Hitchcock's *Notorious*, a film which, perhaps, owes at least part of its powerful impact to the fact that its dénouement should be perceived against the background of at least two other possible outcomes which resonate in it as a kind of alternative history.[23] That is to say: in the first story outline, Alicia wins redemption by the end, but loses Devlin, who is killed rescuing her from the Nazis. In the last scene, back in the USA, she visits Devlin's parents, and shows them a commendation from the President that cites both her and Devlin for their heroic deeds. In a further elaboration of this first version, the climactic party scene was added, and the film was supposed to conclude with it: Devlin preoccupies the Nazis long enough for Alicia to escape, but he is waylaid and killed as she waits outside. The idea was that this act should solve the tension between Devlin, who is unable to admit to Alicia his love for her, and Alicia, who is unable to perceive herself as worthy of love: Devlin admits his love for her without words, by dying in order to save her life. In the final scene, we find Alicia back in Miami with her group of drinking friends: although she is more 'notorious' than ever, she has in her heart the memory of a man who loved her and died for her, and – as Hitchcock put it in a memo to Selznick – 'to her this is the same as if she had achieved a life of marriage and happiness'.

In the second main version, the outcome is the opposite: we already have the idea of a slow poisoning of Alicia by Sebastian and his mother. Devlin confronts the Nazis and flees with Alicia, but Alicia dies in the process. In the epilogue, Devlin sits alone in a Rio café, where he used to meet Alicia, and overhears people discussing the death of Sebastian's wanton and treacherous wife. The letter in his hands, however, is a commendation from President Truman citing Alicia's bravery. Devlin

23   See the fascinating report in Thomas Schatz, *The Genius of the System,* New York: Hold & Co., 1996, pp. 393–403.

pockets the letter and finishes his drink . . . In a further (arguably the worst) version, devised by none other than Clifford Odets, Alicia and Devlin escape Sebastian's house with Sebastian and his mother, who holds the two lovers at gunpoint; however, the mother becomes enraged and shoots her son, and in the ensuing crash she herself dies, so that everything ends well . . . Finally, the version we know was arrived at, with a finale which implies that Devlin and Alicia are now married. Hitchcock then left this finale out, to end on a more tragic note, with Sebastian, who truly loved Alicia, left to face the Nazis' deadly wrath. (Already in the triangle of gazes at the famous party scene, Sebastian's gaze is that of the impotent observer.)

The point is that if we are to grasp the explicit story properly, we should read it in the Lévi-Straussian way, against the background of (and in contrast to) the two alternative stories. That is to say: there is definitely a Hitchcockian shibboleth; beneath the standard notion of Hitchcock – the great commercial entertainer, the 'master of suspense' – there is another Hitchcock who, in an unheard-of way, practised the critique of ideology. The spectator who is not versed in recognizing this Hitchcockian shibboleth will miss the way in which both alternative endings (Devlin's and Alicia's death) are incorporated into the film, as a kind of phantasmic background to the action we see on the screen: if they are to constitute a couple, both Devlin and Alicia *have to undergo the 'symbolic death'*, so that the happy ending emerges from the combination of two unhappy endings – that is to say, these two alternative phantasmic scenarios sustain the dénouement we actually see.

Towards the end of the film, Alicia undergoes a 'symbolic death' in the guise of the long and painful process of slow poisoning which nearly kills her. (Devlin's 'symbolic death' has a different form, that of openly acknowledging his love for Alicia, an act which involves the radical reformulation of his subjective identity: after he does it, he is no longer 'the same Devlin' – to put it in somewhat pathetic terms, the moment he acknowledges his love for her, his old ego dies.) From this brief description it should already be clear how strong the ideologico critical thrust of this Hitchcockian shibboleth is: it reveals the entire problematic of sexism – the way the male identity is threatened by assertive femininity, as well as the traumatic price a woman has to pay in order to become a 'normal wife' (Alicia's ordeal by poisoning – like Melanie's near-death towards the end of *The Birds* – demonstrates how only a subdued, immobilized woman, deprived of her autonomy of action, can enter into the marital link with the hero).[24]

Back to *Meet John Doe*: in what, then, does the resolution of the film consist? A lot has been written about the film's Christological reference (the hero at the end endures his Way of the Cross, the obvious reference to the pietà when he carries his beloved Anna [Barbara Stanwyck], the film's Mary Magdalene). What actually occurs, however, is *not* the Christological gesture of the redemption of the collective through the sacrifice of the Leader: the solution the film proposes is not a religious escape. What we in fact encounter at the end is a different sacrificial gesture, the one patently at work in opera, especially in Mozart. Confronted by the ultimate deadlock, the hero heroically asserts his readiness to die, to lose everything, to put everything at stake, and at this very moment of heroic suicidal self-abandonment, the Higher Power (the King, Divinity) intervenes and spares his life. (In Gluck's *Orfeo*, divinity intervenes and gives Orpheus back his Eurydice at the very moment when he raises the knife to kill himself; in Mozart's *The Magic Flute* the Three Boys intervene at the very moment when Pamina is ready to stab herself, and, later when the desperate Papageno is about to hang himself; in *Idomeneo*, Neptune intervenes at the very moment when King Idomeneo raises his sword to fulfil the sad duty of sacrificing his beloved son; up to Wagner's *Parsifal*, in which Parsifal himself intervenes at the very point when King Amfortas urges his knights to stab him, and thus end his torment.[25])

Capra's solution of saving the hero at the precise moment when he

24   Among Hitchcock's films, *Topaz* also has two other endings which were shot but later abandoned: (1) Granville, unmasked as the Russian spy, leaves for Russia and meets the hero, who is also leaving for America, at the airport; (2) Granville and the hero meet at an empty stadium for a duel, but before the duel starts, he is shot by a hidden KGB hit man . . .

25   See Chapter 5 of Slavoj Žižek, *Tarrying With the Negative*, Durham, NC: Duke University Press, 1993.

displays the seriousness of his suicidal intent (you can have it all only if you pass through the 'zero point,' and agree to lose it all) thus follows an old tradition. This gesture as such is not necessarily mystifying, so the problem with the film is not that it opts for this solution. That is to say: this gesture fits perfectly the fact that, in contrast to the two populist *Mr* films, the hero of *Doe* is not, from the very outset, an innocent nice guy but a confused opportunist, a victim who only gradually, through a painful process of education, grows into his role of Doe: so, in this sense, a suicidal moment has to occur in which the hero casts off the fake position and assumes an authentic position. The position of Gary Cooper in *Meet John Doe* is thus in a way analogous to that of Cary Grant in Hitchcock's *North by Northwest*: in both films the subject occupies, fills in, the empty place in some pre-existing symbolic network: first, there is the signifier 'George Kaplan' or 'John Doe', then the person (Roger O. Thornhill, the anonymous unemployed man) finds himself occupying this place. The difference between the two cases is that Gary Cooper (like de Sica in Rossellini's *General della Rovere*) gradually identifies with this symbolic place and fully assumes it, up to the point where he is prepared to stake his life on it.

This line of development is properly *materialist* it accounts for the process in the course of which what was at the outset a manipulated movement with a faked Leader can outgrow its initial conditions and turn into an authentic movement. That is to say: much more interesting than the idealist narrative of gradually corrupted innocence is the opposite story: since we all live within ideology, the true enigma is how we can outgrow our 'corrupted' initial condition – how something which was planned as ideological manipulation can all of a sudden miraculously start to lead an authentic life of its own. (In the case of religion, for example, the most interesting cases are those – like the Virgin of Guadalupe in Mexico – where the ideological edifice initially imposed by the colonizers was appropriated by the oppressed as a means of articulating their grievances, and turned against the oppressors themselves.)

So there is nothing inherently false in the idea that the hero, by means of his suicidal gesture, is no longer a puppet figure manipulated by the proto-Fascist Norton – that he redeems himself and is free to start his movement anew. The problem lies elsewhere. The film concludes with the promise that now, after Doe's redemption, it will be possible to reassemble the Doe movement, but this time in a pure form, freed from Norton's (i.e. proto-Fascist) manipulation, as an authentic movement of the people themselves; the only content of this movement, however, is empty populist sentimental solidarity and love for one's neighbour – in short, what we get is exactly the same ideology as the one previously promulgated by Norton. To paraphrase Marx's well-known indictment of Proudhon from *The Poverty of Philosophy*: instead of the depiction of actual people caught in and manipulated into an ideological illusion, we get this illusion itself, without the actual people and conditions in which it thrives . . .

What one should bear in mind is the purely *formal* nature of such a gesture of 'authentic contact': it is quite possible to arouse a feeling of truly belonging to a Cause by simply insisting that things are now for real, that we really mean it, without specifying the content of the Cause (see the parodic speech quoted by Adorno in his *Jargon of Authenticity*). Fascism refers directly to this formal emptiness of the gesture of belonging, to the satisfaction provided by the attachment to the form as such: the message is to obey, to sacrifice oneself for the Cause, without asking why – the content of the Cause is secondary, and ultimately irrelevant. In *Kiss of the Spider Woman*, one of the stories told by William Hurt to Raul Julia is about a woman in France during the German occupation, who is in love with a high-ranking Nazi officer but is horrified at the actions of the Nazis; to allay her fears, the Nazi takes her into his office and explains to her the deepest secrets of the Nazi effort (how they are really doing things to help the people, the profound love that moves them . . .), and she understands and accepts his explanation. Of course, we never learn *what* these profound motivations are, but this gesture, in its very emptiness, in the primacy of form over content, is ideology at its purest.

In the same way, the solution of *Doe* is apparently 'radical' (a 'true' populist movement no longer manipulated by – and playing the game of – big Capital), yet precisely as such it is *stricto sensu* empty, a self-referential assertion of authenticity, a kind of hollow container open to a multitude of incompatible readings, from Fascism to Communism: we never learn in what, precisely, this new populism will consist, and this very void *is* ideology. In other words, what is missing is simply the turn towards organizing a labour movement and changing the very material conditions in which people like Norton can thrive. The solution would be authentic if we were to witness the birth of a true radical (Communist) political movement, aimed at destroying the political and economic power of people like Norton, who effectively corrupted the movement in the first place. The emptiness of the existing solution becomes evident if one tries to imagine a possible sequel to the film: what will follow? Will it be possible for the new authentic Doe populism to thrive in the same society which concocted it as a means of manipulation? Or, if we take the well-known allegorical dimension of the film, is Doe a kind of Capra self-portrait (Capra himself was traumatized by his own success; he underwent a kind of 'crisis of investiture' and considered himself a fake, unable as he was to accept the fact that he was the author who could incite such enthusiasm in the public; on the other hand, he considered himself manipulated by the studio bosses, the real-life Nortons)? The resolution proposed by the film is exactly correlative to the fact that Capra himself was allowed to continue with his populist foolery, in so far as he did not effectively question the power of the studio system.

The suspension of the master

The supreme example of symbolic virtuality, of course, is that of (the psychoanalytic notion of) castration: the feature which distinguishes symbolic castration from the 'real' kind is precisely its virtual character. That is to say: Freud's notion of castration anxiety has any meaning at all only if we suppose that *the threat of castration* (the prospect of castration, the 'virtual' castration) *already produces real 'castrating' effects*. This actuality of the virtual, which defines symbolic castration as opposed to the 'real' kind, has to be connected to the basic paradox of power, which is that symbolic power is by definition virtual, power-in-reserve, the threat of its full use which never actually occurs (when a father loses his temper and explodes, this is by definition a sign of his *impotence*, painful as it may be). The consequence of this conflation of actual with virtual is a kind of transubstantiation: every actual activity appears as a 'form of appearance' of another 'invisible' power whose status is purely virtual – the 'real' penis turns into the form of appearance of (the virtual) phallus, and so on. That is the paradox of castration: whatever I do in reality, with my 'real' penis, is just redoubling, following as a shadow, another virtual penis whose existence is purely symbolic – that is, phallus as a signifier. Let us recall the example of a judge who, in 'real life', is a weak and corrupt person, but the moment he puts on the insignia of his symbolic mandate, it is the big Other of the symbolic institution which is speaking through him: without the prosthesis of his symbolic title, his 'real power' would instantly disintegrate. And Lacan's point apropos of the phallus as signifier is that the same 'institutional' logic is at work already in the most intimate domain of male sexuality: just as a judge needs his symbolic crutches, his insignia, in order to exert his authority, a man needs a reference to the absent-virtual Phallus if his penis is to exert its potency.

Swiss bureaucracy provides an illustrative case of this effectivity of virtuality. A foreigner who wants to teach in Switzerland has to appear before a state agency called the *Comité de l'habitant*, and to apply for a *Certificat de bonne vie et mœurs*; the paradox, of course, is that nobody can *get* this certificate – the most a foreigner can get, in the case of a positive decision, is a paper stating that he is *not to be refused* it – a double negation which, however, is not yet a positive decision.[26] This is how Switzerland likes to treat an unfortunate foreign worker: your stay there can never be fully legitimized; the most you can get is the admission which allows you to dwell in a kind of in-between state – you are never positively accepted,

26   I owe this information to John Higgins, Cape Town University (private conversation).

you are just not yet rejected and thus retained with a vague promise that, in some indefinite future, you stand a chance . . .

Furthermore, the very notion of 'interface' has its pre-digital precursors: is not the notorious square opening in the side wall of the restroom, in which a gay offers part of his body (penis, anus) to the anonymous partner on the other side, yet another version of the function of interface? Is the subject not thereby reduced to the partial object as the primordial phantasmic object? And is not this reduction of the subject to a partial object offered in the interspace-opening also the elementary *sadistic* scene? If, however, the dimension of virtuality and the function of 'interface' are consubstantial with the symbolic order, in what, then, *does* the 'digital break' consist? Let us begin with an anecdotal observation. As any academic knows, the problem with writing on the computer is that it potentially suspends the difference between 'mere drafts' and the 'final version': there is no longer a 'final version' or a 'definitive text', since at every stage the text can be further worked on *ad infinitum* – every version has the status of something 'virtual' (conditional, provisional) . . . This uncertainty, of course, opens up the space of the demand for a new Master whose arbitrary gesture would declare some version the 'final' one, thereby bringing about the 'collapse' of the virtual infinity into definitive reality.

Hackers in California practise a computer manipulation of the *Star Trek* series, so that they add to the 'official' TV storyline scenes of explicit sexual encounters without changing any of the 'official' content (for example, after the two male heroes enter a room and close the doors, we see a homosexual play between them . . .). The idea, of course, is not simply to ironize or falsify the TV series, but to bring to light its unspoken implications (the homoerotic tension between the two heroes is clearly discernible to any viewer . . .).[27] Such changes do not depend directly on technical conditions (the computer's capacity to create lifelike images); they also presuppose the suspension of the function of the Master on account of which – potentially, at least – there no longer is a 'definitive version'. The

27   I owe this information to Constance Penley, UCLA (private conversation).

moment we accept this break in the functioning of the symbolic order, an entirely new perspective on traditional 'written' literature also opens up: why shouldn't we start to produce rewritings of canonic masterpieces to which, without changing the 'explicit' content, one would add detailed descriptions concerning sexual activity, underlying power relations, and so on, or simply retell the story from a different perspective, as Tom Stoppard did in his retelling of *Hamlet* from the standpoint of two marginal characters (*Rosencrantz and Guildenstern Are Dead*)? *Hamlet* itself immediately gives rise to an entire host of ideas: Hamlet is seduced by his mother into incest (or is he himself raping her)? Ophelia kills herself by drowning because she is pregnant by Hamlet? Wouldn't it also be enlightening to rewrite canonic love texts from the feminist standpoint (say, to produce the diaries of the *woman* who is the object of male advances in 'The Diary of a Seducer' from Kierkegaard's *Either/Or*)?[28]

In Germany, a whole collection of short stories was written recently, retelling great Western narratives from Oedipus to Faust from the standpoint of the woman involved (Jocasta, Margaretha); even more interesting is the case of the new version of a novel written by a woman and from the romantic woman's perspective, which shifts the focus to another woman – like Jean Rhys's *Wide Sargasso Sea*, which retells Charlotte Brontë's *Jane Eyre* from the standpoint of the 'madwoman in the attic', the insane Bertha, Rochester's first wife, imprisoned on the third floor of the Rochester manor house – what we learn, of course, is that, far from simply fitting the category of evil destroyer, she was herself the victim of brutal circumstances . . .

Since the writer who exemplifies restraint and reliance on the unspoken is definitely Henry James, in whose work tragedies occur and whole lives are ruined during what appears to be a polite dinner-table conversation, would it not also be enlightening to rewrite his masterpieces in order to explicate their latent sexual tensions and political content (Strether from

28   Incidentally, Kierkegaard *did* plan also to write 'hetaira's diary', a diary of seduction from the perspective of the seductress (who is, typically, conceived of as a 'hetaira', i.e. a prostitute).

The Ambassadors masturbating late in the evening in his hotel room – or, better still, engaged in homosexual play with a young rent boy – to relax after his busy daily social round; Maisie from *What Maisie Knew* observing her mother's lovemaking with her lover)? Once the dam of the Master-Signifier collapses, it opens up the way for the flood of ideas, some of which can be not only amusing but also insightful in bringing to light the underlying 'repressed' content. The problem is, however, that one should also not lose sight of what gets *lost* in such a procedure: it relies on the transgressive move of violating the boundaries of some canonic work – once the canonic point of reference loses its strength, the effect changes completely. Or – to put it in a different way – the effect of some content is entirely different if it is only hinted at as the 'repressed' secret of the 'public' storyline, as opposed to being openly described.

Franz Kafka's *The Castle* describes the hero's (K.'s) desperate attempts to get into the Castle, the mysterious seat of power. A new CD-ROM, *The Castle*, turns Kafka's novel into an interactive game: the player is invited to guide the hapless K. past Klamm, the mysterious gatekeeper, and into the dark and dank corridors of the castle . . . The point here is not to deplore the vulgarity of this idea but, rather, the opposite: to emphasize the structural analogy between K.'s endless attempts to enter into contact with the Castle and the never-ending feature of the interactive computer game, as if that which was, in the case of Kafka, a nightmarish experience turns all of a sudden into a pleasurable game: nobody really wants to enter the Castle fully; the pleasure is provided by the endless game of gradual and partial penetrations. In other words, nightmare turns into pleasurable game the moment the function of the Master is suspended.

The decline of this function of the Master in contemporary Western societies exposes the subject to radical ambiguity in the face of his desire. The media constantly bombard him with requests to choose, addressing him as the subject *supposed to know what he really wants* (which book, clothes, TV programme, holiday destination . . .): 'Press A if you want this; press B if you want that'; or – to quote the slogan of the recent 'reflective' TV publicity campaign for advertisement itself – 'Advertisement – the right to choose'. At a more fundamental level, however, the new media deprive the subject radically of the knowledge of what he wants: they address a thoroughly malleable subject who has constantly to be told what he wants – that is, the very evocation of a choice to be made performatively creates the need for the object of choice. One should bear in mind here that the main function of the Master is to tell the subject what he wants – the need for the Master arises in answer to the subject's confusion, in so far as he does *not* know what he wants. What happens, then, in the situation of the decline of the Master, when the subject himself is constantly bombarded with the request to give a sign of what he wants? The exact opposite of what one would expect: it is when there is no one there to tell you what you really want, when all the burden of the choice is on you, that the big Other dominates you completely, and the choice effectively disappears – is replaced by its mere semblance. One is again tempted to paraphrase here Lacan's well-known reversal of Dostoyevsky ('If there is no God, nothing at all is permitted'): if no forced choice confines the field of free choice, the very freedom of choice disappears.[29]

Informational anorexia

The suspension of the function of the (symbolic) Master is the crucial feature of the Real whose contours loom on the horizon of the cyberspace universe: the moment of implosion when humanity will attain the limit that is impossible to transgress; the moment at which the co-ordinates of our societal life-world will be dissolved.[30] At that moment, distances

29   However, one is also tempted to claim that there is a way in which, in cyberspace, the foreclosed dimension of the symbolic Master 'returns in the Real': in the guise of supplementary characters who exist only as programmed entities within the cyberspace (like Max Headroom from the TV series of the same name – see Chapter 6 of Stone, *The War of Desire and Technology*). Are not such figures the exemplary cases of what Lacan calls *l'Un-enplus,* the One which adds itself to the series, the direct point of subjectivization of the anonymous order which regulates relations between 'real' subjects?

30   For an outline of this unreachable limit, see Paul Virilio, *Cybermonde, la politique du pire,* Paris: Textuel, 1996.

will be suspended (I will be able to communicate instantly through tele-conferences with any place on the globe); all information, from texts to music to video, will be instantly available on my interface. However, the obverse of this suspension of the distance which separates me from a faraway foreigner is that, due to the gradual disappearance of contact with 'real' bodily others, a neighbour will no longer be a neighbour, since he or she will be progressively replaced by a screen spectre; general availability will induce unbearable claustrophobia; excess of choice will be experienced as the impossibility to choose; universal direct participatory community will exclude all the more forcefully those who are prevented from partic-ipating in it. The vision of cyberspace opening up a future of unending possibilities of limitless change, of new multiple sex organs, and so on, conceals its exact opposite: an unheard-of imposition of radical closure. This, then, is the Real awaiting us, and all endeavours to symbolize this Real, from utopian (the New Age or 'deconstructionist' celebrations of the liberating potentials of cyberspace) to the blackest dystopian ones (the prospect of the total control by a God-like computerized network . . .), are just that: so many attempts to avoid the true 'end of history', the paradox of an infinity far more suffocating than any actual confinement.

Or – to put it in a different way – the virtualization cancels the distance between a neighbour and a distant foreigner, in so far as it suspends the presence of the Other in the massive weight of the Real: neighbours and foreigners are all equal in their spectral screen presence. That is to say: why was the Christian injunction 'Love thy neighbour as thyself' so problematic for Freud? The proximity of the Other which makes a neigh-bour a neighbour is that of *jouissance*: when the presence of the Other becomes unbearable, suffocating, it means that we experience his or her mode of *jouissance* as too intrusive.[31] And what is contemporary 'post-modern' racism if not a violent reaction to this virtualization of the Other, a return of the experience of the neighbour in his or her (or their)

31   For a more detailed account of the other's unbearable proximity, see Chapter 2 above.

intolerable, traumatic *presence*? The feature which disturbs the racist in his Other (the way they laugh, the smell of their food . . .) is thus precisely the little piece of the Real which bears witness to their presence beyond the symbolic order.

So – back to the deadlock involved in the act of filling in the gaps in a canonic narrative (*Star Trek, Hamlet, The Ambassadors* . . .): as it has often been said, Virtual Reality is a kind of Orwellian misnomer. What is threatened in its rise is the very dimension of virtuality consubstantial with the symbolic order: the universe of VR tends to brings to light, to realize on the textual surface, the underlying fantasy – that is, to fill in the gap which separates the symbolic surface texture from its underlying fantasy, which is merely surmised or indicated in a canonic text (What takes place when the door closes behind the two main heroes of *Star Trek*? What is Strether doing alone in his hotel room in *The Ambassadors*?). The canonic text's consistency relies on the delicate balance of what is said and what is merely implied – if we 'say it all', the effect is not simply that of truth. Why? We must focus on what gets lost when these voids in the text are filled in – what gets lost is the real presence of the Other. Therein lies the paradox: the oppressive and simultaneously elusive presence of the Other subsists in the very absences (holes) of the symbolic texture. In this precise sense the commonplace according to which the problem with cyberspace is that reality is virtualized, so that instead of the flesh-and-blood presence of the Other we get a digitalized spectral apparition, *misses the point*: what brings about the 'loss of reality' in cyberspace is not its emptiness (the fact that it is lacking with respect to the fullness of the real presence) but, on the contrary, its very excessive fullness (the potential abolition of the dimension of symbolic virtuality). Is not one of the possible reactions to the excessive filling-in of the voids in cyberspace therefore *informational anorexia*, the desperate refusal to accept information, in so far as it occludes the presence of the Real?

We are thus a long way from bemoaning the loss of contact with a 'real', flesh-and-blood other in cyberspace, in which all we encounter are digital phantoms: our point, rather, is that cyberspace is *not spectral enough*.

That is to say: the status of what we have called the 'real presence of the Other' is inherently spectral: the little piece of the Real by means of which the racist identifies the Other-*jouissance* is a kind of minimal guarantee of the spectre of the Other who threatens to swallow us or to destroy our 'way of life'. To take another example: in 'phone sex', the very narrowness of the communication band (our partner is accessible to us only in the guise of a disembodied and, as such, all-pervasive voice) elevates the Other, our partner, into a spectral entity whose voice directly penetrates our interior. When (and if) we finally encounter our phone-sex partner in real life, the effect is often precisely what Michel Chion called *désacousmatisation*:[32] the Other loses his spectral quality, he turns into an ordinary worldly being towards whom we can maintain a normal distance. In short, we pass from the spectral Real to reality, from the obscene ethereal *presence* of the Other to the Other who is simply an object of *representation*.

One of the tendencies in theorizing cyberspace is to conceive cybersex as the ultimate phenomenon in the chain whose key link is Kierkegaard, his relationship with Regina: just as Kierkegaard rejected the actual proximity of the Other (the beloved woman) and advocated loneliness as the only authentic mode of relating to a love object, cybersex also involves the nullification of the 'real-life' object, and draws erotic energy from this very nullification – the moment I encounter my cybersex partner(s) in real life is the moment of *desublimation*, the moment of the return to vulgar 'reality'. Convincing as it may sound, this parallel is deeply misleading: the status of my cyberspace sexual partner is *not* that of Kierkegaard's Regina. Regina was the void to which Kierkegaard addressed his words, a kind of *'vacuole' weaved by the texture of his speech*, while my cyberspace sexual partner is, on the contrary, *over-present*, bombarding me with the torrential flow of images and explicit statements of her (or his) most secret fantasies. Or, to put it in another way: Kierkegaard's Regina is the cut of the Real, the traumatic obstacle which again and again unsettles the smooth run of my self-satisfying erotic imagination, while cyberspace presents its exact

32   See Michel Chion, *La Voix au cinéma*, Paris: Cahiers du cinéma, 1982.

opposite, a frictionless flow of images and messages – when I am immersed in it, I, as it were, return to a symbiotic relationship with an Other in which the deluge of semblances seems to abolish the dimension of the Real.

In a recent interview, Bill Gates celebrated cyberspace as opening up the prospect of what he called 'friction-free capitalism' – this expression encapsulates perfectly the social fantasy which underlies the ideology of cyberspace capitalism: the fantasy of a wholly transparent, ethereal medium of exchange in which the last trace of material inertia vanishes. The crucial point not to be missed here is that the 'friction' we get rid of in the fantasy of 'friction-free capitalism' does not refer only to the reality of material obstacles which sustain any exchange process but, above all, to the Real of the traumatic social antagonisms, power relations, and so on, which brand the space of social exchange with a pathological twist. In his *Grundrisse* manuscript, Marx pointed out how the very material mechanism of a nineteenth-century industrial production site directly materializes the capitalist relationship of domination (the worker as a mere appendix subordinated to the machinery which is owned by the capitalist); *mutatis mutandis*, the same goes for cyberspace: in the social conditions of late capitalism, the very materiality of cyberspace automatically generates the illusory abstract space of 'friction-free' exchange in which the particularity of the participants' social position is obliterated.

The easiest way to discern the set of social relations which overdetermine the mode of operation of cyberspace is to focus on the predominant 'spontaneous ideology of cyberspace', the so-called *cyberevolutionism* which relies on the notion of cyberspace (or World Wide Web) as a self-evolving 'natural' organism.[33] Crucial here is the blurring of the distinction between 'culture' and 'nature': the obverse of the 'naturalization of culture' (market, society, etc., as living organisms) is the 'culturalization of nature' (life itself is conceived as a set of self-reproducing items as information – 'genes are

---

33   I draw here on Tiziana Terranova, 'Digital Darwin', *New Formations* 29 (Summer 1996), London: Lawrence & Wishart.

memes'). This new notion of Life is thus neutral with respect to the distinction between natural and cultural or 'artificial' processes – both Earth (as Gaia) and global market appear as gigantic self-regulated living systems whose basic structure is defined in terms of the process of coding and decoding, of passing on information, and so on. The reference to the World Wide Web as a living organism is often evoked in contexts which may seem liberating: say, against the state censorship of Internet. This very demonization of the State, however, is thoroughly ambiguous, since it is predominantly appropriated by right-wing populist discourse and/or market liberalism: its main targets are the state interventions which try to maintain a kind of minimal social balance and security – the title of Michael Rothschild's book (*Bioeconomics: The Inevitability of Capitalism*) is indicative here. So – while cyberspace ideologists can dream about the next step of evolution in which we will no longer be mechanically interacting 'Cartesian' individuals, in which each 'person' will cut their substantial link to their individual body and conceive themselves as part of the new holistic Mind which lives and acts through him or her, what is obfuscated in such direct 'naturalization' of the World Wide Web or market is the set of power relations – political decisions, institutional conditions – within which 'organisms' like the Internet (or the market or capitalism . . .) can only thrive.[34]

Saving the appearance

This brings us back to the problem of the Master-Signifier: a Master-Signifier is always virtual in the sense of involving some structural ambiguity. In *The X Files*, the relationship between the extraterrestrials interfering with our lives and the mysterious government agency which knows about it is utterly ambiguous: who actually pulls the strings, government or extraterrestrials? Is the government using the extraterrestrials to increase its hold over the

34   The other foreclosure, correlative to that of social antagonism, is that of sexual difference. cyberevolutionism strives to replace sexual reproduction with models of direct cloning (of the self-reproducing genes).

population, or is it passively collaborating in order to prevent panic, since it is helpless and held in check by them? The point is that the situation has to remain open, undecidable: if the gaps were to be filled in here, if we were to learn the true state of things, the entire symbolic universe of *The X Files* would disintegrate. And it is crucial that this ambiguity turns around the problem of power and impotence: symbolic authority is virtual, which means that it functions as a threat which should never be put to the test – one can never be sure if one's father (on whose symbolic authority one relies) is truly so powerful or just an impostor. Symbolic power is thus effective only as virtual, as a promise or threat of its full display. This, perhaps, also provides the ultimate resort of the figure of 'the man who knows too much': he knows too much about authority – that is, the secret he knows is that authority is an imposture, that Power is really impotent, helpless. What the emptiness of the Master-Signifier conceals is thus the inconsistency of its content (its signified): the shark in Spielberg's *Jaws* functions as a symbol only in so far as its fascinating presence obfuscates the inconsistent multitude of its possible meanings (is it a symbol of the Third World threat to America? A symbol of unbridled capitalist exploitation? and so on) – were we to obtain a clear answer, the effect would be lost. And again, this virtual status of the Master-Signifier is what gets lost in cyberspace, with its tendency to 'fill in the gaps'.

The suspension of the Master, which reveals impotence, in no way gives rise to liberating effects: the knowledge that 'the Other doesn't exist' (that the Master is impotent, that Power is an imposture) imposes on the subject an even more radical servitude than the traditional subordination to the full authority of the Master. In his analysis of Paul Claudel's Coufontaine trilogy, Lacan elaborates the distinction between classical and modern tragedy: classical tragedy is the tragedy of Destiny, of the subject guilty without his active participation; guilt is inscribed into his very position in the symbolic network of Destiny. The modern, post-Christian tragedy, on the contrary, takes place in a universe in which 'God is dead' – that is, our lives are no longer preordained by the cosmic frame of Destiny. Lacan's point here is that this absence of Destiny, of the symbolic frame which determines our guilt in advance, not only does not make us free, but imposes on us an even more radical tragic guilt – as he puts it, the subject's tragic fate hinges on the fact that he becomes the hostage of the Word.[35]

The supreme example of this new tragic predicament is the fate of the sacrificed Stalinist Communist: this example makes it clear how – to put it succinctly – the subject is called upon to sacrifice himself *in order to save the appearance* (of the Master's or Leader's omnipotence and knowledge) – to prevent the Master's impotence from becoming visible to all the world. When, in the post-classical universe, no one 'really believes' in the universal Destiny inherent in the cosmic Order (be it Christian Faith or Communism) – when, to put it in Hegelese, Faith loses its substantial weight – it becomes crucial to *maintain the appearance* of Faith. When a true believer in Stalinist Communism is asked to confess his deviancy, or even his treason, the underlying line of argumentation is: 'We all know that the big Other doesn't exist (that our Leader is not perfect, that we have made a lot of mistakes, that there are no iron laws of History, that the Necessity of Progress towards Communism is not as inexorable as we pretend), but to acknowledge this would add up to a total catastrophe. The only way to save the appearance – to safeguard the Party and its Leader as historical Reason incarnate, to avoid imputing to the Leader and the Party the responsibility for our evident failures – is for *you* to assume the responsibility for our failures – that is to say, to confess your guilt.' This underlying logic of the Stalinist show trials thus bears direct witness to the fact that Communism is no longer a substantial Faith, but a modern Faith relying on the subject's readiness to sacrifice himself and to assume guilt in order to keep hidden the fact that 'the father is humiliated', that the Leader is impotent. The subject is not called upon to sacrifice himself for the Truth of the Faith: he is called upon to sacrifice himself precisely so that the fact that 'the big Other doesn't exist' will continue to be invisible, so that the idealized figure of the Leader embodying the big Other will remain intact and unblemished.

In this sense, the subject is 'the hostage of the Word': 'Word' stands

35   See Lacan, *Le Séminaire, livre VIII: Le transfert.*

here for the ideological doctrine which has lost its substantial bearings, it has the status of a pure semblance, but which – precisely as such, as a pure semblance – is essential. The subject is blackmailed and, as it were, cornered by being told that if he doesn't forget about his individual rights, his innocence, or even his honour and dignity, and confess, the Word which guarantees the semblance of Meaning will disintegrate. In other words, he is asked to sacrifice himself, the innermost kernel of his being – not for the True Cause, but for a pure semblance. Furthermore, this retreat of substantial Destiny, of the symbolic Law regulating our existence, also coincides with the shift from *symbolic Law* to *superego*: the agent who imposes on the subject the sacrifice which should 'save the appearance' (say, the confession at the show trial 'needed by the Party to forge its unity and mobilize its members') is clearly a superego figure amassing the *jouissance* of which the subject is deprived: the appearance of Destiny to which this subject refers (in the case of Stalinism, as the 'inexorable progress towards Communism') is a mask concealing the *jouissance* of the subject who reserves for himself the position of the object-instrument of the big Other.[36]

What can meteorology teach us about racism?

What, then, is the nature of the difference between the narrativist post-modernism and Lacan? Perhaps the best way to approach it is via the gap which separates the modern universe of science from traditional knowledge: for Lacan, modern science is *not* just another local narrative grounded in its specific pragmatic conditions, since it does relate to the (mathematical) Real beneath the symbolic universe.

Let us recall the difference between modern satellite meteorology and

36 'So, when the God of destiny is dead, instead of assuming this death and fulfilling its mourning, one substitutes oneself to it and *perpetuates* with regard to the other a will-to-castration, conferring on this will the figure of destiny in order to mask one's own maligned *Jouissance*' (Philippe Julien, *L'Étrange jouissance du prochain,* Paris: Seuil, 1995, p. 137). Do not these lines, written to illustrate the position of Father Badillon in Claudel's *L'otage,* perfectly fit the position of the Stalinist party executioner?

the traditional wisdom about the weather, which 'thinks locally'. Modern meteorology assumes a kind of metalanguage view on the entire atmosphere of the Earth as a global and self-enclosed mechanism, while traditional meteorology involves a particular viewpoint within a finite horizon: out of some Beyond which, by definition, remains beyond our grasp, clouds and winds arrive, and all one can do is formulate the rules of their emergence and disappearance in a series of 'wisdoms' ('If it rains on the first of May, beware of drought in August', etc.). The crucial point is that 'meaning' can emerge only within such a finite horizon: weather phenomena can be experienced and conceived as 'meaningful' only in so far as there is a Beyond out of which these phenomena emerge, following laws which are not directly natural laws – the very lack of natural laws directly connecting actual weather here and the mysterious Beyond sets in motion the search for 'meaningful' coincidences and correlations. The paradox is that although this traditional 'closed' universe confronts us with unpredictable catastrophes which seem to emerge 'out of nowhere', it none the less provides a sense of ontological 'safety', of dwelling within a self-enclosed finite circle of meaning where things (natural phenomena) in a way 'speak to us', address us.

This traditional closed universe is thus in a sense *more 'open'* than the universe of science: it implies the gateway into the indefinite Beyond, while the direct global model of modern science is effectively 'closed' – that is to say, it allows for no Beyond. The universe of modern science, in its very 'meaninglessness', involves the gesture of 'traversing the fantasy', of abolishing the dark spot, the domain of the Unexplained which harbours fantasies and thus guarantees Meaning: instead, we get the meaningless mechanism. This is why, for Heidegger, modern science stands for metaphysical 'danger': it poses a threat to the universe of meaning. There is no meaning without some dark spot, without some forbidden/ impenetrable domain into which we project fantasies which guarantee our horizon of meaning. Perhaps this very growing disenchantment with our actual social world accounts for the fascination exerted by cyberspace: it is as if in it we again encounter a Limit beyond which the mysterious domain of phantasmic Otherness opens up, as if the screen of the interface is today's version of the blank, of the unknown region in which we can locate our own Shangri-las or the kingdoms of *She*.

Paradigmatic here are the last chapters of Edgar Allan Poe's *Gordon Pym*, which stage the phantasmic scenario of crossing the threshold into the pure Otherness of the Antarctic. The last human settlement prior to this threshold is a native village on an island with savages so black that even their teeth are black; significantly, what one encounters on this island is also the ultimate Signifier (a gigantic hieroglyph inscribed into the very shape of the mountain chain). Savage and corrupt as they are, the black men cannot be bribed into accompanying the white explorers further south: they are scared to death by the very notion of entering this prohibited domain. When the explorers finally enter this domain, the ice-cold polar snowscape gradually and mysteriously turns into its opposite, a domain of thick, warm and opaque whiteness . . . in short, the incestuous domain of primordial Milk. What we get here is another version of the kingdom of Tarzan or *She*: in Rider Haggard's *She*, Freud's notorious claim that feminine sexuality is a 'dark continent' is realized in a literal way: She-who-must-be-obeyed, this Master beyond Law, the possessor of the Secret of Life itself, is a white woman ruling in the midst of Africa, the dark continent. This figure of She, of a woman who exists (in the unexplored Beyond), is the necessary phantasmic support of the patriarchal universe. With the advent of modern science, this Beyond is abolished, there is no longer a 'dark continent' which generates a Secret – consequently, Meaning is also lost, since the field of Meaning is by definition sustained by an impenetrable dark spot at its very heart.

The very process of colonization thus produces the excess which resists it: does not the mystery of Shangri-la (or of Tarzan's kingdom, or of the kingdom of *She*, or . . .) lie precisely in the fact that we are dealing with the domain which *has not yet been colonized*, with the imagined radical Otherness which forever eludes the colonizer's grasp? Here, however, we encounter another key paradox. This motif of *She* relies on one of the key mythical narratives of colonialism: after white explorers transgress a certain frontier which is taboo even for the most primitive and cruel aborigines, and enter the very 'heart of darkness', what they encounter there, in this purely phantasmic Beyond, is again the rule of a mysterious White Man, the pre-Oedipal father, the absolute Master. The structure here is that of a Moebius band – at the very heart of Otherness, we encounter the other side of the Same, of our own structure of masterhood.

In his formidable *Fear in the Occident*, Jean Delumeau draws attention to the unerring succession of attitudes in a medieval city infested by plague: first, people ignore it and behave as if nothing terrible is really going on; then they withdraw into privacy, avoiding contact with each other; then they resort to religious fervour, staging processions, confessing their sins, and so on; then they say to themselves, 'What the hell, let's enjoy it while it lasts!', and indulge passionately in orgies of sex, eating, drinking and dancing; finally, they return to life as usual, and again behave as if nothing terrible is going on.[37] However, this second 'life as usual' does not occupy the same structural role as the first: it is, as it were, located on the other side of the Moebius band, since it no longer signals the desperate attempt to ignore the reality of plague, but, rather, its exact opposite: resigned acceptance of it . . . Does not the same go for the gradual replacement of (sexually, racially . . .) aggressive with more 'correct' expressions, like the chains *nigger – Negro – black – African-American* or *crippled – disabled – bodily challenged*? This replacement functions as a metaphorical substitution which potentially proliferates and enhances the very (racist, etc.) effect it tries to banish, adding insult to injury. In analogy to Delumeau, one should therefore claim that the only way actually to abolish the hatred-effect is, paradoxically, to create the circumstances in which one can *return to the first link in the chain* and use it in a non-aggressive way – like following the patterns of 'life as usual' the second time in the case of plague. That is to say: as long as the expression 'crippled' contains a surplus, an indelible mark, of aggressivity, this surplus will not only be more or less automatically transferred on to any of its 'correct' metaphorical

37   See Jean Delumeau, *La Peur en Occident,* Paris: Albin Michel, 1976.

substitutes, it will even be enhanced by dint of this substitution. The strategy of returning to the first link, of course, is risky; however, the moment it is fully accepted by the group targeted by it, it definitely can work. When radical African-Americans call each other 'niggers', it is wrong to dismiss this strategy as a mere ironic identification with the aggressor; rather, the point is that it functions as an autonomous act of dismissing the aggressive sting.[38]

A further thing to note about the white Master who rules in this phantasmic domain of radical Otherness is that this figure is split into two opposites: either the horrifying embodiment of 'diabolical Evil' who knows the secret of *jouissance* and, consequently, terrorizes and tortures his subjects (from Conrad's *Heart of Darkness* and *Lord Jim* to the feminine version, Rider Haggard's *She*) or the saint who rules his kingdom as a benevolent theocratic despot (Shangri-la in *Lost Horizon*). The point, of course, lies in the 'speculative identity' of these two figures: the diabolically evil Master is 'in himself or for us' *the same* as the saintly sage-ruler; their difference is purely formal, it concerns only the shift in the perspective of the observer. (Or, to put it in Schelling's terms, the saintly wise ruler is, in the mode of potentiality, what the evil Master is in the mode of actuality, since 'the same principle carries and holds us in its ineffectiveness which would consume and destroy us in its effectiveness'.)[39] What the hundreds-of-years-old monk who runs Shangri-la, and Kurtz from *Heart of Darkness*, share is that they have both cut their links with common human considerations and entered the domain 'between

38   In the course of my military service, I became very friendly with an Albanian soldier. As is well known, Albanians are very sensitive to sexual insults which refer to their closest family members (mother, sister); I was effectively accepted by my Albanian friend when we left behind the superficial game of politeness and respect, and greeted each other with formalized insults. So when we met each other in the morning, I usually greeted him with: 'I'll screw your mother!', to which he regularly responded: 'Go ahead, you're welcome – after I've finished with your sister!' The interesting thing was how soon this exchange lost its openly obscene or ironic character, and became formalized: after only a couple of weeks, the two of us no longer bothered with the whole sentence; in the morning, upon seeing him, I just nodded my head and said 'Mother!', to which he simply responded 'Sister!'.

39   F.W.J. Schelling, *Die Weltalter Fragments. In den Urfassungen von 1811 und 1813,* ed. Manfred Schroeter, Munich: Biederstem, 1946 (1979 edn), p. 105.

the two deaths'. As such, Kurtz is the Institution in all its phantasmic purity: his very excess merely realizes, brings to an end, the inherent logic of the Institution (the Company and its colonization of the wilderness of Congo).[40] This inherent logic is concealed in the 'normal' functioning of the Institution: the very figure which literally realizes the logic of the Institution is, in a properly Hegelian way, perceived as an unbearable excess which has to be finished off.

This, however, in no way implies that today's racism is a kind of remainder of the traditional open/closed universe, with its structure of the Limit and its phantasmic Beyond (the place of what one usually refers to as 'enchantment'), which gets lost in the modern 'disenchanted' universe. Today's racism is strictly (post)modern; it is a reaction to the 'disenchantment' inflicted by the new phase of global capitalism. One of the commonplaces of the contemporary 'post-ideological' attitude is that today, we have more or less outgrown divisive political fictions (of class struggle, etc.) and reached political maturity, which enables us to focus on real problems (ecology, economic growth . . .) relieved of their ideological ballast – however, it is as if today, when the dominant attitude defines the terrain of the struggle as that of the Real ('real problems' versus 'ideological chimeras'), the very foreclosed political, as it were, *returns in the Real* – in the guise of racism, which grounds political differences in the (biological or social) Real of the race.[41] One could thus claim that what the 'post-ideological' attitude of the sober pragmatic approach to reality excludes as 'old ideological fictions' of class antagonism, as the domain of 'political passions' which no longer have any place in today's rational social administration, is the historical Real itself.

40   I owe this idea to Ed Cadava, Princeton University. In his cinema version of *Heart of Darkness* (*Apocalypse Now*), Francis Ford Coppola distorts the Kurtz figure by giving it a New Age twist: Coppola reads Kurtz as a Fisher King figure awaiting (and thus accepting) his death as a ritual which will lead to his subsequent regeneration.

41   Here I follow ideas developed by Jacques Rancière (in a private conversation). Such a gesture which draws the line of separation between 'real problems' and 'ideological chimeras' is, from Plato onwards, the very founding gesture of ideology: ideology is by definition self-referential – that is, it always establishes itself by assuming a distance towards (what it denounces as) 'mere ideology'.

What, then, does all this tell us about cyberspace? Cyberspace, of course, is a thoroughly technological-scientific phenomenon; it develops the logic of modern meteorology to extremes: not only is there no place in it for the phantasmic screen, it even generates the screen itself by manipulating the Real of bytes. However, it is by no means accidental that *modern science, including meteorology, inherently relies on the interface screen*: in the modern scientific approach, processes are *simulated* on the screen, from the models of atomic subparticles, through the radar images of clouds in weather reports, up to the fascinating pictures of the surface of Mars and other planets (which are all manipulated by computer procedures – added coloration, etc. – in order to enhance their effect). The outcome of the suspension of the dark spot of Beyond in the universe of modern science is thus that 'global reality' with no impenetrable dark spot is something accessible only on screen: the abolition of the phantasmic screen which served as the gateway into the Beyond turns *the whole of reality* into something which 'exists only on screen', as a depthless surface. Or, to put it in ontological terms: the moment the function of the dark spot which keeps open the space for something for which there is no place in our reality is suspended, we lose our very 'sense of reality'.

The problem with today's social functioning of cyberspace is thus that it potentially fills in the gap, the distance between the subject's public symbolic identity and its phantasmic background: fantasies are increasingly immediately externalized in the public symbolic space; the sphere of intimacy is more and more directly socialized. The inherent violence of cybersex lies not in the potentially violent content of sexual fantasies played out on the screen, but in the very formal fact of seeing my innermost fantasies being directly imposed on me from without. A painful and disturbing scene from David Lynch's *Wild at Heart* (Willem Dafoe invading the private space of Laura Dern, touching her intimate parts, forcing her to say 'Fuck me!', and after she finally does so, replying 'No, thanks, I don't have time today, but on another occasion I would do it gladly')[42] perfectly

---

42   For a closer analysis of this scene, see Appendix I below.

illustrates the obscene violence of cybersex in which, although (or, rather, precisely because) 'nothing really happens in our bodily reality', the phantasmic intimate kernel of our being is laid bare in a much more direct way, making us totally vulnerable and helpless.

The prospect of the accomplished digitalization of all information (all books, movies, data . . . computerized and instantly available) promises the almost perfect materialization of the big Other: out there in the machine, 'everything will be written', a complete symbolic redoubling of reality will take place. This prospect of a perfect symbolic accountancy also augurs a new type of catastrophe in which a sudden disturbance in the digital network (an extra effective virus, say) erases the computerized 'big Other', leaving the external 'real reality' intact. We thus arrive at the notion of a purely virtual catastrophe: although, in 'real life', nothing whatsoever happens, and things seem to follow their course, the catastrophe is total and complete, since 'reality' is all of a sudden deprived of its symbolic support . . . As is well known, all large armies are today more and more playing virtual war games, winning or losing battles on computer screens, battles which simulate every conceivable condition of 'real' war. So the question naturally crops up: if we have virtual sex, and so on, why not virtual warfare? Why shouldn't 'real' warfare be replaced by a gigantic virtual war which will be over without the majority of ordinary people being aware that there was any war at all, like the virtual catastrophe which will occur without any perceptible change in the 'real' universe? Perhaps, radical virtualization – the fact that the whole of reality will soon be 'digitalized', transcribed, redoubled in the 'big Other' of cyberspace – will somehow redeem 'real life', opening it up to a new perception, just as Hegel already had a presentiment that the end of art (as the 'sensible appearing of the Idea'), which occurs when the Idea withdraws from the sensible medium into its more direct conceptual expression, simultaneously liberates sensibility from the constraints of Idea?

APPENDICES

Appendix I

From the Sublime to the Ridiculous:
The Sexual Act in Cinema

In his essay 'Humour', Freud refers to the opposition between unconscious and superego in order to explain the difference between joke and humour, the two modalities of the comical: a joke is 'the contribution made to the comic by the unconscious', while humour is 'the contribution made to the comic through the agency of the superego'.[1] The connection between joke and unconscious seems easy to grasp: in a joke, a preconscious thought is given over for a moment to unconscious revision; how, however, are we to grasp the connection between humour and superego, this 'severe master' of the ego which is usually associated with the opposite features of cruel, sadistic repression and culpabilization?

The 'malevolent neutrality' of the superego consists in the impossible position of pure metalanguage, as if the subject can extract himself from his situation and observe himself from the outside. This split is the split between superego and ego: when the subject adopts this neutral position, his ego, with all its problems and emotions, is suddenly perceived as something petty and insignificant, *quantité négligeable* . . . Englishmen, who allegedly specialize in such an indifferent attitude towards one's own predicament, excel in the humour of 'understatement'; recall the scene from Hitchcock's *The Trouble with Harry* in which the old gentleman drags

1 'Humour', in *The Pelican Freud Library*, vol. 14: *Art and Literature*, Harmondsworth: Penguin, 1985, p. 432.

Harry's corpse along a forest path and encounters an elderly woman who kindly asks him 'What seems to be the trouble?'; over the corpse, they fix their first date. It is this distance which separates humour from jokes, or from what is simply funny. That is to say: in contrast to a person who becomes caught up in his mask and loses his distance from it (as in the story of the old man lying in the sun who, in order to get rid of the children running and shouting around him, tells them: 'Run to the other side of town – don't you know they're giving out free candies there?', and then, after some reflection, says to himself: 'What am I doing here? I want some free candies too!' and runs after them . . .), in humour, a person maintains the distance where one would not expect it – he acts as if something which we know very well exists, does *not* exist.

Therein lies the humour of Buñuel's *That Obscure Object of Desire*: the elderly lover (Fernando Rey) acts as if he does not notice that his beloved consists of two women (played by two actresses). According to the standard feminist reading, the poor man is so blinded by his phantasmic image of Woman that he is unable to take note of the fact that there are really two of them. However, one should oppose to this two other, perhaps more productive readings: (1) he *knows* there are really two women, yet he *acts* as if there is only one, since his fantasy determines his acts irrespective of his conscious knowledge. What we encounter here is the fundamental paradox of the Marxian notion of commodity fetishism: 'commodity fetishism' designates not a (bourgeois) theory of political economy but a series of presuppositions that determine the structure of the very 'real' economic practice of market exchange – in theory, a capitalist clings to utilitarian nominalism, yet in his own practice (of exchange) he follows 'theological whimsies' and acts as a speculative idealist . . . (2) What if there is truly only one woman, and the male subject simply projects on to her the dichotomous split between whore and faithful maternal wife which determines the male patriarchal perception of woman, so that, because of the phantasmic frame of ideological co-ordinates, one and the same 'real' woman is (mis)perceived as two?

Undoubtedly the greatest masters of humour in cinema (as opposed to the Marx Brothers' jokes) are the works of Monty Python.[2] An episode from their *Meaning of Life* takes place in a couple's apartment. Two men from the 'live organ transplants' business ring the bell and demand the husband's liver. The poor husband resists: they have the right to take his liver only in the event of his death; but the two men assure him that in any case he is not likely to survive the removal of his liver . . . The two men then set to work, dragging bloody organs out of the victim's viscera with cold indifference. The wife cannot stand the sight and leaves the room for the kitchen; one of the men follows her and demands her liver too. She refuses; however, a gentleman then steps out of the refrigerator and escorts her out of the kitchen on a promenade across the universe, singing about the billions of stars and planets, and their intelligent dispositions within the universe. After she realizes how small and insignificant her problem is compared to the universe, she gladly agrees to donate her liver . . . Is this scene not literally *Kantian*? Does it not evoke the Kantian notion of the sublime which emphasizes how the 'view of a countless multitude of worlds annihilates, as it were, my importance as an animal creature, which must give back to the planet (a mere speck in the universe) the matter from which it came, the matter which is for a little time provided with vital force'?[3]

The sentiment of the sublime, of course, arises from the gap between the nullity of man as natural being and the infinite power of his spiritual dimension. In the late-Victorian age, this mechanism accounted for the ideological impact of the tragic figure of the 'Elephant Man', as the subtitle of one of the books about him (*A Study in Human Dignity*) suggests: it was the very monstrous and nauseating distortion of his body which revealed the simple dignity of his inner life. And is not this same logic the crucial ingredient of the tremendous success of Stephen Hawking's *A Brief History of Time*? Would his ruminations about the fate of the universe, his endeavour to 'read the mind of God', remain so attractive to the public if

2   I draw here on Alenka Zupančič, 'The Logic of the Sublime', *The American Journal of Semiotics* 9: 2–3, 1992, pp. 51–68.

3   Immanuel Kant, *Critique of Practical Reason*, New York: Macmillan, 1956, p. 166.

it were not for the fact that they emanate from a crippled, paralysed body, communicating with the world only through the feeble movement of one finger and speaking with a machine-generated impersonal voice? Yet this same gap can also produce the effect of ridicule: 'Du sublime au ridicule, il n'y a qu'un pas!', says an Englishman emphatically. 'Oui, le pas de Calais', retorts a Frenchman acidly. Monty Python's *Meaning of Life* is a kind of English revenge on this joke: the film is simultaneously sublime and ridiculous – ridiculous in the mode of humour.

How does sex fit into all this? In so far as sex is that which disturbs, throws off the rails, it also calls for the position of an indifferent observer, in the eyes of whom it appears trifling and ridiculous. One need only remember the famous publicity photo of Hitchcock sneezing indifferently, while close to him Grace Kelly and Cary Grant are engaged in a passionate embrace . . . Another episode, about sex education, in Monty Python's *Meaning of Life*, expresses perfectly not only this impossible position of neutral distance towards one's own engagement, but also the fact that the superego is the injunction to enjoy. The teacher questions the pupils on how to arouse the vagina; caught in their ignorance, the embarrassed pupils avoid his gaze and stammer half-articulated answers, while the teacher reprimands them severely for not practising the subject at home. With his wife's assistance, he thereupon demonstrates to them the penetration of penis into vagina; bored by the subject, one of the schoolboys casts a furtive glance through the window, and the teacher asks him sarcastically: 'Would you be kind enough to tell us what is so attractive out there in the courtyard?'. . . The teacher's examination of the disinterested children is so uncanny precisely in that it exhibits, in broad daylight, the usually concealed truth about the 'normal' state of things: enjoyment is not an immediate spontaneous state, but is sustained by a superego imperative – as Lacan emphasized again and again, the ultimate content of the superego-injunction is 'Enjoy!'

Perhaps, the briefest way to render the superego paradox is the injunction 'Like it or not, enjoy yourself!' Take the proverbial father who works hard to organize a Sunday excursion and, after a series of postponements, tired of it all, shouts at his children: 'Now you'd better enjoy it!' On a holiday trip, it is quite common to feel the compulsion to enjoy; one 'must have fun' – one feels guilty if one doesn't enjoy it. (In the Eisenhower era of the 'happy' 50s', this compulsion was elevated to an everyday patriotic duty – or, as one of the White House aides put it: 'Not to be happy today is un-American.') The Japanese have perhaps found a unique way out of this deadlock of the superego: they bravely confront the paradox by directly organizing 'fun' as part of one's everyday duty, so that, when the official, organized fun activity is over, you are relieved of your duty and are finally free *really to have fun*, really to relax and enjoy . . . The impossible ideal would then be that of a perfect prostitution in which sexual satisfaction and business absolutely coincide: by doing it for money (in a wholly externalized way, without being subjectively engaged), I at the same time fulfil my superego duty to enjoy, so that when I am over with my business, I am finally really free, delivered of the pressure to earn money in terms of my livelihood, as well as the confines of the superego.

The gesture of bringing to light this paradox of enjoyment grounded in the superego injunction, so that freedom is ultimately not freedom to enjoy but freedom from enjoyment, is what allows us to insert Monty Python in the series of 'overconformist' authors who subvert the ruling ideology by taking it more literally than it is ready to take itself.[4] When Malebranche 'revealed the secret' (the perverted truth) of Christianity (it was not that Christ came down to Earth to deliver the people from sin, from the legacy of Adam's Fall; on the contrary, *Adam had to fall in order to enable Christ to come to earth and dispense salvation*), is his gesture not strictly analogous to Money Python's procedure? Does not Monty Python bring to light again and again the similar structural paradoxes and short circuits which underlie our desire?

Humour is thus one of the modes of defence against the dimension of the traumatic Real which pertains to the sexual act. Of course, in the good

4   For a more detailed discussion of this 'subversive overconformism', see Chapter 2 above.

old days of the Hayes Code, from the 1930s to the late 1950s, even an oblique reference to the sexual act was prohibited (in the bedroom, the beds of husband and wife had to be separated; when the marital couple was shown in the bedroom, they had to be dressed in full pyjamas . . .). Under these conditions of severe censorship, the only possibility was to use, in a reflective way, this very hole which signalled the absence (and thus, at another level, the presence) of the act. The supreme example of the comical use of this gap is found in Preston Sturges's *Miracle in Morgan Creek* – the true miracle is how this film passed through the censorship. Its story is organized around a hole, a central absence (what happened during the night when Betty Hutton went to the farewell party for the soldiers?) – the dénouement (the birth of sextuplets) clearly suggests a group orgy ('gang bang') with six men who were her companions that fateful night. The eclipse during the fateful night (from the moment Betty Hutton hits her head on the heavy lights, till the time early next morning when she wakes up in the car on her way back to her home town) is thus what Lacan calls *aphanisis*, the self-erasure of the subject when she approaches her fantasy too closely.[5] With the liberalization of the 1960s, when at least oblique references to the sexual act became admissible, we obtain three modes of this reference: comicality, perversion, pathos. These three modes fit the three types of object found in the schema from Lacan's seminar *Encore* reproduced opposite.[6]

Let us first explain the schema itself. The three angles of the triangle stand for the three fundamental dimensions which, according to Lacan, structure the human universe: the Real (the 'hard', traumatic reality which resists symbolization), the Symbolic (the field of language, of symbolic structure and communication), and the Imaginary (the domain of images

5   The pure absence, the hole at the place of the sexual act, is also found in Stalinist cinema. Incidentally, we find an exemplary case of the same attitude even in Hollywood, in *North Star* (written by Lillian Hellman): when the happy kolkhoz couple (Anne Baxter and Farley Granger) dream about their future together, they see themselves surrounded by a throng of grandchildren, *not* children – the first generation of the descendancy is passed over in silence, censored, since it none the less implies sex between the parents!

6   See Jacques Lacan, *Le Séminaire, livre XX: Encore,* Paris: Éditions du Seuil, 1975.

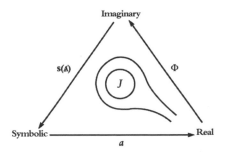

with which we identify, and which capture our attention). 'J' in the middle of the triangle designates *Jouissance*, the abyss of traumatic/excessive enjoyment which threatens to swallow us up, and towards which the subject desperately endeavours to maintain a proper distance (like the hero in Poe's 'A Descent into the Maelstrom', who barely succeeds in not being dragged into the maelstrom). The three objects on the sides of the triangle specify the three ways in which to 'domesticate' or 'normalize' this horrible Thing in the middle, to perceive it in a way which is no longer directly threatening: $S(\cancel{A})$ is the signifier of the barred Other (*Autre*), and marks the inherent inconsistency of the symbolic order, the fact that there is something (*jouissance*) which resists symbolization and causes gaps and ruptures in the symbolic order; *a*, the Lacanian *objet petit a*, is the partial object which sets in motion the metonymic movement of desire (nose, feet, hair . . . in perversion); the capital Phi is the fascinating image which represents the impossible Thing (the *femme fatale* in the *noir* universe, for example).[7]

7   The same triad of Phi, *a* and $S(\cancel{A})$ is clearly discernible in the three cinema hits of summer 1996 (*Twister, Independence Day, Mission Impossible*); in each, an object gives body to the dimension of the Real. The vortex of the tornado in *Twister* is obviously Phi, the horrifying object which stands for the real Thing. The other two cases, albeit less obvious, are perhaps more interesting. In *Independence Day*, contact with the invading aliens is established by a *virus* planted in their computer. Does not a computer virus – a foreign intruder, a parasite which renders the computer inoperative, an 'organ without a body' which causes the penetrated body to 'run amok' and to function inconsistently – exemplify the Real in

The matrix of these objects accounts for the three modes of depicting the sexual act: comicality, perversion, pathetic ecstasy. In the comic mode, the gap which separates the sexual act from our everyday social interaction is rendered palpable; in perversion, the focus is displaced on to a partial object which acts as a stand-in for the impossible-unrepresentable act itself (for Lacan, the ultimate example of such a partial object is *the gaze itself*: what ultimately fascinates the pervert is the gaze transfixed by some traumatic Thing which can never be rendered present, like the stare of Medusa's head); finally, one can endeavour to erect a fascinating image destined to render present the pathos of the act.

So let us, for a brief moment, return to comicality. The sexual act and the comical: it seems that these two notions exclude themselves radically – does not the sexual act stand for the moment of the utmost intimate engagement, for the point towards which the participating subject can

---

the domain of cyberspace, the Real *qua* S($\mathbb{A}$); that is to say, is not the computer virus the ultimate figure of the *signifier of the Other's (computer's) inconsistency*, the signifier on account of whose intervention the cyberspace big Other (the software rules) loses its consistency? Symptomatic here is the very term 'virus', which stands for the ultimate threat in cyberspace as well as in 'real life' (from the ebola virus to AIDS).

DePalma's *Mission Impossible* is emblematic of the new material sensibility of today's cinema: on the one hand the ultra-complex plot, with its double and triple reversals (the very agent who is supposed to unmask the plot and solve the problem is the real traitor), with a multitude of technological gadgets (glasses which make the subject's view directly transmissive, etc.); on the other hand, strictly correlative to this overcomplex plot, the accentuated enjoyment in material texture – the presence of smooth surfaces where every detail of bodily humanity or animality can be catastrophic (like the unexpected rat in the air vent or the tiny bead of sweat in the famous CIA burglary scene) – that is to say, a kind of hyperrealistic texture where the material objects are deprived of the vulgar materiality of bad smells and corruption, yet at the same time overpresent in their clean, smoothly functioning ethereal modality. The rat in the air vent and the bead of sweat are not ordinary bodies but, precisely, *objet petit a*, a kind of sublime remainder/excrement of the very reduction of the vulgar body to the smoothly functioning machine. The tiny bead of sweat which falls from Cruise's head when he hangs from the ceiling of the CIA's ultra-secret computer room, and threatens to expose his presence to detectors if it touches the floor, is no longer an ordinary bodily excrement but a kind of ethereal materialized sign of presence, absolutely clean in its glasslike transparence. (In contrast to this spectral bodily presence, the body of the CIA computer specialist who throws up and sweats is an ordinary dirty material body.)

never assume the attitude of an ironic external observer? For that very reason, however, the sexual act cannot but appear at least minimally ridiculous to those who are not directly engaged in it; the comical effect arises out of the very discord between the intensity of the act and the indifferent calm of everyday life. To the external 'sober' glance, there is something irreducibly funny (stupid, excessive) in the sexual act – it is impossible not to recall here the unforgettable Earl of Chesterfield's dismissal of the sexual act: 'The pleasure is momentary, the position ridiculous and the expense damnable.'[8]

The sexual act in its ecstatic dimension is thus properly *unrepresentable.* It is not simply a question of a pure ecstasy beyond rules which can never be captured by an external, disinterested gaze. The encounter between (symbolic) rules and pathos is by definition a failed one: not only does following the rules never guarantee the desired effect; sometimes the opposite procedure, a direct surrender to ecstasy, is even more catastrophic. Any good sex manual tells us that in the case of impotence, the worst thing a man can do is to follow the injunction 'Forget all the rules and just relax! Let yourself go!'; far more effective is to approach it in a purely instrumental way, to treat it as a difficult task to be performed, and to discuss it from a faked disinterested distance, even put it down on paper as a kind of strategic battle plan (Shall I first lick you down there? How many fingers should I put in? What will you do with your mouth and fingers during this time? ...) – then, all of a sudden, we might find ourselves engaged, transported ... The 'real' dimension lies in this radical undecidability: following the rules *may* ruin the charm, yet it may also enhance

8   Milan Kundera effects a similar inversion from pathetic sublime to ridiculous. Already in his first novel, *The Joke,* the love of the narrator's youth, now a mature woman, wants to commit suicide, yet she grabs the wrong bottle, so that instead of the intended toxic pills she swallows a strong laxative – all that results from her pathetic act is that she has to run for the lavatory ... In his latest novel, *La Lenteur,* a biologist from the Czech Republic who participates at an international symposium in France after the breakdown of Socialism wants to introduce his intervention with a brief recall of totalitarian horrors; however, the pathos of his remarks makes him forget to deliver his scientific paper – he steps down from the podium after the applause which follows his introductory political remarks in praise of freedom ...

it; giving ourselves over to ecstasy *may* work, yet it may also make the thing ridiculous. In other words, the point is not that the sexual act is a kind of Kantian thing-in-itself beyond representations, but that it is always-already split from within. In other words, the 'comical' is in a way the sexual act 'as such', 'in itself', in so far as there is no 'proper' way to do it, in so far as the way we do it is by definition always a matter of learning, of rules that we imitate from others. So my point is that the split between the sexual act and its representation affects this act itself – which is why it is always possible that this act, all of a sudden, also appears ridiculous to those who perform it . . .

The ultimate proof of this unrepresentability is provided precisely by pornography, which pretends to 'show everything'; the price it pays for this attempt is the relationship of 'complementarity' (in the quantum physics meaning of the term) between the narrative and the sexual act: the congruence between the filmic narrative (the unfolding of the story) and the direct display of the sexual act is structurally impossible: if we choose one, we necessarily lose the other. The next paradox of pornography, following logically from this 'complementarity' between narrative and act, is that this genre, which is supposed to depict the most spontaneous of all human activities, is probably also the most codified, down to the most intimate details: the face of the actress during intercourse, for example, allows for four codified expressions: (1) indifference, signalled by ignorant, bored staring into space, chewing gum, yawning . . .; (2) the 'instrumental' attitude, as if the subject is in the midst of a hard task which demands high concentration: eyes turned down, towards the region where things are happening, the tightened lips signalling concentrated effort . . .; (3) the provocative stare into the eyes of the male partner, whose message is: 'Give me more! Is this all you can do?'; (4) ecstatic rapture, with half-closed eyes. Incidentally, do not these four expressions correspond to the four discourses articulated by Lacan: is not the first, indifferent attitude that of the Master? Does not the second, 'instrumental' attitude signal the discourse of the University embodied in technical knowledge, *savoir-faire*? Is not the third attitude that of the hysterical provocation and defiance of the Master? And, finally, does not the fourth position of ecstatic rapture stand for what Lacan calls 'subjective destitution', identification with the object-cause of desire characteristic of the position of the analyst?

The antagonism which is the most difficult to sustain in pornography is that it presents the 'unity of opposites' at its most radical: on the one hand, pornography involves the total externalization of the most intimate experience of pleasure (doing it for money in front of the camera); on the other, pornography is, on account of its very 'shamelessness', probably the most utopian of all genres: it is properly 'Edenic' in so far as it involves the fragile and temporary suspension of the barrier that separates the intimate/private from the public.[9] For this reason, the pornographic position is untenable: it cannot last too long, since it relies on a kind of magic suspension of the rules of shame which constitute our social link – a properly utopian universe where the intimate can be made public, where people can copulate in front of others . . .

Two key features of pornography are repetition and look. First there is the urge to repeat the same scene again and again, as if to convince ourselves that this impossible suspension of the Other regulating our (social) reality 'is really out there'. Furthermore, the picture or scene we are looking at must openly 'return the gaze' – therein lies its 'shamelessness'. This is why one is ashamed to look at it directly – one avoids the gaze emanating from the pornographic scene; it is this gaze which makes the scene obscene and shameless, in contrast to proto-medical close-ups of sexual organs. The zero-level pornographic picture is that of a woman displaying her genitals *and* defiantly returning the gaze: what she displays is ultimately her lack, 'castration', like the castrato Farinelli (in Corbiau's film), 'shamelessly' looking into the public who, ashamed, avoid his gaze – it is the spectator, not the object, who feels ashamed . . . (Do we not encounter the same phenomenon in the everyday scene of a crippled or dirty homeless person who is amused by *our* uneasiness in his presence, and shamelessly stares back while *we* are ashamed and avoid his gaze?)

9   For this point I am indebted to James McFarland, Princeton University.

The proto-pornographic scene thus seems to take place in a kind of curved space: the copulating couple bend in order to make sexual organs and zones visible to the gaze of the camera, so that we sometimes obtain a truly Cubist anamorphic condensation of multiple perspectives (the woman looks into the camera and simultaneously curves her hips and spreads her legs, so that her sex is also visible). The camera's eye here is the object-cause which curves the space, the third intruder which 'spoils the game' (the 'natural' sexual act in which partners are directly immersed in each other). The illusion, of course, is that without this intruder one would obtain 'full sex': one way to read Lacan's 'il n'y a pas de rapport sexuel' is that this very intruder who seems to spoil the game *effectively crystallizes its enjoyment* – what one would have without this intruder is a flat scene bereft of *jouissance*.

The true enigma of pornographic sexuality lies in the fact that the camera not only does not spoil *jouissance*, but enables it: the very elementary structure of sexuality has to comprise a kind of opening towards the intruding Third, towards an empty place which can be filled in by the gaze of the spectator (or camera) witnessing the act. This elementary pornographic scene (a woman, twisted in an anamorphic way, displaying her sex to the camera as well as looking at it) also confronts the spectator with (what Lacan calls) the split between eye and gaze at its purest: the actress or model staring at the spectator stands for the eye, while the open hole of the vagina stands for the traumatic gaze – that is to say, it is from this gaping hole that the scene the spectator is witnessing *returns the gaze* to him. The gaze is thus not where one would expect it (in the eyes staring at us from the picture) but in the traumatic object/hole which transfixes our look and concerns us most intensely – the model's eyes staring at us here are, rather, to remind us: 'You see, I'm watching you observing my gaze . . .'

The lesson of pornography is thus more important than it may appear: it concerns the way in which *jouissance* is torn between the Symbolic and the Real. On the one hand, *jouissance* is 'private', the kernel which resists public disclosure (look how embarrassing it is to us when our intimate modes of enjoyment, private tics, etc., are publicly disclosed); on the other hand, however, *jouissance* 'counts' only as registered by the big Other; it tends in itself towards this inscription (from public boasting to a confession to one's closest friend). The discord between the two extremes is irreducible: between the In-itself of the purely 'private pleasure' excluded from the public gaze and the For-itself of a wholly externalized sex, of a sex openly staged for the public gaze – there is always 'something missing' in the first one, while the second one is always experienced as 'faked'. This inherent reference to the Other on account of which 'there is no Don Giovanni without Leporello' (Don Giovanni obviously rates the inscription of his conquests into Leporello's register higher than the pleasure provided by the conquests themselves) is the theme of a low-class joke on a poor peasant who, after enduring a shipwreck, finds himself on a desert island with Cindy Crawford. After having sex with her, she asks him if he is fully satisfied; his answer is yes, but none the less he still has a small request to make his satisfaction complete – could she dress herself up as his best friend, put on trousers and paint a moustache on her face? In response to her surprised reaction and suspicion that the poor peasant is a hidden pervert, he comforts her that this is not the point at all, as she will immediately see . . . So, after she fulfils his request, he approaches her, elbows her in the ribs and tells her, with the obscene smile of male complicity: 'You know what just happened to me? I had sex with Cindy Crawford!'. This Third, which is always present as the witness, belies the ideal of hedonism – that is, it introduces the moment of reflexivity on account of which unspoiled innocent private pleasure is never possible: sex is always minimally 'exhibitionist', it relies on the gaze of an Other.

This tension between the Symbolic and the Real is best exemplified by the paradoxical effects of the well-known 'politically correct' endeavour to formalize the rules of sexual interplay: prior to each further step, the man should ask the woman for explicit permission ('May I unbutton your blouse?', etc.). The problem here is double. First, as today's sex psychologists tell us repeatedly, even before a couple explicitly state their intention to go to bed together, everything has already been decided at the level of innuendos, body language, and the exchange of glances, so that the explicit formulation of the rules is in a way *superfluous*. For that reason, far from clarifying the situation, such a procedure of preceding each step by explicitly asking for permission introduces a moment of radical ambiguity; it confronts the subject with the abyss of the Other's desire ('Why is he asking me that? Didn't I already give him a proper signal?'). On account of this ambiguity, the explicit formulation of rules opens up a new space for aggressivity – for much more refined modes of humiliating the partner; imagine a man who, after asking his feminine partner 'May I unbutton your blouse?' and effectively doing it, asks her 'May I now button up your blouse again?' – a cruel act of rejection after 'inspecting the merchandise', masked as politeness . . . What we encounter here, once again, is the structure of the failed encounter which is constitutive of the symbolic order: either the message (the permission to go further) is implicit, and as such always prone to misunderstanding, or the very attempt to render it explicit makes it again radically ambiguous.

Another way to put it is to say that in the pornographic utopia, the unity of bodily self-experience is magically dissolved, so that the spectator perceives the bodies of the actors not as unified totalities but as a kind of vaguely co-ordinated agglomerate of partial objects – here the mouth, there a breast, over there the anus, close to it the vaginal opening . . . The effect of close-up shots and of the strangely twisted and contorted bodies of the actors is to deprive these bodies of their unity: a little like the body of a circus clown which the clown himself perceives as a composite of partial organs which he fails to co-ordinate completely, so that some parts of his body seem to lead their own separate lives (recall the standard stage number in which the clown raises his hand, but the upper part of the hand doesn't obey his will and continues to dangle loosely). This change of the body into a desubjectivized multitude of partial objects is accomplished when, for example, a woman is in bed with two men and does fellatio on one of them, not in the standard way, actively sucking his penis, but so that she lies flat on the bed and leans her head over the edge downwards into space – when the man is penetrating her, her mouth is above her eyes, the face is turned upside-down, and the effect is one of an uncanny change of the human face, the seat of subjectivity, into a kind of impersonal sucking machine being pumped by the man's penis. The other man is meanwhile working on her vagina, which is also elevated above her head and thus asserted as an autonomous centre of *jouissance* not subordinated to the head. The woman's body is thus transformed into a multitude of 'organs without a body', machines of *jouissance*, while the men working on it are also desubjectivized, instrumentalized, reduced to workers serving these different partial objects . . .[10]

Comicality, of course, can slide into perversion at any moment, in so far as the pervert attitude involves the 'instrumental' approach to sexuality – that is, performing 'it' from an external distance, as an externally imposed task, not just 'for the sake of it'. Perhaps the ultimate proof of how perversion necessarily lapses into the comical is provided by the last episode in Woody Allen's *Everything You Always Wanted To Know About Sex*, which answers the question 'What goes on within the body during the sexual act?': the inside of the body is presented as a complex company; in the head, managers observe outside reality through a periscope, as in a submarine, then give orders through megaphones to the lower parts of the body, all of it reminding the spectator of a factory under Stalinist Socialism: when a manager relays the order 'Erection to 45 per cent!', workers down there start to push gigantic pipes of blood into the penis, singing rhythmic songs to raise their spirits; the erection target is not met and everything is in chaos until the secret police discover a sabotage (a reactionary priest from the Conscience Department blocking the effort, since the intended intercourse was not with the wife). After the saboteur is arrested, and with renewed effort from the workers, the production target of 45 per cent is soon met . . .

One of the first explicit suggestions of the sexual act in Hollywood,

10   In so far as drive relates to desire as partial object to subject, this 'desubjectivization' involves the passage from desire to drive: desire aims at the subject, at the void which is the core of other's subjectivity; while drive does not take into account the whole person, just the partial object around which it circulates (shoes, anus . . .):

the seduction scene in Billy Wilder's *Some Like It Hot*, mixes comedy with perversion. On the yacht, Marilyn Monroe seduces Tony Curtis (the poor musician who pretends to be an impotent millionaire), while at the same time, in a nightclub on the land, the millionaire who is the true owner of the yacht tries to seduce Jack Lemmon (Tony Curtis's friend, dressed up as a girl) by means of a passionate tango . . . The perversion of the 'normal' ritual of seduction here is double: it is the woman who plays the active role, while the other man who actively seduces a woman is actually seducing another man dressed up as a woman.

Perversion is also a constant feature of sexual activity in Hitchcock's films. Recall the famous scene from *Vertigo*, in which Judy (Kim Novak) finally appears to Scottie (James Stewart), dressed up as the allegedly dead Madeleine. The first perverse feature here is the necrophiliac dimension of the scene: Scottie wants to sleep with a dead woman; Judy fascinates him as the living embodiment of the dead Madeleine. Furthermore, the very direction of the seduction process is inverted: instead of undressing his beloved, Scottie is dressing her up. The way Scottie casts anxious and simultaneously shy glances at the corridor from which the properly dressed Judy is supposed to emerge expresses the impatience of the lover waiting for his beloved to return naked from the bathroom. After Judy's return, Scottie is visibly disappointed because she has not done her hair properly; in his conversations with Truffaut, Hitchcock himself pointed out that the libidinal economy of this disappointment fits perfectly that of a lover who is disappointed when the girl returns from the bathroom not quite naked, but with her panties still on. No wonder, then, that Hitchcock's first direct presentation of the sexual act (in *Frenzy*) coincides with murder: the necktie murderer strangles his victim during the very act of rape – a direct confirmation of Truffaut's notion that Hitchcock shoots the sexual act as if it were a murder and murder as if it were a sexual act . . .

One can see here how perversion is inscribed into the very act of censorship: the very displacement from the 'proper' to the supplementary object or activity (from undressing to dressing, from living to dead, from copulating to killing . . .) which takes place under the pressure of censorship

– that is, in order to avoid the direct depiction of the act – makes things even worse, adds to the act a supplementary perverse dimension. Another version of the same paradox is at work in obsessional neurosis, in which the 'prohibitions of the erotic [in censorship] are always at the same time, and despite themselves, the eroticization of prohibition':[11] the neurotic's compulsive rituals which enact defensive measures against his unacknowledged/ repressed (erotic) desire become themselves extremely eroticized, as is proved by the fact that they bring about an intense satisfaction.

Because of all these erratic deadlocks, Hollywood gives preference to the third version, that of 'romantic' pathos, which endeavours to conceal these deadlocks by expressing sexual ecstasy through metaphors, musical accompaniment, and so on – the danger which lurks here all the time is, of course, that things will all of a sudden turn ridiculous. Suffice it to recall the love encounter between Sarah Miles and her illicit lover, the English officer, in David Lean's *Ryan's Daughter*: the depiction of the sexual act in the midst of the forest, with waterfall sounds supposed to express their subdued passion, cannot but strike us today as a ridiculous bric-à-brac of clichés. Of crucial importance here is the pathetic sound accompaniment, since its role is profoundly ambiguous: by emphasizing the ecstasy of the sexual act, its exemption from prosaic everyday reality, these sounds (or passionate music) in a way 'de-realize' the act; they deliver us of the oppressive weight of its massive *presence*. A small mental experiment is sufficient to make this point clear: let us imagine that, in the middle of such a pathetic rendering of the sexual act, the music cut out all of a sudden, and all that remained was quick, snappy gestures, their painful silence interrupted by the occasional rattle and groan, compelling us to confront the inert presence of the sexual act. In short, the paradox of the scene from *Ryan's Daughter* is that the waterfall sound itself, with its massive presence, functions as the phantasmic screen obfuscating the Real of the sexual act.

This ecstatic rendering of the sexual act is to be located within the logic

11   Judith Butler, 'The Force of Fantasy', *Differences* 2: 2, 1990, p. 111.

of the 'production of the couple', whose culminating moment is provided by Warren Beatty's *Reds*. *Reds* integrates the October Revolution, the most traumatic historical event for Hollywood, into the Hollywood universe by staging it as the metaphorical background for the sexual act between the movie's main characters, John Reed (played by Beatty himself) and his lover (Diane Keaton). In the film, the October Revolution takes place immediately after a crisis in their relationship: by delivering a fierce revolutionary oration to the aroused crowd, Beatty fascinates Keaton's gaze; the two exchange desirous glances, and the cries of the crowd serve as a metaphor for the renewed outburst of passion between the lovers. The crucial, mythical scenes of the Revolution (street demonstrations, the storming of the Winter Palace) alternate with the depiction of the couple's lovemaking, against the background of the crowd singing the 'Internationale'. The mass scenes function as vulgar metaphors of the sexual act: when the black mass approaches and encircles the phallic tramway, is this not a metaphor for Keaton who, in the sexual act, plays the active role – is on top of Beatty? So, at the end, the happy couple is created, even with a Christmas tree – Lenin himself, addressing the deputies in a great hall, appears as the paternal figure who guarantees the success of the sexual relationship ... Here we have the exact opposite of Soviet Socialist Realism, where lovers experience their love as a contribution to the struggle for Socialism, making a vow to sacrifice all their private pleasures for the success of the Revolution, and to submerge themselves in the masses. In *Reds*, on the contrary, revolution itself appears as a metaphor for the successful sexual encounter.

Our point, of course, is that the singing of the 'Internationale' in *Reds* plays exactly the same role as the waterfall sound in *Ryan's Daughter*: the role of the phantasmic screen which enables us to sustain the Real of the sexual act. The standard situation in which, whatever we are doing, we are 'thinking about *that*' – about sexuality as the universal hidden reference of every activity – is inverted here: it is real sex itself which, in order to be palatable, has to be sustained by the 'asexual' screen of the October Revolution (instead of the proverbial 'Close your eyes and think of

England!', we have 'Close your eyes and think of the October Revolution!').
The logic is the same as that of a Native American tribe whose members
have discovered that all dreams have some hidden sexual meaning - all,
except the overtly sexual ones: here, precisely, one has to look for another
meaning. (In his recently discovered secret diaries, Wittgenstein reports
that while masturbating at the Front during World War I, he was thinking
about mathematical problems . . .) And our key point is that *it is also the
same in reality*, with so-called 'real sex': it also needs some phantasmic screen
- as we have already seen,[12] any contact with a 'real', flesh-and-blood other,
any sexual pleasure that we find in touching *another* human being, is not
something evident but something inherently traumatic, and can be
sustained only in so far as this other enters the subject's fantasy-frame.

What happens, then, when this screen dissolves? The act turns into
ugliness - even horror. An excellent illustration is provided by Alan Parker's
Angel Heart: Mickey Rourke and a beautiful Creole teenage girl make love
passionately on a rickety bed in a decaying room; along the walls and
through the holes in the ceiling, water is dripping into pots placed there
to capture it, since outside the house torrential rain is falling. All of a
sudden, the raindrops turn red, the water changes into blood which falls
on the couple, their copulating becomes more and more wild and turns
literally murderous when the bloodied Rourke begins to strangle the girl
. . . More interesting than the 'psychological' explanation of this scene
(Rourke plays a split personality unaware of the fact that he murdered the
girl), is its purely visual impact: the spectator does not perceive the blood
which gradually overflows the room as simply part of the scene; this blood
functions, rather, as a stain which gradually washes over the very borders
of the frame through which the spectator observes reality on the screen.

The truly traumatic aspects of this scene are thus not the flashback
memory fragments of the ritual killing in which, years ago, the hero
exchanged his identity, but the stain itself, the mediator-intruder between
the two levels, the present (sexual act) and the past (ritual killing). It is

12   See Chapter 2 above.

not the stain which evokes the traumatic past; rather, it is the memory of the past itself which serves as the screen obfuscating the intrusive presence of the stain. This stain thus undermines the position of the spectator who, from a safe distance, has observed the depicted events, and somehow takes him in, directly involves him in what is happening on the screen, as if something has emerged in this depicted reality which is 'too strong' and threatens to break through its frame. Paraphrasing Derrida, one can say that the stain of blood functions here as part of the (depicted) scene which enframes its frame itself. It is unnecessary to add that we have thereby approached the mysterious capital J in the midst of Lacan's schema: the expanding stain of blood announces the abyss of lethal *jouissance* which threatens to engulf us, to draw us into a psychotic night in which we are bombarded from all sides by an excessive, unbearable enjoyment. The sexual act is thus asserted as ugly, as that which disturbs and undermines the frame of reality. In other words, what takes place here is the disintegration of the phantasmic support of our relationship to reality.

There is, however, something which is even worse than being swallowed by the pre-ontological Real of the sexual act not sustained by the phantasmic screen: its exact opposite, the confrontation with the phantasmic screen deprived of the act. As we have seen, this is what occurs in one of the most painful and troubling scenes from David Lynch's *Wild at Heart*. In a lonely motel room, Willem Dafoe exerts a rude pressure on Laura Dern: he touches and squeezes her, invading the space of her intimacy and repeating in a threatening way 'Say fuck me!' – that is, extorting from her a word that would signal her consent to a sexual act. The ugly, unpleasant scene drags on and on, and when, finally, the exhausted Laura Dem utters a barely audible 'Fuck me!', Dafoe abruptly steps back, assumes a nice, friendly smile, and cheerfully retorts: 'No, thanks, I don't have time today; but on another occasion I would do it gladly . . .'

The uneasiness of this scene, of course, lies in the fact that the shock of Dafoe's final rejection of Dern's forcibly extorted offer gives the final pitch to him: his very unexpected rejection is his ultimate triumph and, in a way, humiliates her more than her direct rape. He has attained what he really wanted: not the act itself, just her consent to it, her symbolic humiliation. What we have here is rape in fantasy which refuses its realization in reality and thus further humiliates its victim – the fantasy is forced out, aroused, and then abandoned, thrown upon the victim. That is to say: it is clear that Laura Dern is not simply disgusted by Dafoe's (Bobby Peru's) brutal intrusion into her intimacy: just prior to her 'Fuck me!', the camera focuses on her right hand, which she slowly spreads out – the sign of her acquiescence, the proof that he has stirred up her fantasy. The point is thus to read this scene in a Lévi-Straussian way, as an inversion of the standard scene of seduction (in which the gentle approach is followed by the brutal sexual act, after the woman, the target of the seducer's efforts, finally says 'Yes!'). Or – to put it in another way – Bobby Peru's friendly negative answer to Dern's extorted 'Yes!' owes its traumatic impact to the fact that it makes public the paradoxical structure of the empty gesture as constitutive of the symbolic order:[13] after brutally wrenching out of her the consent to the sexual act, Peru treats this 'Yes!' as an empty gesture to be politely rejected, and thus brutally confronts her with her own underlying phantasmic investment in it.

How can such an ugly, properly repulsive figure as Bobby Peru stir up Laura Dern's fantasy? Here we are back at the motif of the ugly: Bobby Peru is ugly and repulsive in so far as he embodies the dream of the non-castrated phallic vitality in all its power – his whole body evokes a gigantic phallus, with his head the head of a penis . . .[14] Even his final moments bear witness to a kind of raw energy which ignores the threat of death: after the bank robbery goes wrong, he blows off his own head not in despair, but with a merry laugh . . . Bobby Peru is thus to be inserted in the series of larger-than-life figures of self-enjoying Evil whose best-known (although less intriguing and more formulaic than Bobby Peru) representative in Lynch's work, of course, is Frank (Dennis Hopper) in *Blue Velvet*. One is tempted to go even a step further here and to conceive the figure

13   See Chapter 1 above.
14   See Michel Chion, *David Lynch,* London: British Film Institute, 1995.

of Bobby Peru as the last embodiment of the larger-than-life figure on which all Orson Welles's films are focused:

> Bobby Peru is physically monstrous, but is he morally monstrous as well? The answer is yes and no. Yes, because he is guilty of committing a crime to defend himself; no, because from a higher moral standpoint he is, at least in certain respects, above the honest and just Sailor, who will always lack that sense of life which I shall call Shakespearean. These exceptional beings should not be judged by ordinary laws. They are both weaker and stronger than others . . . so much stronger because they are directly in touch with the true nature of things, or perhaps one should say, with God.

In this famous André Bazin description of Quinlan in Welles's *Touch of Evil*,[15] I have merely changed the names, and the description seems to fit perfectly . . .

Another way of accounting for the uncanny impact of this scene from *Wild at Heart* is to focus on the underlying *reversal* of the standard division of roles in the heterosexual process of seduction.[16] One could take as the starting point the emphasis on Dafoe's all-too-large mouth with its thick wet lips, spitting its saliva around, contorted in an obscene way, with ugly twisted dark teeth – do they not recall the image of *vagina dentata*, displayed in a vulgar way, as if this vaginal opening itself is provoking Dern into 'Fuck me!'. This clear reference to Dafoe's distorted face as the proverbial 'cuntface' points to the fact that beneath the obvious scene of the aggressive male imposing himself on a woman, another phantasmic scenario is played out: that of a young, blond, innocent adolescent boy aggressively provoked and then rejected by a mature, overripe, vulgar woman; at this level, sexual roles are reversed, and it is Dafoe who is the woman teasing and provoking the innocent boy. Again, what is so unsettling about the Bobby Peru figure is its ultimate sexual ambiguity, oscillating between the non-castrated raw phallic power and the threatening vagina, the two facets of the pre-symbolic life-substance. The scene is thus to be read as the reversal of the standard Romantic motif of 'death and the maiden': what we have here is 'life and the maiden'.[17]

How, then, are we to grasp the 'No, thanks!' of Bobby Peru, one of the great ethical gestures in contemporary cinema? Perhaps the proper way to do it is to contrast the setting of this scene from *Wild at Heart* to another well-known scene from real life, to what was perhaps the most humiliating racist ritual in the American Old South: a white gang cornering an African-American and forcing him to commit the first gesture of insult. While the African-American is held tightly by his associates, a white racist thug shouts at him: 'Spit on me! Tell me I'm scum!', and so on, in order to extort from him the 'occasion' for a brutal beating or lynching – as if the white racist wanted to set up retroactively the proper dialogical context for his violent outburst. Here we encounter the *perversity* of the injurious word at its purest: the proper order of succession and implication is perverted; in a mocking imitation of the 'normal' order, I compel the victim to insult me voluntarily – to assume the discursive position of the offender and thereby to justify my violent outburst.

It is easy to perceive the analogy with the scene from *Wild at Heart*: the point of this repulsive racist ritual is not simply that white thugs compel the well-meaning humble Uncle-Tomish African-American to offend them

17 Another key feature is the obvious theatrical exaggeration in Dafoe's harassment of Dern: the scene involves a third gaze for whom it is staged, like the wild shouting and gesticulation of Dennis Hopper while he is brutally harassing Isabella Rossellini in the famous scene from *Blue Velvet* – Hopper's ridiculous theatrics are also clearly addressed to the observer in the closet, the obvious stand-in for the spectator. Peru's final friendly rejection of Dern's 'Fuck me!' is incomprehensible without the reference to this third gaze, and the entire scene is so uncomfortable for the spectator precisely because he is compelled to occupy the place of this third gaze – because his position as witness is directly inscribed into the scene: the final rejection functions as a 'bad joke' which provokes uneasy laughter in the spectator (not in Dern), releasing the energy the spectator was saving for the juicy scene of copulation which should have followed Dern's extorted 'Fuck me!'. In other words, the scene is so uneasy not because we are embarrassed on account of Dern's humiliation, but because we are caught red-handed in our own phantasmic expectation.

against his will – both parties are well aware that the besieged African-American does cultivate aggressive fantasies about his white oppressors, that he *does* consider them scum (quite justifiably, considering the brutal oppression he and his race have been exposed to), and their pressure serves to awaken these fantasies, so that when the African-American finally spits on the white thug or tells him 'You're scum!', he in a way lets go of his defences, his sense of survival, and displays his true desire, cost what it may . . . exactly like Laura Dern in *Wild at Heart* who, in saying 'Fuck me!', yields not only to external pressure but also to her phantasmic kernel of *jouissance*. In short, the poor African-American is beaten (probably killed) for his desire.

There is, however, a crucial difference between the two scenes. After extorting her consent from Laura Dern, Bobby Peru does not pass to the act itself; on the contrary, he reads her consent as a truly spontaneous act, and gently rejects it. In contrast, the racists molesting the African-American, after extorting the 'You're scum!' from him, use this as a legitimate excuse actually to beat up or even lynch him. In other words, if Bobby Peru were to act like the Ku Klux Klan racists, he would simply rape Laura Dern violently after obtaining the forced consent from her; and vice versa, if the KKK racist were to act like Bobby Peru, he would follow the African-American's 'You're scum!' by simply retorting 'Yes, we probably are!' and leaving him alone . . . Or – to put it in yet another way – in the scene from *Wild at Heart* one should be attentive to the way Lynch turns on its head the standard procedure of male seduction, in which the gentle process of verbal coaxing is followed by the forceful physical act of sexual penetration, once consent is obtained: in Lynch, the violence is entirely displaced on to the process of verbal seduction itself, which functions as a nightmarish mockery of 'proper' gentle coaxing, while the sexual act itself simply fails to materialize.

The traumatic impact of these two scenes thus relies on the gap between the subject's everyday symbolic universe and its phantasmic support. Let us approach this gap through another disturbing phenomenon. When attention is drawn to the fact that women often *do* fantasize about being handled brutally and raped, the standard answer is either that this is a male fantasy about women or that women do it in so far as they have 'internalized' the patriarchal libidinal economy and endorsed their victimization – the underlying idea being that the moment we recognize this fact of daydreaming about rape, we open the door to male-chauvinist platitudes about how, in being raped, women only get what they secretly wanted: their shock and fear only express the fact that they were not honest enough to acknowledge this. To this commonplace, one should answer that (some) women may actually daydream about being raped, but this fact not only in no way legitimizes actual rape – it makes it even more violent.

Let us take two women – the first, liberated and assertive, active; the other secretly daydreaming about being brutally handled, even raped, by her partner. The crucial point is that, if both of them are raped, the rape will be much more traumatic for the second woman, *on account of the very fact that it will realize in 'external' social reality the 'stuff of her dreams'* – why? (Perhaps a better way to put it would be to paraphrase yet again Stalin's immortal lines: it is impossible to say which of the two rapes would be worse – they are *both worse*; that is to say, rape against one's will, of course, is in a way *the worst*, since it violates our personality; on the other hand, the very fact that a rape might be done in accordance with our secret proclivity makes it *even worse . . .*).[18] There is a gap which forever separates the phantasmic kernel of the subject's being from the more 'superficial' modes of his or her symbolic and/or imaginary identifications – it is never possible for me fully to assume (in the sense of symbolic integration) the phantasmic kernel of my being: when I approach it too boldly, when I come too close to it, what occurs is the *aphanisis* of the subject: the subject

18   In this mental experiment, of course, we have radically simplified the mechanism: the relationship between a certain type of public, intersubjective behaviour and its phantasmic support is never direct; that is, we can easily imagine that a woman who is aggressive and assertive in her relations with men secretly fantasizes about being brutally mishandled; furthermore, we can easily imagine a woman who daydreams about being submissive in order to conceal a more fundamental fantasy of a much more aggressive nature . . . The conclusion to be drawn is that in contacts with another human being, one can never be sure when and in what way one will touch and disturb his or her fantasy.

loses his/her symbolic consistency, it disintegrates. And perhaps the forced actualization of the phantasmic kernel of my being in social reality itself is the worst, most humiliating kind of violence, a violence which undermines the very basis of my identity (of my 'self-image').[19]

Another way to make the same point about rape – about how the woman's fantasizing about being brutally mishandled in no way legitimizes actual male rape – is to focus on the radical *asymmetry* between sadism and masochism.[20] As Deleuze emphasized, the stupid joke about a masochist asking a sadist to beat him up cruelly, and the sadist answering him with a malicious smile: 'No, never . . .', completely misses the point: the relationship between sadism and masochism is not complementary; that is to say, the sadist and the masochist definitely do not form an ideal couple; their relationship is definitely not a relationship in which each of the two partners gets from the other what he wants (in which the masochist's pain is directly the sadist's satisfaction, and vice versa). (In so far as masochism is usually identified as feminine and sadism as masculine, the belief in their complementary nature is also yet another way to perpetuate the illusion that there is a sexual relationship.) The asymmetry lies in the fact that masochism is not simply the attitude and practice of the masochist subject himself: it involves an elaborate *mise-en-scène* with a specific position to be occupied by the executioner (say, the Dominatrix), a position which is in no way simply that of a sadist, but the much more ambiguous position of the enslaved Master who, on a contractual basis, executes the orders of his masochist partner. *Mutatis mutandis*, the same goes for the sadist, who also wants his victim to occupy a specific position which is definitely not that of the subject who, as part of the contract, accepts his pain and enjoys it – it is part of the sadist's pleasure that his victim is appalled by the horror of what is taking place. Or – to put

19   Another way to make the same point is to draw attention to the crucial fact that *men who actually perform rapes do not fantasize about raping women* – on the contrary, they fantasize about being gentle, about finding a loving partner; rape is, rather, a violent *passage à l'acte* emerging from their incapacity to find such a partner in real life . . .

20   See Gilles Deleuze, *Coldness and Cruelty,* New York: Zone Books, 1989. I owe this point to Renata Salecl, New York

it in yet another way – the crucial question is: which, exactly, is the dimension of his identity that the victim wants to expose to pain and humiliation by means of the masochist ritual?

As Deleuze emphasized, this dimension concerns the paternal identification: what the masochist wants to see humiliated and tortured is the internalized figure of the (paternal) authority – not the Name-of-the-Father, but the figure of the obscene humiliated father the subject is ashamed of. By means of the masochist ritual, it is the 'father in myself which' I expose to ridicule. This, however, is definitely not what the sadist targets in his victim: what he targets is, rather, the exact opposite: the 'noble' symbolic dignity of the subject. One can now see in what precise sense the male logic according to which a woman who is actually raped merely gets her fantasy realized is wrong: even if she actually was fantasizing about being raped, she does *not* get what she wanted in the case of the actual rape, since her masochist fantasy is not realized.

The four modes of presenting the sexual act in cinema (compulsive distance in *The Meaning of Life*; phantasmic screen in *Ryan's Daughter* and *Reds*, the stain which undermines reality in *Angel Heart*; the direct manipulation of the fantasy in *Wild at Heart*) are thus like the different versions of the lavatory (German, French, American) discussed on pp. 3–4 above: in both cases, the problem is how to accommodate oneself to an excess (of shit, of sex). For this reason, it would be easy to construct a Greimasian semiotic square accounting for these four modes: *The Meaning of Life* and *Reds* present two opposite modes of maintaining a distance (compulsive isolation-neutralization, i.e. suspension of libidinal investment, versus phantasmic screen); in *Angel Heart* we get the act in all its horror, deprived of its phantasmic support, while in *Wild at Heart* we get fantasy deprived of the act. The crucial paradox is that we come closest to the Real in *Wild at Heart*, where the act itself does not occur: the very absence of the act in reality confronts us with the Real of the subject, with the innermost kernel of her *jouissance*.

Appendix II

Robert Schumann:
The Romantic Anti-Humanist

1

What is music at its most elementary? An act of *supplication*: a call to a figure of the big Other (beloved Lady, King, God . . .) to *respond*, not as the symbolic big Other, but in the real of his or her being (breaking his own rules by showing mercy; conferring her contingent love on us . . .). Music is thus an attempt to provoke the 'answer of the Real': to give rise in the Other to the 'miracle' of which Lacan speaks apropos of love, the miracle of the Other stretching his or her hand out to me.[1] The historical changes in the status of 'big Other' (*grosso modo*, in what Hegel referred to as 'objective Spirit') thus directly concern music – perhaps, musical *modernity* designates the moment when music *renounces* the endeavour to provoke the answer of the Other.

One of the easiest ways to discern this inherent historicity of music is to follow the vicissitudes of operatic ensembles. In Mozart's great operatic ensembles (paradigmatically in the long finale of Act II of *Le nozze di Figaro*), for a brief moment, at least, the utopian possibility of 'non-repressive' *intersubjectivity* shines through: every voice retains its full individuality, and is none the less included in the ensemble in a frictionless way; the harmony is not the harmony of an imposed uniform order, but the harmony of the conflict itself. Already in

1 See Jacques Lacan, *Le Séminaire, livre VIII: Le transfert*, Paris: Éditions du Seuil, 1991.

Beethoven, such a harmonious multitude-in-conflict becomes impossible – recall, at the very beginning of *Fidelio*, the quartet 'Mir ist so wunderbar', a kind of direct homage to Mozart: despite the 'beauty' of the music, the properly Mozartian magic has already evaporated, and the quartet cannot but strike us as somehow contrived, a mechanical application of the formula. At the end of this road lies the quintet 'Morgenlich . . .' from Act III of Wagner's *Meistersinger*: here inter-subjectivity proper is completely lost, and what we get in exchange is a kind of ecstatic immersion in which the multitude of voices is drowned in the same flow.

Our point, however, is that this passage from Mozart to Wagner does not entail merely a loss: what is clearly gained in it is *the 'depth' of subjectivity*. Suffice it to recall – again, in *Fidelio* – Pizarro's great aria 'Ha! Welch'ein Augenblick!' from Act I, which bears witness to a violent passion and fury of subjectivity unimaginable in Mozart. That is to say: in Mozart, as Ivan Nagel has pointed out,[2] stage characters remain 'flat' and in a sense *wholly externalized*, which means that the truly modern 'demoniac' Evil (whose first personification was the Byronic hero) is not yet present here: a Mozartian evil character (Osmin in *Die Entführung aus dem Serail* or Bartolo in *Le nozze*) openly *displays* his Evil in a way which is never far from ridicule, since his very cunningness and deception are thoroughly conspicuous (even Mozart's Don Giovanni, who already announces Romantic Evil, lacks proper 'depth': he remains a machinelike parasite deprived of any individuality). Although Beethoven's Pizarro discloses an intense destructive fury for which there is no place in Mozart's universe, he still openly *declares* his Evil in a way which precludes the post-Classicist 'depth' of character. For that one has to wait for Alberich in Wagner's *Rheingold*: Alberich's great monologue 'Bin ich frei? Wirklich frei?' involves the psychological complexity of a universe in which even an evil person is not simply

2   See Ivan Nagel, *Autonomy and Mercy,* Cambridge, MA; Harvard University Press, 1991.

evil, but, together with his victim, caught in a cobweb of passions and fate beyond his control, and thus a victim himself.[3]

Furthermore, music is not historical merely in the abstract sense according to which each determinate type of music is 'objectively possible' only within a given epoch, but also in the sense that each epoch, in a kind of 'synthesis of imagination', self-reflectively relates to preceding epochs. This reflectivity is posited as such in Romanticism – say in Liszt's *Réminiscences de don Juan*: what we get through the series of fragments-variations on Mozart's opera is *one epoch's remembrance of another epoch* – that is to say, Liszt's view of Mozart's Don Giovanni, who is already the reinterpretation of a previous configuration. We thus have three Don Giovannis: (1) the pre-Romantic *burlador*, the combination of libertine, buffoon and trickster, who dashes from one adventure to another in search of pleasure; (2) Mozart gives this figure a Romantic twist by turning him, at his end, into a proto-Byronic 'demonic' hero, the personification of diabolical Evil, a kind of negative ethical hero (from this perspective, all his adventurous conquests pave the way for the encounter with the Stone Guest, when Don Giovanni bravely endures the ordeal and refuses to renounce his lifestyle); (3) this Romantic 'demonic' hero is not to be confused with Liszt's late-Romanticist Don Juan, who is a little bit like Liszt himself – a decadent and reactionary mixture of abstract spirituality and flabby perverse sensuality.

The easiest way for today's listener to sample *in vivo* the historical character of our most elementary musical experience is to listen carefully to a popular baroque piece like Pachelbel's *Canon*: the first notes are today

3   Here one can also perceive clearly how historical development proper differs from mere natural evolution: in an evolutionary process, one shape passes into another, and the intermediate stage is simply the gradual transformation of one shape into another, while in the historical development proper a kind of impossible limit intervenes between stages A and B, and is missed by both. (The literary counterpart to this passage is perhaps the passage from Jane Austen to Emily Brontë.) While Mozart's intersubjectivity lacks the 'depth' of subjectivity, Beethoven pays for his access to the 'depth' of subjectivity with the loss of intersubjectivity proper which, in his hands, turns into a kind of externally imposed mechanical device; as if the 'deep' subjects were all too aggressive and intense for their interaction to be co-ordinated in a harmonious ensemble. The passage thus turns around the impossible-Utopian point of intersubjective harmony between 'deep' subjects.

automatically perceived as the accompaniment, so that we wait for the moment when the melody will emerge; since we get no melody but only a more and more intricate polyphonic variation on the pre-melodic accompaniment, we feel somehow 'deceived'. Where does this horizon of expectation, which sustains our feeling that the melody proper is missing, come from? Perhaps melody in today's accepted sense, involving the difference between the main melodic line and its background, emerges only with Viennese Classicism: after the retreat of Baroque polyphony. Complementary to this emergence of the melody is its gradual disappearance signalled by the often-observed fact that a decade after Beethoven's death, a long, 'beautiful', self-enclosed melody all of a sudden becomes 'objectively impossible'; this observation provides the proper background to the well-known vicious quip that Mendelssohn's melodies usually begin well but finish badly, losing their drive and ending in a 'mechanical' resolution (his overture 'Fingal's Cave', or the beginning of the violin concerto which marks a clear melodic regression with respect to Beethoven's violin concerto). Far from being a simple sign of Mendelssohn's weakness as a composer, this failure of the melodic line bears witness, rather, to his sensitivity towards the historical shift; those who were still able to write 'beautiful melodies' were kitsch composers like Tchaikovsky. On the other hand, for that reason Mendelssohn was precisely not yet a full Romantic: Romanticism 'arrives at its notion' (to put it in Hegelese) only when *this failure is included in, and becomes a positive factor of, the desired effect*. César Franck's *Prelude, Choral and Fugue,* the supreme case of religious kitsch, none the less provides a nice example of 'impossible longing' in the guise of the melody which endeavours to reach the climax, but is again and again forced to abandon its effort and, as it were, to fall back.[4]

4   At a level entirely different from Romanticism proper, one of course already encounters this same complicity between failure and truth in Mozart: the very structural necessity of the failure of the finale of *Così fan tutte* (i.e. the fact that the final reconciliation fails) is the moment of its truth. See Mladen Dolar, 'La femme-machine', *New Formations* 23 (Summer 1994).

2

This failing melody condenses the innermost logic of Romanticism.[5] Romanticism in its opposition to Classicism can be best grasped through the different logic of memory: in Classicism, memory recalls past happiness (the innocence of our youth, etc.), while the Romantic memory recalls not a direct past happiness but a past period in which future happiness still seemed possible, a time when hopes were not yet frustrated – memories here are 'those of absence, of that which never was'.[6] The loss deplored in Classicism is the loss of what the subject once had, while the Romantic loss is the loss of what one never had. Therein lies the Hegelian 'loss of a loss'; another way to put it is to paraphrase the Gospel – in the double renunciation, the subject loses that which he does not possess. That is to say: what the subject does not have is not simply absent, but is an absence which positively determines his life: when, for example, I do not have the desired object, this lack structures my entire life, and it is this determining and structuring lack which becomes suspended in the 'sacrifice of sacrifice'. In one of Roald Dahl's stories, filmed for TV by Hitchcock, the heroine – whose husband died young soon after their marriage, disappearing in an avalanche – does not marry again, but dedicates her entire life to his memory, elevating him to an idealized figure; however, when, twenty years later, the snow melts and the husband's frozen body is recovered, they find at his breast a small photo of another woman, the dead husband's true love. Thus, the wife's lifelong mourning has been in vain – through this belated discovery, she *lost what she never had*: she lost the loss itself, the image of the lost husband which sustained her life . . . One finds the same reversal in *La Princesse de Clèves*, when it is revealed that Madame de Tournon, mourned and idealized by Sancerre, was unfaithful to him in the most brutally calculating way.[7]

5   Here I draw on Charles Rosen's admirable *The Romantic Generation,* London: Harper Collins, 1996.

6   Ibid., p. 175.

7   Significantly, this truth is articulated in the guise of a *story within a story* (this story is narrated to the Princess de Clèves by her husband); as in Goethe's *Elective Affinities,* where the proper ethical attitude of 'not compromising on one's desire' is articulated in the story about two youthful lovers from a small village, told by a visitor to the mansion.

For that reason, Romanticism is closely linked to the motif of melancholy. Crucial to the concept of melancholy is the distinction between loss [*perte*] and lack [*manque*]:[8] lack is co-substantial with desire, while loss designates the moment at which desire loses its dialectic (the famous 'dialectic of desire') by being transfixed by some positive object which is missing. The lost object is thus precisely *not* lacking: it is identical to itself; the subject possesses it in the very mode of loss; his desire is fixed in/on it. (Incidentally, the Derridean critique of Lacan according to which, in Lacan, 'the lack has its proper place [*le manque a sa place*]', has to miss this distinction and to conflate loss – which, indeed, *does* have its place – and lack.) For this reason, melancholy is deeply related to drive: it is, in a way, *desire itself, perceived within the horizon of the (death) drive.* As such, melancholy is the counterpoint to what Bernard Baas calls 'pure desire [*le désir pur*]', a desire which is not desire for something, a definite object, but a direct desire for the lack itself (say, when I truly desire another person, I desire the very void at the centre of his subjectivity, so that I am not ready to accept any positive service in return).[9] That is to say: there is an intersection between drive and desire, and this intersection acquires a different shape when viewed either from the perspective of drive or from that of desire: if melancholy is desire viewed from the perspective (perceived within the horizon) of drive, 'pure desire' is drive viewed from the perspective (perceived within the horizon) of desire – that is, within the logic of lack.[10] Is not Hitchcock's *Vertigo* the study in melancholic loss which also

8   See Brigitte Balbure, the entry 'Mélancolie', in *Dictionnaire de la psychanalyse,* ed. Roland Chemama, Paris: Larousse, 1993.

9   See Bernard Baas, *Le Désir pur,* Louvain: Peeters, 1992.

10   Another concept closely linked to melancholy is that of *depression*: in its most elementary form, the depressed subject has severed his links with the universe of intentions and meanings, his embeddedness and active participation in intersubjective activity; as Heidegger would have put it, what 'depression' suspends is the attitude of active engagement, of 'care [*Sorge*]'. This link with Heidegger is further substantiated by the changed status of temporality: according to Heidegger, in 'care', past, present and future are interwoven (the subject's present consists in the way he projects his future out of his being-thrown, through his past, into his determinate situation), while in depression, time is reduced to a uniform, monotonous duration.

demonstrates how this loss is not the worst that can happen to the subject? That is to say: the film's thesis is that, in melancholy, the object is none the less 'possessed' in its very loss, as lost; while the true horror, worse than melancholy, is that of the 'loss of a loss': this occurs when the film's hero (Scottie) is forced to accept that the lost object which transfixes his desire *never existed in the first place* (that Madeleine herself was a fake).

The structure of this double loss ('symbolic castration') is then concealed by means of fetishizing the longing itself: the typical Romantic gesture is to elevate the longing as such, at the expense of the object one longs for. It is easy to discern the narcissistic satisfaction derived from such a reflective reversal: we have only to recall the Romantic infatuation with the artist who is subjected to everlasting longing which will never be satisfied . . . At a more fundamental level, what we are dealing with here is the positivization of an impossibility which gives rise to the fetish-object. For example, how does the object-gaze become a fetish? Through the Hegelian reversal from the impossibility of seeing the object into an object which gives body to this very impossibility: since the subject cannot directly see *that*, the true object of fascination, he accomplishes a kind of reflection-into-self by means of which the object that fascinates him becomes *the gaze itself*. In this sense (although not in an entirely symmetrical way), gaze and voice are 'reflective' objects, objects which give body to an impossibility (in Lacanian 'mathemes': *a* under minus small phi). In this sense, Hegelian 'self-consciousness' is also a reflection which arises against the background of a certain impossibility, of the inaccessibility of the Thing: I (am compelled to) become aware of myself, of my activity, I am forced to turn my gaze back on to myself, only and precisely when this activity malfunctions, that is, *fails* to achieve its goal.

With regard to the couple of Night and Day, this infinite longing, of course, stands for the Night of the Soul as opposed to the Clarity of the Day. In the philosophy of German Romanticism, Schelling's basic insight was that prior to its assertion as the medium of rational Word, the subject is the pure 'night of the Self', the 'infinite lack of being', the violent gesture of contraction that negates every being outside itself. Was not this withdrawal-into-self already accomplished by Descartes, in his universal doubt and reduction to *cogito*, which also involves a passage through the moment of radical madness? Are we thus not back at the well-known passage from *Jenaer Realphilosophie* where Hegel characterizes the experience of pure Self *qua* 'abstract negativity', the 'eclipse of (constituted) reality', the contraction-into-self of the subject, as the 'night of the world'? This notion of the 'night of the world' as the kernel of subjectivity is profoundly 'Schellingian' in that it subverts the simple opposition between the Light of Reason and the impenetrable darkness of matter: the in-between, no longer pre-subjective animal instinctuality and not yet the Light of Reason, is the moment of '*cogito* and madness', this radical dimension of subjectivity, the subject as Night – not the Day opposed to the abyss of subjectless Night, but the moment of absolute contraction into the pure Self. And the irony is that the Subject becomes Night, the demoniac in-between, at the very moment when, in social reality, the Night, in its massive presence, disappears with the emergence of electricity.[11]

3

At the highest artistic level, the structural failure of full melody finds its ultimate expression in Schumann's songs. Schumann and the 'religious kitsch' of Berlioz, Mendelssohn, Franck, Wagner, and so on, are the two opposed versions of the dissolution of Viennese Classicism, of the classical sonata form which, as Adorno insisted again and again, stands for the utopian moment of reconciliation between individual and society, love and Law. Religious kitsch attempts to retain authentic collective experience in the guise of massive works of sacred music; however, the price of its pretension to realize this impossible endeavour is the kitschy aestheticization of the religious experience: religion is reduced to a thrilling sensation, its truth-claim is suspended, all that matters is the aesthetically

11   For a more detailed account of this 'night of the world', see Slavoj Žižek, 'The Abyss of Freedom', in F. W. J. Schelhng, *The Ages of the World*, Ann Arbor: Michigan University Press, 1997.

'satisfying' awareness that we are participating in a sacred event. (This aestheticization, of course, culminates in Wagner's *Parsifal*, which directly aims at constituting the community of spectators as a pseudo-religious community participating in a sacred rite.)

Schumann, on the contrary, stands for the desperate individual experience bereft of its support in the community and, as such, condemned to ultimate madness. (This turn is already confirmed by the simple fact that Schumann's true masterpieces are his songs and pieces for solo piano: his attempts to gain respect by composing symphonies and concertos do not reach far beyond a rather academic respectability.) In contrast to Berlioz who, as Mendelssohn put it, 'with all his effort to go stark mad, [he] never once succeeded', Schumann tried desperately to remain sane, but was violently drawn into madness. The paradox, of course, is that the attempt of religious kitsch to render collective experience ends up in radical subjectivism (in the reduction of authentic communal life to the thrilling subjective 'experience' of the religious ritual), while Schumann's radical reduction to subjectivity comes much closer to expressing the deadlock of the individual's objective social position.

Schumann's crucial contribution lies in the way in which he 'dialecticizes' the relationship between the sung melody and its piano accompaniment: it is no longer the voice which renders the melody, with the piano reduced to accompaniment or, at best, secondary variations on the main melodic line (as it is still with Schubert). With Schumann, the privileged link between melody and voice is broken: it is no longer possible to reconstruct the full melody from the solo vocal line, since the melody, as it were, promenades itself between vocal and piano lines – there is no single line, neither vocal nor piano, in which the melody is 'played out in full'. It is as if the melody's proper place is on some elusive, intangible third level which merely echoes in both of the levels that the listener actually hears, vocal and piano.

It is crucial to distinguish this absent or suppressed melody from the pre-Classicist status of 'unheard melody'. In Bach, for example, we are dealing with the gap between the musical structure and its material actualization; this gap occurs in two opposite forms: (1) a composition is written as a formal structure which is relatively neutral with regard to the medium of its actual performance, as a kind of formal matrix which does not prescribe all the details of its performance (say the Goldberg Variations, which can be performed on piano, on harpsichord, on organ . . .); (2) secondly, and more interestingly, the polyphonic structure is so complex that it is simply impossible to follow it directly by ear; the ideal listener must be at least minimally acquainted with the complexity of the composition – the discernment of this complexity in its necessarily imperfect material realization is the main source of the listener's satisfaction. The supreme example is perhaps the second movement (fugue) of Bach's three sonatas for solo violin, in which the entire polyphonic structure is condensed in one instrumental line, so that although we 'actually' hear only one violin line, in our imagination we automatically supplement it with other unheard implicit melodic lines, and seem to hear the multitude of melodic lines in their interaction. However, the actual condensation to one single line is thereby by no means simply suspended: the key element of the artistic effect is that we are aware all the time of how we actually hear only one line. (Incidentally, that is why the transcriptions of Bach's solo sonatas for organ or the string trio or quartet, even when they are of the highest quality, retain an element of 'vulgarity,' even obscenity, as if, when we 'hear it all', some constitutive void is filled in – the elementary definition of kitsch.)

The Romantic return to the 'unheard melody' which follows the Classicist attempt to establish the perfect transparency of the structure, in which every musical line is potentially audible, is the exact opposite of this pre-Classicist polyphony: what has to remain unheard here 'is not the abstract form but the sensuous conception'.[12] an impossible sound. Therein lies the central paradox emphasized by Rosen: the very fact that Romanticism abolishes the gap between the formal structure and its realization, that it suspends the autonomous status of the formal

12   Rosen, *The Romantic Generation*, p. 11.

structure and makes the material-vocal actualization of the composition, up to the details of the performance, part of its very conception, gives rise to an uncanny surplus at the level of the sound itself – 'the primacy of sound in Romantic music should be accompanied, and even announced, by a sonority that is not only unrealizable but unimaginable'.[13] Rosen quotes a passage from 'Abegg' variations, Schumann's Opus I, in which the impossibility arises:

> because Schumann is thinking of the motto in terms of almost pure sound, in terms of release and attack as well as of pitch and rhythm . . . : a note can be attacked twice, but a double release without a second attack is nonsense on the piano.[14]

This 'absolutely inaudible' sound provides an exemplary case of the Lacanian *objet petit a*, in so far as it is *irréel* in the precise sense that Lacan uses this term apropos of his myth of *lamella*: 'This organ must be called "unreal," in the sense that the unreal is not the imaginary, and precedes the subjective it conditions, being in direct contact with the real.'[15] As such, of course, *irréel* coincides with its opposite, with the Real. That is to say: the Lacanian real is not simply the pre-symbolic natural substance but, rather, the mythical part-organ standing for what is lost when the pre-symbolic substance is symbolized. 'Irréel' is *the Real itself* in so far as it has the status of a pure semblance and can never become part of reality: for that reason, Lacan determines the *irréel lamella* as 'incorporeal' (here one should be able to discern the echo of the incorporeal status of the Event in Stoic logic). The alien from Ridley Scott's movie of the same name, for example, is 'real' precisely as the pure elusive semblance whose shape changes again and again; the same goes for trauma, the traumatic event, in psychoanalysis, which is also *irréel* in the sense of a phantasmic formation – for Lacan, the

---

13   Ibid.
14   Ibid.
15   Jacques Lacan, 'Position of the Unconscious', in *Reading Seminar XI*, ed. Bruce Fink et al., Albany, NY: SUNY Press, 1995, p. 274.

Real is not primarily the horrible formless maternal substance beneath symbolic semblances, but is, rather, itself a pure semblance.

4

One can now see in what the 'event Schumann' (to use Alain Badiou's term[16]) consists: the 'unreal' dimension of music (the unrealizable sonority, etc.) which, before it, belonged to the 'empirical' grey zone of liminal confusion and limitation of our perception, is now elevated into the *structural principle* of the 'unheard voice'; the 'true voice' is now explicitly posited as Silence itself, as an 'impossible' object which, for a priori reasons, cannot be heard and around which, like a traumatic kernel, the musical sounds actually produced circulate. The empirical failure is thus transformed into a 'transcendental' Limit; the philosophical point here is that this object-voice which coincides with Silence itself is strictly correlative to the 'barred' subject (the Lacanian $ as the Void of self-relating negativity). Schumann's entire musical strategy can be accounted for as an endeavour to realize all imaginable versions of this undermining of the privilege of the melodic line, of this dialecticization of the relationship between vocal melody and its piano background, up to the most radical variation in which the voice is simply absent or fails to appear.[17] Here are the main versions of this dialecticization in Schumann:

- In 'In the glorious month of May', the very first song of *Dichterliebe*, the proper, orderly succession is somehow mixed up, so that we do have a beginning, a middle and an end, but not in that order (to quote Godard): the song begins and ends with what is, according to

16   See Alain Badiou, *L'Être et l'événement,* Paris: Éditions du Seuil, 1988.

17   The first steps in this direction had been taken already by Schubert, say, in his *Death and the Maiden*: the main death motif is first played on the piano alone; the maiden's voice – which answers with a different, more active and lively, melodic line – thus functions as a kind of escape from or desperate defence against it; the voice of death then takes over the motif first played on the piano, gently inviting the girl not to be afraid and to surrender herself to it.

standard rules and expectations, the middle part, so that its very structure displays an infinite, unsatisfied longing. Furthermore, in this song, and even more markedly in 'Twilight' (from *Liederkreis* Opus 39), the non-synchronization between voice and piano accompaniment (the delays, overtakings and other barely perceptible forms of rhythmic noncoordination between vocal line and piano line, as well as between the two hands of the piano part itself) gives the song an uncanny, dreamlike atmosphere. What we have here is a kind of musical equivalent of Orson Welles's wide-angle focus shot which distorts the face in close-up and simultaneously transforms the background into a de-realized, dreamlike landscape. Instead of guaranteeing the reality (as well as the psychological 'normality') of the set-up, the piano accompaniment thus de-realizes the situation and colours it with a tinge of pathology . . . no wonder 'Twilight' ends with a recitative panic warning: 'Take heed, be watchful and await!', as if, in its closing moment, the singing subject all of a sudden withdraws from its immersion into the seductive lure of the song, and warns us against surrendering to the madness of the loss of reality (which, in 'Twilight', is signalled by the uncannily hypnotic, circular, childlike character of the melodic line).

- Song 8 of *Dichterliebe* ('And if the little flowers only knew . . .') is in this sense a kind of inversion of 'Twilight': the warning fails in its protective function, so that when the words are over, the piano conclusion explodes in an excessive outbreak of fury. We are not dealing here with the standard coda which adds itself to the 'official' conclusion of the melodic line (two outstanding examples: Beethoven's *Fidelio* overture and, in Mozart's *The Magic Flute*, the conclusion of Tamino and Pamina's duet after the ordeal of water and fire); in Schumann, this outbreak involves a precisely defined reversal. The first three stanzas of the song express the standard poetic contrast between the innocent beauty of external nature and the desperate state of the poet's soul due to his broken heart (if only flowers [nightingales, stars . . .] knew his sorrow, they would also shed tears with him and give him comfort). The last stanza, however, introduces a sharp contrast: although none of them can know it, there is one who *does* know it, and she will *not* shed tears, because the one who knows has *herself* torn his heart asunder, and is thus the very cause of his sorrow – it is at *this* point that the rage breaks out in the excessive coda. Schumann demonstrates his mastery in the way the softly melancholic, almost pastoral, mode of the first three stanzas changes into the fury of the last stanza, which explodes the very frame of the song; what is at stake in this rage is knowledge: she *knows* and doesn't care . . . In the background of this reversal, of course, is the poet's wounded narcissism: he is in search of compassion and consolation – that is, he is in search of an Other from whose point of view he would be properly pitied. Unfortunately, the very one who is in a position to pity him is the cause of his trouble; for this reason, the poet's feigned passive and docile sadness turns into the aggressive rage which, after smouldering below the surface for a long time, suddenly flames out. What we have here is the fundamental Schumann invention of 'an absolute coincidence of words and music, but a coincidence reached by a paradox':[18] the explosion of piano rage stands for the poet's (subject's) rage, which becomes so strong that it can no longer be verbalized, sung by the voice – that is to say, the piano gives form to the silence of the subject suffocated by his rage . . .

- We encounter an even more refined example of this 'coincidence of words and music reached by a paradox' in 'I can't understand it' (from *Frauenliebe und Leben*), where the melody loses its vocal autonomy: at the high point the singer's voice disappears, the line continues only on the piano, so that the impossibility for the subject to grasp what goes on 'is translated into music by the impossibility of realizing the conception vocally'.[19] Here, in a properly structural

18   Rosen, *The Romantic Generation*, p. 67.
19   Ibid., p. 68.

way, 'the significance arises from the impossibility of musical realization' – the very failure to transmit the proper message transmits
the message of shock and incomprehensibility. Here again we meet
the 'barred' subject which emerges through the very failure to find
adequate expression, through the impossibility of an adequate
signifying representation; a subject which is not the symbolic subject
(the 'content' expressed in the symbolic chain which represents him)
but, rather, an 'answer of the Real' to the very failure of symbolic
representation.

- In the last poem of *Frauenliebe* ('You betrayed me'), where the woman
  bemoans her lover's death, we have a case of suppressed melody. At
  the moment of greatest pathos, after the words 'I withdraw silently
  into my inwardness, / The curtain falls / There I have you and my
  lost happiness / You [are] my world', the singer remains silent and
  the piano alone replays the first song of the cycle, the memory of
  the woman's first sight of her beloved – not the song itself, but its
  accompaniment. The crucial point not to be missed is that in the
  first song, at the climactic point of its melody ('Tauchst aus tiefstem
  Dunkel' 'rises from deepest darkness'), it is the voice alone that is
  heard, as the accompaniment retreats for several bars. In the repetition, when we hear only the accompaniment, the climactic moment
  is missing; however, since we do remember it, its very absence makes
  it even more palpable: 'the motif actually arises in the listener's
  mind out of the void left by the piano'.[20] Again, the *absence* of the
  full melody, of its climax, renders it more present than its pure
  presence . . .

- In a similar song from the male cycle *Dichterliebe* ('I wept as I
  dreamed'), the same structure of absence is brought to its extreme.
  Three times, the poet reports the content of his dream, which has
  moved him to tears and caused his violent awakening: in the inverted
  temporal order, he first laments the death of the beloved girl, then

20   Ibid., p. 114.

the fact that she abandoned him unexpectedly; finally, he dreams that she still loves him. We thus recede from the future through the present to the past (the present in which the song's narrative takes place, of course, is the predicament of the abandoned lover: the dream about the beloved's death is clearly the realization of the poet's death wish). Again the accompaniment is crucial here: in the first two stanzas it is extremely sparse, just a couple of tones which punctuate the vocal melodic line without actually following and redoubling the voice; in the third stanza, when the poet's imagination is animated by the memory of the happy past, he is finally 'in his element', he truly comes to life. The change is signalled by the sudden animation of the piano accompaniment which turns into a continuous, louder and louder, more and more energetic melodic line of its own – here, things are for real, we have obviously touched the centre of emotional gravity. However, when the awareness that, in the present, all this is lost imposes itself again, the vocal line breaks down at its very climax, and what follows is *merely the piano accompaniment to the first two stanzas*: a long silence is interrupted by a couple of short tones, followed again by an excessively long silence which, in its turn, is interrupted by two short piano tones which conclude the song. The status of these sparse tones interrupting the silence is radically ambiguous: they can be read as a *da capo senza fine*, a strangely protracted conclusion which none the less brings about an 'effect of closure', and, simultaneously, as a fragmentary remembrance of the absent melodic line – that is, a gesture which makes palpable the final breakdown of the vocal melodic line, which resonates all the more powerfully in the listener's mind for not being heard . . .[21]

21   The comparison of this song with the last song of *Frauenliebe* also compels us to raise the question of sexual difference with regard to how the subject reacts to the loss of the beloved. Man's reaction is one of wounded narcissism: he inflates and displaces the

5

Humoresque, arguably Schumann's piano masterpiece, is to be read against the background of this gradual loss of the voice (although most of his song cycles were composed after his great piano pieces): it is not a simple piano piece but a *song* without the vocal line, with the vocal line reduced to silence, so that all we actually hear is the piano accompaniment. (This disappearance of the voice is strictly equivalent to the 'death of man', and what is crucial here is not to confuse man ['person'] with the subject: the Lacanian subject *qua* $ is the very outcome of the 'death of man'. For Lacan, in clear contrast to Foucault, humanism is something which emerged in the Renaissance, and was disposed of with the Kantian break in philosophy – and, we might add, with Schumann in music.) This is how one should read the famous 'inner voice [*innere Stimme*]' added by Schumann (in the written score) as a third line between the two piano lines, higher and lower: as the vocal melodic line which remains a non-vocalized 'inner voice', a kind of musical equivalent to the Heidegger-Derridean 'crossed-out' Being. What we actually hear is thus a 'variation, but not on a theme', a series of variations without the theme, accompaniment without the main melodic line (which exists only as *Augenmusik*, music for the eyes only, in the guise of written notes). (No wonder Schumann composed a 'concert without orchestra', a kind of counterpoint to Bartók's 'concert for orchestra'.) This absent melody is to be reconstructed on the basis of the fact that the first and third levels (the right- and the left-hand piano lines) do not relate to each other directly – their relationship is not that of an immediate mirroring: in order to account for their interconnection, one is thus compelled to (re)construct a third, 'virtual' intermediate level

---

fact that the girl has abandoned him through sudden unexpected death, and then goes on to mourn her, remaining transfixed on her loss and thereby transforming its lament into a new source of satisfaction; woman, on the contrary, undergoes the 'loss of a loss', that is, she retreats into herself, into the 'Night of the World', surrenders to the vortex of 'feminine depression', and is thus reunited for ever with her lost lover, who finally, after she has disconnected from external reality, becomes for her her entire world . . .

(melodic line) which, for structural reasons, cannot be played. Its status is that of an impossible-real which can exist only in the guise of a writing; that is to say, physical presence would annihilate the two melodic lines we hear in reality (as in Freud's 'A Child is Being Beaten', in which the middle fantasy-scene was never conscious and has to be reconstructed as the missing link between the first and the last scene).

Schumann brings this procedure of absent melody to an apparently absurd self-reference when, later in the same fragment of *Humoresque*, he repeats the same two actually played melodic lines, yet this time the score contains no third absent melodic line, no inner voice – what is absent here is the absent melody, that is, *absence itself.* How are we to play these notes when, at the level of what is acutally to be played, they exactly repeat the previous notes? The actually played notes are deprived only of what is *not* there, of their constitutive lack – or, to paraphrase the Bible, they lose even that which they never had. Again it is this difference between 'structuring absence' (of the 'inner voice') and pure absence which provides the co-ordinates of modern subjectivity: this subjectivity hinges on the absent melody – that is to say, the modern subject emerges when its objectal counterpart (in this case, a melody) disappears, but remains present (efficient) in its very absence: in short, the subject is correlative to an 'impossible' object whose existence is purely 'virtual'.

When the vocal melody which is supposed directly to 'express' the subject's inner life disappears – that is, when all that remains is the piano accompaniment deprived of the vocal line – this disappearance, far from signalling the 'death of the subject', signals its exact opposite, the *emergence* of the 'barred' subject. When, however, this absence itself is lacking, we enter the domain of *drive*: in drive, the loss itself is lost, so we no longer have the infinite longing for the lost object constitutive of desire (for that reason, *Humoresque* is a strangely joyous and exuberant piece, free of any remainder of flabby romantic longing). And in so far as the subject's very being hinges on the efficient absence of an impossible 'lost object', the 'loss of a loss' in drive equals what Lacan calls 'subjective destitution'.

Is not the 'inner voice' as the paradox of a voice which cannot be materialized thus an exemplary case of the Lacanian *objet petit a*? As we have just seen, we have in *Humoresque* two series of notes which, at the level of their positive features (of what is actually played), are exactly the same; the difference lies only in a different relationship to their constitutive absence, to the missing 'inner voice'. In a good performance of *Humoresque*, these two series of notes somehow 'sound different', although they are exactly the same – is this not the very definition of *objet petit a*, in so far as *objet petit a* is the unfathomable X, the mysterious *je ne sais quoi* which is to be found nowhere in positive reality, yet whose presence or absence causes this positive reality to appear 'entirely different'?

One is also tempted to say that Schumann, in his 'variations without a theme', exemplifies the Deleuzian notion of subjectivity as *le pli*, the fold of the substantial content: it is only when we have variations without a melody, a series of folds without a firm substantial content, that the subject is no longer a(nother) Substance. In the traditional Romantic song, the subject is still defined by the substantial content of the inner wealth expressed by his voice, to which the piano provides the background fold; all that remains in Schumann is the fold itself, deprived of the melody, which is rejected as too 'substantial' to be able to express the void of subjectivity in an appropriate way. The only way to evoke the subject properly is to express it as a void around which the fold of 'variations without a theme' circulate.

Another way to put it is to say that Schumann was the first 'anti-humanist' in music: what his musical practice accomplishes is the passage from 'human person' (which expresses the wealth of his substantial emotions in the melody) to subject *qua* $, a passage strictly in analogy with Kant, who was the first to introduce the split between *subject* (the void of pure negativity) and *person* (the particular wealth of emotional, etc., 'pathological' content), and was therefore the first philosophical anti-humanist. Humanism is pre-modern, pre-Cartesian, reducing man to the high point of creation, instead of conceiving of him as a subject which stands *outside* creation. Our argument is thus that *the very formal structure of Schumann's music expresses the paradox of modern subjectivity*: the bar – the impossibility of 'becoming oneself', of actualizing one's identity – on account of which 'infinite longing' is constitutive of subjectivity. No wonder, then, that one finds in Schumann the musical counterpart to the Hegelian process of the 'subjectivization of substance', of the integration of the immediate substantial content into subjectivity.

In order to maintain a minimum of consistency, the subject has to append his being to some 'little piece of the Real' which is 'ex-timate' in the Lacanian sense of the term: an external, contingent, found element which simultaneously stands for the subject's innermost being. This paradox of extimacy is clearly discernible in the way in which Schumann manipulates fragments of melodies borrowed from other composers (or from his own previous work, as with the 'Papillon' motif in 'Florestan' from *Carnaval*): a foreign body is first intruded as a meaningless trace, a trauma interrupting the flow of the 'proper' melodic line; gradually, however, this intruder is 'perlaborated', fully integrated into the composition's main texture, so that at the end it loses its external character and is reproduced as something generated by the inner logic of the composition itself. Take the first movement of *Phantasie in C Major*, in which the borrowed melody (a reference to Beethoven's *An die ferne Geliebte*), whose concealed echoes are discernible throughout the piece, is 'repeated' (fully performed), and thus brings about the pacifying effect of resolution only at the very end: what at first appeared as the foreign body disturbing the proper melodic line is revealed as the innermost kernel of the piece, (the external) reference changes into self-reference; what is borrowed (from another composer) is gradually generated from within, *the presupposition* (the content which is 'presupposed', borrowed from another composer) *is posited* – is this not 'Hegel in music'? Furthermore, does not this unique procedure provide a kind of musical counterpart to the Freudian gradual integration of some traumatic intrusion (a meaningless memory-trace) into the subject's symbolic life-texture in the course of psychoanalytic interpretation? It is crucial to maintain the radically ambiguous status of the fragment (foreign intruder), its *undecidability* between presupposition and something posited: as we have learned from Freud, a trauma as the kernel of the impossible-real which sticks out and resists symbolization is none the less a retroactive product of this very process of symbolization.

6

Carnaval, another of Schumann's piano masterpieces, is an excellent example of the Deleuzian rhizomatic structure: its twenty-one sections intertwine in multiple ways, each of them a kind of 'variation' on others, related to others through melodic or rhythmic echoes, repetitions and contrasts, whose logic cannot be grounded in a single universal rule. In Classical variations (say, in Beethoven's *Diabelli* variations) we first get the theme 'as such', followed by the multitude of its variations: as one would expect in Schumann, the 'theme' is simply lacking. However – and it is here that Schumann's practice differs from the 'deconstructionist' notion of a play of variations without the original – these 'variations' do not all possess equal weight: there is a section which clearly 'sticks out' because of its elementary character of a musical exercise rather than a full-blown composition, 'The Dancing Letters [*Lettres dansantes*]'. Furthermore, the comparison of the piece actually performed with the written list of the sections provides another enigmatic excessive element: the eighth section ('Réplique') is followed by 'Sphinxes', a section which is merely written and cannot be performed. What are these mysterious 'sphinxes'?

The subtitle of *Carnaval* is 'Miniature scenes on four notes [*Scènes mignonnes sur quatre notes*]', and 'Sphinxes' provides these four notes, the musical cipher of *jouissance* which condenses a series of mnemonic associations: the young pianist Ernestine von Fricken, Schumann's girlfriend at the time when he composed *Carnaval*, came from the Bohemian town of Asch, a name whose four letters are identical to the only letters of the word 'Schumann' which have note equivalents in German musical terminology (where 'H' stands for B, and 'B' for B flat). Moreover, if we read 'As' as A flat, we get another variant of the musical cipher, so that we obtain three brief series: SCHumAnn (E flat – C – B – A); ASCH (read as: A flat – C – B); ASCH (read as: A – E flat – C – B). In his *Psychanalyser*, Serge Leclaire[22] reports on a psychoanalytic treatment which produced the cipher of enjoyment in his patient: the enigmatic term *poord'jeli*, a condensation of a multitude of mnemonic traces (the patient's love for a girl called Lili, a reference to *licorne*, etc., etc.). Do we not encounter something of the same order in Schumann's 'Sphinxes'?

The multitude of *Carnaval* is thus arranged around two nodules: 'Sphinxes' – which, as it were, provides the impossible-real 'cipher of enjoyment' present only in the mode of mute writing – and 'Lettres dansantes', which are exactly what the title indicates, the presentation of this cipher in the guise of a 'preparatory' playful miniature. The entire piece thus pivots around 'Sphinxes' as its absent, impossible-real point of reference: a series of bare notes without any measure or harmony – to put it in Kantian terms, they are not musically 'schematized', and therefore cannot actually be performed. 'Sphinxes' is a pre-phantasmic *synthome*, a formula of enjoyment – not unlike Freud's formula of trimethilamin, which appears at the end of the dream of Irma's injection. As such, the absence of 'Sphinxes' is structural: if 'Sphinxes' were actually to be performed, the fragile consistency of the entire piece would fall apart. In short, 'Sphinxes' is the *objet petit a* of *Carnaval*, the section whose very exclusion guarantees the reality of the remaining elements. In some recordings, 'Sphinxes' is actually performed: less than half a minute of a dozen protracted tones. The effect is suitably uncanny, as if we had stepped 'through the looking-glass' and entered some forbidden domain, beyond (or, rather, beneath) the phantasmic frame – or, more properly, as if we had caught sight of some entity outside its proper element (like seeing a dead squid on a table, no longer alive and gracefully moving in the water). For this reason, the uncanny mystery of these notes can all of a sudden change into vulgarity, even obscenity – it is no wonder that the most outstanding proponent of performing 'Sphinxes' was none other than Rachmaninov, one of the exemplary kitsch composers of serious music.

---

22   See Serge Leclaire, *Psychanalyser*, Paris: Éditions du Seuil, 1968.

Taking into account the central role of the term 'butterfly' in Schumann's universe (not only is one of the *Carnaval* pieces called 'Papillons', but *Papillons* is the title of another of his great piano masterpieces, and, as we have already seen, 'Florestan' from *Carnaval* gradually integrates into its texture a fragment from *Papillons*), one should emphasize how this term attracted Schumann's attention not only as a metaphor for a fragile and passing spark of beauty, but also as a term which involves the opposition to larva as its not-yet-fully-developed form, as well as to the moth as a 'butterfly of the night [*papillon de nuit*]' (which, incidentally, is the biological meaning of 'sphinx' – so, for Schumann, 'sphinx' does not refer only to the enigmatic statue-riddle!). 'Sphinxes' contains the kernel of the whole *Carnaval*, as it were, in its larval, pre-ontological state, and, in 'Papillons', a dynamic piece which immediately follows 'Sphinxes', it actually seems as if a butterfly has got rid of the inertia of a larva, and started to fly wildly.

One should evoke here the quite respectable philosophico-ideological lineage of larva and butterfly: Aristotle's biological writings bear witness to a fascination with the larva, which is designated as a living dead, a body deprived of soul [*psyche*], and the transformation of larva into butterfly stands for the soul which sheds bodily inertia and takes off (in Greek, *psyche* also means 'butterfly'!). What larva (or, on a different level, the moth) stands for is the uncanny pre-ontological, not-yet-symbolized texture of relations first approached by Plato who, in his late dialogue *Timaeus*, conjectured about *chora*, a kind of matrix-receptable of all determinate forms, governed by its own contingent rules – it is crucial not to identify this *chora* too hastily with the Aristotelian matter [*hyle*].

Much later, German Idealism outlined the precise contours of this pre-ontological dimension which precedes and eludes the ontological constitution of reality (in contrast to the standard commonplace according to which German Idealists pleaded the 'panlogicist' reduction of all reality to the product of the Notion's self-mediation). Kant was the first to detect this crack in the ontological edifice of reality: if (what we experience as) 'objective reality' is not simply given 'out there', waiting to be perceived by the subject, but an artificial composite constituted through the subject's active participation – that is, through the act of transcendental synthesis – then the question crops up sooner or later: what is the status of the uncanny X which *precedes* transcendentally constituted reality? It was Schelling, of course, who gave the most detailed account of this X in his notion of the Ground of Existence – of that which 'in God Himself is not yet God': the 'divine madness', the obscure pre-ontological domain of 'drives', the pre-logical Real which remains forever the elusive Ground of Reason which can never be grasped 'as such', merely glimpsed in the very gesture of its withdrawal . . .

For an idea of this pre-ontological dimension, we can again recall the scene from *Brazil* in which, in a high-class restaurant, the waiter recommends the best items from the day's menu to his customers ('Today, our tournedos is really special!', etc.), yet what the customers receive on making their choice is a dazzling colour photo of the meal on a stand above the plate, and on the plate itself a loathsome excremental pastelike lump: is not this split between the image of the food and the Real of its formless excremental remainder – between the ghostlike substanceless appearance and the raw stuff of the Real – strictly analogous to the gap that separates the raw stuff of 'sphinxes' from the multitude of 'butterflies', these brief sparks of spectral appearances? This gap thus 'de-realizes' the solid, firm reality, changing it into a fragile mask beneath which palpitates a horrifying life-substance; on the intersubjective level, the psychological reality of 'another person' also dissolves into a multitude of masks.

It has often been remarked that the universe of *Carnaval* is not the universe of 'real people', but the universe close to the stories of E.T.A. Hoffmann or the expressionist paintings of Edvard Munch: a carnival in which we encounter a multitude of masks whose Beneath is uncertain, oscillating between mechanical dolls and the horrifying substance of undead Life (ghosts). There is only one piece in *Carnaval* in which this 'de-realizing' quality dissolves, so that we seem to be dealing with the universe of 'real people', not with uncanny masks of ghosts and living dolls: 'Reconnaissance', another piece which, as it were, sticks out from the totality of

Carnaval in so far as it is arguably the most 'beautiful' of all the pieces; that is, the closest to an easily memorable and recognizable popular tune. Schumann himself described this piece as a 'lovers' meeting': a dream of a finally fulfilled sexual reunion. As if to signal the phantasmic quality of such a reunion, Schumann uses an ingenious acoustical trick here: the entire melody is doubled in rapid notes an octave lower, generating a kind of shimmering effect; undoubtedly a kind of musical equivalent to the standard Hollywood kitsch procedures of blurring a love scene with unfocused lenses, sweet 'Romantic' music, and so on. The paradox is thus that the only piece in *Carnaval* which brings us back to everyday 'firm reality', is the very piece whose 'beauty' comes dangerously close to musical kitsch.

7

What, then, do all these paradoxes tell us about Schumannian subjectivity? One unfailing rule about Schumann is that one cannot understand anything at all about his songs without taking into account their codas. In his *Dichterliebe*, for example, the key to the entire cycle is provided by the long coda which concludes 'In the Rhine, in the holy river', the song in the midst of the cycle which compares his beloved to the mysterious painting of the Madonna in Cologne cathedral on the banks of the Rhine.[23] The vague but none the less profoundly disturbing effect of this coda hinges on the fact that it puts into music the gradual breakdown of sublimation – that is, the movement from the sublime Madonna (evoked in the words of the song) to the treacherous and repulsive woman, the object of the next song, 'I do not complain', in which the shattered poet heroically refuses to mourn her loss. So, back to our starting point about

23   Schumann refers to the Rhine as to the father-river ('Vater Rhein') which shelters in its depths the image of the beloved; the barely concealed lethal dimension of this image is directly evoked in Song 7 of the *Liederkreis* (Opus 24) cycle, which presents the Rhine (calm and kind on the surface, but hiding night and death in its depths) as the image of the beloved whose appearance of joy and kindness conceals perfidy and decay. When the contours of this figure become discernible in the river, summoning us to its depths, we effectively witness the call of death – Woman as one of the Names-of-the-Father.

music as the entreaty addressing the Other to stretch out his or her hand to us: what becomes obvious in Schumann is the utter ambiguity of this entreaty, the way it also involves its opposite: yes, answer my call, stretch out your hand, but *not too far* – keep your distance!

To conclude, let us jump to the other end, to the dissolution of the Romantic subject – there is a unique musical piece which stages the disappearance of the Romantic subject: Schoenberg's *Gurrelieder*, which not only 'out-Wagners Wagner himself', but also marks the progress from late Romanticism to properly modern music. *Gurrelieder* is a strange piece, distinguished by a double split: its melodic line was composed in 1901–02, when Schoenberg was still a late Romantic, and instrumentalized in 1910, after Schoenberg's atonal break; this discord between the late-Romantic melodic line and the atonal orchestration accounts for the piece's uncanny effect on the listener. *Gurrelieder* is furthermore split in its very narrative line: the main part tells the archetypal late-Romantic story of the deadly passion which lasts beyond the grave (after his beloved Tove is killed, King Valdemar rises against God Himself, and is punished for this blasphemy by returning restlessly with his band of soldiers as undead spectres); towards the end, however, the heavily pathetic late-Romantic singing is replaced by the melodrama (spoken song, *Sprechgesang*) which announces the regeneration of Life, the transformation of the *nightly* spectral roaming of the 'undead' into the celebration of the new *daylight*, of reawakened 'sane' nature. At this precise point, the Romantic subject which stands for the 'night of the world', whose innermost being consists in phantasmic spectrality, retreats and is replaced by the new daylight – but, what kind of daylight? Definitely not the old, pre-Romantic daylight of the serene Classicist Reason. True, the Romantic passion, melancholy and rising up against God, is replaced by a renewed optimistic beatitude – but, again, what kind of beatitude? Is not this beatitude uncannily close to the one caricatured in the archetypal cartoon scene in which, after a cat or a dog is hit on the head with a heavy hammer, it starts to laugh blissfully and to see birds twittering and dancing around its head?

The daybreak with which *Gurrelieder* concludes thus designates the moment when Romantic infinite longing and pain break down in utter insensitivity, so that the subject is in a way desubjectivized and reduced to a blessed idiot capable only of uttering meaningless babble. For this reason, there is definitely something terrifyingly-obscene about the excessively pathetic declamation of the Speaker's *Sprechgesang* which concludes *Gurrelieder*: an utterly denaturalized nature, a kind of perverted, mocked innocence, not unlike the corrupted debauchee who, to add spice to his games, mimicks a young innocent girl ... The unique achievement of *Gurrelieder* is that it renders the very *passage* from late-Romantic excessive expressionist pathos to the desubjectivized idiotic numbness of the *Sprechgesang*.

Appendix III

The Unconscious Law:
Towards an Ethics Beyond the Good

1

Today the philosophical approach to ethics seems to be split between three options: attempts to provide a direct ontological foundation for ethics via some substantial (communitarian, for example) notion of supreme Good; attempts to save ethical universalism by sacrificing its substantial content and giving universalism a proceduralist twist (Habermas, Rawls); and the 'postmodern' attitude, where the quintessential and only all-encompassing rule is to be aware that what we perceive as 'truth', our own symbolic universe, is merely one in a multitude of fictions, and thus not to impose the rules of our game on the games of others – that is, to maintain the plurality of narrative games.

These three options form a kind of Hegelian triad: first the immediacy of substantial ethics, grounded in the reference to some supreme Good; then its 'negation', the grounding of ethics in some purely formal frame of rules (the criticism according to which this formal proceduralist universality of rules is never truly neutral but effectively always gives preference to some positive content is quite accurate); finally, the 'negation of negation', the postmodern renunciation of universality itself, so that the only universal ethical precepts are the negative ones (allow for the plurality of games, respect the otherness of the Other, do not impose your language game as universal . . .). It should be superfluous to emphasize how this last attitude also involves its own paradoxes: first, it effectively functions as a subspecies of the second position, imposing a second-level set of formal rules (of tolerance, of accepting the irreducible *différend*, etc.); secondly, for that reason, it also *de facto* privileges a certain positive content. It is Lacan's position in relation to this triad, however, which enables us to break out of it by articulating a *fourth* position: an ethics grounded in reference to the traumatic Real which resists symbolization, the Real which is experienced in the encounter with the abyss of the Other's desire (the famous '*Che vuoi?*', 'What do you want [from me]?'). There is ethics – that is to say, an injunction which cannot be grounded in ontology – in so far as there is a crack in the ontological edifice of the universe: at its most elementary, ethics designates fidelity to this crack.

The crucial point on which the consistency of Lacan's position hinges is thus the difference between reality and the Real. If the Lacanian Real is simply another version of 'reality' as the ultimate and unsurmountable point of reference of the symbolic process, then Lacan's endeavour to formulate a new 'ethics of the real' effectively amounts to a return to pre-modern substantialist ethics. Let us, then, tackle this key distinction via a detour through Judith Butler's notion of sexual difference as performatively enacted.[1] Its background is Foucauldian: by means of repetitive interpellative procedures, the social text in which subjects are embedded performatively enacts a series of standardized features (normative constructs) of 'man' and 'woman' as fixed subject positions; what is thus imposed on subjects is the notion (and material practice) of 'sexual difference', the opposition of 'man' and 'woman' as fixed and 'naturalized' subject positions. For Lacan, however, sexual difference is something radically different – paradoxically, it *precedes* the two differentiated positions, 'masculine' and 'feminine': sexual difference is the Real of an antagonism/deadlock that the two positions, 'masculine' and 'feminine'

---

1   See Judith Butler, *Gender Trouble,* New York: Routledge, 1990; *Bodies That Matter,* New York: Routledge, 1993.

endeavour to symbolize, but can do so only by way of getting involved in their own inconsistencies.

Against the criticism that the Lacanian Real continues to function as the ultimate referent which fixes/limits the play of signifying displacements, one should thus insist on the distinction between the Real and (objective) reality – to put it succinctly, the trauma *qua* real is not the ultimate external referent of the symbolic process, but precisely that X which forever hinders any neutral representation of external referential reality. To put it more paradoxically, the Real *qua* traumatic antagonism is, as it were, the *objective factor of subjectivization* itself; it is the object which accounts for the failure of every neutral-objective representation, the object which 'pathologizes' the subject's gaze or approach, makes it biased, pulls it askew. At the level of gaze, the Real is not so much the invisible Beyond, eluding our gazes which can perceive only delusive appearances, but, rather, the very stain or spot which disturbs and blurs our 'direct' perception of reality – which 'bends' the direct straight line from our eyes to the perceived object.

Therein lies the unsurmountable divide that forever separates dialectical materialism from discursive idealism, as well as from non-dialectical ('vulgar') materialism: for the latter, subjective perception is a distorted, 'pathologically' biased, 'reflection' of 'objective' reality which, ontologically fully constituted, exists outside, 'independently' of the subject; for transcendental idealism, 'objective' reality itself is constituted through the subjective act of transcendental synthesis. The true point of idealism is not the solipsistic one ('there is no objective reality, merely our subjective representations of it'); idealism claims, on the contrary, that the In-itself of 'objective reality' is definitely to be distinguished from mere subjective representations – its point is only that it is the synthetic act of the transcendental subject itself which transforms the multitude of representations into 'objective reality'. In short, idealism's point is not that there is no In-itself, but that the 'objective' In-itself, in its very opposition to subjective representations, is posited by the subject.

Lacan (dialectical materialism) accepts idealism's basic ontological premiss (the transcendental subjective constitution of 'objective reality'), and supplements it with the premiss that this very act of ontological positing of 'objective reality' is always-already 'stained', 'tainted' by a particular object which confers upon the subject's 'universal' view of reality a particular 'pathological' twist. This particular object, *objet petit a*, is thus the paradox of a 'pathological a priori', of a particular object which, precisely as radically 'subjective' (*objet petit a* is, in a way, subject itself in its 'impossible' objectality, the objectal correlate of the subject), sustains constitutive transcendental universality itself; in other words, *objet petit a* is not only the 'objective factor of subjectivization' but also the very opposite, the 'subjective factor of objectivization'.

Let us clarify this key point apropos of trauma as the Real. Claude Lanzmann's film *Shoah* alludes to the trauma of the Holocaust as something beyond representation (it can be discerned only via its traces, surviving witnesses, remaining monuments); however, the reason for this impossibility of representing the Holocaust is not simply that it is 'too traumatic', but, rather, that we, observing subjects, are still involved in it, are still a part of the process which generated it (we need only recall a scene from *Shoah* in which Polish peasants from a village near the concentration camp, interviewed now, in our present time, continue to find Jews 'strange' – that is, repeat the very logic that brought the Holocaust about . . .).

The traumatic Real is thus that which, precisely, prevents us from assuming a neutral-objective view of reality, a stain which blurs our clear perception of it. And this example also brings home the *ethical* dimension of fidelity to the Real *qua* impossible: the point is not simply to 'tell the entire truth about it', but, above all, to confront the way we ourselves, by means of our subjective position of enunciation, are always-already involved, engaged in it . . . For that reason, a trauma is always redoubled into the traumatic event 'in itself', and into the trauma of its symbolic inscription.[2]

2   'On the one hand, there's a cataclysmic event, which produces symptoms and calls for testimony. And then it happens again, when the value of the witness in the testimony is denied, and there's no one to hear the account, no one to attend or respond – not simply to the event, but to its witness as well' (Tom Keenan, 'The AIDS Crisis Is Not Over', in *Trauma: Explorations in Memory*, ed. Cathy Caruth, Baltimore, MD: Johns Hopkins University Press, 1995, p. 23).

That is to say: when one is caught in a trauma (a concentration camp, a torture chamber . . .), what keeps one alive is the notion of bearing witness – 'I must survive in order to tell the others (the Other) what really went on here . . .'. The second trauma takes place when this recognition of the first trauma through its symbolic integration necessarily fails (my pain can never be fully shared by the other): it then appears to the victim that he or she has survived in vain, that their survival was meaningless. The victims of rape in the Bosnian war, for example, were traumatized again by the denial of symbolic recognition – that is to say, when the narrative of their ordeal was either dismissed as fantasizing, or perceived as a sign of their complicity (whores deserve it, they are stigmatized, dirty . . .); most of the suicides of these victims occurred at *this* point, not in the direct aftermath of the original traumatic experience.

Or – with respect to truth: the Real *qua* trauma is not the ultimate 'unspeakable' truth which the subject can approach only asymptotically, but that which makes every articulated symbolic truth forever 'not-all', failed, a bone stuck in the throat of the speaking being which makes it impossible to 'tell everything'. This is also how the Real of antagonism ('class struggle') functions within the social field: antagonism, again, is not the ultimate referent which anchors and limits the unending drift of the signifiers ('the ultimate meaning of all social phenomena is determined by their position in class struggle'), but the very force of their constant displacement – that on account of which socio-ideological phenomena never mean what they seem/purport to mean – for example, 'class struggle' is that on account of which every direct reference to universality (of 'humanity', of 'our nation', etc.) is, always in a specific way, 'biased', dislocated with regard to its literal meaning. 'Class struggle' is the Marxist name for this basic 'operator of dislocation'; as such, 'class struggle' means that there is no neutral metalanguage allowing us to grasp society as a given 'objective' totality, since we always-already 'take sides'. The fact that there is no 'neutral', 'objective' concept of class struggle is thus the crucial constituent of this notion.[3]

3   For a more detailed account, see Slavoj Žižek, 'Introduction', in *Mapping Ideology*, London: Verso, 1995.

Exactly the same goes for sexual difference *qua* real in Lacan: sexual difference is not the ultimate referent which posits a limit to the unending drift of symbolization, in so far as it underlies all other polarities and provides their 'deep' meaning (as in pre-modern sexual cosmologies: light against darkness, fire against water, reason against emotion, etc.; they are all, in the last resort, *yin* against *yang*, the male principle against the female . . .), but, on the contrary, that which 'skews' the discursive universe, preventing us from grounding its formations in 'hard reality' – that on account of which every *symbolization* of sexual difference is forever unstable and displaced with regard to itself. To put it in a slightly speculative way: sexual difference is not some mysterious inaccessible X which can never be symbolized but, rather, the very obstacle to this symbolization, the stain which forever keeps the Real apart from the modes of its symbolization. Crucial to the notion of the Real is this coincidence of the inaccessible X with the obstacle which makes it inaccessible – as in Heidegger, who emphasizes again and again how Being is not simply 'withdrawn': Being 'is' *nothing but its own withdrawal* . . .

In what precise sense, then, is the Real not the last vestige of the fixed unhistorical referent? Let us quote Ernesto Laclau's concise formulation: 'the limits of signification can only announce themselves as the impossibility of realizing what is within those limits'.[4] In this precise sense, real (antagonism) is inherent to the symbolic (system of differences), not the transcendent Beyond which the signifying process tries to grasp in vain: in the case of real antagonism, external opposition is always internal; the antagonistic opposition of B to A prevents A from realizing its full self-identity, truncates it from within (for example, sexual difference is antagonistic in so far as the opposition between men and women, far from being complementary, prevents women from achieving their identity, from developing their autonomous identity). This also allows us to conceive of the Fascist strategy as a desperate attempt to construct a purely differential hierarchical system of Society by condensing all negativity, all antagonistic

4   Ernesto Laclau, *Emancipation(s)*, London: Verso, 1996, p. 37.

tension, in the external figure of the Jew. And the Real cannot be signified not because it is outside, external to the symbolic order, but precisely because it is inherent to it, its internal limit: the Real is the internal stumbling block on account of which the symbolic system can never 'become itself', achieve its self-identity. Because of its absolute *immanence* to the symbolic, the Real cannot be positively *signified*; it can only be *shown*, in a negative gesture, as the inherent failure of symbolization: 'if what we are talking about are the limits of a *signifying system*, it is clear that those limits cannot themselves be signified, but have to *show* themselves as the *interruption* or *breakdown* of the process of signification'.[5] Crucial here is Laclau's implicit reference to the Wittgensteinian opposition between signifying and showing: the real as impossible can be shown (rendered) only as the failure of the process which, precisely, aims at signifying it . . .

Perhaps this also opens up a new approach to phenomenology, redefined as the description of the ways in which the breakdown (failure) of symbolization, which cannot be signified, *shows itself*. Furthermore, perhaps, this is how we should read Hegel's determination of art as the (sensible) appearing – that is, showing – of the Idea: what appears in art, what art demonstrates, is the Idea's *failure* to signify itself directly.

In his reference to phenomenology, Lacan moves through three stages. Early Lacan is a hermeneutical phenomenologist in that for him the domain of psychoanalysis is the domain of meaning – that is to say, the goal of psychoanalytic treatment is to integrate traumatic symptoms into the domain of meaning. The middle 'structuralist' Lacan aggressively devalues phenomenology: in Jacques-Alain Miller's classic formulation,[6] phenomenology is determined as the imaginary science of the Imaginary; as such, it is unable to approach the senseless structural mechanism which generates the phenomenal effect-of-meaning. Later, with the shift of emphasis on to the Real, fantasy is no longer reduced to an imaginary formation (over)determined by the absent symbolic network, but

5   Ibid.
6   See Jacques-Alain Miller, 'L'Action de la structure', *Cahiers pour l'Analyse* 9, Paris, 1966.

conceived as the formation which fills in the gap of the Real – as Lacan put it, 'one does not interpret fantasy [*on n'interprète pas le fantasme*]'. Phenomenology is now reasserted as the description of the ways in which the Real shows itself in phantasmic formations, without being signified in them: it is the description, not interpretation, of the spectral domain of mirages, of 'negative magnitudes' which positivize the lack in the symbolic order. We are thus dealing here with the paradoxical disjunction between phenomenology and hermeneutics: Lacan opens up the possibility of a radically non-hermeneutical phenomenology – of a phenomenological description of spectral apparitions which stand in for constitutive non-sense. In so far as the respective domains of *meaning* (accessible to hermeneutics) and symbolic *structure* (accessible through structural analysis) form two circles, the phenomenological description of fantasy is thus to be located at the *intersection* of these two circles.

2

The philosopher who opened up this problematic of the 'phenomenology of the Real' is none other than Kant. In Kant's philosophy, Beautiful, Sublime and Monstrous [*Ungeheure*] form a triad which corresponds to the Lacanian triad of Imaginary, Symbolic and Real: the relationship between the three terms is that of a Borromean knot, in which two terms are linked *via* the third (Beauty makes possible the sublimation of the Monstrous; sublimation mediates between Beautiful and Monstrous; etc.). As in Hegelian dialectics, each term, brought to its extreme – that is fully actualized – changes into the next: an object which is thoroughly beautiful is no longer merely beautiful, it is already sublime; in the same way, an object which is thoroughly sublime turns into something monstrous. Or, to put it the opposite way: a beautiful object without the element of the Sublime is not truly beautiful; a sublime object which lacks the embryonic dimension of the Monstrous is not truly sublime, merely beautiful . . . [7]

7   Here I draw on Jacob Rogozinski, *Kanten*, Paris: Éditions Kime, 1996.

This interconnection provides the key to the paradoxical relationship between the (sublime) Law and the horror of the Monstrous in Kant: the suprasensible Law, as well as the Monstrous, belongs to the domain of the noumenal, and what Kant is not ready to accept, the conclusion he endeavours to avoid at any cost, is the ultimate *identity* between the two, the fact that the sublime Law is *the same as* the Monstrous – all that changes is the subject's perspective on it. That is to say: one has to distinguish the In-itself as the monstrosity of the Real from the In-itself of the sublime Law which is already For-us (what the moral subject experiences as the kingdom of universal rational Goals which bears witness to his noumenal freedom): this second In-itself emerges only when the subject views the Real, as it were, from the proper phenomenal distance – the moment we come too close to the Law, its sublime majesty turns into obscene abhorrent monstrosity. This implicit reversal of the traditional theological justification of Evil and disharmony ('What our finite mind perceives as disturbing stains are, in the eyes of God's infinite mind, details which contribute to the global Harmony') condenses the entire Kantian revolution: what our finite mind perceives as the sublime majesty of the moral Law is in itself the monstrosity of a crazy sadistic God.

Kant's thesis that the limitation of human experience to the phenomenal domain is a necessary condition of ethical activity (since a direct insight into noumena would make ethics superfluous) is thus much odder than it may seem: its underlying premiss is that the status of the ethical Goals is in a way *anamorphic* – that is to say, the divine monstrosity appears as the kingdom of rational Goals only when it is viewed from a certain (finite human) angle.[8] Or – to put it another way – it is not only the experienced material reality that results from the combination of two heterogeneous levels (the transcendental a priori of the categories of pure Reason and the way that transcendent things affect our mind); the noumenal rational kingdom of ethical Goals is itself the product of the combination of the monstrous, unbearable 'true In-itself', and its pacifying distortion by the perceptive framework of our finite mind.

8   For a more detailed account of this aspect of Kant's philosophy, see Part 1 of Slavoj Žižek, *Tarrying With the Negative*, Durham, NC: Duke University Press, 1993.

This tension between the two aspects of the noumenal, the (moral) Law and the Monstrous (with the *superego* as their intersection, i.e. as the disturbing apparition of a *monstrous Law*) is already at work in pure reason, in the most elementary synthesis of imagination (memory, retention, temporality). That is to say: what Kant fails to appreciate is the extent to which this synthesis constitutive of 'normal' reality is, in an unheard-of and simultaneously most fundamental sense, already 'violent', in so far as it consists in an order imposed by the subject's synthetic activity on the heterogeneous disarray of impressions.[9] If the synthesis of imagination were to succeed without a gap, we would obtain the perfect self-sufficient and self-enclosed auto-affection. However, the synthesis of imagination necessarily fails; it gets caught in an inconsistency in two different ways:

- first, in an inherent way, through the imbalance between apprehension and comprehension, which generates the mathematical sublime: the synthetic comprehension is not able to 'catch up' with the magnitude of the apprehended perceptions with which the subject is bombarded, and it is this very failure of synthesis which reveals its violent nature;
- then, in an external way, through the intervention of the (moral) Law which announces another dimension, that of the noumenal: the (moral) Law is necessarily experienced by the subject as a violent intrusion which disturbs the smooth self-sufficient running of the auto-affection of his imagination.

In these two cases of the violence which emerges as a kind of answer to the preceding violence of the transcendental imagination itself, we thus encounter the matrix of mathematical and dynamic antinomies. This is the exact *locus* at which the antagonism between (philosophical)

9   See Rogozinski, *Kanten*, pp. 124–30.

materialism and idealism is discernible in Kant's philosophy; it concerns the question of primacy in the relationship between the two antinomies. Idealism gives priority to the dynamic antinomy, to the way the suprasensible Law transcends and/or suspends from the outside the phenomenal causal chain: from this perspective, phenomenal inconsistency is merely the way in which the noumenal Beyond inscribes itself into the phenomenal domain. Materialism, in contrast, gives priority to mathematical antinomy, to the inherent inconsistency of the phenomenal domain: the ultimate outcome of mathematical antinomy is the domain of an 'inconsistent All', of a multitude which lacks the ontological consistency of 'reality'. From this perspective, the dynamic antinomy itself seems like an attempt to resolve the inherent deadlock of mathematical antinomy by transposing it into the coexistence of two distinct orders, the phenomenal and the noumenal. In other words, mathematical antinomy (i.e. the inherent failure, collapse, of imagination) 'dissolves' phenomenal reality in the direction of the monstrous Real, while dynamic antinomy transcends phenomenal reality in the direction of the symbolic Law – that is, it 'saves phenomena' by providing a kind of external guarantee of the phenomenal domain.[10]

As Lenin emphasized, the history of philosophy consists in an incessant, repetitive tracing of the difference between materialism and idealism; what one has to add is that, as a rule, this line of demarcation does not run where one would obviously expect it to run – often, the materialist choice hinges on how we decide on a seemingly secondary alternative. Within the horizon of Kant's philosophy, 'materialism' does not consist in clinging to the Thing-in-itself (allegedly the last vestige of materialism which poses a limit to the idealist thesis on the subjective positing of reality), as Lenin himself incorrectly claimed, but, rather, in asserting the primacy of mathematical antinomy, and conceiving dynamic antinomy

10   For a more detailed account of the connection between the Kantian antinomies and Lacan's paradoxes of non-All, see Chapter 2 of Žižek, *Tarrying With the Negative*.

as secondary, as an attempt to 'save phenomena' through the noumenal Law as their constitutive exception.[11]

3

So – back to our starting point: how does this dialectical materialist reference to the Real affect our reading of Kantian ethics? According to the standard pseudo-Hegelian criticism, Kantian ethics fails to take into account the concrete historical situation in which the ethical subject is embedded, and which provides the determinate content of the Good: what eludes Kantian formalism is the historically specified particular Substance of ethical life. However, one should counter this criticism by claiming that the unique strength of Kant's ethics lies in this very formal indeterminacy: moral Law does not tell me *what* my duty is, it merely tells me *that* I should accomplish my duty. That is to say, it is not possible to derive the concrete norms I have to follow in my specific situation from the moral Law itself – *which means that the subject himself has to assume the responsibility of 'translating' the abstract injunction of the moral Law into a series of concrete obligations.* In this precise sense, the point of Kant's ethics is (to paraphrase Hegel) 'to conceive the moral Absolute not only as Substance, but also as Subject': the ethical subject bears full responsibility for the concrete universal norms he follows – that is to say, the only guarantor of the universality

11   The same goes for the relationship between (social) antagonism and the 'ontological' gap between the Real and reality. How do the two relate to each other? Perhaps we encounter here the ultimate line of separation between idealism and materialism. That is to say: idealism locates the ultimate horizon of human experience in the gap that separates the ontological Void from constituted reality. The ultimate idealist problematic is that of the content which fills in the Void which gapes in the midst of reality (is this Void filled in merely by fantasies?), while materialism conceives of the Void (or 'primordial Lack') as the indicator of the primordial repression of the antagonism. So the ultimate idealist gesture of 'demystification' is that of denouncing each and every positive content as a contingent filler (place-holder) of the transcendental Void, while materialism endeavours to enter the dimension beyond (or, rather, beneath) this Void. And does not this opposition rely on the contrast between drive and desire? Drive involves a purely ontic antagonism, and is therefore strictly pre-ontological, while desire is 'ontological', maintained by the void in the midst of the ontic.

of positive moral norms is the subject's own contingent act of performatively assuming these norms.

It is therefore Kant's very 'formalism' which opens up the decisive gap in the self-enclosed ethic and/or religious Substance of a particular life-world: I can no longer simply rely on the determinate content provided by the ethical tradition in which I am embedded; this tradition is always-already 'mediated' by the subject; it 'remains alive' only in so far as I effectively assume it. The way to undermine ethical particularism (the notion that a subject can find his or her ethical Substance only in the particular tradition out of which he grew) is thus not via reference to some more universal positive content (like the unfortunate 'universal values shared by all humanity'), but only by accepting that the ethical Universal is in itself indeterminate, empty, and that it can be translated into a set of positive explicit norms only by means of my active engagement, for which I take full responsibility . . . thus there is no determinate ethical universality without the contingency of the subject's act of positing it as such.

That is also the actual thrust of Hegel's critique of Kant: Hegel is not a contextual traditionalist who claims that I must 'irrationally' accept the particular content of my ethical community; he definitely endorses the need to break out of the constraints of particular identity. What Hegel effectively rejects is merely the notion of categorical imperative as the abstract testing device which enables me to establish, apropos of every determinate norm, if it is my duty to follow it or not: Hegel's implicit point is precisely that there is no universal moral Law which would free me of the responsibility for its determinate content. Or – to put it more precisely – what Hegel draws attention to is the fact that actual Universality is not only the abstract content common to all particular cases, but also the 'negative' power of disrupting each particular content. The fact that the Subject is a Universal Being means that, precisely, he cannot simply rely on some determinate substantial content ('universal' as it may be) which would fix the co-ordinates of his ethical activity in advance, but that the only way for him to arrive at Universality is to accept the objective indeterminacy of his situation – I become 'universal' only through the violent effort of disengaging myself from the particularity of my situation: through conceiving this situation as contingent and limiting, through opening up in it the gap of indeterminacy filled in by my act. Subjectivity and universality are thus strictly correlative: the dimension of universality becomes 'for itself' only through the 'individualist' negation of the particular context which forms the subject's specific background.[12]

The full acceptance of this paradox also compels us to reject any reference to 'duty' as an excuse: 'I know this is difficult, and might be painful, but what can I do? It's my duty . . .'. The standard motto of ethical rigour is 'There is no excuse for not accomplishing one's duty!'; although Kant's '*Du kannst, denn du sollst!* [You can, because you must!]' seems to offer a new version of this motto, he implicitly complements it with its much more uncanny inversion: 'There is no excuse for *accomplishing* one's duty!'[13] The reference to duty as the excuse for doing our duty should be rejected as hypocritical; we need only recall the proverbial example of a severe sadistic teacher who subjects his pupils to merciless discipline and torture – of course, his excuse to himself (and to others) is: 'I myself find it hard to exert such pressure on the poor kids, but what can I do? It's my duty!'. The more pertinent example is that of a Stalinist politician who loves mankind, but none the less carries out horrible purges and executions; his heart is breaking while he is doing it, but he cannot help it, it's his Duty to the Progress of Humanity . . . What we encounter here is the properly *perverse* attitude of adopting the position of the pure instrument of the big Other's Will: it's not my responsibility, it's not me who is effectively

12   One can see how Ernesto Laclau's notion of *hegemony* is perfectly suited to this Kantian ethical frame: the positive content of the empty universal is provided by the subject who, by an act of abyssal decision, *identifies* the (empty) Universal with some particular content which hegemonizes it (say, in the case of a successful Nazi ideological hegemony, 'to be a true German' *equals* 'rejecting liberal individualism as well as the principle of class struggle on behalf of the vision of society as a corporate body whose members – classes – co-operate harmoniously').

13   For a more detailed account of this key feature of Kant's ethics, see Chapter 2 of Slavoj Žižek, *The Indivisible Remainder*, London: Verso, 1996.

doing it, I am merely an instrument of the higher Historical Necessity . . . The obscene *jouissance* of this situation is generated by the fact that I conceive of myself as exculpated from what I am doing: isn't it nice to be able to inflict pain on others in the full awareness that I'm not responsible for it, that I am merely fulfilling the Other's Will . . . *this* is what Kantian ethics prohibits. This position of the sadist pervert provides the answer to the question: How can the subject be guilty when he merely realizes an 'objective', externally imposed necessity? By subjectively assuming this 'objective necessity' – by finding *enjoyment* in what is imposed on him.[14]

4

Perhaps a reference to Pascal is of some help here. For Pascal, as we have already seen,[15] ideology is not only 'irrational obedience' beneath which critical analysis must discern its true reasons and causes; it is also the 'rationalization', the enumeration of a network of reasons, which masks the unbearable fact that Law is grounded only in its own act of enunciation: argumentation is for the crowd of 'ordinary people' who need the illusion that there are good and proper reasons for the orders they must obey, while the true secret, known only to the elite, is that the dogma of power is grounded only in itself. And Kant's notion of duty has an analogous structure. That is to say: one should invert the standard pseudo-Freudian approach to Kant which endeavours to discern secret 'pathological' motivations beneath what appears to be an ethical act accomplished purely out of duty ('You think you did it out of duty, but you were actually doing it to satisfy your vanity, to impress your peers, to gain the love of your prospective mistress . . .'): Kant himself would be willing to accept this point, since he emphasizes how we can never be sure if we have acted for the sake of duty alone. What, however, if we follow the illusion that we have acted for some 'pathological' reason (to satisfy our vanity, to impress

14   See Alenka Zupančič, *Die Ethik des Realen. Kant mit Lacan*, Vienna: Turia & Kant, 1995.
15   See Chapter 2 above.

our peers...) in order to avoid the traumatic fact that we did it 'for nothing'
– that is, for the sake of duty alone?

The true horror of the act resides in this self-referential abyss – or, to
put it another way, it is crucial to bear in mind the gap between the act
and Will: the act occurs as a 'crazy', unaccountable event which, precisely,
is not 'willed'. The subject's will is, by definition, split with regard to an
act: since attraction to and repulsion against the act are inextricably mixed
in it, the subject can never fully 'assume' the act. In short, what Lacan
calls 'act' has the precise status of an *object* which the subject can never
'swallow', subjectivize – which forever remains a foreign body, a bone
stuck in his throat. The standard subject's reaction to the act is that of
aphanisis, of his/her self-obliteration, not of heroically assuming it: when
the awareness of the full consequences of 'what I have just done' hits me,
I want to disappear. At this precise point, Lacan (and already Freud's notion
of the death drive) parts with the Romantic ideology of a 'demonic' self-
destructive Will: the death drive is *not* a 'will to die', radical Evil is *not* a
'diabolical' intention that seeks pleasure in inflicting pain on one's
neighbour ...

In Max Opuls's undeservedly neglected melodrama *Caught*, there is a
unique moment of ethical decision in which the act coincides with *not*
doing it: Leonora, the heroine, silently observes Smith, her husband, lying
in convulsions (from a faked hysterical heart attack) on the floor, and
ignores his desperate pleas for water and pills – she simply withdraws
silently, actively wishing for him to die (as she later acknowledges). (The
scene uses a depth-of-field shot, with the husband in the front and her
in the background.) She then also gets rid of the child (the last legacy from
the husband), and is at the very end effectively reborn, ready to start a
new life with her true love, Doctor Quinada. This scene is one of those
moments in which Hollywood passes the threshold of the ideologically
permissible – one wonders how it got past the Hayes Code.[16] In Lacanese,

16   Another such scene is definitely James Mason's – who is also in *Caught* – famous
line 'God was wrong!' (in preventing Abraham's slaughter of Isaac at the last moment)
from Nicholas Ray's *Bigger Than Life*.

Leonora's choice enacts the disjunction between the Good and the proper ethical stance, since it is the choice between the Good (human compassion and matrimonial ideology, which both direct her to help her suffering husband in distress) on the one hand and the ethical stance of the death drive on the other, and she chooses the death drive. After making this choice, Leonora literally undergoes *aphanisis* – she passes out, is totally immobilized, overwhelmed by feelings of guilt (i.e. unable to accept her full assertion of death drive); finally, she is reborn, delivered of the pressure of guilt, and ready for a new beginning. In this precise sense, *act* has for Lacan the status of an unbearable object which the subject is unable to assume and subjectivize.

Of course, as Mary Ann Doane has shown in her penetrating analysis,[17] the end of the film brings about an overtly oppressive patriarchal closure. Paradigmatic here is the scene in an ambulance towards the end in which sirens wail as Quinada tells Leonora how free she can be if the child dies. The intrusive closeness of Quinada to Leonora, who lies immobilized on the ambulance stretcher, is matched by the no less intrusive proximity of the camera to her – her liberation is thus literally staged as her entry into the new (medical) order of subordination. In other words, her 'liberation' consists in being passed from one man to another. It is also a man (Quinada's older colleague) who enacts for her, on her behalf, her liberation from the symbol of her enslavement to Smith, as well as in general to the idea of the wealth and culture of images (a mink coat), by ordering a nurse to get rid of Leonora's mink. Leonora is thus not only reduced to an object of exchange between the two male protagonists; her liberation from the lure of wealth is also false, because it endorses the notion that one should not transgress class boundaries in marriage (in contrast to the rich Smith, Quinada is of her own class). But the act of refusing to yield to compassion, this moment of the open assertion of the death drive, none the less remains her own, and is merely taken over after the act by the 'new man in her

17   See Chapter 6 of Mary Ann Doane, *The Desire to Desire*, Bloomington: Indiana University Press, 1987.

life'. The woman's paralysis is thus not simply the indicator of her subordination; rather, it bears witness to the *aphanisis*, to the subject's self-obliteration which always accompanies the act on account of its suicidal dimension. So – back to the ambulance scene: it is crucial to read its claustrophobic character with a sense of (medical) urgency, intensified by the sound of sirens which provide a strange background to the scene's intimacy – perhaps Quinada is reduced here to his role of obstetrician, and this intimacy, rather, signals the passage through (symbolic) death and consequent rebirth.

The oppressive intimacy of the scene in the ambulance directly recalls the same kind of intimacy at the end of Hitchcock's *Notorious*, when Cary Grant carries the drugged and half-paralysed Ingrid Bergman down the stairs to freedom (i.e. to their happy matrimonial future): here, also, the woman is ultimately the object of exchange between two men. Is not the ultimate Hitchcockian version of this in the climax of his two Tippi Hedren movies, *Birds* and *Marnie*? In both films, the heroine – who, at the outset, is an active, self-assertive young woman who exerts a hold on her life (albeit in a 'superficial' or 'pathological' way: the manipulative socialite in *Birds*, the kleptomaniac in *Marnie*) – is reduced at the end to a paralysed, numbed mummy: now, after her 'non-authentic' hold on her own life has been violently crushed, she is ready to enter the matrimonial link . . .[18] Again, the self-evidence of such a feminist reading is to be put in question: true, what we are witnessing here is the heroine's symbolic death; however,

18   Elisabeth Bronfen (see Chapter 8 of *The Knotted Subject*, Princeton, NJ: Princeton University Press, 1997) draws attention to how Tippi Hedren's final confrontation with the birds (in *The Birds*), which reduces her to an incapacitated mummy capable only of hysterical wild defensive gestures of waving her hands, replays the scenario of Gothic novels *à la* Radcliffe, in which the young and innocent heroine finally dares to go up the stairs and enter the room in the attic, the place of forbidden secrets which emits whispers and cries during the night – in a kind of ironic reversal of the formula, Hedren herself is reduced to the 'madwoman in the attic'. The scene of her going up the stairs is strictly analogous to the scene of the detective Arbogast climbing the stairs of the mother's house and then being attacked by the mother-figure in *Psycho*: a further confirmation of the fact that the attacking birds stand for the unleashed force of the maternal superego . . . The room in the attic with a mysterious opening in its roof is thus literally the place of

the question remains open as to what the final outcome of her confrontation with the traumatic Thing will be – that is, in what guise she will be 'reborn'.

5

How, then, does Kant's notion of the moral Law compel us to rethink the opposition between Good and Evil? In *Coldness and Cruelty*, Deleuze provides an unsurpassable formulation of Kant's radically new conception of the law:

> the law is no longer regarded as dependent on the Good, but on the contrary, the Good itself is made to depend on the law. This means that the law no longer has its foundation in some higher principle from which it would derive its authority, but that it is self-grounded and valid solely by virtue of its own form . . . Kant, by establishing THE LAW as an ultimate ground or principle, added an essential dimension to modern thought: the object of the law is by definition unknowable and elusive . . . Clearly THE LAW, as defined by its pure form, without substance or object of any determination whatsoever, is such that no one knows nor can know what it is. It operates without making itself known. It defines a realm of transgression where one is already guilty, and where one oversteps the bounds without knowing what they are, as in the case of Oedipus. Even guilt and punishment do not tell us what the law is, but leave it in a state of indeterminacy equaled only by the extreme specificity of the punishment.[19]

---

ex-timacy: the place in the very centre of the house which nests the threatening exterior (the attacking birds). The 'secret' is thus that the true *locus* of the threatening exterior is well within the house, which is why no wooden planks can protect us from it: in a Freudian reading, the room in the attic Hedren approaches is, of course, the parental bedroom.

19   Gilles Deleuze, *Coldness and Cruelty*, New York: Zone Books, 1991, pp. 82–3.

The Kantian Law is thus not merely an empty form applied to a random empirical content in order to ascertain if this content meets the criteria of ethical adequacy – rather, the empty form of the Law functions as the promise of an absent content (never) to come. Or – to put it in a slightly different way – the form is not only a kind of neutral-universal mould of the plurality of different empirical contents; the autonomy of the Form, rather, bears witness to the uncertainty which persists with regard to the content of our acts – we never know if the determinate content which accounts for the specificity of our acts is the right one: that is, if we have really acted in accordance with the Law and have not been guided by some hidden pathological motive. Kant thus announces the notion of Law which culminates in Kafka and in the experience of modern political 'totalitarianism': since, in the case of the Law, its *Dass-Sein* (the fact of the Law) precedes its *Was-Sein* (what this Law is), the subject finds himself in a situation in which, although he knows there is a Law, he never knows (and a priori *cannot* know) *what* this Law is – a gap forever separates *the* Law from its positive incarnations. The subject is thus a priori, by virtue of his very existence, guilty: guilty without knowing what he is guilty of (and for that very reason guilty), infringing the law without knowing its exact regulations.

What we have here is, for the first time in the history of philosophy, the assertion of the Law as *unconscious*: the experience of Form without content is always the index of a repressed content – the more intensely the subject sticks to the empty form, the more traumatic the repressed content becomes. This also holds for art history: since the very beginnings of bourgeois art, artistic formalism has been nothing but a stigmatized-coagulated emergence of some repressed antagonistic content, too traumatic to be directly assumed – that is to say, the insistence on a pure form, and the paranoiac resistance to concrete social content (from Gautier onwards), serves as the unmistakable signal of the presence of some traumatic repressed content. In this precise sense, formalism is a kind of elementary *Konversionshysterie* – that which was repressed at the level of content returns in the guise of 'autonomous' form. The same applies to the symbolic order itself as the universal Form: as a first step, of course, one should oppose any quick reduction of the symbolic form to its content (the basic lesson of so-called 'structuralism' was that the symbolic form is never simply an expression of its content). To subordinate the symbolic form directly to its content in such a way is to fall into the trap of 'reification' and to misrecognize the structuring role of this form itself with regard to its content: what the term 'form' stands for is the signifying process which generates the signified 'content' . . . The next step, however, is to focus on how the symbolic form which seems to precede content emerges by means of a primordial repression of some traumatic kernel of 'content' which, precisely, can never become the explicit content of this form.

And does not the same also hold for the Kantian moral Law as pure universal Form? What, then, in this case, is the repressed 'secret' of Kantian ethical formalism? The answer is provided by Kant himself. Jacob Rogozinski[20] describes in detail how, in each of his three *Critiques*, Kant repeatedly produces a concept which he then almost immediately feels compelled to reject as impossible and/or self-contradictory: the Monstrous [*das Ungeheure*] in the critique of judgement; 'diabolical Evil' (Evil elevated into an ethical principle) in the practical reason (Kant's favourite example of this 'diabolical evil' is the *crimen inexpiabile* of putting to trial and passing a legal sentence on the very bearer of the legal order – the King – in the political sphere).[21] After indicating the contours of this concept, Kant quickly withdraws and offers another, supplementary concept in exchange, a concept which already 'pacifies' the unbearable dimension of the first one: the Sublime (instead of the Monstrous); radical Evil (instead of diabolical Evil) . . . This excessive/impossible concept, in all its different versions, points towards the 'repressed' kernel of the Real which philosophy is never able to confront – its encounter is, by definition, a failed one.

20   See, again, Rogozinski, *Kanten*.
21   On the notion of 'diabolical Evil', see Chapter 3 of Žižek, *Tarrying With the Negative*; on the *crimen inexpiable* of the judicial murder of the Monarch, see Chapter 5 of Slavoj Žižek, *For They Know Not What They Do*, London: Verso, 1991.

There, in the different modalities of avoiding this encounter, lies the difference between Kant and Hegel: Kant is 'not-yet' there; he stops short of the ultimate horror of the monstrous Thing and avoids it; while Hegel is 'no-longer' there – he only feigns fully to embrace radical negativity, to 'tarry with the negative', since the dialectical machinery guarantees the happy outcome, the 'magic' (Hegel's own term) reversal of the Negative into the Positive (of the radical negativity of political Terror into the inner Call of conscience, etc.) in advance . . . In short, the impossible *content* of the moral Law as pure *form* is 'diabolical Evil'. The empty moral Law is thus the supreme example of what Lacan endeavours to isolate as the kernel of the Freudian concept of *Vorstellungs-Repräsentanz*: the (symbolic) *representative* of (or, rather, stand-in for) the impossible, foreclosed *representation* – that is, of (for) the *content* of the Law which must be foreclosed if the Law is to function normally (in a non-psychotic way). One can also see how the concept of *Vorstellungs-Repräsentanz* allows us to explain the Lacanian notion of the subject's *aphanisis*, self-obliteration: the subject disintegrates, obliterates itself, the moment it comes too close to the impossible Thing whose symbolic stand-in is in the empty Law: that is to say, the moment when, instead of the injunction of the moral Law, the subject directly confronts the obscene Thing itself, the foreclosed content of the Law.

As a good Kantian, Rogozinski, of course, conceives of Kant's refusal to go right to the end, his stopping short of the abyss of the Monstrous, as a positive condition of the Ethical – the moment one chooses to cross this threshold, one falls into nihilism and commits a kind of ethical suicide, since the very limit which separates Good from Evil is thereby suspended. According to Rogozinski, the proof *a contrario* of this suspension is provided precisely by Hegel who, in his dialectic of the 'cunning of Reason', subordinates Evil (egotistic interests, etc.) to Good as a means of the latter's realization. Hegel thus effectively undermines the very foundations of morality, and opens up the path to the catastrophes of the last two centuries whereby the worst atrocities have been legitimized by means of a reference to historical Necessity or Progress – in this way, Hegelian dialectics regresses beneath the level of modernity to the pagan fascination with a dark God who demands sacrifices.

Joan Copjec goes even further in her heroic attempt to prove that *radical Evil (man's ineradicable propensity to Evil) is actually more radical than diabolical Evil*: the latter already phenomenalizes/positivizes the Law.[22] That is to say: the noumenal Law is phenomenally accessible to us, finite humans, only in a negative way, in the guise of the feeling of guilt, in our awareness that we have betrayed its call, that we have not lived up to our ethical duty – never in a positive way, 'as such'; and this necessity which makes us 'a priori and forever guilty' is the sole content of 'radical Evil'. In other words, without radical Evil, the moral Law would lose its formal character and phenomenalize itself in a set of positive regulations which would tell us at all times where we stand – that is, whether we are guilty or not. Diabolical Evil is thus impossible for the same reason as the position of a saint is untenable: the 'diabolically evil subject' is the Romantic phantasmic image of a negative hero, a kind of inverted saint who fully realizes that what he is doing is evil, and consciously elevates Evil into his ethical principle.

It seems, none the less, that such a reading of Hegel misses its target. Hegel's (and Lacan's, incidentally) point is that it is possible to move 'beyond Good and Evil', beyond the horizon of Law and constitutive guilt, into *drive* (which is the Freudian term for the Hegelian 'infinite play of Idea with itself). Hegel's implicit thesis is that *diabolical Evil is another name for the Good itself*, for the concept 'in itself', the two are indistinguishable; the difference is purely formal, and concerns only the point of view of the perceiving subject. Kant himself was already on the track of this uncanny identity – take the enigmatic conclusion of Part I of the *Critique of Practical Reason*, in which he asserts the (epistemologically) inaccessible character of the moral Law – that is, man's epistemological limitation and/or finitude – as the positive condition of our ethical activity: if we

22   See Joan Copjec, 'Introduction: Evil in the Time of the Finite World', in *Radical Evil*, London: Verso, 1996.

gained direct access to the noumenal sphere, we would be confronted with the 'terrible majesty' of God in His *Ungeheure, horrifying Real.* The effect of this look would be no less petrifying than that of Medusa's gaze: as to the content of his acts, the subject would act morally, but as a lifeless marionette, not as a free living being . . . In *this* sense, Sade is the truth of Kant: here, Kant is forced to formulate the hypothesis of a perverse, diabolical God.

The Hegelian answer is thus that *it is the very opposition between radical Evil and the call of moral Law which is all too 'phenomenal'*, in so far as it is conceived as 'real opposition' – that is, structured according to the feature which, according to Kant, is the most fundamental feature of what we experience as (phenomenal) reality. What is so unbearable about the notion of diabolical Evil is that, far from phenomenalizing Evil, it makes the ethical Good and Evil *indistinguishable* – the problem with diabolical Evil is that it meets all the criteria of the transcendental definition of a morally good act . . . Far from being the inadmissible phenomenalization of Law, diabolical Evil is the non-phenomenalizable Real, the impossible point of intersection between Good and Evil, the 'vanishing mediator' between the two, which has to be presupposed if we are to account for the tension between Good and Evil which is a part of our phenomenal life. In other words, the only true phenomenalization of diabolical Evil (i.e. the way in which diabolical Evil appears to the finite subject, is experienced by him) is *the Good itself,* the call of the moral Law. Diabolical Evil is therefore not to be confounded with its false phenomenalization, with the narcissistic figure of the Byronesque hero who, in a melancholically heroic way, elevates Evil into a sublime metaphysical entity, and assumes it as his End-in-Itself (see Milton's 'Evil, be Thou my Good'): this figure already suspends the impossible-real dimension of diabolical Evil, reducing it to the narcissistic economy of a hero who likes to see himself as evil. In short, 'diabolical Evil' is simply Kant's name for what Freud later endeavoured to approach in the guise of the *death drive* which subverts the duality of the egotistic striving for pleasure and ethical duty: to deny 'diabolical Evil' is, within the psychoanalytic frame, strictly equivalent to denying the death drive.

Or – to put it in yet another way – as Hegel pointed out, the Kantian moral act is ultimately *impossible* to accomplish; one can never be certain of excluding all pathological motivations – that is, one becomes effectively aware of one's duty only through one's awareness of one's failure to carry it out in full. Just as Kant states that moral law is the *ratio cognoscendi* of my noumenal freedom (I become aware of my freedom only through the experience of how, on behalf of the moral law, I am able to withstand the pressure of the pathological motivations which tie me to innerworldly phenomenal causality), one can say that the *failure* to do one's duty, the experience of one's *inadequacy* to act in full compliance with the moral law, is the *ratio cognoscendi* of the moral law itself. Consequently, the argument according to which the notion of 'diabolical Evil' should be rejected as involving a gesture of impossible phenomenalization misses the mark: it is already the moral act as such (in so far as it is not merely the inner intention to act, but an effectively accomplished act) which is evil, since in it the gap that separates noumenal from phenomenal, the pure noumenal ethical injunction from a positive worldly act which fails to realize it, is by definition suppressed. This is the unavoidable conclusion Kant is not ready to accept: *the very formal structure of an act is 'diabolically' evil.* Or – to put it in yet another way – the obverse of Kant's insistence of how the pure moral act is impossible, of how one can never be sure that one is acting solely out of consideration for duty, is the far more uncanny fact that the moral act, precisely as *impossible*, is simultaneously *unavoidable*, that which is in a way impossible to transgress. One can transgress only positive moral prescriptions and norms, while, as we have already seen, with regard to a pure moral act the suspicion that I have yielded to pathological motivations is only the obverse of a more radical suspicion that what appeared to me as a simple pathological act was actually an act of pure reason, accomplished for 'no good (pathological) reason at all'.

Here, we once again encounter the reversal typical of obsessional economy: the Kantian moral subject seems to search for the pathological motivations of his acts in the hope that he will find none, and thus finally accomplish a true ethical act. What, however, if he desperately searches for pathological motivations and is relieved when he finally finds one, satisfied that 'this was not yet it,' that the dreadful encounter with the Act has been successfully postponed yet again? The thesis according to which the experience of one's *inadequacy* to act in full compliance with the moral law is the *ratio cognoscendi* of the moral law itself thus appears in a new, much more unsettling light: it is only my failure to act ethically which guarantees that I remain an ethical subject, since were I to accomplish a pure ethical act, I would change into a being of diabolical Evil (into a Sadeian Supreme-Being-of-Evilness [*Être-suprême-en-Méchanceté*]). Here also the logic of proper distance described above holds: when I approach the ethical act too closely, it turns into its opposite, into diabolical Evil.

This also enables us to reject the standard Hannah Arendt variation on the theme 'Kant and Nazism', which focuses on the alleged totalitarian potentialities of Kantian ethical criticism: was not an unconditional formalist attitude of 'do your duty for the sake of duty, do not think about its content and possible consequences for the Good of the people affected', practised by the executors of the Holocaust – that is, in the historical form of violence which comes closest to Kant's notion of 'diabolical Evil'? In contrast to this line of reasoning, one should emphasize that the Nazi practice was by no means 'formalist': it violated the basic Kantian precept of the primacy of Duty over any notion of Good, since it relied on a precise notion of Good (the establishment of a true community of German People) with regard to which all 'formal' ethical injunctions were instrumentalized and relativized (it is proper to kill, torture . . . *if* it serves the higher goal of the German community). The element which suspended the 'formalist' character of Nazi normativism was the very reference to the Führer: like the Stalinist Leader, the Führer is the one who *knows what is for the Good of the People* and, consequently, whose word overrides all 'formalist' ethical considerations. Horrifying as it was (and precisely *because* it was so horrifying), the Nazi Holocaust (or, within a different socio-symbolic economy and practice, the Stalinist gulags) is *not* an example of 'diabolical' or 'radical' Evil – when we designate it in this way, we use 'diabolical Evil' in a common sense, as a term for 'evil which is horrible beyond measure,' not in the strict Kantian sense.

In spite of Arendt's rejection of any profound affinity between her notion of the 'radical Evil' of the Nazi crimes against Jews and Kant's notion of radical Evil (as opposed to the simple egotistic evil in which we neglect our duty for the sake of some selfish motive, pleasure or personal gain), it may seem that they do share a crucial common feature: the lack of what Kant called a clear 'pathological' motivation (greed, lust for power, even sadistic pleasure in inflicting pain on other human beings). That is to say, the feature which troubled Arendt apropos of the Nazi crimes was the discrepancy between the monstrosity of the deeds and the lack of evil intent on the part of the subjects who committed these deeds, as if these subjects were totally blind to the human dimension of what they were doing – that is, completely unable to pause for a moment and simply *reflect* on the human dimension of what they were doing. Let us quote Arendt's description of the change in the functioning of concentration camps which occurred when SS units took over their administration from the populist-lumpenproletarian SA units:

> Behind the blind bestiality of the SA, there often lay a deep hatred and resentment against all those who were socially, intellectually, or physically better off than themselves, and who now, as if in fulfillment of their wildest dreams, were in their power. This resentment, which never dies out entirely in the camps, strikes us as a last remnant of humanly understandable feeling . . . The real horror began, however, when the SS took over the administration of the camps. The old spontaneous bestiality gave way to an absolutely cold and systematic destruction of human bodies, calculated to destroy human dignity; death was avoided or postponed indefinitely.[23]

Richard Bernstein is thus fully justified in emphasizing how Arendt's notions of 'radical Evil' and the 'banality of Evil' are not contradictory, but fully compatible:[24] what makes the Nazi crimes against Jews 'radical' is the very fact that they were not committed by 'larger-than-life' monsters,

---

23   Hannah Arendt, 'The Concentration Camps', *Partisan Review* 15: 7, July 1948, p. 758.
24   See Richard Bernstein, *Hannah Arendt and the Jewish Question*, Cambridge: Polity Press, 1996, p. 147.

by proto-Romantic 'geniuses of Evil' who, borne by a superhuman *hubris*, in a kind of demoniac perversion of the 'normal' human will, fully willed their crimes and heroically assumed their monstrous Evil – they were ordinary, 'decent' people who carried out monstrous acts as if they were just another technical-administrative measure to be implemented. Arendt's insistence that figures like Eichmann were not 'perverted sadists' misses the point in so far as it refers to the pre-theoretical, common-sense notion of a 'sadist' as a person who fully wills and enjoys the suffering he inflicts upon his others. In clear contrast to this common notion, Lacan insists that the fundamental feature of the pervert's subjective position is the attitude of radical self-instrumentalization, of turning oneself into the pure instrument-object of the Other's *jouissance*: for Lacan, the sadistic pervert is not a passionate figure of demoniac evil but a thoroughly depersonalized 'bureaucrat of Evil', a pure executioner – there is no psychological depth in his personality, no complex cobweb of traumatic motivations.

The first thought that imposes itself here is the affinity between the perverted sadist's attitude and the basic Kantian ethical attitude itself – that is to say, the attitude of accomplishing one's duty for the sake of duty alone, and not for the sake of any 'pathological' motivations, even if they are of a noble nature (compassion, love of one's neighbour). Are we thus not back with the theme of 'Kant avec Sade', elaborated from different perspectives by Adorno and Horkheimer, and by Lacan: sadistic perversion as the hidden truth of Kantian ethics? Does not the commonplace according to which the Nazi 'banality of Evil' can be legitimized in Kantian terms (the commonplace evoked by Eichmann himself during his trial in Jerusalem) as a dispassionate fulfilling of one's duty for the sake of duty alone, with no regard for any 'pathological' considerations, therefore contain a grain of truth? In other words, does not Kant, when he endeavours to obliterate from the notion of moral duty all traces of 'pathological' affects (compassion, concern for our neighbour's well-being . . .), inadvertently open the doors to an evil much more radical than common selfish evil – an evil which, moreover, becomes indistinguishable from the Good, from ethical activity as defined by Kant himself?

The standard way to counter this suspicion is to emphasize how Kant distinguishes between *radical* and *diabolical* Evil: while he fully endorses the notion of 'radical Evil' (i.e. the innate, eternal propensity to evil as a kind of anthropological constant which is consubstantial with the very human condition), he rejects as impossible the notion of 'diabolicial evil', of evil elevated into an ethical principle – that is, of evil accomplished for no 'pathological' principles, but just 'for the sake of duty': for Kant, such a perversion of the human will is unthinkable. The obvious temptation here is to claim that the Nazi Holocaust presents a historical actualization of this very notion of 'diabolical Evil' rejected by Kant as unthinkable – the position elaborated in detail by John Silber in his thought-provoking essay on 'Kant at Auschwitz':

> Kant's ethics is inadequate to the understanding of Auschwitz because Kant denies the possibility of deliberate rejection of the moral law. Not even a wicked man, Kant holds, can will evil for the sake of evil.[25]

> Milton, in presenting Satan in his solitary defiant rage, consumed by hatred of everything God-like save God-like power, presents a compelling example of the genuinely demonic. This is the evil we confront in Auschwitz – evil that far transcends the conceptual limits of Kant's theory.[26]

These two opposed readings of Kant in relation to the Holocaust epitomize the two opposed ways in which the post-Hegelian critique of German Idealism approaches the topic of 'German Idealism and Evil'. That is to say, this critique (notably already in late Schelling) oscillates between the two theses. First, (radical or diabolical) Evil is posited as a radical outsider, as an outbreak of wild negativity which the Idealist machinery of the

25   John Silber, 'Kant at Auschwitz', in *Proceedings of the Sixth International Kant Congress*, ed. G. Funke and T. Seebohm, Washington, DC: Center for Advanced Research in Phenomenology, 1991, p. 198.
26   Ibid., p. 200.

subjective mediation-internalization is unable to 'swallow', to sublate, to contain, to posit as an inherent moment in the theodicy of the absolute Spirit: in radical Evil, the philosophy of absolute subjectivity, of the notional mediation-sublation of all positive content, encounters its ultimate limit, something which remains forever incomprehensible, the absolute Otherness to the Notion. The idealism of absolute notional mediation/reflection is thus unable to confront, fully to acknowledge, the positive meaningless reality of the Evil whose sudden emergence can undermine the edifice of Reason at any moment. On the other hand, however, it is absolute subjectivity itself, with its pretension to assert itself as the power of absolute mediation, devouring/internalizing all independent positive content, transforming this content into its own subordinate moment, which is the highest expression of Evil – that is, of the assertion of unconditional selfishness.

The Hegelian solution to this aporia, of course, is to assert the ultimate (speculative) identity of the two approaches: the Otherness of Evil which eludes the grasp of the subject is not an In-itself, but the very kernel of the subject's own absolute negativity, its own excessive founding gesture. Absolute subjectivity is thus simultaneously that which ignores radical Evil, and that which is itself the highest Evil – that is, the highest egotistical denial of the subject's dependence on an irreducible Otherness. And is not the ultimate example of this simultaneity the fate of political subjectivity, as conservative criticism of revolutionary attempts tries to convince us? The revolutionary attempts which endeavour to impose on the world their vision, based on their belief in the fundamental goodness and rationality of humankind, not only fail to take into account the essential frailty and meanness of human nature, they themselves unleash the powerful force of an unheard-of destructiveness (like the Terror of the French Revolution). Hegel himself seems to tend in this direction – not so much in his famous remarks on the revolutionary Terror in *Phenomenology* but, rather, in his *Lectures on Aesthetics*, where he comments on the fact that 'evil in the abstract has no truth in itself and is of no interest':

For the purely negative is in itself dull and flat and therefore either leaves us empty or else repels us, whether it be used as a motive for an action or simply as a means for producing the reaction of another motive. The gruesome and unlucky, the harshness of power, the pitilessness of predominance, may be held together and endured by the imagination if they are elevated and carried by an intrinsically worthy greatness of character and aim; but evil as such, envy, cowardice and baseness are and remain purely repugnant.[27]

Here Hegel is referring to Satan in Milton's *Paradise Lost*, which is of such interest precisely because it elevates evil (rebellion against God) into the consistent ethical attitude of a strong character. The only thing to add is that purely one-dimensional evil (a simply egotistical mean person) *is not true Evil at all*: true Evil involves precisely the blurring of distinctions between Good and Evil – that is, the elevation of Evil into a consistent ethical Principle. A revolutionary terrorist, for example, is of aesthetic interest if he is not merely a bloodthirsty executioner killing and torturing out of pure egotistical baseness, but a sincere idealist ready to sacrifice everything for his Cause, convinced that he is doing a service to humanity, and thus caught in the tragic deadlock of his predicament. So a Schellingian reminder to Hegel would be that such an 'ethical evil' *is* the true diabolical Evil, much worse than the evil of simple egotistical baseness: the cleaner you are (the more your motives are selfless-humanitarian), the greater your evil. Furthermore, the Arendtian reminder to both of them would be that the Nazi executioners were neither creatures of selfish baseness nor distorted heroic idealists.

So – back to Kant: our solution to this alternative (the formalist rigorism of Kantian ethics as a possible legitimization of the Nazi executioners; the Nazi evil as a phenomenon which transcends the horizon of Kant's ethical theory) is to reject both its terms. On the one hand, one should fully endorse the notion according to which Kant's rejection of 'diabolical Evil'

27   *Hegel's Aesthetics*, Oxford: Oxford University Press, 1975, p. 222.

is a theoretically incoherent disavowal of the necessary consequence of his own thought: the inherent logic of his thought effectively compelled him to posit 'diabolical Evil' as the paradox of an evil prompted by no pathological motivations, but just 'for the sake of it', which – on a certain level, at least – renders it indistinguishable from the ethical act. On the other hand, against Silber's position, one should categorically deny any connection between the Kantian 'diabolical Evil' and the horrible reality of the Nazi Holocaust: the Nazi Holocaust crimes have nothing to do with the Kantian 'diabolical Evil' (with the 'demonic' explicit willing of monstrous deeds for the sake of it, because they are evil).

Although the Nazi Holocaust crimes were 'banal' in the precise way described by Arendt, they are none the less *not* deprived of all pathological motivations. In so far as one calls 'pathological' any positive, ultimately contingent content which supplements ethical formalism and permits us momentarily to suspend the universal ethical commandments, one should assert that the Nazi ideological universe definitely involves reference to such a positive content: Eichmann did not act 'for the sake of duty', but for the sake of the German Fatherland, clearly posited as the Supreme Good of the Nazi ideological universe. Without this massive, all-pervasive reference to the German Fatherland (to be defended against the Jewish threat), without this logic of 'My country, right or wrong!' brought to its extreme, it is not possible to account for the utter thoughtlessness of the Nazi executioners, for their inability to *reflect* upon the human dimension of their deeds: it was the reference to the highest interests of the Fatherland, not to some abstract Kantian sense of 'duty for the sake of duty', which enabled the 'ordinary, decent German' to suspend elementary ethical judgement.

In other words, although it is true that the place for the Nazi Holocaust is opened up by the gap between formal Duty and the positive notion of Good, this does not mean that the attitude of the Nazi executioners was grounded in the principle of 'Do your duty, irrespective of any considerations for the Good of the people!' – quite the opposite, it was grounded in the principle of 'Do everything for the Good of your Fatherland, even if you are compelled to commit what, in the terms of the abstract notion of ethical duty, look like horrible crimes – the very fact that you will be able to commit such crimes is the ultimate proof of your devotion to the Good of the Fatherland!' The Nazi crimes were not the ultimate consequence of the modern formalist ethics of 'doing one's duty for the sake of duty', which obliterates all reference to some positive, substantial notion of the Good; but, on the contrary, the most radical example of ethical anti-formalism, of the ethics of the Supreme Good, the reference to which justifies the obliteration of any reference to the formal notion of ethical duty. The Nazi reference to the Good of the Fatherland, of course, was in a sense a mere mask; nevertheless, if this mask were to fall, the entire edifice of the Nazi machine would have disintegrated – the Nazi machinery could not have continued to function in its 'naked state', as a pure killing apparatus.

6

Rogozinski is fully justified in discerning the first version of the Kantian excess already in the *Critique of Pure Reason*, around the key notion of 'transcendental imagination'; however, he seems to miss its true focal point when he identifies this excess with the violence involved in the act of the transcendental synthesis which unifies the dispersed sensible data into reality. In contrast to Rogozinski, one is tempted to locate this primordial excessive violence at the very heart of transcendental freedom which precedes the (moral) Law – in the 'unruliness' of the human subject which Kant mentions in his *Anthropology*. Is not this 'unruliness' the primordial manifestation of 'diabolical Evil', of the unconditional drive which compels the subject to 'go right to the end', beyond every (human) measure? And is not ethics, in its most radical dimension, the endeavour to contain *this* drive? Kant's insistence on the *epistemological* inaccessibility of the noumenal domain to us, finite human beings, is thus to be read as 'You cannot, *because you should not*', as an *ethical* prohibition, as the fundamental 'no trespassing', as the caution against getting enmeshed in the self-destructive vortex of 'unruliness' which disrupts the self-sufficient reproductive cycle of animal life. There is something, an uncanny domain, *between* the animal life regulated by the search for pleasure, and the rule of moral Law – this something is 'transcendental freedom', the unthinkable direct intervention of the noumenal into the phenomenal in the guise of a violent tearing up of the chains of the natural causality which is not yet kept in check by the moral Law.

This Kantian deadlock finds its clearest expression in the passage (already mentioned) towards the end of the *Critique of Practical Reason*, where Kant asserts how God Himself wisely limited our cognitive capacities (i.e. rendered the noumenal domain inaccessible to us) in order to enable us to act morally – it is not only Kant but God Himself who has to 'limit the scope of our knowledge in order to make room for morals'. Does not Kant's own description of the catastrophic ethical consequences of man's gaining access to the noumenal domain, however, indicate the only consistent answer to the enigma of diabolical Evil, which is that this diabolical Evil is none other than 'God-in-itself,' i.e. *God Himself in His noumenal dimension*, the God of an obscene superego Law which coincides with perverse *jouissance*? Behind the opposition of Law and the lethal Thing, behind the notion of Law as the prohibition which enables us to maintain a proper distance towards the Thing, there is thus the monstrous dimension (not of the Thing-in-itself beyond the scope of Law, but) of the *Law itself as a Thing*, of a terrible Law which is itself inscribed into the dimension which it tries to keep out of our reach.[28]

28   Alain Juranville (see 'Du Malin Génie au Surmoi', in *L'Âne* 64, October 1996, pp. 35–40) opposes the superego *qua* the obscene law which imposes enjoyment, to the 'true' symbolic Law by means of which we open ourselves to the Call of the authentic Other beyond narcissistic distortions. In this perspective, the 'Oedipus complex' (whose outcome is superego) is no longer the necessary matrix of 'socialization' (of the subject's integration into a sociosymbolic universe), but a paradigmatic pathological *distortion* of the normative process of the subject's entry into the symbolic order. From our perspective, however, such an opposition between the 'proper' symbolic Law and its 'pathological' superego distortion is the very ideological operation (or 'idealist falsification') to be avoided: the fundamental lesson of psychoanalysis is precisely that *there is no Law without superego* – the superego is the obscene stain which is structurally unavoidable, it is the shadowy supplement to the 'pure' symbolic Law which provides its necessary phantasmic support.

Or – to put it in another way – Rogozinski demonstrates conclusively how, beneath the official-academic image of Kant as the philosopher who asserts the ethical autonomy of the subject, one should discern *another Kant,* a Kant who focuses on the enigmatic donation of the Law which enables the subject to maintain a proper distance towards the monstrous Thing, and thus avoid being swallowed up by its abyss. We thus get a Kant for whom the main problem is not how to avoid immersion in pathological empirical interests and follow the call of the noumenal Law, but (one is almost tempted to say: on the contrary) how to maintain a minimal distance from the monstrous noumenal Thing. What the moral Law is bound to constrain is thus not primarily our fixation on pathological motivations referring to contingent phenomenal objects but, rather, the 'unruliness' which Kant, in his *Anthropology,* defines as the specifically human stubborn insistence, the cling-ing to wild egotistical freedom unbound by any constraints (discernible in young children), this impossible point of direct phenomenal appearance of noumenal freedom which has no parallel in the animal kingdom and has to be broken and 'gentrified' by the pressure of education.

So there definitely *is* 'another Kant' beneath the official academic Kant – *however, does not the same also apply to Hegel?* And does Rogozinski not commit the same error with regard to Hegel; does he not accept too hastily the official academic image of Hegel as the philosopher of dialectical wizardry which enables him magically to invert the experience of radical negativity into the positivity of the theodicy of the absolute Idea? Is there not also *another Hegel?*[29] And is it not that, in both cases, this other

29   It is therefore crucial, for the relationship between Kant and Hegel, to break out of this double constriction: from the 'naturalized' pseudo-Hegelian position from which Kant appears as a self-contradictory philosopher who did not think his own conjectures through to the end, and thus got involved in meaningless inconsistencies, as well as from the standard Kantian position according to which Hegel misperceives the limit which for Kant is constitutive, as a mere limitation to be overcome, and so regresses back to traditional metaphysics. The point here is not to engage the two philosophers in a 'dialogue' in which each would 'respect' the other's true contribution, but much more radical: the traditional Kantian criticism of Hegel is the screen which prevents us from gaining access to the truly subversive dimension of Kant's philosophy itself (to outline the consequences of his 'limit-notions' like diabolical Evil, the Monstrous, etc.); and vice versa: the standard Hegelian critical (mis)perception of Kant is a screen which obfuscates the unheard-of real kernel of Hegelian dialectics themselves.

dimension which eludes the standard academic image of the philosopher is focused on the enigma of 'diabolical Evil', of the impossible Real of an unthinkable act of Evil which takes the form of its opposite, of the Good? Precisely as unthinkable/impossible, this act *has to be presupposed* if one is to account for the fact of the ethical subject: 'diabolical Evil' is not the unattainable *telos* of Evil, its extreme point which can never be reached, but, rather, something which *always-already has happened* the moment we are within the ethical domain, its 'primordially repressed' founding gesture, a kind of 'vanishing mediator' between natural/instinctual innocence and the domain of moral Law and guilt.

One could also express it like this: why does Kant introduce the notion of 'diabolical Evil' in the first place, before he rejects it? Because the reference to 'diabolical Evil' is necessary if one is to distinguish 'radical Evil' itself from the traditional notion of evil as a mere weakness of the will, as the will's incapacity to resist temptation. That is to say: Kant's crucial point is that Evil is not a mere lack of Good, a mere weakness of the will, but an active, positive force resisting the Good, an attitude adopted by the subject by means of his/her eternal noumenal act of choosing his/her eternal character – and is not such an act necessarily, by definition, 'diabolical'?

One should be careful here not to miss the complexity of the Kantian operation as it is reconstructed by Rogozinski: this operation turns around the standard Hegelian criticism according to which Kant 'does not go right to the end' and thus remains stuck halfway – stops just before the abyss of radical negativity. According to Rogozinski, the fundamental gesture of the 'true Kant' beneath the academic semblance of 'Kantian philosophy' lies precisely in a *refusal to go right to the end*: when he 'goes right to the end', the subject is swallowed up by the abyss of total self-disintegration, he accomplishes the impossible step into diabolical Evil, morality breaks down, reality itself dissolves into the Monstrous. In clear contrast to the misleading image of Kant's 'ethical rigorism', one can see how, for *this* Kant, the last support of ethics consists not in the attitude of unconditional persistence ('do not give way', go right to the end, *fiat iustitia pereat mundus*), but in the subject's capacity to restrain himself, to stop before the abyss. 'Law' is the name for the limitation the subject imposes on himself – say, with regard to another human being, the name for the 'respect' which enjoins me to maintain a distance towards him or her, to abstain from trying to penetrate all of his or her secrets . . .[30]

Although the Kantian radical ethics of unconditional injunction is usually opposed to the Aristotelian ethics of the proper measure and of avoiding the two extremes, we encounter here, in this notion of the properly ethical attitude (as involving the avoidance of the extreme of simple immersion in the pathological universe of empirical objects, as well as the avoidance of directly lethal immersion in the impossible noumenal Thing), the unexpected Aristotelian side of Kant. At a level more fundamental than his notorious moral rigorism, Kant thus reasserts the ethics of proper distance, of consideration and self-limitation, of avoiding the temptation to 'go right to the end'. Approached from this Kantian standpoint, Lacan's *ne pas céder sur son désir* (the ethical injunction not to compromise on one's desire) in no way condones the suicidal persistence in following one's Thing; on the contrary, it enjoins us to remain faithful to our desire as sustained by the Law of maintaining a minimal distance towards the Thing – one is faithful to one's desire by maintaining the gap which sustains desire, the gap on account of which the incestuous Thing forever eludes the subject's grasp.

Translated into ethical terms, the opposition between desire and drive is thus the opposition between the attitude of 'No trespassing', respecting the secret of the Other, stopping short of the lethal domain of *jouissance*, and the reverse attitude of 'going right to the end', unconditional insistence which follows its course irrespective of all 'pathological' considerations. And is this not also the opposition between modernity and postmodernity? Is not the uncompromising attitude of 'going right to the end' the basic feature of modernist rigorism, while the postmodernist attitude is

---

30 Along the same lines, the Lacanian desire grounded in symbolic Law is also a defence against the lethal *jouissance*.

characterized by the radical ambiguity of the subject's 'impossible' relationship to the Thing – we derive energy from it, but if we approach it too closely its lethal attraction will swallow us up? Like the unfortunate narrator of Poe's 'A Descent into the Maelstrom', who survives the shipwreck and, by deftly steering the wreck on which he is stuck, which circulates around the maelstrom, miraculously avoids being swallowed up by the gigantic maelstrom's eye, the postmodernist subject must learn the artifice of surviving the experience of a radical limit, of circulating around the lethal abyss without being swallowed up by it ... Is not Lacan's entire theoretical edifice torn between these two options: between the ethics of desire/Law, of maintaining the gap, and the lethal/suicidal immersion in the Thing?

Index